how to succeed with women

RON LOUIS
DAVID COPELAND

PARKER PUBLISHING COMPANY

Library of Congress Cataloging in Publication Data

Copeland, David.
    How to succeed with women / David Copeland, Ron Louis.
      p. cm.
    ISBN 0-13-095091-2 (hardcover). — ISBN 0-7352-0030-0 (pbk.)
    1. Dating (Social customs)—United States. 2. Women—United
State—Psychology. 3. Man-woman relationships—United States.
I. Louis, Ron. II. Title.
HQ801.C716 1998
646.7'7—dc21   98-27038
                                                CIP

© 1998 by Prentice Hall

Printed in the United States of America

10 9 8 7 6

ISBN 0-13-095091-2 (hardcover)   ISBN 0-7352-0030-0 (pbk.)

ATTENTION: CORPORATIONS AND SCHOOLS
Prentice Hall books are available at quantity discounts with bulk purchase
for educational, business, or sales promotional use. For information, please
write to: Prentice Hall Special Sales, 240 Frisch Court, Paramus, New Jersey
07652. Please supply: title of book, ISBN, quantity, how the book will be used,
date needed.

PARKER PUBLISHING COMPANY
West Nyack, New York 10994

On the World Wide Web at http://www.phdirect.com

Introduction

We were no different than you might be. Our relationships with women were dependent upon two things: luck and the whim of women who happened to be attracted to us. When either of us had sex, it was because we quite literally "got lucky," and a woman decided to have us. We had little choice or power over when we had sex and relationships and what women we had those interactions with. Sex and relationships, it seemed, were a crap-shoot. Perhaps we'd meet someone, perhaps we wouldn't. Needless to say, we got tired of it.

Finally, we decided that we would do whatever it took to find out what worked with women. We wanted to know how to seduce women and more—we wanted to know how to develop relationships with women that would be fulfilling for both us and them.

That was five years ago. We set out dating as much as we could and comparing notes after each and every interaction with women. Looking back, many of our interactions with women seemed unskilled or even laughable to us now, but we stuck with it through the failures, frustrations, and successes. We found that as we kept at it and kept working together, we began to see the underlying structures of successful dating interactions. We found that we could start to predict how interactions would go and how certain women would respond to us. We began to take our interactions with women less seriously and to have more fun. We started to see how most of our problems with women had been generated by our own behavior. We began to develop the set of principles that has evolved into this book.

Now we know that we can have as many women as we desire simply by using the technology outlined in this book. For instance, we understand the messages we send to women through our personal styles (Chapter Three) and how to make those messages as seductive as possible. We know how to get women to naturally think of us as possible romantic material when they first meet us, rather than relegating us to the role of "friends" (Chapter Two). We know how to flirt successfully and how to use that flirting to get the first date (Chapter Five). We know how to take a coffee date (Chapter Seven) and make it into a full blown seduction (Chapter Eight). We know how to go for the first kiss—and more (Chapter Nine). We know how to handle problems when they arise (Chapter Eleven), how to develop a relationship (Chapters Twelve and Fourteen), and how to cut one off effectively (Chapter Thirteen). Our lives with women are much easier and more successful than they ever were before, simply from using these techniques.

Over the course of writing this book, we often found ourselves saying to each other, "If only I'd had this book ten years ago I'd have made so many fewer mistakes!" This book contains a program that can change your life with women, forever. To get the most out of it, you may want to take on the following practices:

Be coachable. It won't do you a bit of good to read this book if you go through the entire thing rejecting everything we say before you have even tried it out. Of course, you will inevitably disagree with some of the things that we tell you to do or when we explain what has worked for us or our students. But, don't worry about it.

Think of us as your personal dating coaches. Part of a coach's job is to push you into trying something new. Imagine a professional basketball player who argues with his coach every time the coach tried to teach him a new move or critiques his performance. The player would fight a lot and get nowhere. As a man being coached, you have to be willing to set aside what you know to be true and to try out something different once in a while. So, if you want to get the most out of this book, don't run mental arguments with us as you read it. Pretend what we are saying is true and try it out, at least for a while, and see how something new works for you. After all, if you already know everything about success with women and have exactly the sex life you want, why are you reading this book?

Have a "study partner." Do you know why, on the average, Asian students get better grades than non-Asian students? According to the experts who study this kind of thing, it is not because they are inherently smarter. It is because they are much more likely to study together than alone. Students who study with other students master the material faster, have more fun, and get better grades than students who study alone. You would do well to take advantage of this principle.

If you know another man who you can study seduction with, then by all means study with him. You can discuss the chapters and the ideas together and egg each other on to try out the techniques that we will teach you. A study partner can be someone to get pumped up with before an interaction with a woman and someone to debrief with after. He will be able to give you feedback and coaching on e-mail you send to women, love letters you write, and how to handle the variety of experiences you will have with women once you start using your program. He will be able to celebrate your successes with you and help you quickly get over your disappointments.

It worked for us. We developed the material in this book by working together. We were able to master the various distinctions faster through our conversations, and we were able to learn from each other's experiences.

The only trick of this is to find the right guy to work with. He needs to be someone you can kick back and have a good time with, who won't be offended by the idea of studying ways to romance women. He should not be a blabbermouth. If he tells everyone that you are studying seduction, he is likely to put off women you might want to seduce. You do not need to be overly secretive, but no useful purpose is served by telling everyone. You will find that having someone to work with you while studying this material, although not essential, will help you quite a bit.

Write in this book! We know that you were probably taught to never write in a book. To this we way fiddlesticks! Feel free to customize this book to make it work best for you. Underline things you think are important and take notes in the margins of ideas or questions you might have. This will help your retention of the material substantially and make it easier to find parts that you may want to refer back to later.

We have learned that good intentions and being a good guy are not enough. These qualities are important, but, by themselves, they will almost never generate romance with a woman. If you are gong to have success with women, you must be able to create romantic structures. You must be able to intentionally create interactions, conversations, events, dates, and moments that, by their very nature, make women feel romantic feelings and think romantic thoughts about you. Sometimes these structures just happen, but, with a little know-how, you can insure that they happen consistently and with the women you desire. You must know how to construct them. Fundamentally teaching you to do just that is what this book is about.

Remember, dating is a game. It is an important game, but it is a game. All games are frustrating when you are first learning the rules, and dating is no different. But, like other games, dating becomes fun as you master it. Stick with it through the first few tries and the possible confusion. Keep at it, and it will become fun.

Much of the material in this book comes from questions we have received from our students. We have been conducting individual coaching sessions and courses for the past few years. If you find the material in this book useful, you, too, can participate directly with us, the masters of seduction. To get in touch with us, visit our website at www. .com or write to us at P. O. Box 55094, Madison, WI 53705.

Contents

chapter three... 55
The Elements of Style:
Dress and Confidence

chapter four...
Where the Girls Are;
Meeting Women for Sex
and Relationships

chapter five...
Flirting Without Disaster

chapter six... 177
A Crash Course in Romance/
How to Sweep Her Off Her Feet
and into Your Bed

chapter seven... 205
The Priming Date

chapter eight... 237
The Seduction Date

chapter nine... 273
Closing the Deal:
The First Kiss and More

chapter ten... 293
Being the Man of Her Dreams
In Bed

chapter eleven... 319
When Babes Attack:
Handling Problems Women Cause

chapter twelve... 365
After the Date—Keeping
Up the Pursuit

chapter thirteen...   387
Breaking Up Is Easy to Do

chapter fourteen...   413
From Casual to Committed

chapter fifteen...   435
Conclusion

Index   444

chapter one...
So You Want Success with Women

Greg came to us with a problem. "I can't seem to get women to like me," he told us. "I mean, they like me as a friend, but when I try to make things more romantic, it never works out. I haven't had sex in over a year. What should I do?"

We hear stories like Greg's all the time. All sorts of men come to us with their dating problems. Some are young, some are middle-aged, some are older. Some are salesmen, some are computer programmers, some are executives. We've worked with college professors, as well as men who are their students. We've worked with men who've never been married, and men who are divorced. We've worked with rich men and poor men, attractive men and ugly men. We've worked with men from as many different walks of life and socio-economic strata as you can imagine.

All of them have come to us with the same problem: they can't seem to get women to have sex and relationships with them. They desperately wish they could be successful with women, but they aren't, and it seems like the harder they try, the worse things get. Greg says "I've all but given up dating because I'm so tired of the pain and humiliation." His feelings are common among these men.

These are good men. They are sincere and honest and would make good lovers, boyfriends, and husbands. But they can't seem to get women to even give them the time of day. They all find themselves living in hope—hoping that someday they will meet a woman who likes them, hoping that someday they will magically figure out how to attract women, hoping that someday they will, through some mysterious process, turn into super-studs.

Obviously, living in hope doesn't work, especially about something important like relationships with women. It's like hoping that your apartment will get clean, but not cleaning it. It's like hoping that you will have enough money for your retirement, but not saving for it. You have to take the proper actions consistent with your commitments, not just live in hope.

Very occasionally you may meet a woman with whom everything goes right, no matter what you do, but such occasions are rare. Romance rarely "just happens." Hope alone will not give you the relationships you want with women. Leaving it to chance will very likely cause you to end up alone. You've got to take continuous action.

But what to do? What can a man do that will make him so attractive to the women he's interested in that they'll not only like him, but that they'll want to take their clothes off and rub their bodies against him? Answering that question is the subject of this book.

We won't lie to you, or hold out some ridiculous claim that simply reading this book will instantly make you into a super-stud who can go from meeting a woman to getting her into bed in 10 minutes or less. That's snake-oil salesmanship, and not part of our program. Effectively seducing women is work. The reason this book will change your life is that it will show you, for the first time in your life, *exactly* what the work is. It's up to you to follow through and to implement the "science" we'll teach you (though we'll show you exactly how to do that, too). If you are willing to do the work, the tools we'll teach you in this book *will* work for you, just as they have worked for us and the many men we've taught. The principles are simple and extremely useful. The steps are easy to learn and easy to remember. With practice you will master them, and will be more successful with women than you ever imagined.

WHAT THIS BOOK WILL TEACH YOU

This book will teach you, step by step, how to find women, meet them, seduce them, and build relationships with them. We'll cover every aspect of seduction, so at each step you'll know where you are, where you've been, and what there is for you to do next.

This book will give you the ability to pursue and date as many women as you want, and to pick and choose from among them the one that works for you long-term.

We'll teach you:

The Seven Habits of Highly Effective Seducers

There are a number of habits that all master seducers follow. We'll show you what successful seducers do every single day that makes them consistently successful with women. We'll also show you how to stop making the most common seduction mistakes, which you probably are making continuously. When you take on the habits of successful seducers and stop making these few common errors, you'll be more effective with women instantly.

The Elements of Style

Your deepest communication to women is carried out by your personal style and your level of confidence. What you "say" to a woman through these two key areas can easily make the difference between a successful and a failed seduction. We'll show you how to develop a personal style, both through how you dress and how you behave, that is a genuine expression of who you are and that women will find absolutely compelling.

Flirting Without Disaster

You use *flirting* to go from seeing a hot woman to making her your date. You build the basic structure of your relationship through the quality of your flirting. Will you be a woman's lover, or will you be her friend? Much of that will be decided by how you flirt. If you don't know how to flirt well, you will screw up your future with a woman and not even know you did it. We'll show you how to flirt your way to the date, effectively overcoming her natural fear of you, and building a bond of fun and excitement between you. We'll then show you how to effortlessly turn that connection into an accepted invitation for a date.

A Crash Course in Romance

Many "practical minded" men don't know how to be romantic in a way that will really make a woman feel special. Furthermore, romance seems passé; in this age of equality, a man shouldn't have to romance a woman, should he? Well, yes, he does. You have to be romantic because it can be a fun way to make a woman see you as special and exceptionally attractive. We'll show you how to do it.

The Priming and Seduction Dates

We'll teach you about the two kinds of dates, priming and seduction. We'll show you how each is a different, yet critical, part of effectively seducing a woman. You'll learn how to find what she desires in a man, and how to fulfill those desires by bringing those parts of you alive. You'll learn how to reliably make romantic conversation, and how to construct romantic experiences that will turn her on, connect her to you, and that she'll remember for the rest of her life.

Closing the Deal: Going for the First Kiss and More

Done properly, the first kiss is easy. Done improperly—which is the way most men do it—the first kiss seems more like pulling teeth. We'll show you exactly how to create an experience in which the woman is thinking about the kiss, and desires it. We'll teach you the specifics of how to go for that first kiss, and how to take it much, much farther immediately.

How to be the Man of her Dreams in Bed

The master seducer understands that he must always be improving his ability to enjoy sex and to please a woman. We'll show you how to improve three key areas—your communication, your attitude, and your technique. We'll show you how to create that moment when the date turns sexual, how to excel at foreplay and afterplay, and what to say and not to say during sex.

When babes attack: handling problems women cause

Sadly, not all of your interactions with women will be easy. In our experience, and in the experience of our students, the same basic problems tend to show up again and again. We'll teach you the nine secrets of handling the problems women cause, and walk you through, step by step, handling the most common dating difficulties. Because women are only half the problem (if that), we'll also show you how to handle the problems *you* cause in dating situations.

Keeping her

After you've seduced a woman, you have to maintain your connection with her if you want to be able to have sex with her again. We'll show you the ABC's of maintaining romantic relationships, and the specific steps you must take to keep her warmed up, happy, and waiting for you.

Breaking up with her

All short-term relationships come to an end, sooner or later. We'll show you how to figure out when it's time to end it, and how to break up in the most merciful way possible so you end up friends. We'll also show you how to determine if she might be a good candidate for a long-term relationship.

Going from casual to committed

Most men like to "play the field" for a while, then move on to a long-term relationship. We'll teach you the most important "do's and don'ts" for creating a relationship that stays passionate, fun, and loving for the long-term.

Along with all this, we will ask you to be responsible for your life. We will constantly show you how many of the problems you blame on women or on "life" are actually caused by your behavior.

Not to worry, though, we'll also show you how to change your behavior to make you more responsible for your life, and to get more of what you really want. As you learn and use this material you will naturally become less whiny. You will become more of a man who is able to go for what he wants, both with women and in other aspects of his life.

At its core, this book is about generativity—your ability to be creative, inventive, results-producing and fun. As you take on the practices we will teach you in this book, you will naturally become more so in your life. This is important because it is this characteristic—your ability to create a life that turns you on—that will ultimately attract women to you. All the exercises, steps, and processes we'll show you are simply means to the end of turning you into an exciting, generative man. You'll find enhancing this trait will make your entire life better, not just your relationships with women.

THE SEVEN DATING MYTHS

You are ready to do the work to get women into your bed; now all you need is for us to tell you what the work is. But before we tell you the secrets to creating an abundant sex life, we must explore and dispel the seven dating myths. You've probably bought in to most or all of them; the first thing to do now is to clear them away.

Myth 1. If you are nice enough and interesting enough, you will get a woman

It's great to be nice and interesting, but it is not enough; it's not the same as being seductive. Most men don't understand this. Your average man thinks that if he likes a woman, and she says that he is "sweet," "interesting," or "a wonderful friend," that he's moving the relationship toward eventual romance. He isn't, because, as we've said, being nice and interesting is not the same as being seductive.

If you don't believe us, then just look around at all the jerky men who have plenty of women to have sex with. Women certainly aren't panting around these men because they are so nice and so interesting. They are panting around them because they are exciting and romantic and fun. When you learn how to be exciting, romantic and fun, you too will be surrounded by willing, interested women. You won't have to give up being nice and interesting in order to do this; just remember that being nice and interesting isn't what turns women on.

Myth 2. You are a nice guy, who only has nice thoughts and desires

Men who believe that they are really nice guys, who only have nice thoughts and nice desires, often break women's hearts the most cruelly. Men who know that they aren't always sweet, and who know that they don't always have kind thoughts and desires, are often much more humane.

How can this be? After all, men who are committed to always being nice in every way should actually be nicer, shouldn't they? Sadly, it doesn't work out that way.

Look at it this way: Over the course of any relationship, you have the opportunity to feel a wide variety of feelings and behave in a wide variety of ways. Statistically speaking, you can't always be at your best. Sometimes you'll be at your best, most of the time you'll be at your average, and some of the time you'll be at your worst.

When you are at your worst, sometimes you'll have feelings and desires that aren't very nice. Actually they will probably be downright unkind. You'll want to retaliate against something the other person said, or you'll feel angry about how the other person's behaving. If you believe that you are a nice person who only has nice thoughts and desires, you'll be less able to be responsible for your behavior. You'll do things that most definitely are *not* nice, but you won't even notice you did them. After all, you'll tell yourself, no way could you be mean: you're a "nice man." You will ruthlessly refuse to admit that you are ever unkind. Women tell us repeatedly that it's the "nice men" they have to watch out for. They tell us that "nice" guys are more likely to express their anger indirectly, and to hurt them emotionally, all the while acting innocent and claiming to be victims themselves.

Men who know they are not always "nice guys," and who know that they don't always have nice thoughts and desires, are much more able to be responsible for themselves. They can acknowledge when they are angry, or when they want to retaliate, and can handle it appropriately. They are much more straightforward and forthright than "nice" men are. Women trust them more and like them more. In the long run, they are much less hurtful to everyone around them.

Some "nice" men pride themselves on being especially sensitive to women's feelings and women's needs. Women often tell them they are "special" or "not like other men." They often consider themselves ardent feminists, and are ever-vigilant for anything that might hurt a woman in any way. They are naturally suspicious of other men, and determined to not be like them. We call this kind of man a "Snag," or "Sensitive New-Age Guy." Don't get us wrong—if you are one of these men, we aren't against you personally. In fact, we relate to you quite well—both of the authors used to have some Snag characteristics, as well.

Here's what we've learned about it, though: You don't have to give up being a good, honest, sensitive man who loves women in order to get sex. A woman has sex with a man because that man is able to fulfill her needs. He may fulfill her need for excitement, he may fulfill her need for romance, or he may fulfill her need for something else. If you are a "nice" and "sensitive" man, yet not getting any sex, you may not be as nice and sensitive as you think. You may be ignoring women's needs, and not fulfilling them. That may well be the reason you're sleeping alone. If you read this book and use the technology we present in it, you will be able to fulfill women's needs even better, and get more sex than ever before.

Myth 3. Just "be yourself" and women will desire you

People who don't understand our method sometimes think that we are teaching men how to be manipulative. "It's wrong to study seduction," they whine to us. "Why can't you just be yourself?"

It's a mistake to think that using the technology in this book is a substitute for being yourself. It isn't. We are not suggesting that at all. It's actually harder to get women into bed if you are trying to be someone else. They notice, of course, that you are acting strangely. Even if you do succeed in getting a woman into bed by hiding your true self, you won't enjoy it as much as you thought you would. You'll know that you, yourself, weren't good enough for her, and that you had to pretend to be someone else. The whole experience will hurt your self-esteem and your self-respect.

We are, however, suggesting that some parts of you are more appropriate in some situations than in others. This isn't such a strange idea. After all, you probably don't swear or burp loudly in church, even if you feel like doing so. You don't put your feet up on the tablecloth at a fancy dinner party, even if you want to. And you don't come on to a woman giving you a job interview, even if it would be an expression of who you truly are at that moment. None of these actions would be appropriate to getting the outcome you desire.

But isn't that being manipulative? After all, if you find the woman at the job interview attractive but you want the job, aren't you manipulating her by not "being yourself" and asking her out? Aren't you just "putting on airs" to try to get a job? And at church, shouldn't people like you without you having to go through all the contortions of dressing a certain way, and repressing certain kinds of behavior? Aren't you just manipulating the people there into accepting you? Shouldn't you just be able to "be yourself"?

Isn't your self-expression being limited at the dinner party by not putting your feet up on the tablecloth if you want to? Shouldn't you be able to "be yourself," and be liked for that? Why should you have to manipulate everybody into liking you with all these special behaviors that might not come naturally to you? Shouldn't you be able to just "be yourself"?

Of course this makes no sense. "Being yourself" doesn't mean that you are utterly impulsive and driven by whatever behavior is most convenient for you in the moment. In different situations, you naturally bring out different parts of yourself. In church you follow a certain "code of conduct," but that shouldn't repress you. It's simply an opportunity to bring out the more formal, religious part of yourself. At the dinner party, you bring out the more cultured, sophisticated part of yourself. At the job interview, you bring out the professional part of yourself. You're not "repressed" because you don't ask her out. You are simply expressing a different part of yourself at that moment.

Our belief is this: It's critical that you bring out different parts of yourself in seduction situations than at other times in your life.

Furthermore, we believe that you probably don't know much about those parts of yourself, and that you will need guidance to bring romantic, seductive behaviors to the forefront.

That's what this book is about. Just as you were probably taught how to behave at a formal dinner, before you act without external guidance, you must learn how to behave when dating. When you do, you'll be able to bring out and explore romantic, seductive, powerful and interesting parts of yourself that you may not have spent much time with before. After all, women do this, too. When they put on make-up and their push-up bras, you could say they are being manipulative. Or you could say that they are bringing out the seductive, sensual side of themselves. That's what we believe, and you must learn how to do it, too. You'll grow and have fun, and women will be captivated by you, all because you were willing to go beyond your normal knee-jerk behavior, and to try something new.

Myth 4. Women know what they want, and they will tell you

Have you ever noticed that women will talk about the kind of man that they want, and end up with someone completely different? It happens all of the time. What women say they want, and what they actually respond to, are often totally different.

This is actually a very human trait: there are probably things you say you want in your life that you only *think* you want. Women are no different.

The bottom line is that women love men who are generative and creative. If they have to tell you how to get them, what to be like, and how to behave every step of the way, they aren't going to be turned on by you. It's your independent nature that gets them going, not your dependency on being told how to act.

Ironically, some of the traits in men that women complain about the most have in them the seeds of the traits women find most attractive. In the film *The Full Monty*, a bunch of out-of-work male steelworkers decide that they will make their money by putting on a strip-show for the local women. The plan has "trouble" written all over it—none of these guys is particularly great-looking. It also speaks to a basically male trait that women find both aggravating and attractive: men are trouble-makers. They take on silly projects, push them to their limits, and even sometimes make them work. This trouble-making quality is the flip-side of the generative creativity that women desire so much in men. If you count on women to tell you what they want, and how to behave in order to get them, you short-circuit this creative, trouble-making nature that women love so much.

Women can't tell you what they want in a man—they can only tell you what they *think* they want in a man. There's a big difference. They also aren't attracted to men who approach as supplicants, begging for the easy keys to melt a woman's heart. Don't fall into the trap.

Myth 5. Be a woman's therapist, and you'll get sex

We'll talk about this more in the next chapter when we discuss the Seven Habits of Highly Effective Seducers. For now we will simply point out that being a woman's therapist is one of the worst ways imaginable to get sex. Many men think it will work, but it almost never does.

Myth 6. Being "honest" means telling her the worst things about yourself

Many men seem to think that the best way to be honest with women is to tell them the worst things about themselves, the sooner the better. "Full disclosure!" seems to be these men's motto. We think this is foolishness.

It's good to be honest. There's only one time that we ever suggest that you not tell a woman the truth. (You'll learn about that in Chapter 7.) The rest of the time, we believe that dealing with the consequences of the truth will almost always be easier than dealing with the eventual consequences of lying.

However, this doesn't mean that you should tell a woman every thought or desire you ever have. That simply isn't useful. A man who believes this myth will often tell a woman his problems right away, or will talk to her about his abusive childhood. He believes that by sharing the worst parts of himself he is being emotionally vulnerable, and that vulnerability will make the woman he is interested in desire him.

Nothing could be further from the truth. A man who "spills the beans" about his problems and his defects right away may bond emotionally with a woman, but she won't desire him. She'll think of him as a friend, but she may also think of him as a nut case. As you'll learn in this book, many men think that if they get any positive emotional reaction at all from a woman, they must be on the way to a romantic encounter. This simply isn't true. While you shouldn't lie about your flaws, you shouldn't share everything right away, either.

Myth 7. Dating should be fair

This one myth gets men in more trouble than almost any of the others. If you are a man who whines about how dating isn't fair, and how you have to do all the pursuing of women, you must stop that right now.

We hear it all the time: "Why can't a woman ask me out for once?" "If women really believed in equality, they'd kiss me first!" "I'm tired of doing all the pursuing with women. It's their turn now." Blah blah blah. If it makes you feel better, you are right: It is unfair that you have to do all the pursuing, and that you have to take all the emotional risks by making all the "first moves."

We've known men who confront women about their not pursuing men. One man named Cameron made it a habit of confronting women who didn't do "their fair share" of the pursuing. He'd tell them in no uncertain terms that, if they wanted to date him, they'd have to do at least half of the initiating, the pursuit, and the emotional risk-taking. "It's the age of equality," he'd explain to them. "You get equal rights, so now take equal responsibilities!" Cameron didn't have many second dates.

Other men we know just complain about it. They whine to their friends about how women just aren't willing to do the work to make a relationship happen. They complain about how, every time a real risk has to be taken, it's "the man's move." They say they are waiting for a woman to pursue them.

Our advice is to get over it. If you don't have the sex life you want, it's *your* responsibility to get it. It is not women's responsibility to take care of you, and to make sure you have what you want in relationships. Expecting them to do so is just immature.

You can also look at it this way: if dating is naturally unfair, and if you have to do all of the initiating, that just means that you get to make it work the way you want it! You can pursue women when you want to, and not pursue them when you don't. You can set up dates for times that work for you, and go for that first kiss when you feel like it. Having to do all the initiating puts you in the driver's seat. Use it as an opportunity to make your relationships the way you want them to be and stop complaining about it.

If you've believed any of these myths in the past, we suggest you stop believing them now. To recap: First, being nice and interesting is great, but it won't get you sex. It will get you women who think you are nice and interesting, which is not at all the same as getting women who think you are arousing. Second, you aren't a nice guy who only has nice thoughts and desires. You'll be much better able to be responsible for your behavior if you admit that sometimes you are nice, and sometimes you are not. Women will also find you more attractive, because you'll be more trustworthy. Third, just "being yourself"—meaning impulsively doing whatever you feel like in the moment—won't get you women. You need help bringing out the more seductive parts of yourself, and the first few times you bring those parts out, they won't feel natural at all. Fourth, even if women did know what they wanted, they wouldn't be attracted to a guy who they had to spell it out for. Women are attracted to men who are generative and creative, not men who come groveling to them, asking how they should behave. Fifth, being a woman's therapist won't get you sex. It simply doesn't work. Sixth, being "honest" does not mean telling her the worst things about yourself right away. "Full disclosure" of everything that might make her dislike you is not necessary. And seventh, dating isn't fair. Men who complain about that fact need to grow up. Men who accept that fact can have as many women as they like.

It's as if dating is a dance. In the past, everybody knew their steps, and could dance together. A man knew that, if he was interested in a woman, he could do certain things to show that interest, and a woman knew the proper responses to show interest or lack of it. In the modern world, those dance-steps have been largely lost, and we have been left on our own to figure them out. Oftentimes, rather than dancing together it feels more like we are crashing into each other, and stepping constantly onto each other's toes.

This book is about changing all of that. By helping you understand the dance women are doing, and showing you how to dance with them, this book will teach you how to put music, rhythm, and grace into your interactions. They will be attracted to you, because you seem to "just know" how to be romantic with them. With this skill in hand, you will be able to have as much success with women as you desire.

chapter two...
The Seven Habits of Highly Effective Seducers

UNDERSTANDING WOMEN'S BIGGEST FEAR

We've been lucky enough to date and befriend many extremely hot and sexy women. Since learning the "tricks of the trade" we've been with women we would have only dreamed of earlier in our lives. We've been with hot blondes, brunettes, women of every description, all from using the material in this book.

On of the authors has a good friend and former lover named Dawn. She is 24 years old, long blonde hair, big blue eyes, tall, great legs, a huge chest, and loves to wear seductive clothes. She also loves sex, hot sex for hours. In short, Dawn embodies many men's fantasies.

Before dating one of the authors she used to go out and flirt with guys at bars. She told us about entering a bar and seeing how the men would stop talking and stare at her, drooling like dogs. She said she enjoyed the attention, but she rarely gave out her phone number to or dated any of the men who came onto her in bars. Why? Because she was afraid. She would be attracted to a man and then get afraid of being physically abused or raped by him. After all, she didn't know him; she just met him at the bar. So she'd stay distant, unattainable by the many men who desired her.

Fear of being abused, hurt or raped by men is *the* biggest concern women have in dating. Dawn and most other women smartly scope out men to make sure they won't be physically hurt by the men they date. They want to be sure they can trust the men they are attracted to before getting physically vulnerable with them.

If you want to have success with women, you must be aware of this most basic female concern. You must deal with the fact that women you meet will be testing you to see if you are "safe," or potentially violent.

We think this concern makes total sense. If we were women we would have the same concerns, and so would you. Put yourself in a woman's position: if you became aware of stories of rape, spousal abuse, torture and murder of women every day in newspapers and on TV, you'd be paranoid, too. Women need to be a bit paranoid because so many men are psycho. It simply isn't worth the risk for a woman to go home with a man who could hurt her. What this means for you is that you must do the things to create trust with a woman, and be sure to move at her pace when pursuing sex and relationships.

YOU CAN BE A NERD AND STILL SCORE

In writing, speaking about and researching dating dynamics, we talked to men from every age group and occupation. We've counseled middle-aged lawyers from farm towns in Wisconsin, and young up-and-coming musicians in New York. We've counseled computer geeks in Washington and writers in San Francisco. In the process, we've observed many of the hidden sexual dynamics between men and women.

The men we talk to often have a laundry list of problems, concerns, and complaints, about their relationships with women, both past and current. Men often come to us in desperation, at the end of their ropes. They've read other books, tried subliminal tapes and pheromone-scented colognes, and nothing has worked. They usually come to us looking for confidence with women. They want to be able to meet women and make them into lovers. We give men the same advice and information you will get in this book: a systematic approach to transforming your relationships with women.

One of our first clients was an attractive man in New York City. We will call him "Todd." Todd was, and still is, a very popular musician who travels all over the country, puts out CDs on major record labels, and is respected by many people in the music industry. He's beautiful, too—the guy even models and has been in commercials. He's a solo guitar singer/songwriter who performs in front of thousands of people each year. Many women find him sexy as he stands on stage, guitar in hand, singing with his amazing, satiny voice. You know as well as we do that women love rock stars. With Todd it is no different.

During our first meeting with Todd, we couldn't believe that this man was having trouble getting women. We looked at each other and laughed out loud. At first glance, we were hoping Todd might give *us* some advice. We hoped he might let us be roadies at one of his gigs so we could meet the women who were attracted to him, and maybe go home with them. But here he was, with a problem!

After just a few minutes of listening to him, we discovered the problem that kept Todd from being successful with women. Todd suffered from a severe lack of confidence. While he was in a situation that many of us would die to be in, constantly surrounded by hundreds of available women, he didn't have the confidence to follow through and seduce any of them. He told us he never knew what to say to women. He would look out in the audience and see lots of attractive women, but, even though he was the big star, didn't have the slightest idea how to start a conversation with any of them. He even admitted that women would wait to talk to him after a gig, but he rarely would go out with them. It was hard for us to restrain from smacking him, that he would dare to have a problem with women in this situation. We put him on a three-month program of coaching, goal-setting, and dating. He had made commitments about how many dates he would go on and how many women he would talk to. It took a lot of effort, but Todd now has sex with as many women as he wants.

Todd is a useful example because he shows that even men who are surrounded by available women can have a profound lack of confidence. At the same time, other men are very confident with women, but are not in situations where they have much contact with them. Some other men are not even all that attractive at first glance, yet embody the Habits of Effective Seducers so well that they have as much success with women as they want.

Blake, for example, is a computer programmer for a large firm in Chicago. He is 38, has epilepsy, and has scars on his arms from an accident as a child. At first glance Blake looks like a computer geek, and is not particularly attractive. His glasses look a bit out of date, and he even has pens in his pocket in a plastic pocket protector. He wears goofy ties and white tennis shoes. He is balding and has a gut. He looks like the type of guy who is much more comfortable with computers than with people.

However, as you get to know him, it is easy to see why he dates as many women as he wants, and even knows some who just like him for sex. It is pretty funny that a computer geek like Blake can have so many women, and a guy who is a successful rock star could hardly get a date to save his life! But it is true.

One of Blake's strong points is that, unlike Todd, he is very easy to talk to. Unlike many computer geeks, he is very personable. He has studied how to be romantic and is able to be sweet to women and seem harmless to them at the same time. Women find Blake attractive because it's easy for them to trust him. Blake has learned that he must pursue many women and he doesn't seem upset when he's rejected. He knows it is all part of getting the sex life he wants.

The bottom line is that if Blake can get sex and Todd can't, then so can you. Yes, we are speaking to you, the one who is reading this right now. Even if you're not a model-quality beauty or are older and balding, you can still have wonderful relationships with as many women as you want. You can cultivate the skills to be a dating machine.

IT'S NOT ROCKET SCIENCE

People tend to make things they don't understand more complicated than they really are. It's only natural. Many people think that using a computer will be so difficult that they are too intimidated to even turn the blasted thing on. Other people are so intimidated by the simple task of balancing their checkbook that they never learn how to do it. We all tend to complicate topics we do not yet understand.

One of the authors gives this example from his childhood. When I was six years old football seemed so complicated. I could understand the basic ideas of the game: the quarterback throws passes and someone catches the ball. Guys try to score touchdowns, block the other team, and make goals. That, I could understand. The rest of the strategies involved, however, didn't make any sense. Even after my father explained it to me dozens of times, the strategy of the game still seemed like a foreign language that I'd never understand. I decided to keep watching games, and have my father continue his explanations. By the time I turned eight, things started to make sense and I began to understand some of the more complicated aspects of the game.

Meeting and dating women is just like any other skill. At first it seems overly complicated and difficult. Most men simply give up because the task seems too large. This is not true. In fact, many men are less successful than they could be because they overcomplicate matters by being overly involved with their own thoughts about how difficult dating is.

Let's introduce you to a man named Bob. He spends hours a day preoccupied with scenarios about women. He carefully constructs imaginary conversations with beautiful women at the pizza place he frequents. He creates come-back lines for all of her reasons why she won't go out with him. He daydreams about seductive conversations with young women he imagines he could meet on the bus. In short, Bob is so "in his head" about talking to women that when he talks to a real, alive, breathing woman, he flips out and becomes tongue-tied. He's made it overly complicated by thinking about seduction too much, and taking action too little. He's made it into rocket science, and left himself unable to deal with it.

We have purposefully written this book in a very straightforward manner. We want you to understand that this material is not rocket science; the first steps to becoming a successful seducer are simple, and you can start today. We want to dissolve once and forever the idea that other men know something that you don't, and that these skills are out of your grasp. That just isn't true. Once you get over the idea that it's complicated and beyond your reach, you'll find you can easily learn and apply our system and get women, no matter what your age or level of physical attractiveness. So let yourself relax, and enjoy learning this material.

YOU'VE GOT WHAT IT TAKES

If you've ever learned any skill, then you can learn how to get women into bed. You've simply never been taught how. Like any skill, once you learn the basics, the rest seems easy.

Most guys try to talk to women and fail. Bob tries and tries, but still can't manage to get a woman in bed. "I'm sincere," he moans. "I'm a good guy. I'm nice. I listen to women and try to give them what they want. Why haven't I had sex in two years?"

So Bob becomes more and more upset. He tries to psyche himself up, to "get out there" more, and to be more confident with women. He resolves that he'll change with women, that *this* time he'll be the confident man he knows he is inside. This time he'll actually go up to that woman he's attracted to and ask her out. But when he does, he gets the same results he always gets: failure, or another female "friend"—the same thing as failing, as far as his sex life is concerned. His self-esteem and self-respect plummet, especially as he tries to be more of a nice guy or a better friend, in the hope that this will inspire women to feel romantic about him.

Exasperated, he has even confronted women about their lack of interest in him. Several years ago he had a woman friend named Susan who told him that she wasn't ready for a relationship. He accepted this, even though he was attracted to her. Susan was young, cute, with long legs, almond eyes and jet-black hair. Hoping to be the first man on the scene when she was finally ready for a relationship, he spent lots of time with her just hanging out. He knew she liked him because she spent time with him. He knew they shared the same interests in music and movies, and were intellectually compatible. He knew he wasn't particularly bad looking. In fact, lots of men who had girlfriends looked much worse than him. He knew he had what it would take, and he hung in there, spending time with her whenever she wanted.

One day she told him in an offhand manner, "Remember what I said about not being ready for a relationship right now? Well, I met a guy who it's really working with, so I guess I was wrong!"

"Wait a minute!" Bob came back. "Why didn't you choose to date me? I'm a good friend! I'm always there for you! Why won't you date me?"

"I don't know," Susan responded. "I just don't feel that way about you. To tell you the truth, there's something weird about you, you seem kind of desperate. I like you and everything, but Joel makes me feel different." Once again Bob has been passed over for another guy who, predictably, he later learns, is not nearly as sensitive as he is.

If you are like Bob, you've had this happen to you. You've resolved to try harder, to be more confident. Secretly, like Bob, you've wondered if there's something basically wrong with you. You've thought that there is something you can't see about yourself, that everyone else sees and that repels women from you, just as Susan was repelled from Bob.

The good news is that nothing could be further from the truth. Sure, you've got problems. Everybody does. But, as you've no doubt seen, plenty of guys with more problems than you are dating women and having sex and relationships. We know a wheelchair-bound paraplegic who has an ample sex life with attractive women. We know a man who was horribly disfigured by fire who has a constant stream of women in his life, who would never dream of thinking of himself as sexually inadequate. There's nothing wrong with you that keeps you from having sex with as many attractive women as you like. If you can communicate at all, even if it's typing out messages with a pencil between your teeth, you can get women to desire you.

What's missing is the simple technical skills required to get women experiencing romantic feelings and thinking romantic thoughts about you. As we said, if you can communicate at all, you can have success with women. But you need to know *what* to communicate, and how to communicate it. Just as important, you need to know what *not* to communicate, and how not to communicate that.

Some men intuitively know this material already. They are the "naturals," who seem to have women all around them no matter what they do. Sadly, they usually can't teach you the technical skills of success with women because they don't know how they are doing it. They just do it. Even if they did understand what they were doing, they wouldn't particularly want to share those secrets with you.

In the *Dilbert* comic strip, someone once comes to Dogbert and asks him the secret of his success. He says, "Sleep with a vat of Jello by your bed. Set an alarm to wake you every two hours. When it goes off, stick your head in the Jello and scream, 'boy, I'm tired!'" He ends the strip saying "Beware of the advice of successful people, for they do not want company." If you've ever gotten useless or even destructive guidance from sexually successful men, you've experienced this personally, and perhaps even let it discourage you. Perhaps you used it as another example of how you don't have what it takes to seduce women. This is completely wrong. You don't need to be a "natural." You just need the technology in this book.

"IT'S AN ATTITUDE"

What would you say if you'd never driven a car before and we told you that driving was all a matter of your attitude? We seat you behind the wheel for the first time in your life, give you the keys, and say "Okay, drive!" First, you look at us like we are nuts. You fumble around and possibly manage to get the thing to turn over a few times before it dies. "Hey," we say, "don't get down. The secret of confidence with driving is having a good attitude, everybody knows that. Look at you, you are getting stressed out. Now try again, but have the right attitude!" You take a deep breath, take on a "good attitude," and try again. Perhaps this time you get the car moving, just enough to drive directly onto someone's front yard. "It's no use," you say. "I can't do it." "Well of course you can't," we come back, "with an attitude like that! We certainly can't help you 'til you get that attitude fixed!"

It's obvious what's missing here: we never told you anything about the technical skills of actually driving a car. We never taught you how to start the car, how to stop it, to steer and to shift. We never taught you the rules of the road and all the skills you'd need to be a confident driver. Of course you didn't have the right "attitude." Of course you failed.

Now imagine that we've taught you everything you need to know before seating you behind the wheel for the first time. You've studied the textbooks, learned about how other drivers tend to behave, and the best ways to interact with them to get what you want. You've spent time in an automotive simulator where you could make mistakes with no real-world consequences, and when you first get behind the wheel, you know exactly what to do. What might your attitude be like then?

We think that saying "the secret of success is to have a better attitude" is about as useful as saying "the secret of success is to have success." In our opinion, the word "attitude" is horribly overused and tells you nothing useful. Attitude and success are both outcomes of doing certain things on a consistent basis. When you understand driving inside and out, know what to do when and how to do it, you automatically have the right attitude and have success. When you understand sex and dating inside and out, know what to do when and how to do it, you again automatically have the right attitude and have success.

Just as it does with driving, the attitude that creates success with women comes from understanding and using tools and technology. When you understand and start to use the tools in this book you will have "the right attitude," which will lead to success. Furthermore, you don't have to somehow come up with it. We'll show you exactly how to create it.

WE LEARNED THE HARD WAY

There's no reason to give up because you haven't known how to get women in bed, or because you don't have some elusive thing called "attitude." As a matter of fact, we used to have the same problems you do. For both the authors, sex was sometimes plentiful, and sometimes elusive. It seemed to be at the whim of luck, or at the whim of whatever women we happened to be around. A few years ago we decided to put an end to the uncertainty, and to discover the fundamentals that separate the master seducers from the men who spend Saturday nights alone.

There was work involved for us, the same as there will be for you. But the difference is, using the material in this book, *you will finally know what the work is.* No more guesswork, no more accidentally destroying budding sexual relationships with rookie mistakes, no more spending Saturday night alone. But it *is* work, and it will take practice.

The thing we *did* do is commit ourselves to experimenting and going about seducing women in new ways, ways we would have never previously dreamed of. We realized that we were getting very few results using our then-current strategies and so we decided to try new approaches. We once heard that the definition of insanity is doing the same thing over and over and expecting different results. We took this advice and set out on a completely new course for seducing women. We are sure that you can do the same thing, probably in much less time than it took us. We'll show you how to master these skills step by step, but you must be persistent.

MODELING SUCCESSFUL SEDUCERS

In our quest to become reliably successful with women, we made use of the concept of *modeling*. Modeling, in this case, does not mean runway models or centerfold models. It means that we modeled our behavior after men we met who seemed successful with women.

Modeling means to imitate someone else. Knowing how to model someone who is successful is an essential skill for anyone who wants to learn a skill someone else has. It is based on the belief that anything someone else can do, you can do, too. You simply need to be able to think the way that person thinks, believe what that person believes and take the same actions that person takes. Do this, and you'll get the same results. Along the way, you will learn what works for you and what doesn't.

For instance, a friend of ours returned to college at age 32. He did this after being out of school for ten years. He decided that, this time, he was going to figure out how to be the most effective student he could be. He wanted to study the least he could, and get the best grades he could. So he set about finding and modeling the most successful students. He observed the best students in his classes. He observed how they took notes, and took notes in the same way. He sat in the same parts of the classrooms they sat in. He studied with them to learn their study habits, and interviewed them about how they thought about going to school. By modeling his behaviors on theirs, he was able to take the same actions they took, and to get the same excellent results.

You can also use modeling in learning about success with women. Say you know a man who always seems to be in romantic relationships with hot women. He never seems to have any problems getting as many women as he wants, and seems to have exactly the sex life he wants. If you were to make this man your model, you wouldn't simply ask him how he does it, because he probably wouldn't know. What you would do is observe him. You'd look at how he dresses and moves, and dress and move the same way. You'd watch how he behaves with women, and try to behave the same way. You'd ask him what he's thinking at different times in a date, and think the same way. You'd ask him about his beliefs about women, and believe the same things. You'd listen to how he talks to women, and use the same words and sentences. In time, you'd have the same success he does. And you would be able to adapt what you've learned from him to best suit you.

As we modeled successful seducers for this book (and in becoming successful seducers ourselves), we noticed trends. We were able to determine the basic habits that are common to all Highly Successful Seducers. If the only thing you get out of this book is that you incorporate these habits into your behavior with women, you will get your money's worth—and a *lot* more sex with women.

THE HABITS OF A HIGHLY SUCCESSFUL SEDUCER

A Highly Successful Seducer never grovels for sex

One of the characteristics of kids age 6-10 is that they whine. If you look at any group of kids, you'll see them whining in an attempt to get what they want. We aren't sure if it is a genetic or cultural trait, but it certainly is true about them. Can't you just hear the irritating sound of a kid saying, "Mommy, I don't want to go to sleep!" Or imagine that same statement screamed at you by a kid who's crying and pounding his fists into the wall next to you. How pleasant!

We were recently at lunch with one of our students, Paul. He had brought his six-year-old son, Benjamin. Paul is a divorced single father and is looking for a woman for a casual relationship. During lunch Benjamin drew quietly while we discussed dating strategies. Just as we paid the check, Benjamin threw a tantrum because Paul wouldn't buy him a second dessert. Benjamin screamed, pounded on the table, and spit on us. People at nearby tables stared. Paul apologized to us and seemed embarrassed. Finally, in desperation, after five minutes of Benjamin's screaming, Paul gave in and ordered him a second dish of ice cream.

Benjamin's throwing a tantrum to get what he wanted was similar to the way many men go about trying to get women to have sex with them. Some men approach seduction like they are needy little boys. If a woman says "no," they try to manipulate and cajole her. Or they become obviously upset, and pout. Another common strategy is to wear the woman down by begging her for sex. All of these behaviors convey a sense of neediness. From our perspective, they are forms of whining.

Clearly, people don't respect whiners. They are seen as childish, not worthy of respect, people who can't take care of themselves, and as wimps who could be taken advantage of. While people often give children what they want just to shut them up, adults judge whiners very harshly. The biggest cost to people who whine is a total loss of respect from others. Though you don't realize it, you've probably groveled for sex in much the same way as kids whine for ice cream.

When you grovel to a woman for sex she thinks you are a worm. If the woman has kids she will automatically think of you as one of their peers. She will lose any respect she had for you. Some women will move you from the category called "man" to the category called "boy." She probably won't have sex with you, and will disqualify you from any possible relationship. She may, moreover, think of you as a chump and take advantage of you.

You know what? Some things are more important than sex. And, to a man's man (which is what you will become if you follow the system in this book), self-respect is far, far more important than a momentary sexual experience. On the one hand, the more self-respect you have, the easier it is to be successful with women. On the other hand, you can sometimes get sex by throwing away your self-respect, and groveling and begging to a woman for sex, which a Highly Effective Seducer would never do.

Let's look at the typical groveling situation. Guy goes out with girl. Guy knows nothing or very little about seduction. Girl has nothing better to do, and allows some kissing and petting to happen. Girl gets turned off at some point, and decides she doesn't want sex after all. Guy begs with "Aw, come on," "Why not," and "you don't know how it hurts a guy," until she finally gives in and lets him have six minutes of unsatisfying—for her—sex. Afterward she looks disgusted and tells him to get the hell out of her bedroom. She thinks he's a jerk, and she's right.

Groveling may get you sex, but let's look at the cost: First, even though groveling may have gotten you sex this time, it won't work in the future. Groveling erodes your self-respect, and a man without self-respect is not sexually attractive to women. So this leads to more groveling and begging for sex, which erodes your self-respect even *more*. Eventually you have no self-respect, no self-esteem, and must live as a worm groveling through every interaction with women. Is that what you really want?

Second, how you are in pursuing sex is how you are in pursuing your life. If you are able to have fun, be playful, and pursue a goal consistently but not be attached to the outcome, you will be successful both in life and with women. However, if you get into the habit of groveling and begging with women, you will be a groveling beggar in the bigger realms of your life. To some degree you'll grovel to your boss, to sales clerks, parents, everybody. You will be a true loser with no self-respect, no self-esteem.

Third (as if that's not enough!), women become sadistic and will take advantage of a groveling, no-self-respect man. They'll take your money, time, and will toy with you sexually, finally ditching you without putting out. In the process they will purposefully make you miserable. One woman told us about a man she dated who would always grovel for sex. The man would snivel and whine whenever he wanted her in a way that she found disgusting. As a result, she made him buy her all sorts of expensive gifts. She even made him give her his credit card so she could use it to buy expensive clothes. The problem with this guy was threefold. One, he didn't realize that he was being exploited and punished for his whining. He lost his self-respect and was too naive to realize it. Two, he didn't notice that he was being overcharged for sex with this woman (we will go into this later). Three, he inevitably lost her. He never really got the sex he wanted, and she got rid of him when she became bored.

While we could focus on the woman in this situation, and examine how exploitative she was, we won't. We want you to take the focus off external circumstances and always bring it back to yourself. Rather than blaming women, we want you to always look for what you could change in yourself, what you could bring to the party, and what you could alter to create the situations you want. Men like to blame women for their problems, but blaming, after all, is just another form of whining. Whining, begging, and groveling for sex are behaviors you must stop if you want to become a Highly Effective Seducer.

A *Highly Successful Seducer* knows it's his job to pursue sex; and that **she** has the final say

Men and women play a very elaborate game of cat-and-mouse. Men pursue and women either accept, reject or play hard to get. As men we often love the process, even though it seems tedious at times. A woman likes to know that you are persistent and worthy of her affections. As men, we love the conquest. We love the accomplishment of taking this woman who at first seemed like an impossibility and of knowing that we now "have her."

As research for this book, we interviewed hundreds of women on their attitudes and experiences with dating. One woman explained why she loves being chased by men. "I like knowing I can turn him down. I like knowing he wants me and would do anything to have me sexually. I love the moment before we kiss, knowing it is the beginning of a long series of interactions. The whole process drives me crazy. I must admit, it leaves me feeling all hot and bothered."

Pursuing is paradoxical. On one hand it is your job to pursue sex and go after what you want. On the other hand, she always has the final say. You must go at her speed and yet push at the same time. Even if it doesn't seem "fair" to you, you must stop when she says, no matter what. Warren Farrell, researcher of men's issues, figured out that men have to initiate over a hundred interactions with women to get them into bed. Men risk rejection each step along the way. These initiations include eye contact, kissing, petting, getting the phone number, and more. You must listen when she says "no" and behave accordingly.

When men don't listen to women's "no" they are risking many severe problems. The biggest one is being accused of rape. This is a real threat.

A *Highly Successful Seducer* doesn't get upset at her "no's"

One of the myths in dating and seduction is that as a man you should be able to just go out and meet a beautiful woman on the street and have her back in your bed in minutes. We can recall times in high school thinking that "a real man" could just go out and pick up a woman effortlessly, which we later realized is a near impossibility. If you are a rock star or already very famous, it could happen, but for most of us there is almost no chance.

We once heard a story about a man who was willing to go to extreme measures for sex. No, he didn't have sex with a prostitute in public like Hugh Grant, he had his own ploy. He would stand at a bus stop in Los Angeles during rush hour and approach every woman getting on the bus, off the bus, or waiting, and would say, "I want to sleep with you." The story goes that he would do this sometimes hundreds of times. Women would laugh at him, spit at him, slap him, and run away in fear. Occasionally, however, there would be a woman who was interested in him. She might talk to him and entertain the idea of going home with him. Even more occasionally a woman would have sex with him.

This guy had no problem accepting a woman telling him "no." While we are not telling you to go out and live out this crazy ploy, the man did act with a kind of bold courage and balls that we could all take on. Of course the guy was a bit off-kilter for risking so much trouble, like getting VD, sleeping with women he didn't know, having enraged women attack him, having boyfriends of the women kicking his ass, risking immediate arrest, and not acting with self-respect. The part that is worth modeling is not being upset when women turn you down.

To meet women and have sex with them is often a lengthy process. Along the way you will have to face all sorts of trouble, problems, rejections, etc. The number one thing that stops most men from being successful is that they give up when women ambiguously or uncertainly say "no." From our vantage point, women most certainly will say "no" along the way. We view the dating scene as a game and part of it is that women will, predictably, say "no" at some point. You have to improvise a way to stay motivated and focused on your goal without pushing them in a way they resent. Just like the one fellow who was nuts about asking every woman for sex, you need to develop a tougher skin regarding rejection.

Most men faced with "no" stop because they feel as though they've done something wrong. Have you ever been with a woman and thought things were going great, only to find out later that they weren't? You were holding hands, having great discussions, staring into her eyes, and just counting down the moments before you went in for the kiss. As your heart raced, you slowly brought your lips close to hers for a long hot French kiss. Just as your lips touched hers, she pushed you away and said, "No. I am not ready for that yet. I can't believe you just did that."

First of all, you are not alone. We all have miscommunications with women and let our hormones dictate our experience. The problem in the above situation is that most men stop at that point and never go back because they fear another rejection. The type of attitude we are teaching would have the man stop when the woman says so, all the while knowing that this was a step along the way, that he has other women he is working on, and that the door is still open for kissing or even having sex with this woman later.

A Highly Successful Seducer knows that rejection is the key to sexual prosperity

You're on the third date. You know it's time to make your move. She seems to like you. But who can tell? Maybe she's still wondering why she decided to go out on a date with you in the first place. But you have to make your move now. After all, *you* are ready. But what if she says "no"?

Or perhaps you aren't even out on a date yet. Maybe you are looking across the room at her, that unmet angel, that wonderful woman who you wish you could bring yourself to talk to. You could go up to her. This could be your only chance. But what if she rejects you? What if she's mean to you? What if she says "no"?

Fundamentally, you are scared of women for one reason only: you are afraid of the pain and humiliation you'll feel if she rejects you. If she says "no," you'll interpret it tomean all sorts of things: that you'll never get a woman, that you're not good enough, and that there's something fundamentally wrong with you. You'll feel humiliation and pain for days, perhaps even longer. Each rejection makes you even less likely to initiate anything with a woman again, which makes the next time you actually do initiate something seem even more important and significant to you. It will be extra-important to you that you not get rejected again, which will make you seem weird to the woman, who will then reject you. Then back to more pain and lonely nights ahead. This chain of events is enough to make your head spin. Many men that we've seen have experienced a similar cycle when they were rejected. The strange part is that most of us are not even consciously aware of these crippling thoughts.

For Bob, doing something as simple as asking a woman out is a very significant task. "If she says no," he muses, "I'll look like a fool. I can just see that horrified look on her face already. I wonder how she'll say 'no'? Then she'll tell all our mutual friends that I, of all people, tried to ask her out. They'll all laugh at me and make fun of me behind my back. My reputation will be ruined."

Bob puts himself in so much pain by picturing the worst possible outcomes that he paralyzes himself with fear. He's picturing all these terrible outcomes when he approaches a woman, and his sheer level of fear alone, if nothing else, makes women say "no" to him. He acts so strangely and so hesitantly that he's at his worst, rather than at his best. Few women would choose to go out with him. Women are not stupid; they can sense hesitation in a man. They don't want to be the source of you becoming depressed if they are not interested in dating you.

Like many people, Bob feels it's his duty to imagine the worst of what could happen in a risky situation, so he can "steel himself against it." He thinks that looking realistically at the "downside" of being rejected is the best way. He is wrong. Drawing lots of unpleasant pictures of being rejected and getting completely absorbed in fear of how you'll feel if you are rejected makes rejection almost inevitable.

The Highly Effective Seducer sees things completely differently. Rather than seeing rejection as a reflection of his value as a man, the Highly Effective Seducer has one rule about rejection: "Rejection is the key to sexual prosperity." An Effective Seducer thinks about rejection differently than does an ineffective seducer. He makes better decisions about what a women's rejection means to him.

For instance, imagine you are at a grocery store, and you flirt and joke with the attractive young woman behind the counter (as we'll teach you to do). Perhaps she says, "Would you like a bag?" You smile and jokingly respond "Oh no...bags are dangerous! Haven't you read the suffocation warnings on them?" She responds with a dark glare. You continue to joke with her, and her only words for you are a cold-sounding "Thank-you-come-again" when she hands you your change. In every way that she can, short of outright insolence, she rejects you.

Let's look into the mind of an ineffective seducer after this interaction. He might be thinking, "Wow, I really blew it with her. I can't believe I said that stuff. I must have been really out of line. Once again, I scared a woman I was attracted to. What's wrong with me? Won't I ever be able to talk to women without something weird happening? She's probably talking about me right now, telling everybody what a jerk I am." The ineffective seducer explains the interaction to himself in a way that causes him humiliation and shame.

To the Highly Effective Seducer, rejection is a stepping stone to massive sexual success because he sees it as one more "no" he doesn't have to hear on the way to an inevitable "yes" with some other woman. After that same interaction, an Effective Seducer might say to himself, "Wow, she sure didn't have much of a sense of humor. I wonder if she's not feeling well. Perhaps she had a friend die from suffocation in a plastic bag. Who knows?" If he does think that she didn't like him, his only thought is "Well, it's a good thing I found out now, before wasting more time and energy on her. Now I can concentrate on all the women who will want to be with me!" The

Highly Effective Seducer explains the interaction to himself in such a way that he feels good about himself. He's gotten one more "no" out of the way, and can move on to the "yes" from some other woman.

When asking a woman out, the Effective and Ineffective seducers think differently as well. Imagine you are at a restaurant, and about to ask your waitress out. You say "Hey, you seem pretty fascinating. What would it be like if we went out for coffee sometime? Could I have your phone number?" She responds, "Gee, uh, no. Would you like some dessert?"

Here's how an Ineffective Seducer might think about this. "Man, how humiliating. I can't believe I did that. What a slap in the face! That's what I get for thinking any attractive woman would want to go out with me. She didn't want me. I mustn't be good enough. I feel like crap. I will never do that again."

Meanwhile, here's how the Effective Seducer thinks about it: "Wow, how 'bout that. She must have a boyfriend or something, or really got hurt somewhere along the line. That kind of thing happens, I know. Perhaps she's just caught up in her own little world. Well, that's one more 'no' I don't have to hear on the way to getting a 'yes' from a woman. Too bad, she was cute. What's on the dessert menu?" The Effective Seducer explains her rejection in a way that's not personal; it doesn't mean anything about him, except that it's one more "no" he won't have to hear again.

Effective and ineffective seducers differ when they are rejected when going for a kiss, as well. Say you've been on a date that went okay, but not great. You were bored and found an excuse to take her home early. In the car in front of her house you look into her eyes, run your fingers lightly through her hair, and, as you begin to move toward her, she says "Please don't try to kiss me."

By now you can probably see the difference already. While the Ineffective Seducer is plunging into depression at her rejection, the Highly Effective Seducer is already planning how he's going to spend the rest of the evening, thinking something like "Huh! I guess she was as bored as I was. That's one more 'no' on the way to 'yes.' What's on TV later?" While the Ineffective Seducer is letting it wreck his evening, the Effective Seducer is planning how to get her out of his car as quickly as possible, so he can get on with his life.

Here are the basic principles the Highly Effective Seducer follows in the face of rejection, which you must also follow. First, he leaves his self-image out of it. He comes up with an explanation for her rejection that has to do with her, or with circumstances, rather than with him. He thinks to himself that "She must have a boyfriend," rather than "I must not be attractive."

Second, he redirects his attention. Rather than giving his brain an opportunity to dwell on the rejection, he thinks about something else instead. He asks "What's on the dessert menu?" or "What's on TV tonight?" If his brain does go back to the rejection, he reminds himself it's one more "no" he won't have to hear on his way to an inevitable "yes." The Effective Seducer does not allow rejections to mean that he is unworthy or bad in any way. Though we dislike the overly new age/positive thinking movement, we saw a poster recently that poignantly sums up our point. It said, "You miss 100% of the shots you don't take."

A Highly Successful Seducer sees dating as a numbers game

Highly Effective Seducers constantly remember that dating, like so many areas of life, is a numbers game. Crass as it may seem, dating women is like selling a product. Instead of selling a vacuum cleaner or some other product, however, you are selling *you*. Salesmen know that they rarely make a sale on the first call they make. They know that if they do it was luck, and they can't count on it again.

Let's watch a top salesman at work. Martin sells insurance, and has for four years. He's 29, and has stunned his company by again and again meeting and beating his sales goals. He's made himself the best salesman in the company by following a simple philosophy. He's learned, through keeping records, that for every seventy-five people he calls, he makes four appointments, and out of those four appointments he makes one sale.

Unlike his associates, who don't sell as much as he does, Martin has accepted these facts of life. He understands that it's not personal when people hang up, or aren't home, or yell at him. It's all part of the numbers game he's playing, a game which he knows will eventually, inevitably, make the sale. All he has to do is keep dialing the phone, and sooner or later he *will* sell some insurance. So he keeps dialing, with that end in mind.

His associates that fail don't see it as a numbers game. They take the rejections and difficulties personally. Instead of knowing that they are working their way through inevitable rejection to get to inevitable success, they get caught up in the momentary bad feelings, and lose sight of their goal. They eventually give up, while Martin goes on to succeed. Martin is like the infamous Energizer Bunny. He keeps going and going, unwilling to be stopped by pitfalls along the way. Sure, Martin gets flustered, upset, and angry when things don't go his way. But he is able to always bring it back to the numbers game he is playing.

Highly Effective Seducers see seduction as a numbers game as well. Even the most successful seducers we know don't bed every women they approach—far from it. They know that most of their "cold calling"—that is, flirting with women—will not lead to anything more than that one interaction.

An Effective Seducer expects that one in ten of the women he flirts with he'll go out with, and that one in four of the women he goes out with he'll have sex with. He's accepted these facts of life. He thinks it's like baseball: those who hit the most home runs also have the most strikeouts. He understands that it's not personal when women say "no" to him, don't show up, or reject his advances. It's all part of the game he's playing which he knows will eventually get him in bed with women he desires. All he has to do is keep initiating, flirting, asking women out, and following the principles in this book, and sooner or later he *will* be having sex. So he keeps initiating, with that end in mind.

Ineffective seducers don't see seduction as a numbers game. They take the rejections and difficulties personally. Instead of knowing that they are working their way through inevitable rejection to inevitable success, they get caught up in their momentary bad feelings. As a result, they lose sight of the inevitability of their goal. They eventually give up, while the Effective Seducer goes on to succeed.

At the beginning, when you are first developing your seduction skills, your numbers may be more daunting. Unlike the practiced seducer, you may have to flirt with twenty-five or thirty women before you ask out three, and of those three only two may decide to go out with you. You may have to date six or seven women before you get one in bed, rather than the two or three needed by a more experienced seducer. You must understand that it doesn't matter when they say "no." As long as you realize that your persistence makes success inevitable, you'll be able to stick with it and keep pursuing women until you finally have the success you want. That success will bolster your confidence, and you will have an easier time getting the next women. As long as you remember it's a numbers game, you will have success with women.

Geoffrey is a student of ours who took this habit to heart. Forty-two years old, divorced, and slightly overweight, he hadn't had sex with a woman since his divorce three years previously. He was a sensitive fellow who'd make a devoted lover, boyfriend or husband. His chances of that were slim, however, as he had been taking any negative sign from women extremely personally. If he made a joke and a woman didn't laugh, he was crushed. Since the last woman who said "no" to him two years ago, he hadn't asked any woman out at all. He was living in hope, wishing that somehow he would find the love and relationship he wanted. Geoffrey was depressed when we met him, desperate for female companionship.

We shared the Habits of Highly Effective Seducers with him, and he changed his approach with women. Instead of seeing their rejections as reflections on him, he kept his mind focused on the numbers game. He told us "I figure I'll have to ask out ten women to get one 'yes,' and date four woman before I'll have sex. Fine, I'll do it!" He even showed us a chart he'd made to keep track of how many women he'd asked out, and how many women he dated.

It turned out that Geoffrey's predictions were overly conservative. Three of the first six women he asked out said yes, and one of those ended up having sex with him within three weeks. "Thinking of dating as a numbers game gave me the ability to move on to the next gal when one said 'no,'" he told us later. He now has a girlfriend he loves, and whom he's planning to marry.

Seeing dating as a numbers game will give you the confidence to go on in the face of anything that happens. From the man who approaches women on the street and asks "Will you have sex with me" to Geoffrey's search for a girlfriend, the numbers game will make you a Highly Effective Seducer.

Some men object to the idea that women's rejections could just roll off their backs. They want to be sensitive men; they think that seeing women's rejections as the key to sexual prosperity somehow gives license to men to be even more insensitive than they are already. After all, don't women complain that men aren't sensitive enough?

We think you should be sensitive to what women say and do, but *not* in the early stages of dating. When you are first getting to know one another, too much sensitivity to what she says or does is sexual suicide. The objection is that if you don't feel bad, you won't do what it takes to keep yourself "in-line." You'll just be an example of the huge male ego we've all heard so much about. If you aren't hurt by her rejections, this line of reasoning goes, you must think you're God's gift to women. At least if you are hurt, you know you're not overly egotistical.

Bob takes this route. When a woman rejects him, he's devastated. If you suggest to him that he might explain the rejection in some other way, he'll worry that then he'll be inaccurate: after all, maybe there really is something offensive about him that he needs to fix! If he keeps feeling good about himself after being rejected, he might be one of those egotistical guys who women sneer at behind their backs! He might become a macho pig, and we wouldn't want that.

Bob doesn't realize two things. First, that women may sneer at those guys, but they also have sex with them (for reasons we'll get to later) more than they do with apologetic men. Second, while he should always be refining his style and approach with women, feeling bad about himself will not help him do that. In the atmosphere of early dating, you simply have no choice but to be insensitive in the face of rejection. If you want any kind of relationship with women, you must be thick-skinned. Simply follow the steps the Highly Effective Seducer follows, realize it's one more "no" you won't have to hear on your way to success, and move on.

A Highly Successful Seducer always pursues more than one woman

In interviewing and modeling the behavior of Effective Seducers, we learned a terrible truth: if you are trying to become an expert seducer, pursuing only one woman is worse for your sex life than pursuing none at all!

Why is this so? Because when you are pursuing only one woman, you have no backup plan. You have all your eggs in one basket. You can't be playful and pursue her unconcerned with outcomes, because if she's your only prospect, she's your only chance for sex. You'll get overly concerned that if things don't work out you won't have anyone else to pursue. It most likely will make you dependent on her in some way. You will likely push her away from this dependency attitude. Further, if after a few dates she doesn't like you, then you will feel that there is something wrong with you. Your inability to relax with her will drive her away and leave you feeling bad about yourself.

Many of our students have fallen into this trap. You can follow all the other habits of the Highly Effective Seducer, but if you pursue only one woman, you will never experience an abundant sex life.

Leo, the manager of a dry cleaner, didn't believe us. When we started coaching him, he hadn't had a date in six months. "It's been so long since I've had sex," he joked with us, "that I think I've forgotten how to do it!" We trained him in the Habits. He followed them all except one. He pursued only one woman at a time. He flirted with one woman, returning to the store she worked at to see her again and again. He fantasized about how wonderful it would be to go out with her, to have her as a lover. Leo ignored other women, not exploring them as we recommended he do. But he had a problem: every time he saw the women he desired, he felt more tense. It became harder for him to joke with her, and he became more afraid of saying or doing something that would offend her. By the time Leo decided to ask her out, he was so nervous he was actually sweating. If she said "no," all his work would be for nothing, and all his dreams with her would be dashed! When he tried to ask her out he stumbled on his words, and blushed. She said, "Gee, thanks, I like you and everything, but I don't think it would work out." Because she was the only woman he was after, her response became so meaningful to him that he lost all ability to relax and be himself. Seeing his tension, she naturally didn't want to go out with him.

Leo returned to us and asked our advice. We told him again how it was important to go after more than one woman at a time.

After all, we asked him, would he seek out only one client for his dry-cleaning business? Of course not. He began following our advice, using the system we outline in this book, and soon had success.

If you do this, too, adding in more all the time and dropping out ones that don't work out for you, no single woman's response to you takes on much significance. You are able to relax, be playful, and unconcerned about her responses to your seduction. You'll be able to say to yourself "Hey, if she doesn't want me, there are plenty of women waiting in the wings to take her place," and know it's true.

Pursuing more than one woman also makes you more patient with the women you are seducing, because you have a variety of women at different points in your seduction. Now it doesn't matter to Leo if one of the women is being uncommunicative, is mean to him one day, or is moody. He knows he doesn't have to rush her in any way, because he has his needs met other places. This makes him an easier man to be around, and much more attractive to women.

Following our advice is also important when you finally are having sex. If you stop going after other women once you have a lover she *will* become your girlfriend, whether you like it or not. Studies have shown that men's body chemistry actually becomes physically addicted to a woman he sleeps with on a regular basis. That's fine if you want a girlfriend, but if you want casual short-term relationships with women you *must* continue to pursue other women, even after you've got the first one in bed.

Women are attracted to men who are relaxed, creative and exciting. Pursuing more than one woman brings out both of these qualities because it keeps you engaged with life in a creative exciting way. When you know the woman you are after is one of many, her response matters less than it would if she were your only hope for sex. You can be more relaxed, because you aren't risking offending your only possible sexual partner. If you do lose her for some reason, you can just move on to the next woman.

A Highly Successful Seducer initiates everything with women

Men frequently fail to initiate with women. They either forget that it is essential, or they resent doing it. Perhaps they've been frequently rejected a lot by women. Perhaps they think they are so special that women will approach them and ask them out. Whatever the reason, here is what Highly Effective Seducers know: the man must *always* make it his responsibility to initiate every step of a romantic encounter. Effective Seducers never forget it! If you slack off, another man will be having sex with the woman of your dreams while you are home alone masturbating.

Men commonly think women give signals of interest the same way they would. This is a big mistake. Most men don't realize that women do *not* do things the way men do. You must understand the crucial differences in how men and women respond to initiation.

For instance, if one of your buddies doesn't call you back when you've initiated getting together, it is fair to assume he doesn't want to accept your invitation. This is not the case with women. Women are trained to play hard to get, and are programmed to give mixed messages. It isn't personal. In fact, you will be a much happier man if you just keep initiating; don't take anything a woman does personally.

A case in point: a hot woman will never ask you out and will rarely call you back. If you really want her, you have to prove your worth. You will have to prove you are persistent and patient, and that there is something that sets you apart from the others. When a friend of ours met a beautiful 20-year-old woman at a bar, he initiated and got her phone number. He called her several times and she didn't call back. He kept initiating phone calls and finally talked to her. They set a date for coffee and she didn't show. He initiated another call and set up a date with her. On that next date he slept with her. His success was built on his persistence and willingness to initiate. What he didn't do was take it personally, resent the woman, whine to her, or give up.

We have known many men who are angry that they have to initiate. They complain that it isn't fair, and that if women really believed in equality, they would approach men. Or they complain that it's scary to approach a woman they don't know and risk rejection. Our advice to these men is to grow up and deal with it. If you are resentful, no woman will want you. Just get over it. This may be more easily said than done, but initiating without resentment is essential if you want success with women. This is the law of the jungle, and you must learn it to survive. You have no chance of changing the terrain, only of adapting to the harsh conditions. A master seducer will have the inner discipline to overcome his fear and resentment to get to his eventual goal of abundant sex.

Try looking at it this way: initiating gives you power. Rather than feeling resentful for having to do all the work to get a woman into bed, an Effective Seducer knows that initiating gives you the opportunity to make dating work for you. If you are the initiator, you get to talk to her when you want to, set up dates for times that are convenient for you, approach any woman you want, and eventually sleep with any woman you are attracted to. You're not powerless; in fact, you have total societal approval to make it work for you! From this standpoint having to initiate is pretty great for men.

Just in case you are totally brain dead, here is a list of initiations you must make: the first eye contact, the first smile, talking to her for the first time, keeping the conversation going, asking for her phone number, calling her up, calling her again when she doesn't call you back, asking her out, asking her out again when she "forgets" to show up, all eye contact and touching on the date, the first kiss, every single sexual initiation, and any subsequent dates. In a short-term erotic relationship you will also have to initiate the breakup.

A Highly Successful Seducer is always prospecting

A Highly Effective Seducer turns every situation with women into a prospecting situation. If you want an abundant sex life, you must learn to do this as well. One of Bob's fatal flaws is that he has tunnel-vision in his pursuit. Though he is consistently unsuccessful, he thinks he "knows" that there are very few places he can meet women. He is wrong. The fact is, women are everywhere. There is no shortage of places to meet them. Some of the best places are ones you are in every day that you don't even yet realize. Because Bob doesn't realize this, he only flirts with women when he feels like it, not as practice. He doesn't turn every situation into a prospecting situation.

Before taking our seminars and reading our book, many of our students stumbled through their days. They were unaware of the multitude of women around them at almost every moment. They constantly thought they were flawed in some way, never aware of the constant flow of sex available to every man as his birthright. If you read this book carefully and follow our advice you will be able to notice who the women are that you have contact with every day and turn many of them into lovers, just as Highly Effective Seducers do.

Effective Seducers are like successful salesmen. Let's examine how a successful salesman views his life. To him, every situation poses the potential for a sale. A hungry insurance salesman, for example, will do many cold calls, ask his friends for leads, call up long lost relatives for leads, put ads in newspapers, leave his business card at restaurants, and do other outrageous things to make sales. He will make whatever it takes to get the sale. The Effective Seducer has a similar type of rigor and intensity about his quest for women.

The Effective Seducer is also like a hunter. A good hunter is constantly outside of his comfort zone. This means that he doesn't hunt only in places that are easiest to get to. He goes to areas where he thinks the deer are, whether or not those places are always convenient. He makes it a higher priority to get his prey than to be in a comfortable situation. He gets up before dawn, hikes in the dark, sits in the cold, and waits patiently for a deer that may or may not come, because he knows that if he is consistent, he will eventually be successful. This is a model for us all.

A hunter scans the landscape looking for any signs, smells, or sounds that might lead him to his prey, just as an Effective Seducer does. He observes the whole landscape and investigates anything that moves. Most lonely men could also use this trait. An unsuccessful seducer, is so caught up with how a woman isn't quite pretty enough that he turns down the opportunity to practice on her, or to use that situation to meet other women. He also fails to scan the landscape and to stay aware of all the women who are potentials. The hunter analogy, though crude, is useful for you to use on your path to becoming a Highly Successful Seducer.

Look at every situation you are in as a potential for meeting women. You can even look at every interaction with a woman, be it at a restaurant, in an elevator, while pumping gas, or at the doctor, as an opportunity to initiate the steps to getting a date and practicing your skills as a seducer.

As we mentioned earlier, even computer geeks who are locked away in offices all day have opportunities to meet women. The difference between Effective and ineffective seducers is that the Effective Seducers know about those opportunities, and follow through on them. In the late 1980s there was a trend for many grocery stores to advertise "singles' nights." In many cities this turned out to be an effective way for stores to profit and for men and women to meet. At the time, this seemed like an outrageous idea. Who would think that singles would meet at such a strange place? Then it became a trend and not so out of the ordinary. The same is true for many of the other places you find yourself in throughout your day.

A Highly Successful Seducer always acts with an outcome in mind

If you were cold-calling for your business, would you call up a potential customer and not have any idea of what you were going to say? If you wanted a raise, would you go into your boss's office and have hours of meandering, meaningless conversation in the hopes that a raise would "just happen"? Would you take a potential client to seemingly random events and social occasions, hoping that for some reason he would decide to make a purchase?

Of course you wouldn't. You'd always act with an outcome in mind. If socializing or conversing were part of getting to your outcome, of course you would socialize and talk. But you'd always have in the back (or even near the front) of your mind the outcome you wanted to produce. You'd do the things that brought you closer to that outcome, and not do the things that had no impact or that might even take you away from your goal.

That's what Highly Effective Seducers do. Successful seductions are built on planning, and having outcomes in mind for every step of the way. Where there is no planning, there is room for problems and breakdowns.

Having an outcome before the date means that, when a man is talking to a woman for the first time, he is focused on giving her romantic feelings or getting her phone number. On the date, the outcome may be to have sex. After the date, the outcome may be to see her again, to keep her feeling special and interested, or to move on. You must always be asking yourself "what is my goal?" and "how do I want her to be feeling?" If you want her to feel safe, you must appear safe and not be too outrageous or scary. If you want her to feel romantic , you must ask her romantic questions and do romantic things. If you don't want her to feel disgusted, you must not burp, make crude jokes or do other disgusting things.

If your goal is the first kiss, and you have that goal in mind, you will automatically tend to choose activities and behaviors in line with that goal. And step by step, your goals will be fulfilled.

Men who don't have an outcome in mind are at the whim of circumstance and are bound to fail and most men fall into this category. They go with the flow and want to "just see where things go." As a man following the Habits of Highly Effective Seducers, you know your outcome, and pursue it.

A Highly Successful Seducer always makes life work for him

You met her last week. Attractive, fit, blonde and in her mid-20s. You had fun talking together, she readily gave you her phone number and agreed to meet for coffee. You arrive ten minutes early and are all ready for her to show up. You are waiting at the time she said she'd be there, waiting ten minutes past that time, and still waiting 30 minutes later. She still hasn't shown up. The question is, did you make it work for you, or didn't you?

A man who makes life work for him has no difficulty in this situation. He's brought some work to do, or some reading that is important for him to complete. He set up the date at a place and time convenient for him, so that if she didn't show up it wouldn't wreck his day. He works and flirts with the other women at the coffee shop and ends up having a good time anyway. After waiting 30 minutes, he left. When he calls the woman who didn't show—and we'll show you the best way to do this in a later chapter—he's not filled with unproductive resentment that she didn't keep her word. He makes life work for him, and has a good time anyway.

A man who doesn't make life work for him is so astounded that she said "yes" in the first place, that he bends over backwards to meet her for the coffee date. He may have canceled something important, rearranged his schedule, and come to an inconvenient place to meet her. He'll have arrived ready to socialize and have no backup plan in place for when she doesn't arrive. Even if she does arrive, 40 minutes late, he's so angry and upset and humiliated that he can't have a good time with her. He's made himself a victim by not making life work for him.

This is a huge mistake that many of our students make. They expect others, or their circumstances, to make life work for them. The man who is victimized by his date not showing up was expecting *her* to make the date work for him. As a result, he was a victim, just as you will be if you leave making your life work for you in the hands of other people.

Steve is a tall, balding man in his late 30s. He has an important presentation to make at 8:00 am the next morning. It could make or break his getting that big promotion. After wrapping up the final details for his presentation he decides to go out with the guys for a couple of drinks. It is now 9:00 pm, the bar seems really hopping. Brenda, an attractive woman in a slinky tight silk dress, is giving him a lot of attention. He dances with her and buys her drinks. Brenda touches him, smiles, and even leans over off her bar stool to kiss him lightly, pressing her breasts into him. "Finally," Steve thinks to himself, "I'm finally gonna get lucky."

Unfortunately for Steve, Brenda has no intention of leaving before closing time: 2:30 am, still three hours away. Steve is tantalized with the prospect of sex dangling before him. He drinks and dances with her until 2:30 am. Then she begs him to take her to an after-hours party until 3:30 am. Finally, he gets her back to his apartment, where they have sex until 6:00 am. Still drunk and exhausted, on one hour of sleep, Steve gives a terrible presentation the next morning. He doesn't get the promotion, and his boss's boss wonders aloud what is wrong with him.

The answer is simple: Steve didn't make life work for him, at least not in this situation. Once a woman comes on the scene, he becomes a victim. He hopes her whims will allow his life to work and that he will still get sex. He becomes a victim of his own unwillingness to take control of his life. He is also blindsided with his own urges and has no ability to prioritize the things in his life. He acts out of desperation, not like a man with a plan.

When Robert, who's worked with us, finds himself in the same situation, his choices are easy. He knows that for life to work for him he must leave the bar by 11:00 pm, whether or not there's a woman on his arm. He tells Brenda he has to leave, and she's disappointed. He tells her he'd love to see her again, and gets her phone number. He leaves, gets to bed early, and aces his presentation the next morning. He gets the raise, and is so pumped up by his success that he goes out that night and picks up another woman and has sex with her all night. Plus, he still has Brenda's number to call later!

The difference between Steve and Robert is that Robert is committed to making his life work for him, while Steve isn't. Steve might say he is, but the possibility of sex makes him throw away his control over his life. If we observe both of them we can see that Steve is more committed to being a victim of his circumstances and to instant satisfaction than he is to long-term gain. Robert sets his intention and moves toward it. He's leaving the bar by 11:00 pm, because he knows that's what it'll take to make his presentation work. His presentation is his top priority. He knows a night of drunken sex isn't worth risking the raise he's been working on for three months. Robert is an Effective Seducer. Steve is not.

Do you make life work for you in every situation, or are you willing to throw away control of your life when there's a possibility for sex? Highly Effective Seducers set up their lives so that they get the kind of life they want, whether women are in the picture or not. They count on themselves to make their lives work, rather than counting on women. As a result they are happier, more in control of their lives, more successful, and more attractive to women.

It is said that sex is the world's most expensive commodity. It often seems that way, for men. Men's need for sex topples empires, loses them jobs, gets them landed in jail. If you've ever done something that hurt your long-term best interests in order to pursue the possibility of sex, then you are not making your life work for you. If you've ever felt like a victim in your interactions with women you've dated or tried to date, then you too haven't been making life work for you. In both situations you haven't been a Highly Effective Seducer.

This habit of Effective Seducers branches beyond dating. Men who are committed to always making life work for them are always asking themselves how they can improve their experience of *any* situation. If an Effective Seducer is on a business trip and gets caught in an airport for a four-hour layover, he doesn't whine about it—or if he does, he gets it over with quickly. He asks himself, "How can I make this work for me?" and he keeps on asking until he comes up with an answer that works for him. He may make calls that need to be made. He may set up his laptop and get some work done. He may find the airport bookshop and find a book he's been meaning to read. He may even call phone sex on his cell phone from an empty bathroom stall.

A man who always makes life work for him is willing to be outrageous to have that happen. He wants a life that he lives fully. When caught in the airport, he may set himself the goal of flirting with ten women and getting one to have sex with him. He may call an ex-lover who lives in the town he's stuck in, and try to seduce her. He decides the quality of experience he's going to have, and creates his life to achieve it.

If you are going to be a man who has a life that works, you must do this, too. Here are some of the questions a Highly Effective Seducer constantly asks himself:

* How can I make this experience work for me?
* What quality of experience am I committed to having, no matter what happens?
* What can I do, right now, to create that experience for myself?
* What's most important to me in this situation?
* How can I get that?
* What would make this situation most fun?

By asking yourself these questions, and committing to making life work for you rather than counting on women to do it for you, you will become the kind of man women are most attracted to.

A *Highly Successful Seducer is never a prospect's therapist or friend*

Pop quiz: The best way to get a woman to desire you sexually is to help solve her problems, listen to her difficulties, and to prove yourself to be an excellent friend. True or false?

Every Highly Effective Seducer we studied knew that this statement is false. Being a woman's therapist, confidant, or pal is one of the *worst* ways of getting a woman in bed. In fact, if you are a woman's therapist, confidant or pal, you almost certainly destroy your chances with her sexually. While you may want to have women as pals on your own time, if the woman is a prospective sex partner, this could be the death blow.

The Therapist ploy. The man who tries to get sex by being a women's therapist thinks that if he solves her emotional problems then she'll naturally want to have sex with him. He bases this faulty reasoning on the fact that if an attractive woman solved *his* problems, he'd want to have sex with her. Given the fact that he'd probably want to have sex with an attractive woman even if she added to his problems, his logic doesn't make sense.

Gary is a man who tries to seduce women by being their free therapist. He was very attracted to Diane, as any man would be; she was blonde and bouncy and smart and large-breasted and everything he was looking for in a woman.

But Diane had problems. She'd had a difficult childhood, and it seemed like she always dated men who ended up being jerks to her. Sometimes she was happy and sometimes she was miserable. Her problems gave Gary something to talk with her about, and he secretly decided that he could get her in bed if he solved her problems. She'd see how wonderful he was, and reward him with sex. He took on being her personal therapist.

So Gary listened to Diane's problems, and gave her wonderful advice. Then he listened to more to her problems and gave her more advice. He thought about her problems all the time, figuring out innovative solutions. He talked to his friends about how difficult she was, how she didn't seem to want to change. Gary encouraged her to call him in the middle of the night if she had nightmares—and she did. Gary was certain that he was getting closer to her, and that she would soon be his. After all, they were so intimate. She called him all the time!

Gary's plan fell apart when he took Diane to a party where he noticed she was very flirty with lots of other men. One of his male friends told him later that she had said to him, "You know, it's odd. I want to have sex with every man in this room, except for Gary!" She ended up going home with Gary's best friend. He was devastated that she didn't desire him. He couldn't figure it out. After all, hadn't he helped her solve her problems?

This is a common story of ineffective seducers. When a man discusses a woman's problems with her, she associates him with her problems. Even if he manages to come up with solutions, he's still the last person who saw her with them. Either way, she'll want to get away from him. Effective Seducers know that women are attracted to men who take them into a different, romantic world, in which they seem to have no problems, and feel wonderful. If a prospective lover shares her problems with an Effective Seducer he may listen, but he will never offer solutions. He'll distract her from her problems by being charming and exciting, and get her feeling the way he wants her to feel, and continue the seduction.

When Jake, a Highly Effective Seducer, meets a woman like Diane, he handles her completely differently. He doesn't take the bait of talking about her problems. Instead, he sets up romantic experiences that blow her mind, and make her associate being with him with feelings of pleasure and attraction. (We'll show you how to do this in a later chapter.) She wants to be with him because he's exciting, not because he's a good therapist. He may even cause problems for her, and she'll put up with it, and keep wanting to see him. She'll complain about him to someone like Gary, but she won't be able to wait to see him again. All because Jake knows not to become her therapist.

The "Friend" ploy. The man who tries to get into a woman's pants by being her friend fails with women just as much as the man who tries to be her therapist. As we will discuss later, women we've interviewed have told us that they often decide if a man will be a lover or a friend in the first two minutes after meeting him. Once you are in the "friend" category, it's very difficult to get out. Donnie was friends with Kathy, whom he met at a personal growth seminar. She thought of him as a friend, and often told him so. He wanted to be her lover, but every time he pursued it, she'd say things like "I like you, but I don't want to spoil our wonderful friendship," or "I just don't feel that way about you. You're more like a brother to me." Effective Seducers understand that if a woman is a prospective lover, a man must avoid being her friend, and let her know about his romantic interest right away. When Jerome, a Highly Effective Seducer, meets a woman like Cathy, he shows his interest right away, as we'll show you how to do in this book. By doing this, he puts himself in the lover, or at least potential lover, category, avoiding the trap of friendship altogether. While Donnie is stuck in the "friend" category, Jerome has a foundation he can build his seduction upon, without her being able to object that romance might spoil their friendship. After all, they never had a friendship in the first place.

Women can be great friends if you have no sexual interest in them. If you are interested in a woman as a lover, take a cue from the Highly Effective Seducers: Don't be her friend or her therapist!

A Highly Successful Seducer is always willing to walk away from the seduction or from the woman

Have you ever seen a man totally at the beck and call of a woman, and miserable about it? Have you ever been that guy who is so dependent on a woman that you've forgotten what you are about and what your boundaries are? Have you ever felt "taken" by a woman?

Once the relationship starts, many men tend to give a woman everything she wants and sacrifice their self-respect in hopes of getting a steady supply of sex. Men often stay in unsatisfying relationships because they don't see any way out. Or they think no other woman will put up with or love them. As a result, they stay in relationships, sometimes for years, miserable and knowing that they should break it off, but somehow never mustering the courage to do so.

Ed, a 30-year-old social worker, dated Pam, a modern dancer, for six years. She came from a wealthy family and paid the rent on their apartment. Ed became semi-dependent on Pam during the four years they lived together. They were even engaged during the last year.

At first, he explained, "things seemed so exciting, and the sex was great. She would often prance around the house in her sexy leotards and we would cherish the nights we had at home." Later, she withheld sex and demanded that he do all the housework because she was paying the rent. He felt trapped in the relationship. He worried that no other woman would love him, and besides, he was dependent on her. He didn't like doing all the work, and didn't pursue his interests in the meantime, but somehow he couldn't turn down her requests.

Highly Effective Seducers are willing to cut off relationships with women if they don't work for them. If you are not willing to leave the relationship, you no longer have any power or say in what happens. If you aren't willing to walk away she will assume that she can walk all over you. A woman, like anyone else, will try to take as much as she can from you if you don't show her the bottom line.

The same principle can be applied in business situations. A man who isn't willing to quit when things become intolerable is at the whim of everyone's opinions and desires. He probably doesn't advance at his job or ask for what he wants because he is so busy being subservient to others that he ignores going for what he wants. The willingness to walk gives a man confidence in himself in any situation, especially with women.

This book will show you how to stay in the drivers seat and get sex whether you are in a committed relationship or not. If you don't want a girlfriend or a committed relationship, you must learn the power of being willing to walk away. If you want a committed relationship, you must be willing to walk away from women who do not seem like the type you want to spend the rest of your life with.

Being willing to walk integrates a hard bottom line attitude while not being cruel. It is not a personal attack on her. In fact you are really saying, "I want 'x.' You can either produce that or I'll replace you." A Successful Seducer knows what he wants and cuts to the chase, saving himself and the woman time and energy. A man who is willing to walk away, even from sex, is respected and cannot be taken off the course he has set for his life.

If Ed had known about our ideas, he could have ended the relationship with Pam much earlier and would have been able to create relationships he wanted with other women.

A Highly Successful Seducer makes it look like he's not working on the romance

What is the one difference between seducing a woman and having a job? At work you need to look as if you are working—in fact, the harder you look as if you are working, the better it is. The Highly Effective Seducer knows that when seducing a woman, the opposite is true: when you are with a woman, you absolutely must make everything look easy, even if you worked hard to set up the perfect romantic evening, or even if you hunted for hours to find the perfect little romantic gift.

One of our students, for example, spent two weeks searching for a T-shirt for Rachel, the woman he was pursuing. He knew she would love the shirt and it would lead to a "reward" of some sort. When he gave it to her at an unexpected moment she threw her arms around him and gave him a huge passionate kiss. The response was better than he could have imagined. Had he told her that he only bought it just to charm her, to make her feel romantic, and that he methodically looked for it for weeks, she wouldn't have been so happy.

A common bonehead mistake an ineffective seducer makes is that he expects a woman to acknowledge and thank him for all the work he's done in seducing her. This is suicide. A woman will rarely, if ever, acknowledge that you have pursued her, called her, created good feelings for her, risked rejection in asking her out, risked rejection in touching her for the first time, kissing her, and every other initiation that you've made. After all, the seduction is happening effortlessly for her, isn't it? It must be effortless! You will be happier to not even expect a woman to understand what you have gone through to make the romance seem effortless. She won't appreciate it anyway. It is best to boast to your friends about your seduction schemes, rather than to your date.

Bringing up the fact that you are putting in effort that she isn't appreciating will offend her. Look at it this way: she expects romance to happen, and the last thing she wants is a guy plotting how to get her. If you tell her about the work you are doing to seduce her, you break the magic spell, and she *will* accuse you of treating her like an object, not really caring about her as a person, manipulating her to get sex, and she will be angrier than you can possibly imagine.

On a recent date with Jennifer, Bob idiotically admitted to her that he believed dating is a matter of "constructing a meticulous plan to charm and romance a woman." They got into an argument about the merits of planning out dates versus "just going with the flow." Bob went on to admit that he believed that romance was "just a matter of working hard enough to get a woman into a sexual mood." To make things even worse, he admitted that he had put lots of thought into his last date with Jennifer—the date on which they ended up kissing in front of his fireplace while her favorite band played on the stereo. Jennifer was shocked and offended that he had worked to set that up. She thought it had "just happened." She became so angry and upset with Bob that she made him leave her apartment and told him that she never wanted to see him again.

When Bob opened up his big mouth and wanted Jennifer to acknowledge the work he had done to seduce her, he made a number of horrid mistakes. First, as you will see later, fighting with a woman will not lead to sex. It usually leads to more trouble. Second, Bob didn't realize that women will not understand that sex and dating is work. While he was correct in realizing it was work, she would never understand this. In fact, she responded appropriately. No one wants to feel manipulated. To admit planning out a date *will* be misconstrued by a woman as manipulation. Last, Bob expected to be acknowledged for all the work and energy he put into the seduction dates he created with Jennifer. When he talked about it he bit off more conflict than he could possibly chew, and it wrecked his chances with Jennifer.

Do what the Effective Seducers do. Make it look like you're not working, and the women you desire will be yours!

chapter three...
The Elements
of Style:
Dress
and Confidence

What kind of woman do you want? What's most important to you in a woman? Is it that she be tall, or short? That she have wonderful breasts? That she be blonde, or brunette? That she be smart, or rich? What exactly do you want?

These may seem like confrontational questions. For men who are living in a sexual desert, the answer may well be "any woman at all"! Strange as it may seem, you'll have better chances of getting a woman if you are looking for one with specific qualities than you will if you are looking for any woman at all. So we ask again, what kind of woman do you want?

Most men to whom we ask this question go a little nuts at first. They get like the proverbial kid in a candy shop. "Nineteen years old with perfect skin and a model's body," one man says. "She's aggressively bisexual, and loves sex." "A *Victoria's Secret* model," says another. "She's so rich, I quit my job and she supports me. We have sex twenty hours a day, every day she's not working! And she sets me up with other supermodels, too!"

When they are allowed to ponder the question, however, most guys calm their desires down. They don't *really* want to date 19-teen-year-olds, but they *do* want to date women who are young and very attractive. They don't *really* want to date *Victoria's Secret* models, and quit their jobs. What they *do* want is women who are more beautiful, more sexual, and more intelligent than they've ever been with before. The supermodel fantasy is just the expression of that desire. The bottom line is that most men don't really desire the extremes, but they *do* desire women who are "out of their league."

So think about it. What kind of woman do you really want? Most men dream about women they wouldn't really want, and end up getting women they would never dream about and don't particularly desire. We want you to get women you would dream about, and want in real life. So let yourself dream, let yourself imagine the kind of women you want. Think "out of your league." What do you get?

Most men we asked desire women who are extremely attractive, young, intelligent, mature, and who love sex. They want women who have a great sense of style, who are confident and outgoing, who take care of their bodies, and who are not snobby or overly obsessed with their own comfort. They want women who fulfill their particular physical desires: great legs, or large breasts, or long hair, or perfect butts. Men usually find they desire women who are well above the level of the women they have been dating, but not actually superstars, or supermodels.

There's an old saying, "If you don't have any destination in mind, any road will take you there." You really have to decide what you want in a woman to make use of the information in this chapter to find out what you need to do—what roads to take—to get her.

Once you have an idea of what you want, here's the next step: Think about the kind of woman you desire. Think about her style, her grace, her beauty. Now ask yourself: "If I were to have a woman like this, what kind of a man would I have to be?"

This question is crucial because it will guide you in your quest. What kind of a man would you have to be to have the kind of women you desire? The first mistake men make in answering this question is that they think they would have to be more than they could ever possibly be. They doom themselves, with answers like "to have the women I really desire, I'd have to be a millionaire," or "to have the women I really desire, I'd have to be a professional basketball player." Or, they come up with criteria that doom them from a physical standpoint: "to have the woman I desire, I'd have to be taller," or "to have the woman I desire, I'd have to be more hand-some," or "to have the women I desire, I'd have to be younger," or "to have the woman I desire, I'd have to not have [whatever you think is wrong with you.]"

That's all nonsense. You don't have to be fundamentally differ-ent from what you are to get the women you desire. You don't have to be richer, or taller, or better looking. Look: the truth about women is very simple. You can have the woman you desire if you can make her feel the romantic feelings she most wants to feel. When we ask "what would you have to be like to have the women you desire," we are simply asking you to think about the parts of yourself you'll have to accentuate if you are to make the women you desire feel romantically about you.

The second mistake men make in answering this question is that they decide that they have to become somebody they are not, fake men, supermen. They imagine they'll have to become basically different from what they honestly are. They think they'll have to become James Bond, or some sort of a "tough guy" action hero who they really aren't. They think that to get women, they'll have to betray themselves. They are afraid of trying to be who they aren't, and for good reason. Most men who approach women trying to be completely different from who they basically are come across like *Saturday Night Live*'s "Wild and Crazy Guys," trying to look hip for the "foxes," but really just looking like fools. As you'll see in this chapter, you'll need to stretch yourself, but not betray yourself.

When you think about the kind of man you'll have to be to get the kind of woman you desire, what kind of answers do you get? Most men we work with say things like Ken did: "Well, I'd have to be more confident, and talkative with women, I think. And I'd have to look sharper, too, I think... If I'm going to be with a woman who looks and dresses as hot as I'd like her to, I'd probably have to be fit and wear clothes that look good on me, too. Hm, I might have to clean my car, and what about my house? I'd probably have to put those pictures up, and water the plants more often, if I'm going to be the kind of guy who gets the woman I desire."

Most men discover that while they don't need to be different from who they really are, they do need to develop who they are more thoroughly. They find that they need to develop their *Personal*

Style which has two parts: *style*, that is, how you dress, and *confidence*, how you behave. While you don't have to change who you are as a person, you will probably find you have to change how you express who you are—your personal style—if you want to get the woman of your dreams.

WHY HAVE PERSONAL STYLE?

Bob doesn't want to change anything about himself to get women. He's sure that if he changes his looks or his behavior in any way, he'll be "being fake." "I want a woman to like me the way I am!" he asserts. Many men tell us things like "If only women could know me, I'm sure they'd want to be with me." But, for some reason, the women they'd like to know never seem to want to know them. When we examine how these men dress and their level of confidence, we find again and again that they dress and behave in ways that put women off.

Sidney was one of these men. Very proud of the fact that he always did things his own way, he called himself "a maverick" and "a rebel." He liked to wear torn-up clothes that looked terrible: his favorite sweatshirt was so shredded that he had replaced one of the sleeves with an old pant leg from a pair of jeans. His clothes were not only torn up, but *wrinkled* and torn up. He prided himself on not owning a clothes dryer, and proudly said "I will *never* iron a shirt!" He didn't care at all about how he looked, and was surprised that women who *did* care about how he looked were never interested in him. Day after day he looked terrible, and day after day he wasn't attractive to the women he desired. Strangely, day after day he was surprised by this fact.

He fared little better in his confidence, that is, his behaviors with women. As we worked with him, we discovered that he worried his way through every interaction with attractive women. He was always asking himself, "What am I doing wrong? Am I offending her? What if she doesn't like me? Am I scaring her?" He never had any idea about what to say to women, and often ended up sputtering and apologizing for "bothering" them. His confidence was terrible, and he never varied his approach. Day after day he approached women in the same ineffective, apologetic way, and day after day he wasn't attractive to the women he desired. Again, day after day he was surprised by this fact.

The funny thing was, Sidney was obviously a great guy. He was well read, well educated, and a great cook. He was a marathon runner, in great shape, and had a lot of interesting ideas. He'd obviously make a wonderful companion, and any woman who was with him would be lucky. But Sidney had a fatal flaw that left him helpless with women: he was unwilling to change anything about his dress or approach. As we said before, a person is insane when he does the same things over and over, and expects different results than he got before. This is exactly what Sidney was doing, and it is what many men, quite possibly you included, do as well.

Think about it. When you have not had the success you've wanted with women, have you tried changing your looks and behavior? We are willing to bet that you probably haven't. Like Sidney, you've probably done what you always do, and not known any different approaches to try. As a result you've behaved insanely, doing the same things over and over with women, expecting each time that perhaps, through sheer luck, something better would happen.

As we taught Sidney the material in this chapter, he began to change. He began to see that, rather than needing to be someone other than who he was, he needed to develop his personal style and confidence to better express who he really was. He learned, as you will learn, that his dress and confidence were ways of expressing himself more fully and attractively, not of hiding or being fake. And as he started developing his personal style and confidence, he began to be the man he'd have to be to get the women he wanted.

DEFINING YOUR STYLE

As we said before, women are attracted to men who make them feel the romantic feelings they so desire. Don't be fooled by the simplicity of this statement; teaching you how to make women feel romantically inclined is the fundamental goal of this book and should be your primary goal as well in all your interactions with them. Everything you can do toward this end, you must do.

Your style—how you dress and your level of confidence—is the first thing a woman sees about you. You must make it work for long-term outcome. You must make your style automatically generate romantic feelings in the women you encounter.

Your personal style is your unique expression. It's your first "advertisement" to the world about who you are and what you are about. Through your style, you tell people what is important to you. Your style is a reflection of your passion.

THE COMMITMENT OF STYLE

Would you go to a job interview in your workout gear? Would you show up at your job wearing torn, dirty, or even smelly clothes? Would you wear a suit and tie to play in your local softball league? Or wear swim trunks on a business trip? Of course not.

The simple fact is that different activities have different uniforms. If you want to be successful at a job interview, you invest the time and money in getting the right outfit for it. If you want to look professional at your job, you invest the time and money in getting the right clothes for it. And if you are playing softball on the local team, you don't wear a suit and tie; you wear the clothes that are proper for the activity.

Your life pursuit is now "getting women." If you are serious about this, you will invest time and money in getting the right clothes for the job. Because every day, every interaction you have with women will be a "job interview" of sorts, you need to wear clothes that are attractive for the job.

What, exactly, those clothes will be will vary from man to man. A man who is a mechanic, for instance, will express his style through clothes that are different from those of an executive. But both men, if they wish to be successful, will make the commitment to thinking about how they look to women every single day.

Our level of success with women skyrocketed when we first understood the importance of proper dress when meeting them. We each developed "dating uniforms" which we knew would make us into the kind of men we'd have to be to get the kind of women we desired into bed. We became willing to spend the time and money on getting the right clothes and keeping them clean, pressed, and mended. This simple commitment has made all the difference in our level of success with women.

WHAT YOU SAY WITH HOW YOU DRESS

A wise person once said "I've never met a person who wasn't carefully costumed." We agree. No matter how you are dressed right now, on some level you have chosen your outfit because it makes a statement you want to make. Sidney, in our example above, wore torn clothes as a way of saying that he was a rebel and a maverick. On a subconscious level, it was more important to Sidney to show what a rebel he was than it was for him to get women.

When women look at how you dress, it makes a statement to them. To women, Sidney's way of dressing said "I want you to look good, but I'm not willing to look good in return." Not surprisingly, women were not very attracted to this. Other men make other statements. One of our clients, Ray, was an older man who had been having trouble getting dates for many years. He wore garish, brightly colored clothes that clashed with each other, and from a stylistic perspective, looked terrible. His ex-wife told him he "made a mockery of style." On top of this, he rarely bothered to bathe or shave, so he often smelled bad. On a subconscious level, by wearing clothes women wouldn't like, Ray was constantly saying "Go to Hell!" to women. He was saying this to his mother, to women in his life now, and to every woman he'd ever felt controlled by. He would complain about how women didn't like how he dressed, and wouldn't date him, but as we got to know him, we saw that it was more important to him to insult women's sensibilities than it was for him to get sex. Because of his style, his mere presence offended women. And he wondered why he couldn't get women into bed!

Men like Sidney make less bold, but still destructive statements to women through the way they dress. At best, they send the message "I don't care about how I look," and at worst, "I'm immature and you don't want to go out with me." When it's more important to Sidney to show what a rebel he is than to get the women he desires, women end up thinking "He's immature, and not a real man."

Other men make more constructive statements to women through the way they dress. Think about some men you know, or have seen, whose style of dress is attractive to women. You might think of John Travolta, playing the character Chili Palmer in the film *Get Shorty*. He always looked good, wore clothes that fit, and had a style that fit him. His style said "I'm an attractive man who knows what he's about. I'm not stuck in making some immature statement. You want me in your life." This is what you want to say, too.

As we worked with Sidney, he changed his style and thereby changed what he was saying to women. He realized that saying he was a rebel was not as important as being attractive to women. He decided that, in order to be the kind of man that got the kind of women he wanted, he'd have to have a style of dress that said "I'm an attractive, mature man," rather than making a teenage statement of rebellion. He made the changes, as you'll learn to do in this chapter, and immediately noticed improvements in his relationships with the opposite sex.

What does your way of dressing say to women? Does it say that you are mature, attractive, in love with your life, confident, and of interest to her? Or does your way of dressing send out a more immature message? Let's find out.

WOMEN DO IT!

Focusing on your style may be new to men, but there's one group of people it's not new to: women. Almost all women spend time thinking about how they look to men, and spend a lot of time trying to improve their attractiveness. Heck, they even put paint on their faces to make themselves look better! We're not suggesting you go that far, but since women spend time thinking about how they look to the other sex, perhaps spending a little time on it yourself is not so unreasonable.

Women actually set an encouraging example. How many women do you know who look noticeably more attractive "done up right" than they do when they don't think about how they look? Probably most. One woman we know, Cindy, is on the low end of average looking when she's wearing torn-up, poorly fitted house-clothes, and her hair is a mess. However, when she makes herself up, does her hair, and puts on attractive clothes she looks great. If you are going to get the women you most desire in bed, you must learn to accomplish the same kind of transformation.

THE THREE HELPERS THAT MAKE YOU LOOK BETTER

If you are like most men (and you probably are, right?) you aren't going to be able to transform your style of dressing without help. We will go over the basics in this chapter, but to really create a transformation in how you look, you'll also need help from other people.

1. Stylish Men

We suggest you look around for the resources you already have to help you develop your style. Who do you know who has a great sense of style? Approach stylish men you know, and ask them for advice. Ask them where they shop for clothes, and where they get their hair cut. Then go to those places and ask the sales clerks to help you with a "new look." They'll often suggest clothing you wouldn't normally get for yourself, but that your style could "grow into."

2. Women

Another intelligent way to shop is to find a stylish woman who you are not interested in sexually, and ask her to go shopping with you. One of our students had a tremendous experience the first time he did this. He went to Cindy, the woman mentioned above, and asked her to go shopping with him. He knew she had an extraordinary sense of style, but also wasn't interested in her sexually, so it wouldn't matter if they became friends. She had only one requirement: he must promise to buy everything she told him to until the three hundred dollars he'd set aside for clothing was gone. It turned out she gave him great advice, and some of the hardest purchases to make, such as spending fifty dollars on a tie, turned out to be some of the best. For months he got compliments from women on how great he looked, all because he was willing to commit himself to looking good. "It was hard at first," he said later. "A lot of the clothes she told me to buy, I didn't really want. But it turned out to be great, and did a lot to help me create my personal style."

3. Male Friends

It's good to go clothes shopping with other men who are also developing their personal style. The right men friends can encourage you to take fashion risks.

In time you will develop relationships with stores you like, where you know you can trust the clerks to suggest new style ideas that will both express your true self and make you even more attractive to women. One of our students who often wears a cowboy hat that looks great on him got the hat that way. "I'd never considered a hat like that before," he says. "But when the clerk brought it over and set it on my head, it looked great. I knew right away it was right for me, and I never would have found it by myself." As you buy more clothes, you will discover what you really like, and what kinds of clothes really make the kind of statement you want to make to women.

THE FOUR RULES OF CLOTHING

Most men are "clothes blind." They don't see dirt in the same way women do, and they don't think about style as much. Here are the basic rules about clothes that men need to learn.

First and foremost, *clothes must fit well!* It doesn't matter how great a shirt is if it looks ill-fitting. It doesn't matter how much a pair of pants has been marked down if it pulls into a pronounced "starfish" shape where the legs meet the crotch. Simple clothing that fits well is far better than fancier clothing that just "doesn't look right."

If you are interested in pursuing a casual ragged, torn-up clothing look, proper fitting is the difference between looking sexy and looking like a slob. Next time you see a man or a woman who looks great in the torn-up style, notice how well the clothes fit them. You'll notice they fit perfectly, which is why the style works.

Some clothing stores are better for the average man than are others. If you are a bit overweight, some of the more hip and upscale stores may not have clothes that fit you well. Very often one store will have an entire line of pants, for instance, that don't fit you well. It's just the way their clothes are cut. Another store, on the other hand, might have a wide variety of pants that fit you. It's a good idea to keep shopping around until you find a store where the clothes fit, they look good, and the salespeople help you expand your style.

How do you know when clothes don't fit well? Often, the salespeople will tell you, though you can't count on that. The men you are shopping with can also tell you. The bottom line is simply this: if you don't feel that the clothes fit, they don't. Don't waste your money, and move on to the next piece.

The second rule of clothing is that *clothes must be clean!* Because most men are "clothes blind," and can't seem to tell when clothes need laundering, let's briefly go over how you know when it's time to wash something.

* If it's underwear, and you've worn it more than once, wash it.
* For shirts and pants, you can be more discriminating. To tell if shirts and pants are dirty, look at them under bright light. Are there any spots or stains? If there are, rub the spot with stain remover (buy it where you buy detergent), and wash. Pants also need laundering when they start to get baggy and wrinkled. Blue jeans are especially susceptible to stretching and getting baggy. When this happens, it's time to wash them.

The third rule of clothing is that *clothes shouldn't be wrinkled!* Yes, you might have to iron your shirts and pants, or have them ironed. Think about it: you are more attracted to women who are wearing clothes that aren't wrinkled and sloppy. Women are no different. Of course, not all clothes need ironing, but if you want to send a message to attractive women that you are the kind of man they want, ironing may be required. Having your shirts and pants laundered professionally is also a possibility for men who can afford it and don't want to iron.

The fourth rule of clothing is that you must *keep clothing in good repair!* Look under "Seamstress" in the local Yellow Pages, and get buttons sewed back on, holes patched and rips mended right away.

Wearing clean, well-fitting, ironed clothes that are in good repair has multiple benefits. Not only do you look good, you also *feel* good. Your style of dressing will naturally send out the message to women that you are attractive, together, and of interest to her.

THE 13-POINT BODY MAKEOVER FOR BEING ATTRACTIVE TO WOMEN

By working with men like Sidney, we've developed a 13-point "body makeover" that focuses men's attention on the particulars of their look. We'll start at the top of your body and work down, giving you time-tested style pointers along the way to guarantee that you will look attractive to women.

Bobby came to us because the women he was attracted to didn't seem to be attracted to him. He was 28 years old and thin and wiry. He was a gifted computer system administrator, and had a style that could best be described as "lazy hippie." His hair was long and unkempt, and his beard was unruly. He had thick-framed glasses that looked old, and he seemed to have to squint a lot to see through them. He wore T-shirts under untucked, unbuttoned button-down shirts, and a variety of old jeans and beat-up sneakers. As we worked with Bobby, it became clear that, through his dress, he was telling women "I'm still a boy. I'm not good enough for you." We took Bobby through our 13-point makeover, and changed his message to women to "I'm together and interesting, and you'd like to talk to me." Here's how we did it:

1. Hair

Bobby looked like a "wild man" when we first met him. His hair was long and shaggy, and it looked like he hadn't had a haircut, or even combed his hair, in months.

Hair has to be taken care of to look good: the movie stars who seem to have rumpled, disorderly hair actually spend a fortune in time and money to get it to look "just so." While short hair doesn't always look better than long, many men who have long hair used to look good with it, but, now that they are getting older, don't anymore. We determined that Bobby looked good with long hair as a teenager, but should try a shorter, more orderly style now. He got a new, shorter haircut, which immediately made him look more professional and, we thought, more in charge of his life.

He also learned to style his hair, something he had resisted for years. He discovered that, for his hair to look best, he needed to blow-dry it with styling gel after washing it, which he began doing on a near-daily basis. He began using conditioner to make it fuller and softer. He noticed an immediate change in his life; women seemed more interested in him. He decided that, in view of the newfound feminine attention, having to use a blow-dryer was not such a big problem.

It's important that your hair look good. It should not be greasy, out-of-control, and you should not have dandruff. Go to a real hair stylist, and get a look that is good for you. Men who are balding have several options. Even if you are balding, your hair can still look good and be styled well. Just watch out for the trap balding men fall into of combing just a few hairs across the bald top of their heads. It doesn't work and women, especially, find it unattractive. Just remember Star Trek's bald Captain Picard, and let your bald head shine.

We've also known balding men who have created a powerful, attractive look by keeping their heads shaven. Admittedly, it takes some guts to do this, but if you have an attractive skull, it can really look good.

2. Eyebrows/Ear hair/Nose hair

Most men don't have a problem with their eyebrows, but it makes sense to check yours and be sure. Some men's eyebrows grow very long and need to be trimmed. Several of our students have gray hairs in their eyebrows that grow, if unhindered, to an inch long or longer. These men must pluck or trim these hairs on a regular basis.

Ear hair and nose hair must be trimmed regularly. You might not notice if this hair grows long, and your male friends might not notice, but women you find attractive *will*. You can use little scissors or special trimmers to trim these hairs at least once every two weeks.

Hair should not protrude from the nose or ears. Stray hairs growing on your ears should also be trimmed.

3. Glasses

Like many men, Bobby wore glasses. His looked old, scratched, and he seemed to need to squint to see through them. We sent him to his optometrist to get his prescription updated, then accompanied him to find the right pair of frames.

If you wear glasses, choosing the right frames is very important. The bad news is, really stylish frames can cost two or three hundred dollars. The good news is that having to wear glasses is a great opportunity to choose frames that will enhance your attractiveness noticeably. It's worth shopping around for the frames that look the best on your face. Go to high-end stores as well as the cheaper ones. Every woman who sees you will see your glasses, so it's worth getting ones that really look great.

4. Snorting and phlegm

Brian had a problem. He was attractive and dressed well, but always seemed to need to clear his throat, and spit. He became so used to this that he hardly even knew he did it anymore, but every time he'd take a big snorting inhale, women noticed, and didn't want to be around him.

Women find snorting and spitting of phlegm *very* revolting. We know you find it disgusting too, but take it from us, what you feel is nothing compared to how women feel about it. If you find that you have problems with phlegm, you must find out why, and solve them. Many people who have excess phlegm have allergies to dairy foods, and find it clears up if they avoid milk products or take enzymes to help them digest lactose. If you have these problems, seek professional help and get the phlegm cleared up, or the message you'll send to women is "I'm disgusting. Stay away from me."

5. Facial hair

Bobby had a beard, and, at first, we suggested that he try shaving it off. Unless a beard is well-kept and trimmed regularly, it won't be attractive on most men. We thought Bobby's beard made him look like a slob, so we suggested he shave it off.

While many men look better without beards, Bobby wasn't one of them. "My God," he said after he shaved it off. "I look like those newspaper pictures of Dave Barry!" We agreed that it wasn't the right look for him, and he grew in a short, well-trimmed beard that went with his hair, and looked great on him.

The biggest problem men have with beards is that they let them get too wild. Pick a style, and keep the beard neat. The biggest problem women tell us that they have with men's beards is that the beards tend to get scratchy. If you do have a beard, be sure to use conditioner on it to keep it soft.

6. Lips

And speaking of soft, if you plan to be kissing women, you need to keep your lips soft. If they are rough women will notice, and not want to kiss you. We know it seems petty, but it's true. Remember, when you are first dating a woman, she has you on probation. Sure, you're exciting, but dating you also puts her at risk of emotional entanglements and getting hurt. While you are thinking of how great it's going to be to have sex with her, she's looking for a reason to send you back into the slammer with all those other guys, so she can get back to her nice, orderly life. For this reason you *must* have your details in order. And for this reason, your lips must be soft. Use lip balm.

7. Teeth

We also sent Bobby to the dentist to get his teeth cleaned, and if you haven't had yours cleaned in the last six months, you should make an appointment, too. Bobby didn't want to go, so we had him create a reward that would motivate him. He decided that as a reward for getting his teeth cleaned, he'd take himself out to the local strip club and have a good time. With the prospect of naked women dangling before him, he was able to get in and have more than five years of crud scraped off his teeth. They looked whiter, and felt smoother and cleaner to him. After all, if you expect a woman to stick her tongue in there, you want your mouth to be as clean as possible.

8. Skin

Smooth soft skin is important to women, especially on your face. If you tend to five o'clock shadow, be sure to shave again before going out on a date. If you have rough hands, start using moisturizer to soften them up. Most women aren't interested in men who have rough, sandpaper-like hands.

9. Smells

It's hard to underestimate the negative consequences of smelling bad to a woman. A surprising number of the women we interviewed said that they had been on dates where they would have had sex with the man, if only he hadn't smelled bad. It is important that you bathe regularly, own deodorant, and use it. Remember, if you think you might smell bad to women, then you do.

You should also know that, as one women we interviewed said, "nothing is more of a turn-off than the smell of feces." If you tend to have gas, then you *must* do something about it. Products like *Beano* can help you pass less gas. You may even need to see a doctor if you have a serious gas problem.

This is no small concern. Studies show that women have a more developed sense of smell than men do. Smells that don't seem too bad to men can be quite repellent to women. If you want to have sex with attractive women, then you must manage your smells. Men who refuse to handle this problem send the message to women that they are more interested in passing gas than they are in having sex with women. Women conclude that such men are immature, and they are right.

(While we are on the topic, you should also be aware that women truly don't appreciate bathroom humor as you might. Save it for your guy friends.)

It's also critical that you have good breath. Again and again, the women we interviewed told us that men who have bad breath turn them off. Reena is typical of these women, when she says "Sure, I can think of a number of guys I was ready to have sex with, but then noticed they had bad breath. I figured I didn't want them after all." You must brush your teeth regularly, and if you think your breath might be bad, it is. Carry mints with you, but don't take them in front of her. For some reason, women seem to think that men who take steps to have good breath are vain, even while they say that men who smell bad are slobs. Excuse yourself to the bathroom and take the breath mint there.

If you use aftershave lotion, be sure to not use too much. As the saying goes, a dab'll do. Women aren't attracted to guys who wear so much lotion that smell rays seem almost to be radiating from their bodies. The man you'd have to be to get the kind of woman you want probably doesn't smell too bad, or too good.

10. Pockets

Just as you can have a wonderful, expensive desk, and overload the drawers to the point where they can't be closed, you can have wonderful, stylish clothes, and overload the pockets to the point where your nice slick clothes make you look like an old lumpy mattress.

While women carry purses that they overfill, men overfill their pockets. If you want to be attractive to women, you must carry as little as possible in your pockets, so you don't look lumpy and your clothes don't get stretched.

Bobby overfilled his pockets. He routinely had so many pens and papers in his shirt pockets that the weight pulled the shirt down, and he overfilled his pants pockets as well. Like many men, he had lots of keys which made a big lump on his leg when he put them in his pocket. We had him remove the keys he didn't need, and carry as few as he could get away with. Other men who absolutely must carry lots of keys have benefitted from carrying them on their belts rather than in their pockets.

Bobby's wallet was also thick, disorganized, and bulging with papers and old receipts. We explained to him that women do check out men's bodies, just as men check out women's, and how a thick wallet made his butt less attractive to women. He got rid of the excess papers, and bought a thinner wallet.

11. Belt

Your belt is one of the small particulars of your dress that you must have under control if you want women to be attracted to you. If you are wearing a cheap cardboard belt, or if your belt is falling apart, you won't be sending an attractive message to women. Likewise, if you are using the biggest or the smallest hole in your belt, you might look silly, and should consider getting a belt that fits you better. If you are at all overweight, it's better to not have too fancy a belt-buckle, as it will draw attention to your waist, which is not where you want women to look. Get a simpler belt-buckle until you've slimmed down.

12. Socks and shoes

If you'll look closely at your socks, you'll find that there is an inside and an outside, and that it's possible to wear them inside out. Though few men would ever notice this, women tell us that they do. Wear your socks the right side out.

Women also evaluate men by the quality of their shoes. It's hard for most men to comprehend the amount of time women spend thinking about shoes. They have conversations with each other about shoes; they spend discreet blocks of time shoe shopping; they sit around thinking about what shoes to wear with what outfits. The more attractive a woman you are interested in is, the more time she probably spends thinking about shoes.

With this in mind, you shouldn't be too suprised to find out that she also judges and think about your shoes. So you should be ready. The sad fact is, you probably need more and better shoes. Bobby had his dirty sneakers, his messed-up dress shoes, and a very uncomfortable pair of dress shoes that he wore the two times a year he put on his only suit. Through his work with us, he realized that, to be the kind of man who attracted the kind of women he wanted, he'd need some new shoes. He visited a number of stylish shoe boutiques and got several pair of sexy new shoes.

He also bought shoe trees, which are brilliant wood or plastic devices that you put in your shoes when you take them off to help them keep their shape and last years longer. He also committed himself to having his shoes shined regularly, and to replacing the shoelaces before they became too frayed. He realized that, just as he didn't want to wear wrinkled clothes, he wouldn't be attractive to women wearing wrinkled shoes.

13. Posture

Bobby had what we call "adolescent posture." He slumped like a teenager, and shuffled when he walked. His shoulders were rounded, and his head was forward. He looked unobtrusive and timid, but realized that he needed to look powerful and decisive to get the women he desired.

There are a lot of kinds of bodywork you can get if you, like Bobby, suffer from poor posture. You may want to explore chiropractic, which is often at least partially covered by insurance, to improve your posture. Other men get regular massage, or go through a process called "Rolfing" or Neuro-Muscular Therapy to improve posture. Bobby started getting chiropractic care and regular massage treatments. He soon was standing straighter and taller, his shoulders seemed broader and less tense, and he walked straighter and more upright. As a plus, his lower back pain cleared up. "I feel more solid now," he told us, "and more able to meet attractive women on their own ground." Better posture made him more into the kind of man who would be attractive to the kind of women he desired.

Bobby followed our 13-point makeover plan, and developed an entirely new look for himself that brought out the parts of him that he wanted to express to women. He looked and felt more confident, mature, adult, and attractive. With his good posture, clean look, and neat, interesting, well-maintained clothes and shoes he said "I'm a together adult man, ready to take on the world. You are interested in being with me." Women noticed this and began responding at once.

DETAILS: THE KEY TO WOMEN'S HEARTS (AND PANTS)

One important key to seducing women which we will return to again and again throughout this book is *details*. Women feel romantic when the little details are taken care of, whether those details are perfect candlelight, clean sheets, or the small particulars of how you dress. You may have noticed how many parts of the makeover focused on the details; that's because properly managed details make women feel romantic.

You've probably heard women talk about how important "the little things" are to them. While women usually don't give useful advice about how to seduce them, in this case they are telling the truth. A man who can manage the details will always get women in bed. In upcoming chapters we'll show you how to manage the details in every aspect of a seduction. Here's how you can make the details of your appearance work for you.

The "little things" in how you dress tell a woman a lot about you, and have a big effect on how she treats you. Evan has the "sloppy attractive" look mastered. He seems to wear torn, ratty clothes, but they look mysteriously good on him. He's constantly surrounded by attractive women. What is his secret?

Evan understands the importance of details. He knows that it's not important that his clothes not be torn; what's important is that the details of his "look" all work together to make him look good. Torn clothes are part of his style. What makes him different from other, unattractive men who wear torn up clothes is how he manages the details of his appearance.

First, even though his clothing may be torn, he still follows the four Rules of Clothing closely. His clothes are clean and orderly; we've seen him iron ripped blue jeans, and throw away clothes whose rips don't look "right' to him.

Second, his details are all wonderful. His style has a Native American air about it, even though he's not Native American himself. His belt is from a Pacific Indian clothing store, and his watch, rings, earrings and necklaces also reflect the same style. This attention to detail makes him look like he's thought about his look, which he has, and sends an attractive message to women no matter what else he is wearing. He never carries much in his pockets, and his glasses fit his face perfectly. He looks like he's just thrown on whatever is around, and looks great. The reason he looks great is that he's thought about and managed the details of his appearance. Women notice, and find him fascinating.

You can use the details of your appearance to stand out from other men. Extra-nice or interestingly coordinated shoes, belts, wallets, backpacks, brief cases, watches or hats are all ways to show women that you pay attention to details and care about looking nice.

Slightly unusual details in your dress can even get women to begin conversations with you. One man we know wears a striking copper bracelet he got in India. Women often ask him about it, and he gets to tell them about the time he spent traveling there. Another man wears an artistic pin on the lapel of his suit, which women comment on. Another man has a cowboy hat that fits his style perfectly, which women often comment on.

Tattoos, if you have them, are another kind of detail of style that can start conversations with women. One man we know has several beautiful tattoos and uses them to start conversations with women who have tattoos and piercings. "I like your tattoo. Where did you get it done?" will often lead to interesting conversations and eventually dates with women he's attracted to.

Details to avoid

Once upon a time, tobacco was cool. You could light up a cigarette, hold it casually, breathe smoke and look suave and intellectual.

Those days are past. Cigarettes are no longer attractive to women and, in our current cultural climate, are actually repellent to many beautiful, health-conscious females. Even many coffee shops, the last hold-outs for roll-your-own sophisticated smokers, have gone smoke-free. While it is true that many young women smoke because they think it will keep them thin, you won't be any less attractive to them if you don't smoke. And you will be less attractive to non-smoking women, who outnumber the smokers. To be attractive to women, you must go smoke-free, too.

Even though cigars have come into vogue in recent years, most women still think they smell like burning commodes, and find men who light them up very offensive. Jake learned this the hard way. He was on a business trip to a distant city, and there he met Anne. Anne was 33, tall, with fiery red hair and remarkably upright, beautiful breasts. He seemed certain to score with her; she knew he was in town for only a few days, but still wanted to be with him. She must want to have sex with him, he reasoned. What could possibly go wrong?

They went out to a fine Japanese dinner together, ate and drank and were enjoying each other's company, when Jake made his mistake. With studied casualness, he took a cigar out of his pocket, and lit it up. "I've never seen a woman's mood change so quickly," he told us later. "She wrote me off immediately, became cold, and couldn't get away from me fast enough. Even after I put it out, she still wouldn't warm up to me. Needless to say, I slept alone that night." Don't make the mistake Jake made. If you smoke cigars, do it around other guys. Don't do it around women you are trying to seduce.

WHAT IF YOU ARE FAT AND OUT OF SHAPE, OR UGLY?

Your style needs to send a message to women that says "I am mature and interesting and you want to be with me." Accomplishing this is more about what you do with what nature gave you, than with how subjectively beautiful you are. We all have seen men who, at first look, are no "feast for the peepers" who are dating very beautiful women. They are able to do this because they make the best of what they have, and have developed their personal style into something they can be proud of.

Carey is one such man. Weighing in at well over 300 pounds, Carey seems, at first look, to be a guy who would only get sex if he was willing to pay cash for it. Nothing could be further from the truth; Carey has a constant stream of women in his life.

How does he do it? Carey has style. He never smells bad, and always looks great. Everyone who knows him agrees that his clothes look great on him, and that he "wears his weight well." He also follows the guidelines of the rest of this chapter, and his home and car look wonderful and are extremely inviting. He also has confidence, which we will also cover later in this chapter. Carey's style shows that he is in love with his life, is a mature man, and that he pays attention to details. Subsequently he is attractive to a variety of women.

Carey is careful to never be apologetic about his weight. "I know I'd be healthier if I was thinner, and I'm working on it," he says. "But I know if I start acting like there's something wrong with me, I'll never get another date again. I just think of myself as a big, attractive guy. The ladies seem to agree." If you express your own true style, it doesn't matter if you aren't naturally beautiful to look at. You'll send the right message to women, they will feel romantic feelings about you, and you'll do well with them.

THREE WAYS TO MAKE YOUR CAR INTO A ROLLING SEDUCTION CHAMBER

By now you've learned what you need to know to give women the right message with how you look. You've learned the importance of developing your personal style, looking good, and taking care of the details. You're looking hot and feeling good. You have a good chance of getting a date, so now it's time to start thinking about the other expressions of your personal style that women will see: your car and your home.

One of the most common lies women tell is that they don't care about men's cars. In a sense, we suppose, they are telling the truth: intellectually, they don't care, and don't think they could be swayed emotionally by such silly things. Women often like to make fun of men's cars as "extensions of their penises" (as if that's a bad thing!). On an emotional level, however, women do respond to the kind of car you drive, and to how clean or dirty you keep it. They'll just rarely tell you the truth about it.

This was brought home to us vividly when Esther, a female friend, started dating a new man. Esther is a powerful, can-do kind of woman. She's very successful in her business, and is known for her hard-edged, no-nonsense attitude. She would often list her requirements in a man to her friends, and was very clear that there was no way she'd have sex with a man right away. Or, anyway, that's what she thought until she met Keith.

Esther put it this way. "We had dinner, and everything was going well. We had met at the restaurant and he was about to give me a ride home. It turns out he has a Cadillac Coupe deVille! When he set me into that plush leather seat, and closed the door with that satisfying 'click,' I said to myself 'I'm having sex with this man!'" Which she did, that very night.

We were shocked by her revelation, but it taught us something important: the experience a woman has in your car can make or break your seduction. Most of us don't have cars as nice as Keith's, but there are still things you can do to make your car a more seductive space for the women you date.

Like your way of dressing, your car sends a message to women. Your car can be an important part of your seduction strategy. Teenagers aren't the only ones who have sex in cars, and many successful sexual experiences start in men's cars, and move to the bedroom later. Here are the three ways to make your car into a rolling seduction chamber.

1. Make your car clean

It'll be hard to create the right romantic mood in your car if it is messy. In this society, where people are increasingly living out of their cars, it's easy to fill it with work projects, books, fast-food garbage, and things you've been meaning to take out, but haven't. If you are going to give a woman a ride somewhere, it's important that your car not seem like a dumpster with wheels. Remember, you are sending a message to women with every expression of your style that you make. Remember also that she is judging your style to see if she wants to have sex with you or not. If your car is clean and comfortable, you've made it past another hurdle. If it isn't, she'll get the message that you are a slob and not in control of your life, and be less attracted to you.

If you do need to carry a lot of stuff, get some organizer baskets to keep in your car. Dwight had to make a lot of overnight trips for his work, and had to keep files, product samples, and personal belongings in his car all the time. Not a naturally organized person, his car was always a mess of papers, trash, and dirty laundry. Though his guy friends didn't mind the mess, women were repelled, and he wondered why he had so few second dates.

We had Dwight buy a number of plastic baskets, tubs and organizers, and simply organize what was in his car. Once everything had its proper place, the car looked neat, even though there was a lot in it. Instead of making him look like a slob, his car made him look like an organized man who was serious about doing his job well.

If a woman sees your car messy, we suggest that you don't bother apologizing. Women are sick of guys who apologize for being slobs rather than having their lives together. Simply take the time to clear room for her, act like nothing is out of the ordinary, and hope you can see her again with a neat car.

2. Make your car romantic

If you are going to use your car as part of your seduction strategy—and you should—you should have the right equipment to make your car romantic. We suggest you have blankets and pillows in the trunk, in case a romantic walk in the woods becomes something more. You should have good romantic music on the stereo, and condoms hidden in the glove compartment.

You should not have anything in the car that will turn a woman off. *Penthouse* air fresheners, complete with naked centerfold pictures, should not be hanging off your rear-view mirror. Ditto for fuzzy dice. Your car shouldn't smell either. The scent of old burritos or stale cigarette smoke is not a turn-on for most women.

You should also get rid of any signs of other women in the car, as we'll show you how to do in a later chapter. One of our students ran into trouble when he was dating several women. One had folded a pretty paper swan for him, and written "Christy and Mike" on the wings. She had given it to him in his car and he put it on his dashboard and kissed her so passionately that they went back to his house to have sex. Unfortunately, after he drove her home later in the evening, he forgot about the paper bird on the dashboard. The next day, when he picked up Jane for their date, she saw it immediately, read the message on it, and took great offense.

Your car should be comfortable, romantic, smell good, and not remind your date of other women.

3. Make your car work

Doors and windows should work on your car; women don't like to have to slide across the driver's seat to get to the passenger's. Also, your muffler should work. A loud car tells a woman that your life is out of control and you can't take care of your property. If you can't take care of your car, how will you take care of her?

We do suggest that you open the car door for any woman you are with, and close the door behind her. It's not necessary to say anything about doing this—in fact, it's better if you don't—but you should do it. When you open the door for a woman, it shows her that you are going to take care of her and treat her like she is special. No matter how much she believes politically that men and women should be equal, on a romantic level she will appreciate you making this gesture.

THE FIVE SECRETS OF A SEDUCTIVE HOME

Think about your home. Think about the kitchen, the living room, your bedroom. Picture it in your mind. Now ask yourself the following questions:

First ask yourself, "Is this a home that will make the women I most desire want to have sex with me?" Most of the men we work with have to answer, "no." When they look at their homes from the perspective of the women they desire, they find they can understand why these women wouldn't want them.

Second, ask yourself, "What's the message my home sends to the women I'm attracted to?" Most men find that their home doesn't send the message they want to send. It sends messages like "I'm still a boy," or "I'm not really going anywhere in my life." If your home doesn't seem like a comfortable place to spend romantic time in, then you are sending a message that "romance isn't important to me."

Now think about homes you've seen that seem to send romantic messages to women. While many of these homes may seem expensive, and expensively furnished, their style follows basic principles you can follow, too, to make your home more inviting and romantic. While this entire list needs to be followed only right before a date, it will be easier for you if the basics are in place all of the time.

1. A Seductive home looks like an adult lives there

A seductive home is not a dorm room, a closet, a warehouse, a garbage dump, or a science experiment. It's not a place for random friends to hang out, or a pornographic poster supply house. Any of these things will leave women thinking that you are still stuck in your adolescence, and they won't desire you.

2. A seductive home is clean

Specifically, the details should be clean. It's best if the mini-blinds are clean, and there are no dust-bunnies in the corners. The areas that are most important to your date should be cleanest, and the areas that are least important, or that you think you can keep your date out of, can be ignored. If she wouldn't see your kitchen unless she spent the night, for instance, you can get away without cleaning it. Because she will already have had sex with you by the time she sees it the next morning, the fact that it is a mess won't wreck your chances with her.

The bathroom, on the other hand, must be absolutely clean. There is no middle ground on this one. One man we know tried to get around this by taking the lightbulb out of the bathroom so his date couldn't see how dirty it was. This only annoyed her. You must clean the bathroom thoroughly before a date comes to your house.

3. A seductive home is properly lit

The lighting should be subdued and controlled. Bright over-head lights will make your date feel tense, like she's being interrogated. Try soft, reflected light. This can be a lamp with a 40-watt bulb, rather than a 100-watt bulb, or candles, or light coming in from the next room. There should be shadows and patterns of light and mystery. It should be welcoming, not antiseptic. This idea is hard for many men to grasp, because they are used to lighting spaces in order to get things done in them. Did you know that some women try to stay out of fluorescent lighting because of how it makes them look? Your seductive rooms aren't workshops. Be sensitive to having romantic lighting.

4. A seductive home is unpacked and set up

It's amazing how many people still live out of boxes years after moving into their homes. One man who's lived in his house for four years still hasn't put up his pictures. When we told him it could make his house more romantic, he replied "What's the point of putting pictures up if the house isn't clean?" While we agree that it's important to have a clean home, it's also important to have a set up home. Unpack those boxes, and hang those pictures!

5. A seductive home has romantic potential

A seductive home makes a woman feel like she's in a place she can relax. The pictures on the walls don't have to be originals, but they should be framed and hung properly. There are flowers (there just for her, but she doesn't have to know that) and healthy-looking plants. The furniture is clean, and if it's old or funky, it has a throw-cover on it. The carpet has been vacuumed recently and there are no piles of paper or random belongings around. The music is soft and sexy. Everything seems to have a proper place, and is in it.

A seductive home has a seductive bedroom. The bed should be made and large, at least a double bed in size. There should be plenty of pillows, pictures on the wall, and, of course, the sheets should be clean.

If you are going to have romantic dates in your home, coordinate your seductions with your roommates beforehand. If you want the living room for the evening, for instance, talk to housemates and see if they'll stay out of the house 'til at least a certain hour. You don't want to be interrupted by people coming in, just when you are going for that first kiss.

And speaking of interruptions, in homes with romantic potential, the volume on the answering machine is set to "zero." More than one of our students has been ready to make that first move when the phone has rung, the answering machine has picked up, and another woman's voice has started blaring through the room! Turn answering machines down, and don't answer the phone when you have a date over.

Your style in how you dress, how you keep your car, and how your home looks tells women a lot about you, and helps them decide whether to make you into a hot lover or a lowly "friend." You must take control of these areas, and make sure that the messages you send with them are attractive, intriguing, mature and adult. Everything else you learn in this book can be undone by poor personal style. Make sure that you have it handled.

HOW TO BECOME CONFIDENT WITH WOMEN

Overcoming the two stumbling Blocks on the Road to Confidence. Confidence stumbling block #1: Fear of Rejection

As we covered in Chapter 2, you are afraid of rejection because of what you make rejection mean to you. While the successful seducer knows that every "no" is only another step on the way to the inevitable "yes," a man who fears rejection fears it because he makes it mean that there is something wrong with him. Here are some solutions:

The Thirty-Day Program for Getting Over Fear of Rejection. You must get yourself so used to rejection from women that it no longer has any negative meaning to you. A simple way to do this is to start small, with our easy-to-follow, thirty-day rejection-stomping confidence-building program.

If you are scared to talk to women and scared of rejection from women, this simple program will get you talking to them daily, and laughing in the face of rejection. It's straightforward, painless, and easy to do. It's based on a simple two-letter word that, when you use it with women, will build your confidence, start you talking, and be the first step in getting women into your life.

Are you ready for the word?

The word is "hi!" To build your confidence with women and to overcome your fear of rejection, for the next thirty days, say "hi" to women in public at least six times a day. That's all there is to it. You are walking down the street, you see an attractive woman, you say "hi" to her, and walk on. You see the next attractive woman, and you say "hi" to her, too. And so on.

Don't be deceived by the simplicity of this program. If you are willing to actually do it, and to actually say "hi" to a number of women out in public every day, your confidence will rise, your fear of rejection will diminish, and your success with women will improve. Here's why:

First, your confidence will improve because you actually will be talking to women. Saying "hi" is wonderful because the interaction

ends quickly. Like some other techniques we'll show you for building confidence, the "hi" interaction doesn't put your ego on the line,
and doesn't give her much chance to reject you. What's the worst
thing she'll do, glare at you as you walk by? Who cares? It's not like
you've risked your whole ego by asking her out or trying to kiss her.
You'll get into the habit of seeing women who attract you, and talking to them. And that's good.

Second, women's responses to you will become less important
to you. You'll find that you are being the kind of man you want to
be, the kind of man who says hello to whatever kind of woman
appeals to him, no matter what her response might be. You'll
become less scared of rejection as you notice that some women
smile and say "hi" back, that some women are in their own world
and don't even seem to notice you spoke, and that some women
glare at you darkly and reach for their police whistle. You'll start to
see that it doesn't matter; all that matters is that you are making life
work for you by starting to approach the women who attract you.

Third, you actually will get into more conversations with
women if you set a precedent of talking to them right away. Have
you ever been in a situation in which you would have spoken to a
woman, but the fact that you've initially ignored her makes it hard
to start? This happened to our friend Bob just the other day. "I was
in a line waiting to buy tickets to a movie. There was a gorgeous girl
in line in front of me, but when I first saw her, I went back into my
old fear mode, and didn't look at her or say 'hi.' After about five
minutes of waiting, I really wanted to start talking to her, but it
seemed a lot more awkward because I hadn't said 'hi' at first." After
you've practice saying "hi" for a few weeks, it'll be second nature for
you to see that woman in line, look her in the face, smile, and say
"hi." You'll be relaxed and not concerned with her response. And it
will then be natural for the two of you to talk more, and for you to
be able to use the tools from the rest of this book to seduce her.

Other ways to overcome the fear of rejection

Have a "piece on the side."   As you begin to develop your
harem of available sex kittens, you are at a disadvantage. As usual,
success breeds success. The more sex you are getting, the more con-

fident about sex you will become and the more new women you will attract. But at the beginning, you don't have the confidence of lots of past success, and that slows down your ability to get that first woman on a date and into bed.

Though it is not available to every man, having a "piece on the side" can generate the erotic confidence that allows you to get even more women. A "piece on the side" is a woman who you have occasional sex with—say, once a month—though you might not really want her very much. She is a woman you *know* you can have, but who isn't attractive enough for you to try to start a relationship with. An occasional sex partner like this can build your sexual self-esteem and enable you to take the risks that get you into bed with the women you really want.

So who could be a potential "piece on the side?" They may be ex-girlfriends, women who are not extremely attractive, much older women, close female friends, women who understand you don't want a relationship, or married women. When you have a "piece on the side," you know you aren't a total loser. If you look hard enough at your life you will usually find at least one woman who would sleep with you. Try her out and see what happens.

We've had students say "Yeah, the date didn't go so well, so afterwards I went to the house of my 'piece on the side.'" They were able to get sex when they wanted it. As a result, they were empowered to pursue the sex they really wanted.

Get your validation from your life, not from women. Too many men rely on women for their sense of validation, self-respect, and self-esteem. They live as if women's opinions of them are what matters. If they have a good interaction with an attractive woman, they feel good about themselves. When an interaction goes bad, they feel badly about themselves. This need to be validated by women in order to feel good about themselves robs these men of their confidence with women.

Bob has this problem big-time. His whole picture of himself is based on his latest interaction with a woman. When he asks a woman out on a date and she says no—as they sometimes do, even to the best seducers—Bob is crushed. He thinks "What a jerk I am. Why do I even bother asking women out in the first place? There must be something wrong with me. I'm a failure. Let's see, how long has it been since I've had a date? What a bummer." He stops being able to concentrate on work, doesn't work out, and generally lets his life go to Hell. On the other hand, if an interaction with a woman goes well, Bob is on top of the world, at least for a while. When he has a date that goes well, or meets a hot woman who seems interested in him, he dances through his life. He thinks "See? I'm not such a bad guy after all! I'm okay! Things are going to be great!" He sets himself up for a letdown by making his self-esteem and validation dependent on his success with women.

We tell men to listen to what former UCLA basketball coach John Wooden used to tell his players. He said "I always told them that I didn't want excess dejection at a loss, or excessive jubilation after a victory, and that I hoped that, after a game, no one could tell whether you won or lost by your behavior." Coach Wooden knew that the best path to success is to get your sense of validation from your life as a whole, not from momentary wins or losses. Wooden's teams' record-setting levels of victory make this approach seem pretty smart.

If you want to have an easy sense of confidence with women, how do you make this work? Practically, this means finding ways to be in love with your own life, and to have the things you are up to in your life be validating for you. Success with women and success with life are similar. Just as women won't go out of their way to bring you sexual success, life doesn't go out of its way to bring you life-success. Just as your sex life is your responsibility to make the way you want it, your life as a whole is your responsibility to make the way you want it. If you want success with women, it makes sense to have long-term goals for your life that inspire you and that you are moving towards, no matter how slowly. If you do this, you'll get your validation from your life, rather than from women.

Don is a good example. As a computer programmer for a large insurance company, it was easy for him to allow his life to get into a rut. Day after day he'd go to work, program, come home, watch TV and go to bed. He had no goals and no direction. He became passive with his life and, not surprisingly, with women. He blamed his company for his lack of enjoyment of his job, and blamed women for his lack of an abundant sex life. His future looked like it would be just like the past. He looked to women for validation in his life, because he couldn't find it anywhere else, and when they didn't validate him, he became depressed. Thus the cycle worsened—the more depressed he became, the more he wanted women to make him feel validated, and, predictably, the less attractive he became. The less attractive he became, the less women validated him, and the more depressed he got.

This was the state he was in when he came to us, complaining about his relationships with women. We taught him the tools in this book, and had him begin to set goals for his life. We had him go to his local bookstore and get a book on goal-setting, and got him to really look at what he wanted his life to be like in ten years, five years, one year. We got him to write down goals that inspired him, and to put them into his date book where he'd see them often. As he began to get excited about what was possible for him in his life, the cycle began to break apart. He started getting his validation from his life, rather than from women. This made him more attractive to women. Rather than wanting to be with women so he could have a life, he began having a life that validated him, whether women were in it or not. Naturally, women were intrigued by his passion for his life, and wanted to be a part of it.

We also advised Don to make more male friends. Don tended to have many female friends and few male ones. We aren't against having female friends, but there are two kinds: the ones you don't want to have sex with, and the ones you do want to have sex with, but who don't want you. When a man has many women in his life who he wants sexually but who only want to be "friends" with him, it's hard on his confidence. Don was always around women who didn't want him, and this made him feel undesirable. It convinced him that women only wanted him as a friend, which really meant that women didn't want him as a man. Being around these women also got him into the habit of being nonsexual "friends" with desirable women, rather than being their lovers. He began treating all women like friends, and they treated him the same way.

At our advice Don stopped spending so much time with women he desired but who didn't desire him, and started spending more time with other men. These male friendships were able to validate him without putting down his sexuality or showing him that he was undesirable. He found he could get a kind of support from men that he could never get from women he desired who insisted on being "friends." This validated him, and made women's reactions to his approach less disturbing.

Women are attracted to men who have passion and fire for their lives. They aren't any more interested in providing the validation for your life than you are in providing the validation for theirs. When you have goals, male friends, and a life that inspires you, you'll be validated by what you are up to, and women will want to be a part of your life. It won't matter to you if they say "yes" or "no" when you ask them out, seduce them, and go for that first kiss. You'll be validated by your life, and easily able to move on to the next woman.

Confidence stumbling block #2: Fear of hurting women

Some men are driven by the idea that their sexuality hurts women. For instance, Walt always felt like there was something bad about his sexual desire. A tall thin man in his early thirties, he grew up with three sisters, his mom, and no father. "I was privy to lots of girl talk about how bad guys were, how much they only wanted women for sex," he told us. "With no men to tell me that sex was great, I only got the picture they gave me—that men were insensitive bastards who only cared about using women for their own gratification. I remember being around when my sisters would come home from dates and put down the men they had been with. I so much wanted to be a good guy, to not hurt women with my sexuality."

When Walt first started dating girls as a teenager, he strove to always be polite. "I wouldn't even think about them sexually, 'cause I knew that would be rude," he says. "I masturbated looking at women in magazines, and I even felt guilty about that! Finally I was lying on top of my girlfriend in her bedroom while her parents were away. We were making out, but I was avoiding touching her breasts, because I didn't want to 'use' her, like those guys did with my sisters. Finally she said to me, 'Do you realize you are avoiding touching my breasts? Don't you desire me?,' and she took my hand and put it on her breast. I'll tell you, that turned my world upside-down."

While most men don't have this fear of hurting women as much as Walt did, many men still have it, and usually don't even know it. They've bought into the myth that men are insensitive bastards who only want women for sex. They've bought into the idea that when a man has sex with a woman he is somehow taking something from her for his own selfish gratification. After all, we say that women "put out" sexually; that must mean that men take what women put out.

Saturday Night Live's Stuart Smalley character, played by Al Franken, has this problem. While he may say that "I'm good enough, I'm smart enough, and dogonne it, people like me," he also believes that women are delicate flowers who he would hurt if he was sexual with them. He tries to be harmless and sensitive. Like Walt, he doesn't get much sex.

Men like Walt or Stuart Smalley are committed to being sensitive to women's needs—not being macho, unfeeling jerks who hurt women. Unfortunately, this fear makes them tepid companions for women, and drains them of their confidence by making them hesitant and self-doubting in all their interactions.

"Sensitive" men wonder too much about what women think of them. They spend their brain-power, which should be spent being charming, assertive, funny and romantic, on self-absorbing concerns about what women think of them.

One of the main fears a man might have is that the woman he is talking to will think he's going to hurt or assault her. As a matter of fact, women you talk to *do* worry that you are going to hurt or assault them. Rightfully so; dating is dangerous for a woman. What these "sensitive," unconfident men don't know is that *indulging her fear of you makes her fear you more.*

Let's look at how this works. When a woman is afraid of you, as most will be when they first meet you, they are looking for signs that their fears either are, or are not, well-founded. If you are afraid that you will hurt her, it gives her the evidence she needs to justify avoiding you. You'll be hesitant, unconfident and self-doubting. You'll treat yourself as if you are dangerous. Of course she'll notice this, and want to get away from you.

If, on the other hand, you *aren't* afraid, you'll be confident and relaxed. She may be afraid that you'll hurt her, but she'll notice that you aren't afraid that you will. Your confidence, your certainty will help her relax, and make you more attractive. This is one of the reasons that jerks get women; they aren't worried about hurting them. They simply don't care. The jerk's lack of fear allows women to relax their fear. It's ironic that jerks—the men who hurt women the most—can get sex by not worrying about it, while men who would never hurt women, who worry about it all the time, can't get sex at all. This happens because men who are afraid don't have the sense of freedom or the confidence they need to be successful with women.

We advise men to get over the fear that, by their mere presence, or by having simple conversations with women, that they are going to be hurtful. It almost certainly will be stressful for women when you first approach them, but the best way to relieve their stress is to model being fearless, not by indulging their fears. Women are tough—if your saying "hi" to her disturbs her, she'll get over it. Relax. We also advise men to realize that if you are afraid you'll hurt a woman, and that fear drives women away, they don't ever get the benefit of being with you romantically. They never get to experience the pleasure you'd bring them, the romantic feelings, the thrills.

Some men lose their confidence because of false ideas about what women want. Men tell us that they are afraid that they'll end up hurting women emotionally, because with most women they meet, they only want short-term, sexual relationships. They are certain that no woman could possibly want this, and so they avoid the entire seduction, so they don't accidentally cause a woman emotional harm.

This is simply not true, for several reasons. First, there are plenty of women who just want to have sex with you and get rid of you just as much as you might want to have sex with and get rid of them. We are reminded of a situation comedy in which a guy decided that he needed to have his first one-night stand. True to the make-believe world of television, he easily accomplished this with a beautiful woman. The next day he was hanging out with his friends, bragging about his conquest. He mooned over how wonderful this woman was, and decided to call her and see her again. He called the number she gave him and—lo and behold!—she had given him a fake number! He was beside himself. "She used me!" he said, "She used me for sex!" A friend asked him, "How does it feel?" After a pause, he responded, "Hm. Pretty good, actually." She only wanted him for sex, then to get rid of him.

Television is rarely an accurate reflection of life, but if you get good at seducing women, you will find yourself in this exact situation. It comes as a shock to many men that a women might want sex without a relationship, because it seems like they never meet those women. Bob moans, "Where are these women who just want sex? I never meet them. Where are they?" Well, they are all around him, all the time. The difference between men who just want sex and women who just want sex is that men who just want sex act like it, while women who just want sex act like they want long-term relationships. As far as we can tell, there's not a reliable way to tell if a woman is up for short-term sex without seducing her. After you've had sex with her, you'll start finding out if she wants to keep seeing you, or get rid of you right away.

We advise men to not worry about dashing women's hopes for long-term relationships, because, at least at the beginning, she may well only be checking you out for sex, too.

But what if she really does want a long-term relationship? Well, she has the same opportunity you do: if she desires you badly enough, then she can try to be wonderful enough to convince you to have a relationship with her. You'll only get to know that as you spend time with her. You are depriving her of a possible relationship with you if you stay away from her because you feel guilty about only being interested in sex.

Some men lose their confidence with women because they are ashamed about being male. They've known women who've been very hurt in relationships, and have decided that there must be something basically wrong with men. These men are often feminists, acutely aware of the violence men do to women, and committed to not being like other men. Other men are ashamed of their sexuality because of their religious upbringing. All this shame makes men unconfident with and unattractive to women.

Overcoming fear of hurting women

We admire men for not wanting to hurt women. Not being a hurtful person, either emotionally, physically, or sexually is rightfully important to many men and is commendable. At the same time, we do take issue with how many men try to keep themselves from hurting women by being constantly worried about it. As we've seen, men who are overly concerned about never hurting women often don't get to have relationships with women at all because they are so hesitant and scared of what they might accidentally do. What can you do if you are one of these overly cautious men?

First, being aware that you are paralyzed by your fear of hurting women can help you start to change. Realize also that you are hurting women anyway, in a sense, because they don't get to have relationships with you and have to have relationships with jerks instead. When you start to see that you really aren't helping women, and are hurting your chances with them, it's easier to let go of fear, and be more seductive.

Second, you can decide to change your belief system about women. You can make the decision that you are no longer going to tolerate thinking of women as helpless delicate flowers, and of yourself as somehow dangerous to them. You can commit yourself to taking on the ideas in this book and making them part of your daily behavior, rather than simply passively reading about them. This will immediately increase your confidence with women.

The first stumbling block on the road to confidence—the fear of rejection—is basically the fear that you will get hurt in your interactions with women. We've shown you how to get over this fear, by saying "hi," talking to women all the time, having a "piece on the side," and getting your validation from your life, not from women. If you follow these steps you will become almost immune to rejection, and be free and confident to initiate with women anytime you want.

While the first stumbling block on the road to confidence is fear of being *hurt,* the second stumbling block is the fear that you will somehow be hurtful to women. We've respected your commitment, and have shown you some ways to still not want to hurt women, but to be able to interact more confidently and freely with them. We've shown you how being afraid that you will somehow hurt women actually makes them more afraid of you, not less, and that if you want to have relationships with women, you must treat them as if they can take care of themselves. We've also shown you how some women just want to have sex with you and to get rid of you. We've also looked at how, even in a short-term sexual relationship, a woman who wants a long-term-relationship with you might be able to convince you to stay with her, and how many long-term relationships started out as nothing more than one-night stands.

OTHER CONFIDENCE BUILDERS: EASY WAYS TO RAISE YOUR CONFIDENCE LEVEL

Be in "The zone"

Peak performers talk about being in "the zone" or in "the flow." You are in the zone when you are at your best, when all your inner resources are available to you, and when you seem to automatically handle everything well.

We've all had these moments. Sometimes they take place during sports, when a rock-climber, for instance, is so engaged in the climb that he forgets about everything else in the world but what he is doing. Surgeons report that when they are doing surgery, they are so involved that it's like they are in perfect harmony with the world around them. If you can remember a time when you effortlessly and peacefully performed beyond what you usually were able to do, you have been in the zone.

People who are falling in love are in the zone. You probably have felt it. When you were with her, it was like time stood still. You could do no wrong, and life, when you were with her, seemed effortless. When you were together you were creative and happy, and not worried about yourself or about your life. This is the zone as well.

Nick had this experience when he first met Kay. "I'd seen her at a couple of parties and been very attracted to her, but from the start I didn't feel tense or nervous around her, like I usually do when I meet women I'm hot for. It was like I knew in my heart that we'd get along fine, and I wasn't worried about it. I felt like, if it was meant to be, then it would happen. I really didn't worry about it.

"I remember running into her at a park, and we talked a bit and sat together on the grass. I didn't feel like I had to say anything, and there were these long periods when neither of us said anything, but I knew it was just fine. I felt present and happy and didn't need to fill the silences.

"After one of those silences, she said to me 'I just want to tell you everything about me.' It was the start of our relationship. I was in the zone that day, that's for sure."

How did Nick do this? What made him so irresistible to Kay that she couldn't help but open up to him, even though he said very little? Nick accidentally did what all peak performers do, and what you can do with women, too. He pursued his outcome (being romantic with Kay) and, *simultaneously*, let go of having to make that outcome happen (having faith that if it was meant to be, it would happen). He stopped worrying about whether she would like him or not, and simply pursued her. Any outcome would have been fine with him. If she had not wanted to be with him, he might have been disappointed, but he wouldn't have been upset. Similarly, he wasn't overly excited about her interest, even though he was pursuing it.

Let's look at the opposite example. Randy was very interested in Donna. He thought she was cute and mysterious and very much wanted to have a romantic relationship with her. It was terribly important to him that all of his interactions with her be great for her, so that she'd like him and want to go out with him. He was so focused on this goal, and on how bad it would be if she didn't like him, that he was weird and distracted when he was with her. "I was such a jerk," he says now. "I so wanted to impress her that I talked a mile a minute, made jokes that weren't funny, and was all-around a tense, jumpy guy." Because he couldn't stop thinking about his outcome—having her like him—he could never be relaxed and unconcerned with her. "I scared her off," he says. "I was so wrapped up in what I wanted to happen with her, I never was present with her when we were together." His inability to pursue his goal with her, and give up worrying about the goal at the same time, made him out of the zone, forced, and not attractive.

Women you have chemistry with are women you are pursuing, but you are not worried about the outcome. For some reason, with certain women, it's easy for you to not worry, and to get into the zone. You can, however, train yourself to worry less and less in your interactions with women by simply making that your intention. You can remind yourself, when you go into interactions with women, that the outcome isn't important. When you do this, you'll find that you are getting into the zone, that you are more relaxed, and that you have better chemistry. When Randy learns to not be worried about how it goes with Donna, and has some faith that everything will be okay, he relaxes, and it makes it easier for Donna to get to know him and to find him attractive. All the rest of the tools you learn in this book—seduction strategies, meeting women, going for that first kiss, and more—will be much easier to practice and have success with if you train yourself to follow this credo.

Make decisions

Decision-making is a muscle that gives you control over and confidence in your life. But you must practice. You don't want to be a control freak with women, but you don't want to be a useless wad of indecisiveness, either. Being decisive means you never, ever say, "Oh, I don't know, what do you want to do?" It means that when those little meaningless choices come up during the date—such as what table to sit at—you decide quickly and easily. If she'd rather sit somewhere else, then you can say "sure," but always make decisions quickly when you are with her. This shows her that you are a guy who is in charge of his life and not wishy-washy, and will put you miles ahead of most of the other guys she meets. This seems obvious and simple, but it builds your confidence and sets the stage for seduction.

FOUR THINGS YOU CAN DO *TODAY* TO BE CONFIDENT WITH WOMEN

1. Groom like a man who is confident with women

Think about your grooming. Today might be a good day to try a new aftershave, or to get a better quality shampoo or conditioner. You may want to make an appointment with a good hair stylist to get your hair cut in a new way. Or you may want to get your teeth cleaned. Wash and style your hair, and trim any unwanted hair in your nose and ears. Notice how much more confident you feel when you are well groomed and looking good!

2. Dress like a man who is confident with women

Go to your closet and look at your clothes. What are the best outfits you have for seducing women, and what are the worst? Notice the shirts and pants that you should wear more often, and those that you should wear less around women. Also look at your details: What are the most attractive shoes you own? The most attractive belt? Hat? What earrings, bracelets, rings or other jewelry do you have that might be attractive to women? What clothes fit your body best, and are in best repair? What clothes make you feel most attractive when you wear them? What is your most attractive outfit?

Be aware that your most attractive outfit may not be the fanciest, or the most expensive. You may not look best in a suit, for instance; you may look best in a well-fitting sports shirt and a pair of clean, ironed jeans, with nice sneakers and a black belt. Whatever it is, put it on and wear it today. If you need to iron it first, do so. Notice the confidence wearing this outfit gives you with women, and commit yourself to developing a wardrobe of clothes that make you feel the same way.

3. Move like a man who is confident with women

At any time, you can change the way you hold and move your body, and change your level of confidence and how you feel. If you don't believe us, try slumping and slouching, letting your shoulders come forward as if you were terribly depressed. Breathe shallowly. If you really take on this posture, you will feel less confident, and will eventually actually *become* depressed!

Fortunately, this works both ways. The same body you can use to make you feel unconfident and depressed, you can use to make you feel just the opposite. Try it now. Take on the posture of a man who is confident with women. Imagine, as weird as it may seen, that you are inside his body. How does he sit? How does he stand? Are his shoulders forward, or back? Put your shoulders there. Is his head up, or down? Put your head that way, too. Does this confident man breathe deeply? Do it! What's this confident man's facial expression? Try it out! It may seem crazy, but if you try it, you *will* notice a difference; you may even want to stand up and practice walking around with the posture of a confident man.

Imagine how useful this could be when you are approaching a woman. Before talking to her you take on the posture that makes you feel more confident and, breathing deeply, tall and relaxed, you approach her. If you practice this posture every day, you'll find it brings out your innate confidence, and becomes natural for you.

4. Pursue like a man who is confident with women

Now groomed, dressed and moving well, commit yourself to having an interaction with a woman today in which you pursue her romantically, while at the same time not worrying about whether your outcome happens or not. Put yourself into the zone, and give yourself the freedom of not worrying about the outcome. You may want to commit yourself to asking a woman for her phone number. You may want to ask a woman out. You may simply want to make it clear to a woman you meet that you are attracted to her. Whatever it is that you do, make it a little more risky than you are comfortable with—and, most important, give up worrying about whether she says yes or no.

Think again about the first questions we asked you at the beginning of this chapter. What kind of woman do you want? What's most important to you in a woman? Is it that she be tall, or short? That she have wonderful breasts? That she be blonde, or brunette? That she be smart, or rich? What exactly do you want?

And then think again about the next questions we asked you: What kind of a man will you have to be to get that woman into your life and into your bed? Are you that kind of man already?

If you are like most men, you've realized that you aren't yet the kind of man you'll need to be to get the kind of women you desire. What you need is to develop your personal style—your way of dressing, and your confidence. You've seen how the way you dress sends a message to women, and have learned how to take control of that message so that it says, "I'm interesting, mature and attractive. You want to be with me." You've learned that it doesn't matter what nature gave you; what matters is what you do with it in how you dress, move, and act. You've learned how to make your car and home romantic, and learned how to overcome the two stumbling blocks to confidence with women—fear of rejection, and fear of hurting women. You've learned the importance of not relying on women to validate you, but rather getting your validation from your life. You've learned how to be in the zone with women by giving up worrying about the outcomes of your seduction, and simply pursuing what you desire, no matter what happens. And you've learned the four things you can do today to be more confident with women than ever before.

As you develop your personal style you will discover many benefits it brings beyond simply being attractive to women. Once you start, you'll find women are more attracted to you than they've been before.

chapter four...
Where the Girls Are; Meeting Women for Sex and Relationships

Imagine this scenario: After reading this book Jim decided to call us because he was filled with questions, and wanted to attend our world-famous "How to Be Successful With Women" workshop. He explained that he was our "number one" fan. He told us he had even recorded a homemade audio tape series of our book so that he could listen to this book while in his car, on the train, and while working out in the gym.

After a few minutes of discussion, we invited him to a course, but we refused to tell him where or when it was being held. We simply told him to get on a plane and meet us, still not telling him the location or the date. Jim got annoyed with us because we didn't give him any useful information. We just kept telling him to come to the course without telling him how or where. He finally screamed into the phone, "If you are not going to tell me any of the specifics, I'm not coming to your damn course!" We replied in a calm and methodical manner: "We're sorry you feel that way. We'd love you to attend the course," yet still refused to tell him when and where it was. We told him what to do, but not how to do it. Of course he eventually went nuts. Anybody would.

This is a good example of how most "authorities" will teach you to meet and date women. They'll do what we did with poor Jim;

they'll tell you what to do, but not how to do it. They will tell you the impractical theory without the telling you how to practice. Just learning principles leaves most people feeling frustrated, empty, and worse off than when they started.

The majority of men we've trained haven't had very good experiences using empty theories like "be more hard to get" or "be more outgoing" to get women. Dating advice usually takes the form of unhelpful locker-room talk and equally useless bombast. Plus, the guys who talk about getting women usually aren't the ones actually getting them. You probably know men who are all talk and no action, always bragging, yet always sleeping alone. The most successful men seem to be surrounded by women with no apparent effort or planning. Remember the guys who got girls in high school? They were not always the brightest of the bunch. Often, they were the bad boys who would skip class and get in fights. Or they were football players who made a routine out of punching your lights out if you didn't do their homework for them. They didn't have theory or any ideas at all, but they had the proper action, and managed to get the girls.

Theory alone will not get you sleeping with the women you desire. You know how hard it is sometimes to take a new idea and actually use it those first few times. This chapter will show you how to integrate seduction into your daily life. We'll also explore where to meet women and fun gimmicks that can provide easy and outrageous alternatives to meeting women in bars.

One common myth among single men is that there is a scarcity of single women. Single men usually fail miserably to notice all the women they have contact with in a typical day. Most men are surrounded with women throughout their daily routines, but are too blinded by the myth of female scarcity to notice. The solution is simple in theory, but much more difficult in practice: You must notice the women around you, ask them out, and create seductions.

This myth is not grounded in reality. Our research shows that there are, at this moment, millions of single women waiting for you. They are not hiding in the mountains or in caves; they are at bookstores, shopping centers, bars, on the street, at work, behind the check-out counter, in restaurants, everywhere. You simply need to contact them. This chapter will show you how to turn every aspect of your life into situations that could lead to seduction.

We will start with a blow-by-blow description of our desperately lonely guy, Bob, and of all of his bone-headed mistakes. We will compare him to our master seducer, Bruce, and show you all the things he does throughout a typical day that attract women.

The fundamental difference between Bob and Bruce is that Bruce has many practices in place that have his success insured. He doesn't only know the theory; he knows how to put the theory into practice. But first, let's look at the typical, non-woman-meeting day of Bob.

7:30 am, Bob wakes up to the loud ringing of his alarm clock.

Bob sits up thinking, "Oh no, another day. Can't I just go back to bed and pretend I'm dead? This is going to be even worse than yesterday. God, I wish I was sick today. Maybe I should call in to work and tell them that I have the flu. I haven't met any women in over two years. "

Bob doesn't take time to shower. He looks around his dirty bedroom floor for a pair of semi-clean underwear. He finds a pair under his bed along with a wrinkled shirt that he puts on. His hair is messy and he tries to make it look nicer by running his fingers through it. He stares into the bathroom mirror and grunts to himself, "I hate this." He finds an old pair of slacks in his closet hamper, puts on his shoes, and off he goes to work.

7:45 am, on the way to work

Bob swears at the other drivers on the road. At a stop sign he stares at a beautiful woman in the car next to him and wishes he could be with her. She catches him looking and glares at him as he looks quickly away. "I should just become a card-carrying fairy," he says to himself.

7:55 am, the drive-through at McDonalds

Bob grumbles to the female employees and orders his normal breakfast. He pays the cute young female cashier. She smiles at him and he rolls his eyes. He drives off. He snarfs down his coffee and quickly takes bites of his Egg McMuffin™. Flakes of the muffin drop onto his shirt and pants. He ignores the greasy flakes and mumbles, "I hate being late! Why am I always late?" as he drives the rest of the way to work.

8:15 am, at work

He enters the door to the office and the receptionist Patty smiles and says "Good morning, Bob." He grunts, "Hi. Traffic sucked this morning. I hate that, all that God-damned traffic!" Having vented his frustration at this attractive young woman, he goes to his desk.

As he gets comfortable in his cubicle, his former girlfriend Laurie calls to invite him to a party she's having later that month. Bob gets angry and says, "Look, Laurie, I don't want anything to do with you or your stupid parties! I hate parties!" She hangs up on him and he gets to his work.

A few male employees stop by to say good morning to him and he tries his best to get rid of them by typing and concentrating on his computer while they talk. On a short break from work he gets onto the Internet and looks at the personals ads in newsgroups. He thinks they are stupid. "I could never meet women that way. I bet they are all psychopaths, or guys pretending to be women." He pops over to his favorite Internet porn sites, drools over the hot women on them, then gets back to work.

12:30 pm, lunch time

Bob does his best to avoid people during his lunch break. He either gets food from the company cafeteria and brings it to his cubicle, or brings a book and reads in a corner. Other people joke and laugh. Bob looks at them with disgust. "What the hell are they so happy about?" he thinks to himself. He stares at Marcia, the most attractive woman at the company. She is sitting with a guy named Bruce and having a great time. "What does that guy have that I don't?" he asks himself. "He's not even that attractive."

Today Bob waits in line to pay for his chicken casserole. He doesn't talk to any of the other employees in line, or the friendly 40-year-old cashier. He looks at women he wishes he could talk to, but knows in his heart that they would just be unfriendly to him. "Besides," he tells himself. "There's a big difference between a conversation and actually finally getting some sex. I can't see why I would even bother." He slumps back to his desk.

1:20 pm, back to work

Martin, Bob's high school pal, e-mails him sexy e-mails from women he has met on-line. Martin wants to know if Bob would be interested in going on a blind double-date with the women Martin has met. Bob thinks that Martin is crazy and e-mails back that he has standards, and would never go on a blind date. "Blind dates are for losers," he explains. "It's like admitting that you can't get a woman any other way." Martin gives up, and finds somebody else.

6:00 pm, time to leave work

Bob goes home to watch TV alone for the rest of the night. He orders a pizza and drinks two beers. He watches a porn video, masturbates, and goes to bed.

From the start to the finish of his day, Bob lives in a vacuum. Even when there are women around, he avoids them and rationalizes his lack of contact by telling himself that the available women aren't good enough, or would never want him anyway. He stays horny, lonely, and depressed.

Now let's look at a day in the life of our hero Bruce, who leads fundamentally the same life Bob does. The only difference is in the approach.

6:00 am

Bruce is suddenly awakened by his very loud and obnoxious radio alarm blasting the Jimi Hendrix song, "Foxy Lady." As the radio blares, our gallant hero tries to smile. He rubs his eyes, stretches his arms in the air, and thinks to himself that today will be a day full of flirting, fantasy, and fun. He sings along with "Foxy Lady" and improvises his own lyrics, "You know you're a sweet little heart breaker. Oh, yea, you are my hot and sexy foxy lady. You turn me on so bad. Oooooooh yea!" He laughs out loud and smiles.

He's unfamiliar with the next song, and it fades into the background as the female DJ's sexy voice says, "The 10th caller will win tickets to the coolest new movie and five new CDs." Bruce, halfway through shaving, grabs his cordless phone and dials with a passion. Though the line is busy he calls and recalls until he gets through. Though he doesn't win the contest, he boldly flirts with the DJ and lets her know that he is a fan. While talking to her, Bruce decides that he will make her his newest "project," and he vows to call her a few times per week. Could he get a date from this?

He brushes his teeth, puts on his clean, well-fitting stylish clothes, and packs up his gym gear and briefcase for the next adventure.

6:38 am, on the way to the gym, in his car

Bruce is feeling good and sings along with songs on the radio. As women pass in their cars he smiles, winks, and waves at them. Some glare, some smile, some ignore him. He doesn't care.

He calls back the lovely DJ on his cell phone and asks her out. She says "no," and Bruce, undaunted, tells her a silly joke. He asks for her address at the station so he can send her a card. By the way, he asks, does she have a boyfriend? Bruce figures, if she does, why push for it if the competition is stiff? If she has a boyfriend, he may as well move on to somebody else.

As he nears the gym a beautiful brunette in a sporty car passes. She has pouty lips and looks like an erotic receptionist who would pose in a "Sexy Secretary" *Playboy* pictorial. Even at this early hour, Bruce is mesmerized with her. They seem to be going in the same direction and Bruce smiles, waves, and winks at her as they work their way through the busy traffic. She smiles and waves back, and Bruce thinks he sees her blushing. He mouths "I love you" to her, and at the next stop light pulls up next to her, writes "I'd love to meet for coffee—please call!" on his business card, and tosses it through her open car window. He takes the next turn, and is almost at the gym.

7:00 am, at the gym.

Bruce goes to the gym at the same time four days a week. Consistently working out at the same time pays off because it lets Bruce know the "regulars" who also work out at that time. He can build on his successes with the women he meets there, and slowly chip away at his seductions.

As he walks up to the door, he flirts with Janet, who is also on her way in. Bruce has seen her in the gym lots of times. She is with her six-year-old son. Bruce says "hi" to the son, opens the door for Janet, and checks her out. "So what if she has a kid," he says to himself. She works out all the time, has a great body, and besides, it's all practice anyway. As he walks in the club, he also smiles and flirts with the girl checking IDs. Her name is Pauline, she's 23, and from a small town. He always jokes with her about going to a bar to watch the local college sports team. She always kids him back, and he knows that they will indeed go out sometime soon. He patiently flirts with her, knowing that if he keeps at it, his success with her is inevitable.

While working out

Bruce changes into workout clothes. Even though he's no perfect physical specimen, he's chosen workout clothes that make him look good. They are clean, look neat, and smell good. While working out on the exercise bikes, he smartly positions himself near a large-breasted, sexy looking, mid-30s woman. Bruce hasn't seen her in the club before. "Are you new here?" he asks, creating an opening for conversation. After he introduces himself she tells him her name is Fiona. They discuss her regular workout schedule. As she gets up to leave, he asks for her phone number. She turns him down, but tells him to meet her back at the club some afternoon next week. He accepts her request and enjoys watching her walk away.

On the way to the weight room, Bruce says "hi" to other cute female regulars. He uses every opportunity to talk to women. Even if the women are not all that hot, he flirts anyway because he is as smart as Bob is dumb. He initiates and maintains conversations with women of all ages and all levels of beauty. Because of his persistence, Bruce has dated and had sex with several women from the gym.

He showers, and prepares for the next adventure.

8:30 am, he goes to his regular coffee shop

Bruce enters The Coffee Hut, his favorite place for flirtation, coffee, and breakfast. He has selected a coffee shop to frequent that is convenient for him and that has a large clientele of women. It doesn't have the best food in town, but Bruce knows that the real focus here is finding women to date, not eating the best food or coffee.

Bruce is already pumped up from his workout and is ready to smile and talk to the lovely 22-year-olds behind the counter. The woman making the coffee drinks is named Vicki. He has nicknamed her "cappuccino mamma." She and several others of the other women working there are very beautiful. Bruce talks to them about some silly item in the news. They laugh and smile. He even thinks they look forward to him coming in; at least they seem happy to see him.

While in line he talks to another woman. She is tall, dark, and conservative looking. He talks about coffee and she seems distant and scared. He introduces himself and talks to her until she gets her coffee. She sits far away from him. Once again, he doesn't care. He knows that the important thing is that he's being the kind of man he wants to be, not how women will respond to him.

He sits down with a muffin, coffee, and a newspaper, his regular routine. He strikes up a conversation with yet another woman who is sitting near him. Having a newspaper helps him, because he can comment on something funny or weird in the news. He gets her phone number and readies himself for work.

9:15 am, our boy wonder arrives at work
The first thing Bruce does upon entering work is flirt with the receptionist, Patty. He leans on her desk and smiles, saying "How's the Goddess of Reception doing this morning?" He knows his company policy on dating and is sure to never appear to be sexually harassing while he flirts with the women at his workplace.

He gets to his cubicle, logs onto the Internet, and checks his e-mail. He has been seducing several women he met on line by e-mail, and several lusty responses are waiting for him. He composes a hot, letters-to-*Penthouse*-type reply, and with only minor changes sends it to both of the women who wrote him, as well as to a woman he had been seducing with whom he's lost contact. Aside from using the Internet, he has also been focusing on placing and responding to personal ads in the local free weekly papers. He has met six women so far this way. He plans to meet a few more before the end of the month. He composes a new ad, uses the office fax to send it to the paper, and gets to work.

A little while later, a cute woman from the local print shop enters the office to drop off brochures. He locks eyes with her and they have a conversation. He finds out the type of movies and music she likes and decides to call her sometime at the copy store to set up a movie date.

Lunch time, 12:30 pm
All this running around and working so hard has made our hero hungry. He goes to one of his favorite lunch spots. While the

food is below average, it is near his office and many business women eat there. Bruce selects his lunch spots just like he selects his coffee spots: He goes where the beautiful women are.

While in line he smiles at two very sophisticated women waiting to be seated. "Isn't it fun to be waiting?" he asks in a sarcastic tone. The two women smile and he introduces himself. As one reaches out to shake hands, he kisses her hand and tells her that it is an honor to make her acquaintance. He offers his business card to her as she is seated.

He sits alone and jots down in his notebook a list of women as possibilities for dating. He can't even remember the names of all the women he is in the process of pursuing. On the way to the bathroom, he talks to the not-so-hot-bartender. She knows his name and he chats for a moment.

Bruce always uses his lunch hour as a time to flirt and practice his seduction skills. Even if he is in a hurry, and has to eat at McDonalds, he makes sure to go inside rather than using the drive-through. Going inside gives him more time to flirt with the young women behind the counter, and to hone his skills even more.

1:20 pm, back to work

Bruce arrives back to work and checks his e-mail again for more responses. A few more bored women, also at work, have responded. He flirts through e-mail and sends them more seductive Internet messages. He has also received a few messages on his home answering machine from women he has asked out who want to see him. (Secretly, the authors of this book wonder how Bruce keeps his job with how little time he actually puts into it.)

6:00 pm, time to leave work

Bruce is already focused on what fun events he will pursue that night. Every week he looks in the "Happenings about Town" section of his Sunday paper, and figures out what options most appeal to him. Maybe he will go to a lecture about dogs, or attend a burlesque convention tonight.

He calls several women on his list and makes a date for 8:00 pm at Suzi's house. Suzi has been an off-and-on lover of his for several months. She's always happy to hear from him, and says that tonight she wants to cuddle in bed and watch videos. Our hero ends up going to her house, having sex for hours, and waking up into a new day.

THE FOUR EXCUSES THAT KEEP YOU FROM MEETING WOMEN

The reason Bob is so unsuccessful is that he lets negative beliefs run his life. He is probably a lot like you, and certainly a lot like us before we learned the secrets of seduction. His negative beliefs and concerns dictate how he acts, which, in turn, dictate how successful (or unsuccessful) he is with women. The concerns and beliefs become excuses that Bob uses to keep himself from pursuing women. The following four excuses are often occupying Bob's mind, and they destroy his success with women. If you don't deal with them, they will destroy your success with women, too.

Excuse 1. "It takes too much time."

Bob looks at his daily schedule and whines that he simply doesn't have enough time. He can't meet women, he claims, because he is always busy. He claims he's not scared of women, just too rushed, overloaded with too many responsibilities. We know this is not true. In fact, meeting women is not as time consuming as you may think, and much of the "dead time" in your life—waiting in lines, for instance—is prime women-meeting time.

As Bruce demonstrated, however, flirting and dating women does take some time; there's no way around it. But it is worth it. While dating women may take time up front, after the women are in place, the time required to maintain the relationships is very minimal.

Bruce doesn't view flirting with and dating women as time-consuming because he enjoys it so much. To him, it is his fun-time. It is one of the things that brings him joy in his day. Occasionally it seems like work, but usually he finds himself naturally interacting with women and talking without any effort on his part.

Mastering any new skill does take an initial time and energy investment. If you want to become a great basketball player, you have to buy the right equipment and put in the time to learn the basic moves and strategies. As your playing gets better, it isn't as hard any more. You can get away with simply maintaining your skills and condition, which takes a lot less time.

The same thing is true of dating. Once you have skills in place, you won't have to spend nearly as much time on them. Bruce has many things he does on a daily basis that keep him in practice and make him succeed in dating. He talks to women, smiles and says "hi," and flirts. These things don't take much time on their own, but the cumulative effect is tremendous.

Excuse 2. "It'll hurt my reputation."

Many men, Bob included, worry too much about their reputations. They fear being "found out." They worry that their friends will think they are desperate, and won't respect them. Many people look down on men who are interested in dating, especially on those who are only looking for short-term sexual relationships. Some men don't even try with women, because of this fear.

You handle this by being careful. You must be discreet and watch your back. It is okay to share your desires with your male friends. One caveat, though, is that they must have earned your respect. In male friendships it is often necessary to test the other for his level of trustworthiness. If you trust another man, then you can tell him about your project of dating; otherwise don't. A good rule of thumb is to keep your dating life and work life completely separate. It will insure your job and the integrity of your work relationships and will give you more freedom when you are with women no one else knows. After a while, if you have a serious girlfriend, then she can visit you at work. Otherwise, no.

Bob uses concerns about his reputation as an excuse to not get out there and talk to women. He says, "What if I do ask out that woman I'm so interested in? I can just see how disgusted she'll be by the idea, and I just know she'll tell all our mutual friends. I can see them now, laughing at me." He also moans that he doesn't like to go to pick-up bars because he fears he will see someone he knows. These fears are totally stupid because if you see someone you know, each of you has the same knowledge of the other. If you keep your mouth shut, so will he. Having a certain level of concern about your reputation is healthy, but a paranoia for all potential situations will not allow you opportunities to meet women.

Excuse 3. "I just can't do it."

All of our students, at some point, have felt as though they were fundamentally inadequate when it came to meeting women and dating. Perhaps they were just beginning to learn how to date women, and it all seemed too overwhelming. Or perhaps they had asked out ten women in a row, all of whom said "no." Maybe the last three women they had seduced had gotten almost to the point of having sex with them, then decided to just be "friends." Whatever the reason, it is only natural to sometimes feel as though you just can't do it.

In a way, feeling like a failure is good because your dissatisfaction can get you in action, ready to fight back and prove that you *can* do it. Seen this way, feeling like a failure is actually an opportunity to prove that you aren't one. You've probably experienced feeling bad about something until suddenly you couldn't stand feeling bad about it any more. People who are depressed often report that this happens; they can't stand being so down anymore, so they begin changing and improving their lives. It's sometimes said that it's best to kick a man when he's down; that way, he'll get up faster. When thinking you can't approach women gets painful enough, you'll naturally start to approach them just to get rid of the pain of feeling like such a wimp.

The main thing you must do if you feel like you "just can't do it" is to get support from other men. Mark found himself in this situation. He was just learning how to seduce women, and it seemed like everything he tried made him fall flat on his face. His attempts at witty banter with women came across like drunken street-person rantings, and his every interaction with women seemed forced. He was ready to give up entirely, and came to us dejected.

"I just can't do it," he said. "It's hard and I'm not good at it and I just can't go on anymore with it." He needed support, so we gave it to him, just as you must be able to get support when your seduction failures get you down. "Look," we reminded him, "of course it's going to be difficult at first. If you hang in there, it will get better."

We went over his interactions with him, and gave him coaching about how they could be improved in the future. By reminding him that his dating problems were temporary, and by going over his recent dates with him looking for problems, we were able to give him the support he needed to get out there and keep trying.

You must make sure you get support when you think you can't do it. If you have men friends who are also reading this book, go to them to be reminded that things will get better, and to be reminded of the long-term goal you are working for. Go to men who will remind you of your successes with women so far, no matter how small they may be. When you have support, you'll be able to keep trying.

Excuse 4. "I don't know how to seduce women."

No one taught you, or any of us, how to meet and seduce women. Some men are just "naturals" at it, while the rest of us have been relying on hope and luck. In a way, "I don't know how to seduce women" is a reasonable concern. After all, it's true, isn't it?

You are holding in your hands the answer to this final excuse. Once you finish this book, and you know what there is to study and practice, all you have to do is keep trying, and you will succeed.

These four excuses keep men from taking action to get the women they want. You must give them up and stop whining if you are going to become a seduction machine. As he goes through his day, Bob indulges in these excuses constantly. Bruce does not.

LESSONS FROM THE MASTER

As you can see, Bruce acts in a masterful manner throughout his day and produces results with women. While Bob acts like a putz, Bruce is unstoppable. He focuses his attention, and his activity, on getting women and having a steady supply of dates.

Bruce flirts with every woman

Many men complain that their one or two attempts to meet women and get dates didn't produce results. These men give up if they don't get instant gratification from women. They think that all the time they spend thinking about sex and admiring women's bodies is the same as being out there flirting and asking for dates. Bruce is not like this. He knows that each woman he comes into contact with is another possibility. He flirts and flirts and flirts. He doesn't count on any one woman to be his source of sex; he is unrelenting in meeting new women. Bruce learned a long time ago that he who hesitates, masturbates, so he flirts with women at every opportunity.

Bruce knows that every seduction is a thousand interactions. Remember when President Bush wanted everyone to join his thousand points of light? We want you to join our new thousand interactions. Whether you want a one-night stand, a long-term relationship, or anything in between, you'll do much better remembering that every seduction is made up of a thousand interactions.

Most men we work with get sloppy in their approach with women and try to complete an entire seduction in a few small interactions. They think that once they've met a woman, or asked her out, the work is done. They fail to realize that successfully keeping a woman happy and romantically interested is a daily, moment-by-moment task. Bruce realizes this and knows that there is always work to do. He never gets complacent with women. He is always doing follow-up calls, e-mailing women, visiting familiar waitresses, and making dozens of other bold moves.

The small consistent steps Bruce makes add up to big seduction success. Always remember that it takes dozens if not hundreds of initiations to get a woman in bed. You must do the work, just as Bruce does.

Bruce turns every situation into a prospecting situation

As mentioned in Chapter Two, a successful seducer is always prospecting. What makes Bruce so successful is that he never gives up; he is constantly making every situation into an opening to meet women and flirt.

All women are potential prospects for you. This means that they are potential dates, girlfriends, one-night stands, marriage partners, mothers of your children, or anything else you desire. When you prospect, you are looking for women to interact with, and interacting with them. You are like a salesman; when a salesman goes out looking for prospects, he is looking for prospective clients or customers. He will likely use any situation he is in to ask for a sale, and ask everyone he knows if they know someone who could be a lead or a potential sale. In this way, he turns every situation into a prospecting situation. You have to do this, too.

One of our students, Derek, was a very successful real estate agent. Over coffee he told us about a famed salesman who makes millions of dollars every year in real estate. "So what?" we asked him. "Lots of people make a killing in real estate. What's the point?" Derek told us that the point was how this man had made his money. This agent, he told us, walked house to house, knocked on every door, and spoke to every single resident of his city. He asked them if they wanted to sell their home, if they were looking for a broker, if they had friends looking for a real estate agent, or if they were looking for a new house. He was relentless in his pursuit, talked to everybody he could about real estate, followed up every lead, and it paid off for him.

You must be like this with women. Bruce is. If Bruce thought that he could get the women he desired into bed by going door to door, he'd do it. He's willing to do whatever it takes to meet women he desires. You must do what Bruce does, and flirt and interact with all women. We know you only want to talk to the really hot ones, but that probably won't be useful in the beginning; you'll be too scared of them to flirt effectively, anyway. We say, talk to all women. At this point in your quest for women, the only quality they need for you to flirt with them is that they must be breathing. It is that simple.

Bruce makes it a game

When we say "game," what do you think of? Many men associate games with competition—often fierce competition characterized by battle, conflict, hard feelings, losing and being upset. Or you may be the type who associates games with intellectual, manipulative ploys. Another type associates games with fun, creative expression, freedom, and wonder.

For the sake of this book, "game" means something that is fun and has no negative consequences if you make mistakes while playing it. For most men, dating is serious, and any screw-ups have negative consequences to their self-esteem. Dating seems difficult, like a test of manhood. We want to change that idea. Dating will be radically easier for you if you take it less seriously and make it fun.

Bruce thinks of dating as a game, and you must, too. Then you create a lightness and a freedom in your life. Bruce's attractiveness with women comes as much from his game attitude as from anything else. He's fun, playful, not too serious, and has a life women want to be a part of.

Here are the rules of the dating game:

Rule 1. Nothing is personal. Have you ever been playing a game with other people when it suddenly stopped being a game, and started being personal? One man tells us about a soccer league he was in. The game was going great, when suddenly one of the players attacked a guy on the other team. "Suddenly it wasn't a game anymore," he tells us. "He took personally a move the other guy made, and just lost it." This is one of the quickest ways to destroy a game; then it starts being real.

No matter what a woman does, don't take it personally. Does this mean you can kiss a woman and grab her body and ignore her saying "no"? Absolutely not. But when you say "hi" to a woman and she glares at you, or when you ask a woman out and she says "no," you should simply not take it personally. If you do, you will suffer and not get the sex you desire.

For example, you may want to tell yourself that a woman's rude response to your smile is because she must have just found out about a death in her family. Or you might tell yourself that she has a hearing problem and didn't hear you when a woman ignores your "hello." You may also blame a woman's coldness on the fact that she has a stomach ache from eating too much chocolate. The point is, you don't really know the reasons why she rejects your advances or blows you off. If you take her behaviors personally, it won't be a game anymore, and it won't be fun.

Bruce isn't pulled off course by women's negative responses. He takes it in stride. When you do the same thing, you will be light-years ahead of most other guys.

On the other hand, if a woman responds favorably to your flirtations, then you should take it personally. You should remember that she is attracted you, and that you are the one who made it happen. So, feel acknowledged when things go well, and don't take it personally when things don't work out.

Rule 2. Be playful. Recently we observed a below-average-looking, 55-year-old overweight insurance salesman pick up on a beautiful young woman. We were at a restaurant and he came in to use the bathroom. He asked the cashier about some of the paintings on the wall and joked with her about how ugly and out of date they were. She laughed and smiled at him. She asked him if he wanted to be seated, and he said that he was going to the nearby grocery store to do his shopping. He reached out his hand to say good-bye to her. She extended her hand and he kissed it slowly and said, "It has been a pleasure meeting such a lovely and beautiful woman." She blushed and fanned herself with a menu pretending that he had made her hot and bothered. She gave him a drink in a to-go cup and asked him to stay and talk to her. Because he was able to be playful, he created an opening to charm her. This guy, even though he is below-average-looking, has learned to swoon women and can easily get women to date and have sex with.

Rule 3. Don't give up. Just like in any game, persistence makes a difference. Even if you don't think you'll win the game, you'll enjoy it much more if you don't give up and you play to win, anyway.

This is Bruce's attitude. It doesn't matter to him if he wins or loses, just how he plays the game, and he plays to win even when the odds are against him. Most of the women he flirts with he never sleeps with, but he doesn't care. He simply pushes each interaction as far as it can go, then moves on to the next one. He knows that if you give up in a game, the game is over. Because he enjoys the game, he wants to stay with it.

Being persistent and playing to win makes you into a man who doesn't give up easily, and being a man who doesn't give up will bring you more success than you ever thought possible. There's a story about a boy in a math class. He had dozed off, and awoke to find the teacher writing a problem on the board. Thinking that the problem was a homework assignment, he scribbled it into his notebook, and took it home with him.

For the next two days, he spent every free waking moment working on the problem. Finally, he got the answer and took it to his teacher. She was shocked—it turned out the problem was supposed to be insoluble, and she had only written it on the board as an example. He was able to solve it because he played to win, and didn't know that he "couldn't." He didn't give up when the going got rough, just as Bruce doesn't.

Rule 4. Use probabilities. One of the great things about sports announcers is that they always throw probabilities into their commentaries. They talk about how well a batter has batted against the pitcher in the past, and compare this to his other averages. Announcers then go off into the minutia, talking about how this batter does against right-handed pitchers and compares this to left-handed pitchers. They talk and talk until no one cares anymore. By that time a new batter is up.

In the dating game, probabilities are fun, too. They make the game more fun and make interactions with women more about numbers than about some huge ego risk. On a particular night you may see a beautiful woman across from you in a bar and use probabilities to create the percent chance that you could go home with her. You might give yourself a 5 percent chance that she will talk to you. There might be a 1 percent chance that you could buy her a drink and a .05 percent chance that you could sleep with her tonight. If she's less beautiful or more drunk, your probabilities may go up. It sounds silly, but using this technique creates a framework of fun.

When you follow the rules, dating becomes more like a game, less threatening and scary, and more fun for everybody. You know games have ups and downs, wins and losses. You don't go into games putting your ego on the line, or feel like there's something wrong with you if you don't win every time.

Have your friends egg you on

As men, whether we admit it or not, we love competition. It is useful to use our innate competitiveness to egg on ourselves and our friends to date more women and to do outrageous things we may not normally think to do.

The authors of this book used this principle frequently to push each other to get out and date more. We would tease each other and dare each other to approach a beautiful woman. We placed bets on each other's success and failure rates.

Once again, it's important to have male friends who are supportive. If the competition becomes something that has you feel like a failure, stop doing it immediately. We are encouraging you to have friends to both console you when things go bad and encourage you when you get scared and are not able to be in action. No one understands all the potential pitfalls, problems, and pleasures of dating better than another man. If you are a guy with few men friends, and mostly hang out with women, this must change. Having male friends egg you on will produce results that far exceed any advice that women will give you.

Bruce relentlessly follows-up leads

Bruce is relentless in his quest for women. He is hitting on so many women in one day that he couldn't care less if one or many don't work out. He is focusing on the long-term goal of having dozens of women he can call in an instant and sleep with that night.

He is constantly following up leads at restaurants, on the phone, e-mail, and in the stores and other places he frequents. Like the hungry salesman, he does what it takes to get as many women as he can.

Bruce knows it's a numbers game

Bruce lives his life from the "numbers game" analogy we discussed in Chapter 2. He knows that like sales, dating is all about numbers. He knows that if he flirts with ten women, one will give him her number. If he sets up ten dates, four women will actually show up. He knows that of those four, he will sleep with at least one. Bruce uses this philosophy to boost himself up when he is rejected. To him it is just one more interaction with a woman that will eventually lead to a "yes."

Bruce flirts with and prospects lots of women

We've explained that master seducers not only play it like a numbers game, but they also don't put all their eggs in one basket. They pursue lots and lots of women.

Even if women are not receptive, the practice is well worth the effort. Bruce views flirting and prospecting women as part of the reason for his success. When you practice something long enough you will develop mastery. By flirting often, you master your speaking skills with women. All of us can point to skills in our lives that we studied for a long, long time until we could do them effortlessly. Riding a bike, tying your shoes and memorizing multiplication tables are all examples.

Flirting with lots of women also generates a high level of vitality and confidence in yourself that is infectious to women. When you are talking to many women your successes build on one another and it helps you to get more dates and be more vital in other areas of your life. One definition of vitality is that it is a reflection of how bold you are in life. It can be measured by how much of a public personality you are, how willing you are to be outrageous. Women want you to be powerful and confident in public and private. Flirting with lots of women will help develop these qualities in you.

Another reason to flirt with lots of women is that it will eventually lead to big results. We believe that small, consistent actions eventually lead to success. We all know the story of how successful the turtle was because he was slow but steady, unlike the hare who was quick but got sloppy and lazy. The same is true with pursuing women. When you constantly flirt with women it will have a multiplier effect, and aid in current and future successes with women.

Bruce pretends he is a world-class stud

We mentioned in Chapter Two about the importance of modeling other men. It is useful to model your dress, approach, lines, and general demeanor, after a highly successful seducer.

One of the things that Bruce does constantly is act like he is *the* man. He acts in a confident manner. Secretly, Bruce models himself after a character John Travolta played in the movie *Get Shorty*. He also uses his friend Sam as a role model. Sam is always surrounded by women and dates frequently. Bruce has learned that if he does what Sam does he tends to be more successful with women than if he doesn't.

Bruce leaves the house ready to party

Looking good at all times, no matter what, is an important part of success with women. Many men make the mistake of leaving the house not ready to meet women. We are not suggesting that you always have to be wearing a suit. However, we are suggesting that you seriously consider what you are wearing and consider whether or not it is appropriate for meeting a woman. You read about this in depth in the previous chapter. Even if you are wearing sweat pants and a T-shirt you can present yourself in a manner that will be attractive to women. Keep it in mind.

Bruce is always ready to flirt, no matter what. It's part of being a world-class stud. Behind all of the flirtation is many hours of preparation. He has memorized seductive questions and opening lines. He has decided ahead of time how many women he will talk to in a day. In later chapters you will learn pick-up lines and approaches to meeting women. Bruce can easily use many different approaches and ways to meet women, so he is ready to flirt in any situation.

Bruce has studied seduction in great detail, like a martial artist who studies and anticipates every situation. Like the martial artist, Bruce prepares for all the different options and is ready to create new alternatives that are easily applicable to any situation that may come his way.

THE FOUR EASIEST PLACES TO MEET WOMEN

Bruce is in the habit of visiting the same places regularly. This practice opens up many opportunities to ask out women and creates a basis for rapport. Social scientists have shown that the more you see someone and have contact with that person, the more attracted you are. This is called attraction by familiarity. This fact alone should inspire you to find ways to interact with the same people on a regular basis. Here's a list of four places you can go on a regular basis to meet women and create an attraction by familiarity.

1. Coffee shops

Coffee shops are rapidly becoming the hottest new place to meet women. Singles all over the country are using them as potential pick-up spots. The trend is not just happening in Seattle. We're sure your local coffee place has a good sampling of women.

Bruce demonstrated how useful it is to become a regular at a coffee shop. They tend to be like small communities. The same cast of characters shows up at approximately the same time every day. It is good for you to get into a routine with a place. This way you can get to know the regulars. A woman may be sipping hot java and hanging out with her friends. Or she may be reading a book or writing in her journal. Knowing many of the employees and regulars will also make it easier to meet other customers.

2. Restaurants

Restaurants are another great place to find dates. Women love to go out to eat. The better the food and more expensive, the more women like it. Again, restaurants put people in a festive mood and they're open to new experiences. Besides, women love to get dressed up and go out. Even if you get rejected, it is good for your self-confidence to be interacting with women who are dressed attractively. The best restaurants in which to meet women are ones with large bar areas and patio seating.

Waitresses are the best part of restaurants. By becoming familiar with a restaurant and the waitresses, you can easily turn food service into sex service. For example, Mark, a 34-year-old science researcher went to the same restaurant three times per week for dinner. Over time he became romantic with Darlene, a waitress. He allowed himself to build the romance with her slowly; after all, he knew where she was, and that she'd be seeing him again. He never was obnoxious or overly flirtatious. One night, he ran into her outside of the restaurant at a nearby bar. They talked and he invited her to a movie. They went out and ended up fooling around. They dated occasionally after that.

3. Gyms

Everyone thinks gyms are crawling with singles looking for dates and sex. This certainly hasn't been our experience. Perhaps working out at the most industrial gym in town doesn't help. Gyms are good, however, for making contacts with women and getting occasional dates. We've often seen our gym full of chubby, married, middle-aged women, who look annoyed when you even glance at them. On the other hand, our students continue to report that they've met women at the gym. They comment that at the gym it is fun just to stare at the tight-bodied females.

We recommend the gym to you because working out improves your body and, hence, your net worth with women. By working out a few times per week you can lose the gut and increase your stamina. It is even said to increases your testosterone levels.

The other advantage is that some women are looking for a man in the gym. By becoming familiar with a woman and her schedule, you can start conversations and work on her over time until you ask her out.

4. Bookstores

Are you looking for a sexy, smart, and untamed woman? By frequenting bookstores you can meet lonely intellectuals. Women you meet in bookstores will often be receptive to you because there you will find women who are smart and can't find a guy. Why do you think women read so many romance novels and weird fiction anyway? Many bookstores are packed with women on Friday night. They are looking for something, and it isn't just another Martha Stewart book.

One of our students met an attractive woman looking at books in the Sex section of a large chain bookstore. Though he thought it was corny, he made a joke about the book she was reading. She was receptive to him and they joked about penis enlargement toys. Later, he got her e-mail address and they e-mailed back and forth for a few weeks, and later dated.

We recommend meeting women in bookstores for all of our intellectual students. The other added bonus about bookstores is that many of them have attached coffee shops, so you can meet a woman and then take her out for coffee right away to continue the seduction.

THE NINE SECRET PLACES TO MEET WOMEN

What follows is a list of places that you probably don't associate as prime woman-meeting spots. However, these are wonderfully secret hidden sources of lonely women waiting for you. We recommend that if you show up at one of the following events or places and there are no women you are interested in, move on immediately. If you quickly move on, and keep going on to the next opportunity, you are destined for success.

1. Yoga classes

Your local yoga class is a great place to meet new-age women. Yoga, in case you don't know, is a form of exercise similar to stretching. Yoga comes from India and was used as a form of transcending the body and mind together. We won't go into any more detail, to avoid scaring you. Over the past few years yoga has become a popular form of exercise among health-conscious women. Most cities have many classes and women are usually the main ones teaching and attending classes. A woman who has been active in yoga for years usually has a wonderfully toned body. That's another added advantage!

Fred attended a local yoga class and found himself in a room full of 20 women and no other men. Since he was a beginner, he failed miserably at the yoga "poses." Fred kept asking women nearby for help. By the end of the hour class, he had four women offering to help him outside of class. Other women were friendly and receptive to him coming back. "It was great," Fred said. "I am all over yoga class, like a hobo on a ham sandwich. I love talking to these calm, airy-fairy chicks. They are fun to talk to and even more fun to look at. I'm even finding some physical benefits from the classes."

2. Cooking classes

Who do you think is attending all the exotic cooking classes? Women, of course. Who do you think is concerned with making good quality food? Women. Remember the cliché phrase, "The way to a man's heart is through his stomach." Women attend classes to make the men in their lives happy. Who do you think is *not* attending most cooking classes? Men. They are the ones missing out on the opportunity to meet women and learn great recipes.

Cooking classes are a great place to meet women for the same reasons as yoga classes are. In these situations, you are a rarity, a scarce resource. You will actually get rewarded for not knowing how to cook and botching up recipes. Women in the classes will end up feeling sorry for you and will often offer their services to help you. You can ask them for cooking dates to get them to your house. Furthermore, being in the class for six weeks or so will give you an opportunity to get to know the women in the class and let the seductions build on one another over time. Oh yea: You'll also learn to cook. Weird, huh?

3. Church

A few years ago we had a student who claimed that church was the ultimate place to meet women. His name was Bart and he was the poster boy for geeks everywhere. He wore '50s-style glasses and outdated pants. However, Bart was always active in his church and a devout follower. He decided to use his faith to get women.

Bart began attending single events on weekends. He confessed to several members of his congregation that he was looking for a woman of faith. Since many churches like to promote dating and relationships from within their communities, many members of his congregation began setting him up.

The thing that amazed us was that these women had sex with him. "Like bunnies," he told us. "Most of them couldn't wait to get into bed." You may want to go to church this coming week and check out the chicks while you pray.

4. Renaissance fairs

Summertime Renaissance Fairs happen everywhere, even in your area. While fairs of any sort are great to meet women, Renaissance ones are the best. These fairs attract the hippie, 1960s women who value peace, love, and freedom. In short, these are the types who will be open to meeting you and tend to be sexually open.

A group of our students attended a local Renaissance fair last summer and had a great time. They quickly located groups of women wearing long flowing dresses and patchouli perfume who seemed open to flirting, talking, and more. After spending a few hours walking around the fair, our students took the ladies to a near-by bar. Our boys proceeded to party until dawn.

Another great place to meet women is with groups like the "Rainbow People." The "Rainbow People," as they call themselves, are basically hippies for the next millennium. They have local chapters in many communities, and the women can be quite, um, open. They also have week-long gatherings in the country at least once a year, where lots of sex occurs. But bring your own water; lots of dysentery occurs as well while people camp.

5. Outdoor music events

What could be more romantic than a concert under the stars? Women eat up this type of event. Depending on the type of musician who is performing, a concert can prove to be well worth the time and money.

Such a music event is a great place to meet women, if you are going alone. Single women attending in small groups are open to meeting men; indeed, many of them go with that as their goal. If the music is jazz, classical, or pop rock (not punk or hard-rock), it will be easier to make a connection. The hard-rock outdoor shows will have lots of drunk underage women. Obviously, you have to watch out for women who look attractive and seem mature, but who in fact are 17. The other problem with hard-rock concerts is that they tend to be so loud, you can't talk.

The authors of this book once attended a jazz festival in Concord, California, called The Concord Jazz Festival. Miles Davis played as the headliner. It was a long day under the sun and when night came it was cold. We used the cold as an opportunity to invite three women sitting near us to cuddle under our blanket; they had worn shorts, and weren't prepared for the cold. Because we had talked to them off and on all day long, they felt comfortable with us. We cuddled with them and later invited them to join us in our hotel room for after-hours action. They accepted.

Because there is no magical solution, you won't always be so lucky. However, you can persistent in going to places and attending events where women will be open to dating, and you will eventually have success.

6. The cooking utensil section of any store

Any gourmet cooking store is likely to have classy women hanging out looking at utensils. These are the places in which you have easy openings to talk. Your best bet is to visit on weekends. You can then approach a good looking woman and ask her questions about cooking utensils. Ask her for her advice on which garlic press is the best and which spatula would be good for French food.

The women shopping in these stores will probably be over 35. This is great if you are looking for marriage-minded women into serious relationships, or for a divorcee who would love some sex. This is not good if all you want is a roll in the hay with a 20-something girl.

It will work well to be flirtatious right off the bat. The fact that you are looking for gourmet items tells a woman a lot about you. It says that you like "fine" food and probably "fine" culture. She will like this because she will inevitably, like most women, be attracted to high-class culture. It is to your advantage to speak about your love of culture in the conversations you have with her. It will also tell her that you are "refined" in the sense that you know what "fine" things are, and you have a respect for them. Your interest will set her hormones into overdrive and she will automatically put you in the "possible serious relationship" category. You can also use this approach at any place that sells expensive items, like a jewelry store, an expensive clothing store, or a furniture store.

7. Dance classes

Dancing close to a woman is still one of the most romantic things you can do. The old time male sex symbols are still popular among women because they possess a flair for charm and romance. Fred Astaire, Bing Crosby, and others are still the fantasy of many women. Part of that charm was their ability to sweep a woman off her feet with dancing and romantic talk. They could be subtle and forward at the same time.

Dance classes are great places to meet women and start a seduction. First, women respect men who learn "old time" romantic activities, like dancing. They will hopefully cut you some slack if you are a crappy dancer—after all, you are attending the class to learn, aren't you? Second, they will likely want to dance with you because so few men take dance classes that you are a rare commodity. And third, you will be able to flirt with them over multiple weeks, and seduce them slowly.

Ballroom dance is a great way to hold women close to you and perform the same moves they've seen master seducers do on TV and in movies. Many people report that they feel "high" because of the aerobic effects of dancing and that it adds to the feeling of romance. Learning ballroom dance will also be helpful for weddings, formal events, and even out in a dance club.

Brian, a 31-year-old computer programmer, used ballroom dancing to meet several women. He was having a problem meeting interesting and sexy women to date. His job forced him to be inside most of the day, and he wasn't into the bar scene. Brian saw an ad for the ballroom dance club on a local college campus. He decided to start attending classes. To him it was good exercise, and a great way to meet attractive students.

After a few months he became quite good at dancing, and many of the women in the club asked him to dance during their events. Brian had been used to having a primarily solitary life, and the new attention was fun and thrilling for him. He became a regular member of the club and attended two dances per week. Brian not only created a new social circle, but eventually began to seriously date one of the women.

8. Bars associated with hotels where traveling businesswomen stay

Businesswomen on the road tend to be open to sexual experimentation and tend to be more promiscuous. The "high end" hotels in your town will likely have many traveling businesswomen hanging out in the bar or lounge area late at night. Yes, they are lonely, and yes, they would love to have company. Just like their male counterparts, they get lonely on the road and want affection, love, and pampering from a man. You know how stressful it is to be on the road, not knowing anyone, and having to be in charge for hours a day at meetings. At the end of the day they want exactly what we want: a warm body, a good beer, and sex.

Jack began hanging out at the most expensive hotel in his town. He wanted to see how many women he could meet in the bar. He started visiting the bar a few nights a week. For the first few weeks all he met were boring computer geeks visiting for business. One night, however, he saw a lonely looking 38-year-old. She was attractive, wearing a business suit, drinking wine and scoping the room for a man. Jack sat next to her and started a harmless conversation, as we'll teach you to do in this book. They seemed to "hit it off" right away. They were both in the same business and she seemed very smart. They talked for hours, until Jack was close to drunk. She asked him up to her room. They had sex all night long, and Jack woke up in her bed the next morning.

9. The Internet

Shy? Scared of talking to women? Scared of showing your romantic interest, taking charge and risking rejection? Of course you are. No problem, though: there is a place where you can practice seducing women where any rejection seems minimal, successes are easy, and you can refine your style and your understanding of seduction. This place is the Internet.

If you are lonely, shy and horny, you must get onto the international sex superhighway called the Internet. The parts of the Internet we are concerned with here are the World Wide Web, Personals Ads Newsgroups, and Internet Chat Rooms.

The World Wide Web. The Web is, by and large, a dumb place to look for lovers. It's also where most men go right away, because of the dirty pictures and stories you can find there. But *finding spanking material is not the same as seducing women.* To actually find women to interact with sexually, you need to leave the Web alone, and concentrate on Personals Ads Newsgroups and Chat Rooms.

Personals Ads Newsgroups. With a "Newsreader" application you can explore "Usenet," a selection of thousands and thousands of special interest "newsgroups." Anyone can post to most of these groups, putting up letters that anyone can read and respond to, either in the group or personally directly to their e-mail addresses. There is a large selection of groups that consist mostly of personals ads, and that's where you want to go to start placing seductive postings for women. We'll talk more about personals ads of all types, and how to write them, in a later chapter.

Chat Rooms. Most easily accessed if you are on a large service like America OnLine, Chat Rooms are places where everybody types at once, and what they write shows up on each other's screens. Most of what goes on in Chat Rooms is infantile ("Hey, who's here?" "Are there any women here?"). But with some looking you can find sex and romance groups in which to talk to women about their experiences of romance.

Can you find a woman you will end up having sex with on the Internet? Possibly, but bear in mind several things. First, you are there to practice. Second, she may very well be fat. You can almost count on it, though it is not a 100 percent fact. Third, she may live far away, be married, or be holding back some other unpleasant surprise. Keeping these three caveats in mind, you can definitely have success seducing women on the Internet:

* You get to practice. We advise all our students to hone their seduction skills on the Internet.

* You get successes. Women who write you erotic letters give you a sense of having an abundant sex life, and that abundance makes you more relaxed around women in real life.

* You can get phone sex. This is a very common benefit. Many of our students have phone sex partners they met on the Internet who they can call at any time, day or night, to get them off. These women live in distant towns but are available for phone sex where it doesn't matter how fat she is. You too can have free phone sex if you follow the Rules and get on the Net!

* You can get real sex. Some of our students have traveled to meet these women, as well. One tells of being in a distant town where one of the women he met on-line lives. He had been having lots of e-mail sex and some phone sex with her. He let her know he was coming to town, and she suggested

they get together. Even though she did try to ruin it at the last moment by saying that they had to be just friends, he persisted. He said being just friends was fine, and got together with her anyway. "When I first saw her, she was dressed so hot," he says now. "I touched and kissed her within the first five minutes, then said, 'I know you just want to be friends, but the chemistry is so strong! I'll stop right now if you want.' She said 'I want you to take me' and we had sex all night long. I found out later she only said the 'just friends' thing because she was afraid I wouldn't want her! We still have sex on the Net and she wants me to stop in next time I'm in her town." Internet seduction can definitely work.

* You can get more! People do find the partner of their dreams on the Internet. It does happen. You simply must be persistent and willing to put the time in.

The bottom line is this: You have no excuse to not be meeting women, even if you are shy. If you offend a woman on the Internet, in a letter, or in voice mail message, she simply doesn't write or call back. So what? The Internet is a place to build your confidence and develop your seduction skill mastery.

BABE BAIT: GIMMICKS THAT MAKE WOMEN WANT TO MEET YOU

Every highly successful ladies' man has some sort of a gimmick. Elvis used his fame, wealth, and charm to get any woman he wanted. JFK used his power as President to sleep with hot babes like Marilyn Monroe. Wilt Chamberlain used his basketball prowess to sleep with thousands of women. Since you probably aren't rich and famous, you will have to come up with more creative ways to attract women's attention. Here are some possibilities.

Dogs/dog related activities

Women love dogs. Dogs remind them of a carefree time in their childhood when they would dream of horses, puppy dogs, and Barbies. Not only do most women think dogs are "cute" (especially puppies), most of the people who go to dog training workshops and attend conventions are women.

Sure, you like dogs. They are fun to play ball with. Maybe you had a big dog when you were a kid, and some of your best memories are of your attempts to get your dog to bite people. While you probably associate them with pleasure, you may not associate dogs with romance, charm, and meeting women. You should. Believe us, dogs can be used as the perfect gimmick for shy guys who have a hard time making the first move.

The gimmick is that you play up your interest in dogs, or have one that attracts women. For example, on a brisk fall walk in a nature park, Clem noticed a spot filled with women and their dogs. Clem approached one of the women and said that he was interested in getting a dog. Did she have any suggestions as to what kind to get? Could she help? He looked at her with his big boyish innocent eyes. She couldn't resist, and they ended up talking for an hour about the advantages and disadvantages of different breeds. At the end of the discussion he asked her for her phone number, requesting that they go to the kennel together. She said "yes" and they went out later that week.

Dog shows, dog training weekends, and dog training classes are all great places to meet women. One of our students went to a dog training weekend where there were 120 women and four men! While not all of these women were attractive, a few were, and he got several dates out of it with ease. Dog shows are almost all women. Go to them, even if you don't have a dog!

Most cities have dog parks, where people can go to run their dogs. You should go there, too. And if you have a dog, for goodness sake take some dog training classes. You'll meet women and have an obedient dog, too!

Go to personal growth seminar

Do you want to meet an emotionally open woman who is willing to see you as a magical solution to her problems? Could this solution include a hot night with you? A personal growth seminar may be your ticket.

One of the key elements of most seminars is the deep level of bonding that quickly happens between participants. At a personal growth seminar, you will be in a group of people who are there to break out of their normal day-to-day routines and try something new. This can be a good environment for you to experiment with new behaviors with women who will be much more receptive than those on the street or in a cafe.

Another element of most seminars is that they stress honesty. Usually this means emotional honesty. People who reveal their innermost secrets are often rewarded by the group leaders and gain the respect of fellow seminarians. This environment is perfect because you can come across as Mr. Sincere and Mr. Emotionally Honest & Available when you are actually just hitting on women.

On a break you could walk up to the most beautiful woman in the room and say something like, "I've never told anyone this before, but I am finally realizing that I am a fully sexual being. A sexual man who has both emotional and sexual needs. Does that make sense to you? Have you ever thought you were not honest with yourself or people in your surroundings about what you really want in relationships?" In an environment that stresses honesty and sharing you can approach many women and honestly express your attraction, ask them out, get to know them better, and practice your new skills.

Another advantage is that most women attending will be open to meeting you, and may even approach you first. Some will actually be attending with the sole purpose to meet a man. Some will even be there just to find sex partners! There will also be women attending because they want to explore some inner turmoil and may suffer from both the "innocent-victim syndrome" and the "unbelievably gullible disease." This is both good news and bad news. It is good because they will be open to dating and sharing with you. It is bad news because they may have psycho tendencies and may end up being more of a pain than they're worth. Later we'll teach you about psycho chicks, and provide you with the necessary diagnostic tools to spot these women. In the meantime, some may be fun to date.

You may find the information presented at the seminar useful, too. We've observed that the clearer a man is in his purpose in life and the more clarity he has about his relationships, the easier time he has with women. A seminar may help you in this task.

The only major downfall of seminars is that they may cost too much money. For the untrained man, the personal growth seminar world is a mess. You have all the new-age crystal healing courses, self-esteem seminars, anger management courses, erection problem support groups (avoid these for meeting women), divorced dads groups, and then companies, like Career Track, which run seminars, too. The prices range wildly, from $50 for a day to $3,000 for a week-long course in how to become a spiritual master. We are suggesting spending, at the most, around $350 for a weekend course.

Remember that some seminars are for men only. You won't meet women there.

Volunteer for causes

Do you remember what the biggest obstacle is when you meet a woman? The correct answer is that she will be concerned about whether or not you are violent and who will harm her. When she meets you at a volunteer event this concern can disappear quickly. What kind of men volunteer to help worthy causes? Guys who are trustworthy, honest, and responsible.

Many opportunities to volunteer for causes will lead to meeting women. You will usually be working side by side with a woman, or will have a woman leading a team of volunteers (this is an added bonus for all the submissive guys out there). Women volunteer for causes much more than men, so in the crowd of women volunteers you will be a novelty. Women will think that you are sensitive, moral, and safe, and your net worth to a woman will increase.

If you follow the Seven Habits of Highly Effective Seducers, you will be a man with direction in his life, and one who consistently focuses on his values and expresses them in the world. This type of inner discipline, determination, and focus will make you stand out to women. Being a volunteer can not only help increase your confidence in yourself, but will lead to having the life in which you love. As a result, you will be that much more marketable to women. When a man does things to help his community, stands up for a cause he believes in, participates in a political campaign, or raises awareness for an issue he feels strongly about, he is seen as a leader and commands the respect of one.

Imagine that you are helping with registration at a 10K Run For Nature. You show up early on a Saturday morning and meet all the hot women there to compete in the race. You flirt openly with them. In the process, you get to check out hundreds of women dressed in tights, short shorts, and various degrees of undress. In the process, you probably work with many women who are there to volunteer and have fun. You meet a woman at a nearby table and talk to her after the race begins and make dinner plans for that night.

José, a 40-year-old divorced father, volunteered to be part of a fund-raising banquet for children. As a father, he wanted to help raise Christmas funds as well as an awareness in his town about child poverty. Besides, he thought, it would help get his mind off women. He was lonely during the winter season and wanted to think about "larger issues." He spent two months attending weekly meetings and calling local restaurants to donate food. At the first meeting he noticed Caroline. She was bubbly, 42 years old, and above average looking with a good body. José decided to work with her on a committee. They were in frequent contact on the phone and José suggested they meet at a bar for meetings. Over the two months José not only solicited several restaurants to donate food, but he also began dating Caroline.

Volunteering is a good way to not only meet women, but to increase you net worth around them. You develop confidence and begin to focus on someone else for a change. This is a skill you will need if you ever want to have a long-term relationship.

Magic Tricks

This gimmick is time consuming on the front end. You have to learn a few tricks and practice them. Your guy friends may think you are a freak, but the women you meet with magic will be charmed.

Women love to be entertained by men. Learning a wide range of magic tricks can prove useful in meeting women in any situation. Brian, a 36-year-old average looking guy who works at a bank, first told us about how useful magic tricks are in meeting women. Brian described them as "ultimate conversation starters with any woman at any time."

Brian uses magic tricks to meet women whenever he has to wait in lines, on airplanes, at a restaurant, even while shopping at the grocery store. Recently, while waiting in a line for movie tickets Brian started talking to two women. His initial opening lines didn't go well. They ignored him and one gave him a dirty look. He asked them if they would be interested in seeing a magic trick, explaining that he was studying magic and practicing for a show at a local club. They said "sure." He pulled out a deck of cards and asked them to each take one. Brian went through an elaborate slight-of-hand trick and the two smiled. They began talking and the women asked him to sit with them during the movie.

Once again, this gimmick made Brian look like a "good guy," someone who was certainly trustworthy. Magic can be used to meet any woman at any time. Also, you can use magic to entertain children so that their mothers will be amused and be interested in meeting you.

Carry something odd

The downtown shopping area is filled with shoppers. Women in groups are window shopping and thrilled to be out spending lots of money at their favorite activity. Then comes you, the man holding the four-foot-tall stuffed bear or dog. The women laugh and want to touch it. "Where did you get it?" they ask.

This gimmick is very simple to use. The only requirement is the purchase or loan of a large stuffed animal. Women will instantly be attracted to you and the animal. It is best if you sit on a bench or situate yourself in an easy accessible area that invites people to talk to you with ease.

Guys will think you are a dork. But while they are thinking that, you will be meeting women. It is best to start long conversations about your stuffed animal. The short conversations will be fun, but will rarely lead to dates. Focusing on longer conversations will insure more dates, and more long-term success.

Babies

Do you want to insure dates tonight? Borrow a friend's baby and women will be all over you. Babies make all men look like great guys and will draw every woman in a 100-yard radius. They will instantly want to be with you and help with taking care of the baby. They will even want to date you just to be around the baby.

The obvious problem is that no sane person will loan you a baby so that you can go out and meet women. Realistically, the best strategy is to go around with a friend in hopes of meeting a woman. Taking a baby on a walk in a stroller with your male friend is much better. Women will want to come up and answer questions for you. If you pretend to be helpless and stupid it will work better.

Hand puppets

We once were sitting on a beautiful public outdoor terrace at the local university on a sunny afternoon, when a guy with a large, muppet-sized hand puppet arrived. We watched amazed as he took this charming puppet to each table, and charmed and entertained everyone there. He talked to all the women there, from the least attractive to the most, and ended up sitting with a group of laughing, giggly women. We never found out what happened to him and whether he got sex, but we admired his willingness to do what it takes to get the attention of women.

Read romantic poetry at poetry readings and open-mike events

With the explosion of coffee cafes, there has also been a rise in poetry readings and open-mike events. These are perfect opportunities to meet artistic women who would like an intellectual man to melt their hearts.

A woman wants to be with the kind of man who writes or recites poetry. She sees this type of man as a challenge. He is artistic, and so isolated from the world that no other woman has been able to reach him. She wants to be *the* one who finally brings him out of his shell.

You can get up and read anything and get women to talk to you. We recommend reading something romantic, as it will improve your chances of seduction. You could read a poem about how war is bad or how sad it is that children starve, but then women will be much less likely to respond. Read about love, and love you will get.

You can find short seductive poetry from books in the library, Shakespeare collections, or better yet, write some of your own. Something cheesy like the following will work well.

> You,
> I saw your lips move as you moved past me
> My heart races as I think of your eyes,
> I wish I could be the air you breathe,
> You,
> I want you
> You,
> I lust in my heart for you
> You,
> In candlelit rooms we enter each other
> We disappear for hours in tender kisses
> You,
> My special angel, I want only you

Reading poetry provides a way for women to talk to you and a reason for you to talk to women. It will give you confidence and let women know you are a romantic guy. As we'll discuss later, when you describe a state of mind or a feeling, like lust and desire, the person you are speaking to will automatically remember what it is like when she feels that state. When you read a romantic poem, all the women in the audience will have to recall times when they felt the feelings you describe in your poems. Those are the feelings you want them to have, and it makes it easier for you to talk to them later.

Gimmicks can get women talking to you. As you develop your ability to come up with gimmicks that attract women and express some special part of yourself, you'll find yourself surrounded by women who want to be with you.

In closing, you no longer can make the excuse that there are no women out there, or that you are too scared, or that meeting them is too hard or takes too much time. You no longer have to wait until you "get lucky," and meet a woman, and you no longer have to live a life of helplessly hoping for better times.

Women are everywhere. You encounter them constantly, and regularly pass up opportunities to surround yourself with them. This is not just "positive thinking," or some other new-age noise. If you give up your excuses, flirt with every woman you see, allow your seductions to build over time as a thousand little interactions, turn every situation into a prospecting situation, make meeting women a game, have friends egg you on and support you, follow up on every lead, and leave your home looking good and ready to party, you'll be ready to meet women. If you frequent a coffee shop, a gym, a restaurant, and bookstores, you'll also find women to meet.

If you take the trouble to go to a yoga class, a new age event, a cooking class, a personal growth seminar, or a renaissance fair, you'll also find plenty of women you could meet. And if you have a gimmick, you can even get women to talk to you first!

You now know *where* to meet women. The next thing you need to know is how to meet them. That is the topic of the next chapter.

chapter five...
Flirting
Without Disaster

SO YOU'VE FOUND THE WOMEN TO TALK TO:
NOW HOW DO YOU DO IT?

Many men are very analytical in their approach to life. They think about life practically, and they think about women practically. They get caught in the paralysis of analysis. This is a huge error. Romance is not practical, logical, or even sensible.

Bob thinks women and romance should be logical. When he's been attracted to women and had the nerve to actually approach them, he's figured that it's best to be direct. "After all," he says, "women like men who are direct and honest. What could be more honest than telling them about my attraction to them?" He's tried to seduce women friends by explaining to them how logical it would be for them to have a relationship. "You say you like me, and I like you. It doesn't make any sense for us to not get involved!" He's never understood why they've said no to him. His practical, logical approach drives women away.

WHAT IS FLIRTING?

To date women successfully you must master flirting. Flirting is not practical or direct. But it does follow basic principles, and once you understand them, you'll be miles ahead of other men in talking to and being successful with women.

Think about kids playing together. They don't try to accomplish anything; all they are interested in is games. They take on roles with each other effortlessly. They play cowboys, and one kid is the cowboy, another is the Indian. Or they play house, and one kid is the father and the other is the mother. Or they play doctor, and one kid is the doctor while the other is the patient. (That's the kind of playing you want to do with adult women!) They dress up to get into the roles better. They let their imaginations run free. It's all ultimately meaningless, but they don't care; they just want to have fun.

They also love games, both pre-made and ones they make up. And most of the time, they aren't overly concerned about winning. Just being together playing is enough to make them happy. Kids relate by playing, and if they can play, they feel related to each other, though they don't think about it that way. Playing is a way of being in "the zone" together.

Adults play differently. First, let's look at how men play with men. We usually don't think of it as play, but watching sports together, or talking about sports, is a way men play with each other. After all, sports are ultimately meaningless: which team wins the NBA title this year really isn't going to make that big a difference in the grand scheme of things. It really isn't. Sorry. But the point is, by caring about it together, by watching the games, yelling and screaming at the players together, and keeping track of the player's statistics, men play together. Because of all this, they are feeling the togetherness and un-self-conscious love for each other that kids feel.

The other way men play together is through joking with each other and playing jokes on each other. The little jokes that men make about each other, the loving insults traded back and forth, are bonding for men.

Men and women, on the other hand, play together differently. As most men have discovered, playing with women the way they do with men doesn't work. Women aren't interested in sports statistics. And the jokes you make with your buddies only offend the women you know. Having learned this stuff the hard way, men decide to not play with women at all. They approach women the way Bob does, logically and practically. And they get no results at all.

Flirting is the way men and women play. If you can't flirt, you can't play with women, and if you can't play with women, they won't be romantically interested in you. Flirting is one of the ways women find out what you'll be like as a lover, and what you'd be like in a relationship. If you aren't playful, imaginative, and fun to be with when she first meets you, what will you be like to date? And what will you be like in bed? Bob impresses the ladies as a cold fish. He seems stiff, analytical and calculating. Even if he can logically show them they should be interested in him, his lack of playfulness doesn't touch them inside. His outcome-oriented approach is anything but playful.

Let's look at how Bruce, an accomplished flirter, handles women he is attracted to. At the bank, for instance, he flirts with the cute female teller as he makes his deposits. "So," he asks with a smile. "Do you get to keep a percentage of all the money you take in each day? It only seems fair, don't you think?" She laughs and says, "Oh, that would be nice, especially on payday." He jokes that "but then you might get docked a percentage of the money that goes out! We can't be having that happen to you!" She laughs again, and notices her connection with him. As he leaves he says, "Thank you, O Banking Goddess!" "It's not a bank—it's a credit union!" she laughs after him. He leaves, and thinks about how happy she'll be to see him next time.

Bruce knows that flirting with a woman creates opportunities. It's a chance to have fun interacting with a woman, to build up to asking her for a date, and to pre-qualify women to see if they are interested in sex and relationships. When Bruce flirts, he has fun and makes women like him. He finds out how responsive they are to him, and prepares them for going out with him. Teaching you how to do this is the focus of this chapter.

YOUR GOAL IN FLIRTING

When Bruce leaves the bank, he's left the teller delighted, and looking forward to seeing him again. Indeed, this is Bruce's goal. In any flirting situation with a woman, your goal is for her mind to connect the idea of seeing you with pleasure. Any effective seducer knows that women respond to their emotions, not to their logical minds. An effective seducer uses flirting to get women to have happy emotions every time they see him.

Flirting makes women happy to see you through a process called "anchoring." Anchoring simply means that a certain stimulus—be it a sight, a sound, a smell, or a person—is always connected to a certain feeling. Most people, for example, see a police car in their rear-view mirror, siren blaring and lights flashing and connect with the feeling of fear. Their feelings automatically respond to the police-stimulus, their heart pumps, and they feel afraid. The two are anchored together.

Similarly, Bruce knows that he is the stimulus, and the feeling he wants to create is happiness in the woman. Just as a person automatically responds with fear to seeing a flashing police light, Bruce wants women to automatically respond to his presence with pleasure. He knows that flirting is the structure in which he makes this happen.

WHAT FLIRTING DOES

Flirting is the key to a successful seduction. If you master flirting, you will also master the art of seduction and vice versa. All masters of seduction also have skills in flirting.

You build rapport

"Rapport" simply means that she likes to talk to you, and feels good doing it. When you are flirting, you usually aren't talking about anything heavy or deep. You are probably talking about something fun, or silly. She feels pleasure, and you feel pleasure. This creates rapport.

You make her feel safe by returning to the same topics again and again

As you'll see in this chapter, in flirting you'll often have a "running joke" with a woman. For example, Frank, a 44-year-old college instructor, has been flirting with a woman at his local health food store for several weeks. She's pretty, red-haired, tattooed, and in her mid-twenties. Frank thinks she's quite beautiful, and that she'd probably be a lot of fun in bed. The first time he met her, she was wearing an old military shirt and jeans, and he joked with her about her being a marine. "Hello, major," he said to her. "I see you are wearing your fatigues. Doing some covert operations here at the health food store?" "Oh yes," she responded, immediately drawn into his silly idea. "I'm here watching everyone, to make sure there are no foreign spies." They joked along this line for a while, and as he left, Frank said, "I'd better leave—I don't want to blow your cover!" and she laughed. Since then, every time he's come in they've built on this comic scene. She's always happy to see him, and loves the special little world they create together. Plus, he always has something to talk with her about.

Flirting lets you get to know her to see if you want her

Contrary to what you might think, you really don't want to get involved with every attractive woman you meet. We'll talk about this more in Chapter 12, but for now, simply understand that flirting is a chance to find out if a woman is dangerously unstable, or a cold fish who is not interested in sex.

Ted found this out the hard way. Carolyn was attractive, drunk, and interested in Ted. He met her in a bar, and they went to bed within fifteen minutes of meeting. "We met, she said, 'I want you,' and we went to my house immediately," Ted relates. "It was cool to get sex so fast, but immediately after we had sex, she said, 'Wow, it's so great to have a boyfriend at last.'"

Ted's personal Hell had begun. From then until he finally got rid of her, Carolyn was a constant, unwanted fixture in his life. She broke into his house and was in his bed when he got home, she called and filled his answering machine with crazy messages again and again. She harassed his friends and wouldn't ever leave him alone. He finally had to call the police to get her out of his life. "I wish, now, I hadn't been so 'successful' with her that first night," he says now. "If I'd taken the time to flirt with her more, I might have found out how crazy she was."

So how do you use flirting to evaluate a woman's stability? First, flirting helps you gauge her fear of you. If she has an enduring fear of you, she might not be worth pursuing. It's important to understand, however, that there is a difference between this enduring fear and the temporary fear that almost all women will experience when they first meet any man.

At first, you'll be flirting through her fear, overcoming it with your certainty that everything will be okay. After your second or third interaction with her, however, she should be lightening up and joking back with you. If she isn't, you can certainly keep flirting with her to keep in practice, but you should probably give up on her as someone who you'd want as a sexual partner. A woman who can't play with you will not be fun to be in any kind of relationship with.

Similarly, you may discover that she is extremely sensitive and easily offended. If your flirting with her makes her angry, or if she delivers a lecture about how "there are some things you just don't joke about," you know that you want to avoid her. Likewise, if she starts to cry, or interacting with her scares *you* or makes *you* want to cry, you should avoid her as well. If Ted had taken the time to flirt with Carolyn, he would have seen her fundamental instability, and steered clear.

Flirting helps her feel safe with you

Remember women's number one fear when they first meet you? They are rightfully worried about whether you are dangerous or not. If you are able to be playful with a woman, she relaxes. Subconsciously she reasons, "He's making me feel good. Therefore, he's not dangerous." Men who can't flirt often scare women because they are so tense and cold that the woman's natural fear of men is amplified, rather than dampened. When you can flirt playfully, you also show women you aren't overly concerned about hurting her, which, as we discussed in Chapter 3, will make her less concerned about getting hurt.

Flirting gets her used to the idea
of being romantic with you

When you flirt with a woman, you create a different, imaginary world for the two of you. It's a small step from this world of flirting to the world of romance.

Flirting gives you opportunities to practice your seduction skills

We suggest that all our students flirt with women constantly. Flirting gives you a chance to nibble away at learning seduction, like a mouse eating cheese, until you have mastered seduction. When you are first learning to flirt, it is important that you do it with all women, not just the ones you are attracted to.

Flirting makes you generative

When you flirt, you are always creatively making up new ways to delight the women who interest you. You can't do this if you are into being depressed, needy, resentful, moody, or shut down. To flirt well you have to be energetic and creative. Ultimately, women like to be with men who are generative. Fortunately, practicing flirting as we describe in this chapter will actually take you out of your moodiness and make you into the alive, vital kind of man who gets women.

Flirting gets you the date!

There's not much more to say. The more you flirt successfully with a woman, the more natural it will be for her to want to go out with you.

FLIRTING WITH HUMOR

Remember this: you want to make women laugh. If you can make a woman laugh (so long as she isn't laughing at your expense) then you are delighting her, and she'll want to see you again. However, as most men know, women often find different things funny than men do. It's easy to misuse humor with women, and to frighten and offend them instead. With that in mind, here's a list of do's and don'ts for flirting with humor.

Don'ts

Don't joke with a woman as roughly as you would with a guy, and don't make jokes about her appearance. This is very important.

When a guy drops something, for instance, it's a funny, bonding joke to say "way to drop that, bozo!" Among men this is great humor, occasions for "high-fives" all around. Such jokes are how we men play together. When a woman drops something, you must be much more gentle on her. It's best to not make fun of her mistakes at all, or she will be offended.

It's also better to not make jokes about her appearance, unless you are sure that the joke can be taken only in a positive way. Women are taught to be paranoid about their looks; if a woman can misinterpret a remark about her appearance, she will. When Robert told Greta "Wow, you've got such a nice, big butt. I like big women," he really sincerely meant it. Greta took offense, and so will every other woman in Western civilization.

Don't joke about violence unless you are absolutely sure she'll like it. And she probably won't. Once again, play among men and play among women is different. Among men, jokes about violence are funny: You might ask a man for some information only to have him reply, "I'd tell you, but then I'd have to kill you." To guys, this is funny. To women, it's scary. There's a big difference. Kenny met Rachel at a day-long personal growth seminar. Afterwards they took his car to a nearby bar. Along the way, Kenny made his error. Thinking he was joking, he said "Oh, what the heck. I think I'll just take you out to the woods and kill ya." Rachel became upset, and only the fact that they were just then pulling into the bar kept her from freaking out entirely. "The thing is," he told us later, "I had used that line on a girl I met at a punk-rock concert a few weeks before, and she thought it was hilarious!" Most of the time, women hear jokes about violence as threats of violence. They aren't flirty, and you shouldn't make them.

Don't use physical humor with women. Guys play with each other using physical humor. They play-punch each other, give each other noogies, and generally get rowdy together. They make physical jokes about pissing, farting, and feces. Men find this great fun, but it doesn't work on women. Just don't do it. These jokes *will* offend her. You have to decide which is more important: joking, or seducing.

Don't make yourself the butt on any jokes. This is very important. Remember what we've said: when a woman is first meeting you, she's deciding what position you will have in her life. Will you be a lover? A friend? Someone she avoids? She's trying to figure out what level of respect to give you, and one way she figures that out is by watching how you treat yourself. If you make jokes at your own expense, she knows that you aren't worth wasting time on.

Some men are so used to making fun of themselves to entertain women that it's hard for them to stop. Jerry was always the class clown, was a little overweight, and was used to making fun of his heaviness as a way of entertaining women. "I learned that if I made fun of myself, they'd laugh," he said. "But I noticed I never got any sex. It was hard to give up being the butt of my jokes, but I did it, and now I've got a girlfriend."

Do's

Do make "creative misinterpretations."   When you approach a woman, you've got to be alert and have your eyes open. Look for the details in her appearance or in what she is doing that you can safely make jokes about. You do this by putting a new spin on something normal. When Bruce asks the bank teller "Do you get to keep a percentage of all the money you take in each day?" he's creatively misinterpreting something in her environment and using it to flirt. When he asks if she gets to keep a percentage, he's being silly in a way she can relate to. It gives them a joke to talk about and creates a little separate world for them together.

Similarly, when Frank jokes to the girl at the health-food store about being a Major in the Marines, he's taking something at hand and creatively misinterpreting it, recasting it as something they can joke and flirt about. Every time he sees her they return to this joke, and she feels more comfortable with him each time.

You should try to make your misinterpretations complimentary to her. For example, misinterpreting the woman collecting the money as you leave a parking garage as "the parking goddess" would be more effective than misinterpreting her as, say, a trash collector who got lucky and got her current job. The first is a joke; the second is an insult. Keep track of the difference.

Do smile and say "hi."   Your expression is an important part of your behavior. When you approach a woman to flirt, it's best to be relaxed and to smile, make eye contact, and say "hi." Too many men approach flirting in a non-playful manner. They are resentful about having to do it, or are indulging a bad mood. The don't look relaxed and they don't sound relaxed.

As we said in Chapter 3, you must overcome adolescent posture. It may be necessary for you to get some bodywork or to take some yoga classes if you habitually radiate tension. When you are relaxed and approach a woman, she sees it on your face and in your eyes.

Do ask them about things they know. Work related questions are good, as are questions about personal appearance. As we'll discuss later, one good line is "What's the story behind that...?" If, for instance, she is wearing an unusual necklace, you might say "What a beautiful necklace you are wearing. What's the story behind it?"

Do ask questions. Along the same lines, it's a good idea to ask questions. After all, you want to find out about her, and asking the right questions can give you important information. It's not an interrogation, so don't badger her with questions, but do make inquiries about what she cares about. For example, if she's holding a flower, ask her about it: "That rose you are holding is beautiful. Why did you pick roses? How do roses make you feel?" Or you could ask "Why do you think women love flowers?" Either way, you are engaging her, through your questions, in a conversation that is about her likes, her dislikes, and her feelings. That's the kind of conversation that could become more romantic later on.

Do describe feelings for her. Your goal in flirting is to get her to think romantic thoughts about you, and to want to act on those thoughts. To do this, you must describe romantic feelings.

Have you ever been with someone who was describing something disgusting? Perhaps a friend had been sick, and later described to you, in intimate, loving detail, every step and every nuance of how it felt to be about to throw up. Can you remember how you felt as he described his sickness? Did you start to get sick, too?

Or have you ever wished someone would stop describing some horrible event or accident, because you are starting to feel how it must have felt? You probably have. These people have used a simple principle on you, that to *describe a feeling to someone makes them experience that feeling.* That's why you feel sick when your friend describes getting ill, or you feel queasy when someone talks about a disgusting accident.

To flirt successfully, you absolutely must take advantage of this principle, only in reverse. You must describe the feelings you want her to have—romance, attraction, arousal—in lush and lavish detail. As you describe these feelings, she'll start to have them.

The principle is simple: when someone describes something to you, you must imagine it to be able to understand what that person is talking about. If I'm describing my new car to you, and tell you that it's a mini-van, and it's blue, you can't help but imagine it. Even if I tell you *not* to imagine something, you have to imagine it to know what not to think about. If I tell you *not* to imagine a minivan, you must think of one, so you know what thought to avoid.

The same thing happens when you describe a feeling to a woman. Whether she wants to feel the feeling you are describing or not, she must feel it to even know what you are talking about. The extent to which she feels it is dependent on how well you describe it. For instance, Sven is talking to the attractive young woman behind the pastry counter. "I can imagine you must feel so great and special behind the counter, goddess of the whole store, and people come to worship you," he says to her. "Those great feelings of people coming to see you must really make you feel wonderful." He's playfully described feelings of specialness to her, and, if she is to evaluate what he's talking about at all, she must go inside and feel those feelings. While looking at Sven, she starts to connect his visits to her store with feeling those special feelings. In time, this will lead her to "naturally" feel attracted to him.

Poets are the get-laid kings of all time. Poetry is a wonderful tool in teaching you how to make beautiful, and detailed, descriptions on romantic things. After all, 99 percent of poetry is about love. If you look at most romantic poetry you'll find it's made up of descriptions of romantic, loving feelings. Romance novels, in much the same way, are unending streams of descriptions of romantic feelings. Learn to speak romantically by describing romantic feelings, and you will be much more successful with women.

Do be confident that your joking is okay. One of the top flirt-ing mistakes men make is that they wait for the woman to be com-fortable with the flirting before they become comfortable with it. We can't emphasize this enough: when a woman first meets you, she is trying to decide if you are dangerous or not. If you are uncertain and hesitant, you come across as though you, too, are afraid that you are dangerous. You act as though you are scared of yourself, and she will become scared, too. You must decide to have certainty that you are not hurting her, are not a threat to her, and that your flirting is fun and relaxed for you both.

Bob has this problem. He tries to flirt, but to him it is such a big deal, and he's so afraid that he's going to scare his prospect away, that he's a big ball of tension. When he talked to Natalie, the dental receptionist where he goes to get his teeth cleaned, he was as fright-ened as a cornered mouse. He has to work himself up to talking to her, and his heart pounds. He keeps asking himself "What if she doesn't like me?," and worries about potential rejection. "So, I guess a lot of people get hurt here," he "jokes" with her, his jaw muscles throbbing with tension. She just stares at him, wondering what kind of a psycho he is. He notices her fear, and becomes more upset him-self. "Uh, I mean, that's a joke," he says weakly. "Oh, heck. When's my appointment?" His fear, and his need for her to not be afraid of him, makes him fail with the receptionist, as he does with all women.

Now let's look at how Bruce handles the same situation. When he sees Natalie, he knows he desires her, and knows that she may or may not be induced to desire him. He knows that she may not respond to him, and doesn't care. Bruce has decided that his joking is fine, and is certain that he is charming, even if she doesn't think so. When he walks up to talk to her, he is smiling and relaxed, radiating confidence rather than tension. "So, you are the guardian of this ba-a-ad, evil place, eh?" he says to her in a laughing way. She looks at him to decide if he's a threat, but he's so relaxed and seems so cer-tain that everything is fine that she decides to laugh in response. "Oh yes, I'm the guardian, all right," she says. He continues in his confi-dent, joking manner, "How could I persuade you to put a spell on me to keep me from harm here? In fact, I think I can feel you putting a spell on me already. You are bewitching me, Natalie," he says, reading her name off her name tag. She laughs at his joking. "Now I feel like I can go in there, protected by the spell you have me under. I'll just say to the dentist, 'the beautiful and charming Natalie put me under a protective spell.' How do you think that will work?" "You can try it," she responds, laughing. "But I'd still take the novocaine." "Oh, I don't need painkiller after seeing you," he comes back. "Have you ever had the feeling of meeting someone, and it's like your heart can only feel good feelings, can feel no pain? After meeting you, I'm sure I won't need anything else." She blushes, "Well, thank you!"

Bruce made this interaction work because he was certain that it would work. If he appeared uncertain, like Bob did, and waited for Natalie to give him approval before he allowed himself to relax, he'd have the same failure Bob had. Because he's not waiting for her to feel good for him to feel good, he's able to create the good feelings for them both.

Do be romantic with your humor. Just being a clown for her isn't enough. You must also make it clear that you find her attractive. In the above example, Bruce doesn't only make Natalie laugh; he also uses their flirting to let her know that he finds her beautiful and charming. He does this by slipping in the occasional compliment, sideways. When he says, "I'll just say to the dentist, 'the beautiful and charming Natalie put me under a protective spell,'" he's telling her that she is beautiful and charming, and that he's thinking of her as more than just a friend. By doing this, he makes her choose what category to put him in, friend or potential lover. If she keeps flirting with him after he says these romantic things about her, then she's accepting the fact that he's a potential lover.

Only if she rejects his compliments will she be able to think of him as just another lowly male friend. But, because she's having so much fun flirting with him, she's unlikely to do that. By being romantic with his humor, he puts himself on the inside track for being her lover. When you look at how Bruce flirts with Natalie, you can see how she would have a hard time thinking of him as "just a friend," because of the romantic quality of his flirting. You, too, can do this, if you show your romantic interest as you flirt.

Conclusion of do's and don'ts of humor

Men make two main errors when they flirt with women: either they play (that is the essence of flirting, after all) with women the way they would with men, or they don't play with women at all, and seem stiff and nervous. If you follow the guidelines we've taught you, you'll never make either of those mistakes again. You've learned how flirting relies on humor and play, how men and women play and joke differently, and how to play and joke so women think of you romantically. You've learned to avoid joking with women as roughly as you would with guys, to not joke about violence, to not use physical humor with women, and to not make yourself the butt of any jokes.

You've learned how to "creatively misinterpret" with women, to engage in romantic "pretend" with them, and to ask them questions. You've learned the importance of describing to a woman the feelings you want her to have, and the importance of your certainty that your joking and flirting are okay, even when she isn't.

Can you see how these skills can be useful in your interactions with women, starting today? Of course, learning to flirt with women will take time, and your first interactions may not be as wonderful as you would like. No matter. All that matters is that you start talking with women, joking with women, and playing with women. As you practice, you'll get better at it. Now that you understand these basics of flirting and humor, you are ready to learn how to flirt your way to the date.

FLIRTING YOUR WAY TO THE DATE

With these basics in mind, we'll now take you, step by step, from meeting a woman all the way through asking her out. We'll look at the specific problems of each step, and show you how to overcome them.

The main problem you face is that women, like everybody else, resist change, even change they would like. It is entirely possible that dating you would be the best thing that has ever happened to the women you desire. It's even possible that having sex with you would be the best thing that ever happened to the women you desire (especially after you've read Chapter 11, "Being the Man of Her Dreams In Bed").

If you do what we teach you in this book, you may well provide a woman with more romantic feelings, passion and happiness than any man ever has before. Even if you are only interested in a short-term sexual relationship, you still might easily provide her with a fling she'll be grateful she had for the rest of her life.

In spite of the truth that you could well bring her nothing but pleasure, she'll resist you because she resists change. You represent the *potential* for pain, discomfort, and, at the very least, unfamiliarity. You are a monkey wrench of disorder in her otherwise orderly life. While you are dreaming of wonderful nights of hot sex with her, she's imagining you leaving your dirty socks around, and messing up her life the way other men have. So even in the best of times, when you meet a woman you'll encounter resistance.

It's really no different than any other sales situation (which seducing a woman fundamentally is). If you've ever been a sales-man, you know that people resist most products and services on principle, even if the products and services you offer would improve their lives. While you are thinking about selling them this great product, they are wondering how badly you are going to rip them off. It's exactly the same with women. Each of the steps below takes you through the process of getting through her fear, and helping her see the desire she has for you.

GETTING HER TRUST

Before you can flirt your way to the date, you must handle her natural fear that you will hurt her. You must show her you are trust-worthy.

From time to time, Bob has noticed that women seemed afraid of him when he first talked to them. He's tried to handle this direct-ly, with horrible results. "I'm not dangerous, you know," he said once to an attractive receptionist at an auto parts store. "I'm just a regu-lar guy. You really don't have to be afraid." She got pale and her eyes got wide with terror. No doubt she was asking herself, "Why is this guy telling me he's not dangerous? Why would he think to say that? What's he gonna do to me?"

As we've said so many times, a woman's first concern is that you are going to assault, rape, or kill her. Saying that you are not dangerous only makes her more frightened and suspicious. You alleviate her fear over time— either over the course of the flirting interaction, or over the course of a number of flirting interactions. As you are persistent in your flirting, and as you consistently cause her to laugh and feel good, she'll naturally start to trust you, and to know that you are safe. To overcome her fear that you are dangerous, you must demonstrate certain qualities. If you don't, you will never get past her fear. It's been sad for us to see so many wonderful men striking out with women because they don't know how to show that they aren't dangerous in a way women can understand.

THE ESSENTIAL QUALITIES YOU MUST DEMONSTRATE FOR A WOMAN TO TRUST YOU AND FEEL SAFE

Build trust by respecting her. Bob thinks he's being respectful when he tells a woman that he's not dangerous. Actually, he's just being scary. Bob's mistake is that he doesn't understand that actions, as the old saying goes, speak louder than words. Have you ever known someone who said they were one way, but actually were another? Of course you have. Perhaps it's been someone who has talked about the importance of being on time, yet who chronically showed up late. His words didn't match his actions, and you probably found yourself suspicious of all his talk about being on time. It's exactly the same with not being dangerous. Talking about it only makes it worse; you must demonstrate it. And the first way to demonstrate it is by being respectful.

Respecting her is not the same as groveling before her, or treating her as if she's better than you, or superior to you. That's not respecting, that's fawning and toadying, and no woman wants to be around it.

Most important, you must respect her when she says "no." A woman likes to move at a certain pace during a seduction. She feels safe knowing that she is in control of the speed. You'll get to know this pace by her use of the word "no." You must back off when she says "no." When you do this, she will feel respected.

When you are first flirting with a woman, you may say something that offends her. She'll look unhappy, or a little irritated, and you'll notice the flow of the flirting interaction slow down or even stop. You must respect this, notice it, and work with it.

Build trust by not being desperate. Nothing makes a woman feel used faster than a man who seems needy for female companionship, lonely, or desperate for sex. Women immediately and correctly decide that the guy isn't really interested in *them*; they decide that he's only interested in *sex*. While you might think it would be great if a woman was only interested in you for sex, take it from us when we tell you that even women who *are* only interested in you for sex will be put off if you are desperate and obvious.

Desperation shows up most often in three situations:

1. When you are only pursuing one woman. As we discussed in Chapter 2, when you are only pursuing one woman, and have all your bets hedged on one horse, you are likely to get desperate. You have no backup plan, so things *must work* with the woman you are with. This "it must work" pressure destroys your ability to act freely. You won't be able to say, "It doesn't matter how it goes with this woman; there are lots of others to choose from." You'll get tense, and she'll feel it and get tense, too. Then you'll get more tense, because, after all, this woman is your only chance. Once you have that thought, it's all over. Unless you can remind yourself forcefully that there are lots of women available to you, you are likely to continue looking desperate.

The solution, of course, is to always be "working on" a number of women, as we discussed in Chapter 2. Having a number of potential lovers "in progress" will keep desperation far away.

2. When you are overly terrified of rejection. When you feel this way, you also become desperate. By this time, we hope we've impressed upon you the importance of overcoming rejection, fear, and that you are committing yourself to taking on the anti-fear practices we described in Chapter 2.

3. When your life is otherwise lonely and meaningless. If you are lonely, and your life seems meaningless, you also appear desperate to women. You must have something you are into, that gives your life meaning, above and beyond a relationship and sex with some woman. If you are trying to get meaning for your life out of your interactions with women, they will always notice it, and not want to be with you. Men too, won't respect you.

You may have noticed that women like successful men. It is true that they are attracted to the money, but that's not the whole story. They are also attracted to men who are passionate about their lives, and have fire and drive. Some of these men have money, but some don't. Money is less important than being a dynamic man, tackling his life head-on.

We've all seen garage-band rock guitarists who get sex easily, even though they never play anywhere but in local bars. Their passion for something in their lives makes both these kinds of men, the businessmen and the guitarists, more attractive to women.

We're not going to walk you through an entire life-overhaul here, but you'll find that the principles of being successful with women are the same as the principles for life-success. You'll notice that the Seven Habits of Highly Successful Seducers are also habits that will serve you in your life outside of your relationships.

It makes sense to act with an outcome in mind, not just with women, but in every area. It makes sense to see life like a numbers game, to not take the events of life personally, and to pursue more than one project at a time. It makes sense to be willing to walk away from work or business situations that aren't paying off, just as it makes sense to be willing to walk with women. And it makes sense to make life work for you, just as it makes sense to make dating work for you.

Keeping these dating principles in mind as you design your life will help you live with passion and success. You'll also be able to use the principles of planning and follow-through, which we will use in upcoming chapters, in creating a life you are passionate about. When you are passionate about your life, and care about something other than sex, you won't be desperate.

Men also become desperate when they are lonely. This especially happens to men who have many female friends, and few male friends. If you don't have buddies who you can kick back and really relax with, you should get some. Having male friends makes interactions with women less important sources of love and validation. It will be much easier for a woman to trust you and be relaxed once she knows that you are not desperate for her attention.

If you have any of these problems, you are in danger of becoming desperate with women.

Build trust by being patient with her. Being patient with a woman is an important way of showing her that you are not dangerous, and worthy of her trust. It's easy, however, to confuse "patient" with "stupid." We don't mean to say that you should let a woman walk all over you, or jerk you around. We are saying that a flirting interaction that can lead to dating and sex requires patience.

You must also be patient in the flirting interaction over time. You must be willing to go see her again and again, and have multiple flirting interactions, before you go out with her. Jim used to think that in one interaction, he could build her trust, interest, and attraction, and ask her out on a date that would end in sex. Although this is certainly not impossible, most women won't be seduced that fast. You must be willing to be patient, and to take the time to have multiple flirting interactions, before you finally go out with her.

Patiently visiting her at her work place or gym also builds her trust in you, because she is seeing you again and again. Flirting with you becomes a normal part of her safe, cozy day-to-day life. Knowing people in common also helps build trust, as long as the people you know in common are not other women who you've "loved and left." If she knows a friend of yours, or if you were introduced by a mutual friend, you have an implicit recommendation from that friend; this too helps her trust you.

You can also build her trust in you by giving her your card. She won't call you, so don't count on that. It can be used as a simple way of showing her that you are willing to not keep your address and identity a secret. It's part of the patient process of getting her trust.

Build trust by avoiding unnecessary conflicts. It's also important that you moderate what you talk about, if you want a woman to trust you. Remember your outcome: you want this woman to desire you. To this end, it's important that you avoid unnecessary conflicts while you are flirting with her. Who cares if she spouts some opinion that pisses you off?

Remember what you are after: romance and sex. When Kurt first went out with Sally, he was doing everything properly...until she started talking about feminism. "Women always get the short end of the stick in this society," she said. "Men have everything, and don't even know it." Kurt, who was involved in the men's movement, got angry at her when she said this. He quoted the statistics about how men really are abused by their wives, how more men die in wars than women do, how men get raped in jail, and about the damage done to men by infant circumcision. Arguably, he was right about everything he said, but it didn't matter.

Sally finally interrupted him: "Hey, you're talking really loud now, and it's really scaring me. I don't like this about you." Kurt wrecked a perfectly good seduction by getting drawn into a fight about men's and women's issues, when he should have been romantic. He never did get into her pants.

You have to decide what's most important to you: arguing with a woman, or having sex. If men's behavior is any indication, the average man is more interested in fighting. He gets into fights about why sports are important to men, or gets drawn into fights about men's and women's issues. You must be different. The correct way to handle a woman's invitation to fight is to let her know that you heard her, and to introduce a different topic of conversation. When Sally spouted her opinion about men and women, Kurt should have taken it in stride. He should have said, "Really? That's interesting. Do you remember how it felt the first time you thought you were in love?" By not arguing with her, and changing the subject, he would have avoided losing Sally's trust, and the seduction would have continued.

Some women want to fight, and will do almost anything to provoke it. Women who are very "into" women's issues, and who love to talk about how much men have hurt women, will want combat with you. If you find you are continually avoiding conflict with her, you don't want her anyway. Get rid of her and move on.

Build trust by showing her you're not weird. Have you ever known a man who was odd, or out of the ordinary, who was successful with women? You probably have. It may be someone you know who is tattooed all over, with green hair, and multi-pierced. It may be someone you know who is very tough looking, decked out with black hair and a leather jacket. It may be someone with some other eccentricity. You notice these men seem to have made their eccentricities work for them. They are comfortable with themselves, tattoos, piercings, green hair, odd tastes and all, and they have no difficulty getting women.

You may also have known a man who was odd, or out of the ordinary, who felt self-conscious and ashamed about it. He may have had unusual tastes in music or dress, not different from the men who are "odd" and still have success with women. You notice that these men seem to be uncomfortable with their eccentricities, and they have trouble getting women.

A man who is "weird" in some way, who is comfortable with it, is an inspiration to women. She sees that he is unashamed of his passions, and sees him as a man who is willing to express himself fully. These are arousing qualities to women, who find such men "cute" or "artistic." They trust such men, because such men trust themselves.

A man who isn't comfortable with his eccentricities, on the other hand, is frightening to women. Because he seems to think there is something wrong with him, women will think so, too. His shame about his passions make women see him as "weird" and untrustworthy. They don't trust him, because he doesn't trust himself.

The solution is to look at any "odd" behavior or mode of dress, decide if you want to keep it, and, if you do, to integrate it proudly into your style. You make this decision by asking yourself, "What message does this send about me?" When Luther wanted to decide if he should keep his ponytail and goatee, he asked that question. He not only asked himself, but also his friends and family. Luther found that many folks found his ponytail to look immature. It sent the message that he was a boy in a man's body, someone unwilling to grow up. After thinking about this feedback, Luther agreed. He cut off his ponytail, shaved his goatee, and found he was happier and people began to interact with him differently. Women suddenly seemed to feel more comfortable around him.

Clarence had a different experience. Even though he lived in a large eastern city, he was always more comfortable in cowboy gear. He constantly wore a cowboy hat, shirt, and cowboy boots—eccentric in the area in which he lived. When he asked his friends what message they thought his hat and boots sent to people, they were all positive. "It just seems like 'Clarence,' to me," one said. "It really seems like you've found your style." Clarence agreed, and kept his cowboy gear. He even accentuated it with a new, flamboyant hat, that he wore proudly. Women were comfortable, because, through his style, he was expressing who he really was. They trusted him. Luther, on the other hand, was expressing his fear of aging with his style. When women saw that, it made him seem weird and untrust-worthy.

Often a man appears this way to a woman because he is look-ing for validation from her. We've been over this again and again: get your validation someplace other than from women. Needing women's validation creates problems in every area of seduction. If a woman needs to take care of your feelings, and you are using her to make you feel good, she's not going to be interested in you as a love.

Many men accidentally come across to women as "weird" by worrying about their eccentricities. They look to women to validate their oddness, and end up seeming weird and scaring women off.

Build trust by leaving her happy. All these practices will make you more trustworthy to a woman. If you respect her, are not des-perate, are patient with her, don't fight with her, and show her you are not weird, she'll have every reason to feel trust in you. If you leave her happy, she'll not only trust you; she won't be able to wait for you to return.

THE THREE STEPS
OF A FLIRTING INTERACTION

Step 1. First meeting her

When Bob first met Brenda at a party, he was terrified. Brenda, a 26-year-old copywriter for an advertising firm, had straight blonde hair, a toned, supple body, a beautiful face, and intelligent eyes— though the first thing he noticed was her ample bust line, truth be told. "I knew I had to make a good impression," he later told his friend, Scott, "So I made sure that I didn't do anything that would scare her off." Bob was so scared that she wouldn't like him, or that she would be offended by him, that he was unable to interact with her normally.

He adopted his usual, unsuccessful approach to attractive women: trying to appear harmless. "What do you do?" he asked Brenda. When she told him, Bob initiated a conversation about work, overtime, and different kinds of computer systems that busi-nesses use. She found him harmless, and mildly interesting, but when he finally got the nerve up to shakily ask her for her phone number, Brenda said, "I like you and everything, but I have to tell you you're not really my type." He was aware that she was initially afraid that he was dangerous, and he had handled that danger. She certainly wasn't afraid of him now. So what went wrong?

It is true, as we've said, that a woman's first concern upon meeting you is that you will hurt her in some way, and that you must handle. This doesn't mean, however, that you should allow her fear to sanitize you, and make you tepid, as Bob does. You must allay her fears, and, if you want to ever have sex with her, you must also let her know about your romantic interest right away.

As we've mentioned before, women decide about men immediately. She determines whether you are a potential lover or a lowly friend in the first few minutes of knowing you. It is important that you take advantage of this fact by presenting yourself as a romantic interest immediately. If you don't do this, making her feel safe only leaves her wanting you to be a friend, while she seeks romantic excitement with other men.

Lines to Use When Approaching Her for the First Time. Students often ask us for lines to use when approaching women, or when asking for the date. They seem to think that there is some magic formula that works with every woman, and if only they can figure out what it is, they'll be successful in asking out women.

The truth is, there is no "right" way to ask a woman out, and no "perfect" opening line. This should make you happy, because that means that whatever you feel like saying—something simple and honest, perhaps—may well be the perfect thing.

Some men favor joke lines. They'll go up to an attractive woman and say, "Wow, did heaven lose an angel? 'Cause I'm seeing one right here!" Our interviews with more than 300 women indicate that they don't like these lines. You might as well say "Wow, did heaven lose a couple of angels? 'Cause I can see them bouncing around inside your blouse," which we also don't recommend. We also don't recommend "If I told you had a beautiful body, would you hold it against me?" All these hokey, adolescent lines tell a woman is that you aren't really a grown-up man. Give them up.

Step 2. She starts to think of you as romantic material

If you've done everything properly in Step One, the woman you are interested in will trust you. She will then start thinking of you as romantic material. You've made your interest known, gotten her feeling safe with you, and left her happy every time you've interacted with her. You've flirted with her using humor, as we outlined earlier in this chapter. You haven't gotten into a stupid fight with her, or scared her in any other way. She's enjoying your company, and knows you are interested romantically. You are thinking you're home free. She's starting to think, "This guy is cool. Why shouldn't I go out with him? Why not?" What could possibly go wrong?

Now that you've overcome her early fears it's time for her to give you the next problem in your seduction. As she becomes attracted, she starts to answer that question, "Why not?" Remember, women are like everyone else—they try to avoid change, even change they would like. As we said before, while you are fantasizing about nights of great sex, she is dreading having to sleep on the wet spot. In order to preserve her orderly life, she starts coming up with reasons to disqualify you. Your next challenge is to overcome these reasons, to continue to give her good feelings, and to move the seduction forward.

So what kind of answers will she have to the question, "Why not?" She'll tell herself—and you—that you are not her type, that she doesn't want to spoil the friendship (more on this later), or that she's still getting over some other guy. Like anyone contemplating trying something new and potentially risky, she thinks up any and every reason to not go out with you. You just have to handle it.

"Why not" problems are usually general, rather than specific in nature. She's not saying "no" because she doesn't like you, or doesn't like something you did; "why not" problems seem to be free-flowing, general problems with whole classes of relationships. "I don't date men shorter than me" is a "why not" problem. So is "you're not my type," as is "I'm not looking for a relationship right now." Other "why not" problems are "I don't have the time," "I don't have a car," and anything along the lines of "I have to wash my hair."

"Why not" problems are different from the problems you have when she simply doesn't like you. If she says to you, "Hey, I don't ever want to talk to you again. I'll never go out with you, and I want you to leave me alone," she doesn't like you. Leave her alone, and move on to women who like you. But if she says something more vague, thrown out as an almost offhand problem, a problem more with the idea of relationships themselves than with you specifically, then you must gently persist with her.

Many of our students are older men who want to date younger women. Predictably, at some point early on, the young woman tells the man that he's disqualified because of his age. This happened to Marvin. At 38 years old, he returned to the university part-time to finish up his undergraduate degree. Suddenly he found himself surrounded by unbelievably hot, stripper-quality 19- and 20-year-olds. He went to work on them immediately, but found them to be very frightened and untrusting. "That first step just takes forever with these girls," he told us, "but I found that if I hung in there, eventually they started to trust me."

The first woman he dated from school, a 22-year-old senior named Jennifer, only went out with him after seeing him in class and talking to him over and over and over. "We were a third of the way into the semester, when I finally decided that she trusted me enough to go out for coffee. I asked her, and she said, 'Well, okay, but there's something I have to tell you, I've thought about it, and I can justify dating a man up to 28 years old, but not a man as old as you are.'" A man who hadn't been taught by us might have given up at that moment, or stupidly begun a fight with her about what she meant by "justify." Marvin knew she was probably just answering the question, "Why Not?" and set up the time and location for the coffee date.

"I knew she might really mean it," he told us, "but that's the breaks of the game. If I tried to kiss her later, and she said 'no,' then I'd know she meant it, and didn't like me. But I figured it was a 'why not' situation, told her I understood, and went on with the date." Three dates later, using the techniques from this book, he had sex with her, which she later told him was "the best experience of my life." Marvin knew that by being persistent, being willing to accept her "no," and staying with it, he could get past her "why not's."

Your persistence in making her feel good is the key to getting past her "why not's." Eventually she'll see how wonderful you are, and want to continue with you. Or she'll decide you are basically an obnoxious jerk, and tell you to get lost. Either way, you are on your way to sex, either with her, or with a woman who does want you.

Step 3. You ask her out, she says yes

There are three different kinds of situations in which you meet women. How quickly you ask them out has to do with which of the situations you are in.

First, there is the emergency situation. You see a woman you are attracted to, and you must ask her out right now, because she's about to leave, and you'll probably never see her again. Have you ever seen those personals ads in the "one-to-one" column where some sad guy is describing some woman he saw, pathetically begging her to call him? "I saw you from across the room, but was too scared to approach you," he might write. "You were tall, blonde, built, and talking to a buff weightlifter. I was the guy cowering over in the corner, pretending to make conversation with the potted plant. Please call me!" Not very likely.

If you don't want to be that sniveling guy, you've got to talk to the woman you may never see again. This can be as simple as approaching a woman at a gas station, for instance, and saying, "Hi, I saw you here, and I just couldn't let you walk out of my life without saying 'hi.' I don't usually do this, but I wonder if I could give you a call sometime?" She may well say no, but she also might say yes. If you are especially scared, you can give her your card, though the likelihood of her calling you is vanishingly small. You certainly have a better chance of dating her if you ask than if you don't ask. After all, if you don't ask, your chance is exactly zero.

The second situation gives you a bit more time. You perhaps have a few hours, or a full day, to work on her. This might be at a party, or at a full-day class, for instance. You can have numerous interactions with her, then, before you both leave, say "You know, you seem cool. What would it be like if we went out sometime?," and set it up from there.

In the third situation, you work the flirting over a period of time. This is the woman you see reliably: the women who work out the same time you do, the clerks at the coffee shop you frequent, the waitress at your favorite restaurant. This is the lowest stress situation, because you can work on the woman over a long period of time. You can give her all the time she needs to get used to you, to feel safe, and to imagine you romantically as part of her life. Then, at your leisure, when the time is right, you can ask her out.

It's important that you figure out which situation you are in with any woman you are attracted to. It does you no good to be full of flirting and seduction skills if the woman of your dreams walks out of your life while you do nothing to stop her. When you figure out which class a woman is in, you can plan the urgency and velocity of your flirting accordingly.

USING THE PHONE TO ASK HER OUT

One of the most common mistakes men make is to think that a woman is not interested when she fails to return phone calls. As a result, guys will stop calling, whine about women's lack of responsiveness, and—worst of all—give up. We know this is not intuitively obvious, but the fact of the matter is that women call when they feel like it. They don't act rationally. Remember, a woman is not here to make your life easy. You will be happier if you stop expecting them to simplify things and call you back, ever.

The secrets of using the phone to ask women out:

* After the second message, hang up if you get her answering machine, and only settle for reaching her in person. Otherwise you start to sound desperate, and become, in her mind, "that guy who's always calling me."
* Leave messages about specific times, dates, and places you want to take her. Say, "I'd like to take you to the planetarium next Wednesday night," not "uh, wanna go out?"
* Don't ramble when leaving messages; be decisive.
* Don't call just to "talk." You'll only create opportunities to do something stupid and screw up your chances. Don't call unless you have something seductive to say or a date to ask her out on.
* Keep all phone calls short.

* Sound friendly when you leave messages. Smiling makes your voice sound friendlier.
* Never call when you are upset with her.

If she doesn't call back, call her again and pretend your first message never happened. Never ask why she didn't call back—it'll call attention to the fact that you are a wimp whom she stood up on the phone who has come back for more. Simply act like the first message never happened.

While you do need to be patient and not expect her to call you back, you don't want to be a doormat, either. You could try the three-call rule: if after three calls she hasn't called back, move on. We sometimes advise men to call her back after she has failed to return the second call and warn her. Say something like, "I'd love to see you again, but you've failed to call me back twice. I hate to do it, but if you don't call me back again, I can't call you back again for a long time." This gives her a message that you like her, but that you aren't willing to sacrifice your self-respect to be with her.

WHAT IF YOU SCREW IT UP?

Your problems aren't over when you finally ask her out, and she finally says yes. You are as capable of screwing it up as she is, if not more so.

The time comes when she is primed. You have a strong connection with her, either in one interaction, or through a series of interactions. You've made your romantic interest clear by showing your attraction to her. She's become used to the idea of thinking of you as a potential romantic partner. You've flirted with her consistently and successfully. She's happy every time she sees you, and you leave her feeling good. It's time to ask her out.

This is where you'll foul it up if you aren't careful. Let's go over the bonehead mistakes you are likely to make, and show you how to avoid them:

You wait too long to ask her out

If you do this, you risk losing your "window of opportunity." If your flirting is building a sense of attraction and connection in the woman you are working on, you must take advantage of it before her mood changes. It's hard to know exactly where this point is; practice will teach it to you. If you wait too long, the woman will decide that you must not be interested in her, and will start to think of you as a friend. So you must make your move when the time is right.

As you become more skilled at seducing women, you'll start to find that there are, in fact, women whom you've started to seduce, in whom you aren't interested. It may not seem possible to you now, but once you start pursuing women using the tools in this book, you really can have more women to date than you have time for. That's not a pipe dream; both of the authors, and many of our students have made this happen. When it happens to you, you'll find that one way you show your lack of interest is by not asking women out in the "window of opportunity." Until you get to this point, make sure you ask women out once you've got her interest.

You don't have a plan for the date

When you ask a woman out, always have a specific idea of where you want to go with her on the date. (We'll talk more about this in the upcoming chapters.) *Never* ask a woman out without a date plan in mind. This means that, in advance, you think about the kind of dating experience you want to have, and think about where you could go together, and what you can do. As you'll see later, there are two kinds of dates, priming dates and seduction dates. When you ask a woman out, you must know which kind you are asking for, and what you will do.

If a woman accepts a date with you, and you don't have a plan in mind, you are probably doomed. You'll end up saying "I dunno, what do you want to do?," which is the worst thing you could possibly say. It makes you look like a sloppy jerk who isn't creative and relies on her for everything. Believe us, she won't find it attractive.

When you ask a woman out, you can say something like, "Hey, you seem cool. How about we go out for coffee sometime?" When she says yes, you then supply the details, and gently direct the conversation toward getting everything worked out. "How about we go to Joe's coffee shop sometime next week? I'm free on Tuesday, after work, say around five-thirty. Would that work for you?" You don't make her supply any of the details, and you make sure the plans are clear.

You are indecisive

One easy way to make yourself into a more powerful, attractive man, is to practice making decisions quickly and with a minimum of fuss. The more easily you make decisions the more successful you'll be in every area of your life, including with women.

You don't want to be bossy, but you should present a clear invitation. If she wants to change it, be flexible, but decide quickly and easily on the details. Setting up the date is an important interaction, in which she learns a lot about how you approach your life. She'll be looking at you to see if you are weak and indecisive, or strong and decisive. Do you expect me to make all the decisions and create the plans, or do you come up with ideas? Remember, women are attracted to men who are generative. This means you must come up with the ideas, and get the details ironed out. If you are indecisive you'll blow all the work you've already done.

You seem too available

Like everybody else, women like things that are rare, and hard to get ahold of. If you ask a woman out and say, "Oh, anytime is good for me," it makes you sound like an unemployed bum who has no social life. Even if you are an unemployed bum with no social life, it's important that you not sound like one. Have a couple of times available, and be reluctant to reschedule other things to be with her. Make sure the date is at a place and time that works for you, too, since it's more than likely that she won't show up anyway. When offering times, you may want to say something like "I can do it at four o'clock Wednesday, but I only have about an hour." If you sound busy, though not inaccessible, you'll be more interesting to her.

If you manage to get through asking her out, and setting up the date without screwing it up, congratulations! You have a date!

If you follow these flirting steps, you will be able to easily overcome the problems that will arise during flirting, and you will get the date. You won't be stopped by her fear of you, her "why not" problems, her specific problems with you, or by yourself. You'll move the seduction forward and do much of the romantic groundwork that will make sex with you seem natural to her later. You'll use flirting, humor and creative role-playing to make her feel connected to you, and happy to see you. You'll play with women in ways that make them desire you, while still being strong, decisive and generative. Do all this properly, and a successful date is almost assured.

Will there be more problems during and after the date? Of course. But don't worry; we'll show you how to handle each and every one of them.

THINGS YOU CAN DO TODAY TO IMPROVE YOUR FLIRTING, NO MATTER HOW TIMID YOU ARE

Now let's give you some specific, useful information about precisely how to flirt with women. What follows are exercises and activities you can do that will build your "flirting muscles," and make you ever more attractive to women.

MEETING WOMEN THROUGH PERSONALS ADS IN NEWSPAPERS AND MAGAZINES

Meeting women through personals ads in newspapers and magazines is another good, low-risk way to practice your flirting skills. Like the Internet, only slower, you can interact with women safely and impersonally before meeting in person.

One of the advantages personals ads have over Internet flirting (covered in Chapter 4) is that the women you interact with through these ads are nearby, while on the Internet they can quite literally be on the other side of the planet. Very much like in Newsgroup personals ads, women are more likely to look at ads and respond than they are to place one themselves, so don't be daunted by the fact that 99 percent of the postings are by men. Your focus must be on creating an ad that gets women reading the listing to write or call. While most of these women will probably be overweight or unattractive to you in some other way, the responses you get are wonderful opportunities to practice your flirting. But don't read personals intending to find a woman posting for you. You must do the work, you must post, and, with skill and luck, the woman you want to flirt with will reply.

Let's talk about creating the ad you place. It should be short for several reasons. First, because short ads are cheaper (and sometimes even free). Many men have the idea that they'll be more successful with women if they blow a lot of money. That's not true (except in the case of buying this book, of course!). Make it work for you, and create a short, powerful ad. Second, long ads put women off. If you've ever read personals, you've probably seen an ad from a guy who goes on and on for twenty or thirty lines. This looks weird, and it is weird. You're not there to tell your life's story. All you want is to inspire her to call or write.

A good ad has four parts. First you describe the feeling you want her to feel. Second, you briefly describe yourself physically. Third, you describe your emotional availability, and fourth, you make an invitation. Let's look at these steps one at a time.

1. Describe the feeling you want her to feel

Because romance is all about feelings, you must describe one in your ad. As we've said before, describing a feeling creates a feeling, because when you describe a feeling, the listener must go inside and feel it to be able to understand what you are talking about. Ask yourself, what kind of feeling do you want the woman reading your ad to feel? Attraction, intrigue, romance, lust, curiosity?

Your first sentence or two should remind her of those feelings, and of how much she likes to feel them. It's good to ask a question, like "Have you ever felt totally connected and utterly loved?" or "Can romance last forever? I think it can!" One of our students, Clevin, began one of his personals ads this way: "Isn't attraction incredible? Imagine relaxing into strong arms holding you, feeling safe and appreciated and intimate, knowing it's totally right." He thought of a feeling that he wanted women to feel, and described it.

2. Briefly describe yourself physically

Clevin then followed his introduction with a few words about himself. "I'm looking, too. SWM, 44, 5'9" tall, fit and attractive."

Describe yourself generously (if people have said you are attractive, you can say it), but don't lie. If you aren't fit, don't say so, but also remember—you don't have to be Arnold Schwarzenegger to think of yourself as fit. It's also okay to omit your less attractive qualities. If you are very overweight, you don't have to mention weight at all. Remember, your goal is to practice your flirting, and to get better at it. If you focus on that, rather than on getting sex, you'll have more fun, be more relaxed, and be more successful with women. You just want women to respond, so you can interact with them.

3. Describe your emotional availability

This is an important step. Women complain that men aren't in touch with their emotions, and are hard to have relationships with. We've found that the phrase, "Am emotionally literate and willing to take risks," works wonders in personals ads (especially if it is true), and Clevin adds this to his ad. If you aren't emotionally literate (that is, you can't tell anger from grief, and the last time you cried was when you dropped a brick on your foot), you can still honestly say "willing to take emotional risks." After all, you took an emotional risk just by placing the ad.

4. Make an invitation

This is where you close the deal, and ask her to communicate with you. Here you want to say something like "if this touches something in you, call," or "if this stirs something in you, call." Emotional talk will stir most women, no matter who it comes from. By asking them to call if they are moved, you are drawing their attention to the feelings they had reading your ad, and making those feelings mean that they should call. Let's look at Clevin's complete ad. Note the four parts.

Isn't attraction incredible? Imagine relaxing into strong arms holding you, feeling safe and appreciated and intimate, knowing it's totally right. I'm looking, too. SWM, 44, 5'9" tall, fit and attractive. Am emotionally literate and willing to take risks. If this speaks to you, please call Box 491.

If you follow this approach, you'll have women calling and writing, with whom you can practice your flirting skills.

OTHER BASIC FLIRTING EXERCISES: YOUR DAILY ROUTINE

Saying "hi"

Remember this exercise from Chapter 3? By simply saying "hi" to six women a day, you'll be interacting with women, and improving your flirting skills.

Winking and waving

Much of flirting is in how you move your face and body, rather than what you say. One of our students tells us about being on a subway in New York City. A gorgeous black woman got on the train, and sat across from him, a few seats up. "I wished I had the nerve to go sit next to her and talk to her," he told us, "but I didn't, so I used the 'wink and wave.' I winked at her, smiled and waved when I caught her eye. She smiled back and, to my amazement, she came over and sat down next to me!" They ended up kissing on that same train ride, and later having sex at her apartment, simply because he was willing to do some simple flirting, the "wink and wave."

Stopping while it's still fun

Men who are shy and learning how to flirt frequently stay at parties or flirt with women for too long. When you are learning to flirt, it's wise to stop while it's still fun.

One of our students, Michael, had this problem. He was shy, but was committed to getting over it, so when he flirted with a woman, he'd make himself stay around her until she basically asked him to leave. "I'd start out pumped up, but as the interaction dragged on and on, I'd feel more and more uncomfortable and humiliated. I didn't know it was okay to leave while I was still having fun with her. I guess I thought that as long as it was going well, I should stay." After learning this, he was able to flirt with more women more successfully, and to have a lot more fun doing it.

The "good-bye" compliment

The "good-bye" compliment works well when leaving while it's still fun. If you are at a party, bar, or other social engagement, the "good-bye" compliment allows you to do some more aggressive flirting, even if you are very timid.

The "good-bye" compliment makes use of the fact that most any man can generate enough confidence to say one flirty thing to a woman. The problem, for some men, comes right after he says something flirty. What should he do then? What if she doesn't like it? What if she gets mad, or looks at him like he's something she scraped off her shoe? How to handle the tension? What to do next?

When you use the "good-bye" compliment, all those problems are solved. When you are ready to leave the bar, party, or whatever social engagement you are at (while you are still having fun, preferably), you simply approach the woman you've been too scared to approach, compliment her, and leave immediately.

These compliments can be simple, such as "I've gotta go, but before I do I just wanted to tell you that you look great, and have a wonderful sense of style." They can also be more aggressive, such as "Wow, you look great. I just wanted you to know that, if I didn't have to leave, I'd stay here and try to seduce you." After the "good-bye" compliment, you leave. It gets you flirting confidently, but with much less stress.

Ask "what's the story behind that?"

Bruce was served at his favorite coffee shop. Sandy, the girl who was getting him his coffee was a cute redhead in her early 20s, probably a coed at the local college. He noticed that she was wearing an unusual necklace; it looked old, and like it might have been from India. "Wow, that's a wonderful necklace," he told her. "What's the story behind that?"

This opened the conversational floodgates. She launched into a three-minute account of how she went to India and got the necklace there in one of the most meaningful experiences of her life. She was open and sharing and he learned a lot about what made her feel good.

For those few minutes she was back in India, having that peak experience again as she told him about it. By the end of her account, and their conversation about it, she was feeling very close to Bruce. He ended by saying to her, "Wow, you seem like a fascinating woman. I'd love to hear more about this sometime, and get to know you better. Can I call you?" She said yes; after all, if he was good enough to tell one of her most intimate experiences to, then he must be good enough to go out with, right?

"What's the story behind that?" is an immensely powerful flirting question. It gets most women to open up immediately, and tell you intimate details about themselves. After they've told you these details, it's harder for them to think of you as a jerk—after all, if you were a jerk, why would they open up so much to you?

When you are talking to a woman, be it a salesgirl behind a counter or a woman at a party, notice if she is wearing anything that looks unusual or personal. It might be a pin, a necklace, a piece of clothing, or a bracelet. Notice it, and ask her "what's the story behind that?" It's a powerful conversation-starter.

You've read a lot in this chapter about the specifics of flirting with women. You've read examples, general principles, and do's and don'ts. You've learned things you can do to start flirting more, today, and hopefully have become inspired about what's possible for your sex life if you start using these tools. We want you to use them, and be successful with women, but our experience shows that one question holds men back from actually using this flirting material: "What do I do if I 'blow it' with a woman?"

Men mean different things by "blowing it," but their fears have some general qualities in common. They are often afraid that they'll become flustered and not know what to say. They are afraid that the woman will just stare at them, terrified, like a deer in oncoming headlights. They are afraid that instead of seeming funny, they'll seem offensive.

Well, first the bad news. If you really are practicing, all this will almost certainly happen to you. Women will respond to your witty openings with stunned silence. Sometimes you'll get flustered. Sometimes women will seem scared of you. It's all part of learning to flirt, and it even happens to master seducers. There's just no way around it.

Look, you have a choice, both with women, and in life. You can choose to not try anything until you are absolutely sure things will go exactly the way you want them to, or you can throw yourself into life, and trust that it'll come out okay. If you wait to flirt with women until you think you can do it "good enough," you will never flirt, and never be a success with women. And, incidentally, if you take this approach to life, and never try anything you aren't sure is going to work, then you'll never be a success in life. You'll be trapped in only doing what you've done before, again and again. That kind of behavior will never take you where you want to go, in any area of your life.

And now, the good news. If you practice, you will succeed. Sure, there will be the occasional problem. But if you hang in there, you will get women.

It makes sense to think about your personal definition of success. We suggest that you define a successful interaction with a woman as an interaction in which you learn something about seduction. If you learned something, the interaction was successful. If you failed to learn something, then you failed, and you can make the interaction a success by figuring out what you learned. If you make this your personal definition of success, no matter what you do, you won't have really "blown it," and you can feel good about yourself.

chapter six...
A Crash Course in Romance
How to Sweep Her Off Her Feet and Into Your Bed

On a beautiful spring afternoon, Simon picked up his girlfriend Molly from her job. Earlier that day he had called her and had suggested they go on a secret outing. "Expect the unexpected," he said. "Only pack a light jacket and bring boots that can get muddied. Leave the rest up to me." Throughout the day Molly looked forward to seeing him, excited about the secret adventure ahead. She even told a few of her friends, "I don't know what to expect. Simon is so unpredictable, not like other guys. He always keeps things so exciting."

As she walked toward his car, Simon got out, hugged her, kissed her lips lightly, and whispered, "You look more beautiful than ever. I've been looking forward to seeing you all day." He then opened the car door. Fresh flowers, a card, and a few Hershey's kisses were waiting for her. As they began driving towards country highways near the outskirts of town, Simon popped in a tape of *her* favorite music.

After driving for nearly an hour down deserted highways, they arrived at a remote nature preserve known for its view from high rock ridges. It was a beautiful spot that would inspire anyone to feel happy, excited, and joyous.

Simon knew that Molly loved nature and wasn't allergic to grasses or pollens. These details are essential when planning the perfect romantic date. (If she was allergic to something in nature Simon would have planned the date totally differently.) This outing was custom designed to melt Molly's heart.

Simon had meticulously planned this event. Every detail was thought of ahead of time. Having all the details handled and planned ahead of time made it easier for Simon to relax and have fun with her. It was in his self-interest to plan.

As they walked together holding hands, Simon was very happy with himself, basking in his successes. After an hour of hiking, Molly wanted to take a break. They relaxed on a park bench overlooking a ravine. Simon pulled the blanket around them and they begin kissing. She thanked him for being such a wonderful boyfriend and for going through all the work to have the date go well.

They finally reached the top of the hill, both a bit winded. The view was breathtaking. Molly wrapped her arms around Simon's neck and they kissed passionately, like hungry lovers. They ended up on top of a huge flat rock with the blanket under them.

After they laid together on the rock for a while, the temperature quickly dropped and they got dressed and pressed on. They laughed together, imagining how crazy their friends would think they were to be in various forms of undress, out in the woods. After they got dressed and warmed up together with the blanket wrapped around them, Simon pulled out another gift for Molly. It was a necklace that fit her perfectly. She was thrilled at the gift.

In the near dark Simon took Molly down an alternative path, one that was much quicker than the one they used to get up the hill. Once again, Simon's planning paid off. They arrived at their car quickly. Molly even commented that she was impressed with how familiar he was with this park.

They soon left the park for the next adventure. Simon pulled out a map and navigated them to an out-of-the-way eatery, an elegant, cozy, and dimly lit restaurant. Simon had made reservations ahead of time. They sat together, held hands, and drank wine while sitting beside a huge window overlooking pine trees and woods.

During dinner Simon pulled out more small gifts. One was a stuffed bear. It was something cute and cheap that he knew she'd like. They had seen stuffed animals in a store window a few weeks before and she had mentioned how much she liked this particular one. The other gift was a book of poetry they looked at, and read from at a bookstore months ago. Simon had kept the title in the back of his mind, waiting for a perfect opportunity to buy it for her. Covertly, he thought it would be great to read the poems to her while they were in bed together.

After a slow-paced meal they left to go back home. Simon drove straight to her place and she invited him in. Simon let her get a head start towards her apartment so he could enter with more secret gifts. A few minutes later, he entered with a few items in wrapping paper. She tore the paper open like a kid on Christmas and discovered sexy lingerie, a bottle of wine, and massage oil, all the fixings for a romantic night alone. Molly unwrapped the gifts and pulled Simon into her bedroom. They proceeded to make love all night long.

LIGHTING THE FIRES
OF ROMANCE

Romance is the focus of this chapter. If you want success with women, you must be skilled in romance. You must understand how to create romantic situations and feelings in women. All women love romance and the attention focused on them. While all women are not looking for the exact same thing and desires vary greatly, all women do want the feelings that come from being romanced. Commonalties, however, do exist. And there are ways to think about situations and interactions that will produce romantic interactions and feelings in the woman. You will learn these in this chapter.

If you want a short-term relationship, romance is a large part of it. You have to sweep a woman off her feet if you want to get her into your bed. She must be taken by the experiences you provide for her if you expect her to want to have sex with you. Romance is the key to melting her heart and having her want to have you. In a long-term relationship, romance is what holds it all together over time. Romance is what will have the intimacy and sex last over years and years together. Romance is what will make the relationship stay "fresh" and fun.

It's a man's job is to bring the romance to relationships with women. If you want a steady supply of sex with a woman, romance is your meal ticket. It is worth making the effort to study this topic and become a romantic master.

We make a distinction between sex symbols and romance masters. Guys like James Dean were sex symbols because of their looks and attitudes on screen, but they had little skill in being romantic. JFK was able to sleep with many women because of his power and status, not his active skill in seduction. Someone like Casanova, however, was able to "be" romantic and embody classic romantic moves. Romance masters like Casanova and Don Juan got the way they were by being generative. They were generous with women and were able to give them exactly what they most want.

In the above seduction, Simon acted masterfully with Molly. He not only swept her off her feet, but created a lasting bond between them that would work to his advantage for a long time to come. He created a memorable experience tailored to her. Molly could later look back on their magical afternoon together as she would a vacation to Florida or a cruise. The best part is that Simon didn't have to spend lots of money or travel very far to achieve these results. And this isn't only applicable in long-term relationships, like Simon and Molly's. A relationship at any stage will be accelerated and sexualized by romance.

For women, romance is an individual, highly personal, intimate, and loving experience. There is a certain "other worldly" quality about romance for women. Because girls often learn to value romance at an early age, they are well-prepared to respond well to your romantic offerings. Books and even cartoons aimed at kids present situations in which women are swept off their feet, saved by daring and brave men, or rescued from castle towers. Women are socialized to expect and desire men to romance them. Men, on the other hand, often try to fight this fact. We, however, have accepted it and used it to improve our relationships with women and to increase our successes. You can fight all you want, but if you want success, you will learn to be consistently romantic.

When Simon took Molly to the bluff and brought out a surprise necklace, Molly felt romanced. When she first entered his car, she could see from the card, candy, and flowers that she was being romanced. The combination of having all the details handled, Simon taking care of her, his generosity and planning, and the excitement of it all, created a feeling inside Molly that was magical and mysterious.

Women love to know you are thinking about them. When they realize that you are, they feel romanced. They want to imagine you are hanging around thinking about them, like they often are of you. Even if you aren't, you need to take actions that make them think you are. They want to know that you appreciate it when they give their bodies to you. They want to be certain that, if they are going to be in a relationship, you respect them. One of the main reasons Molly was so thrilled was that she realized Simon put so much thought into the experience and he was thinking of her while shopping and creating the date. She felt special. In some situations it isn't even the gift itself; it is the fact that you thought of the woman when you weren't with her that has made her happy.

Romance is defined by the woman you are romancing. If you buy her flowers, for instance, and she is allergic to them, that's not romantic. Some women may think of it as romantic if you purchase fake blood, bite her neck, and pretend you are a vampire. It is completely subjective. You need to look to her reaction to determine if you were successful in your romance or not.

For example, Bill dated Karen for a few weeks. They liked each other, but didn't connect as well as either thought they could, and the sex certainly wasn't happening. They had kissed and fooled around a few times, but it never seemed to "click." After attending a day-long seminar with us, Bill realized that he had failed to provide her with any romance. He was trying to push the sex too quickly and never put any attention into "charming her." Bill noticed that he wasn't giving her what she really wanted: romance.

The next week, Bill set up an evening experience for Karen. He purchased a few inexpensive, but nicely wrapped gifts, and took her out to dinner. He did the things he thought *she* would like, and kept his attention on her. He restrained himself from talking about work and how much he looked forward to deer hunting season a few weeks away. Immediately, they seemed to get along much better, and had "deep" conversations. After dinner, they went to his house and talked and kissed in front of his fireplace. That night, they had sex for the first time.

Ironically, when Bill stopped focusing on his own needs, sex just happened naturally without any pressure on his part. We propose that sex will just seem to happen as soon as you refocus onto the woman. Romance is the way you shift this focus.

A form of psychology called Neuro Linguistic Programming (NLP) contends that people experience love and appreciation in different ways. Some women feel loved when you touch, or hug them. They connect through physical contact. Other women experience love when you say certain things to them. Certain words and phrases are what gives them the feeling of love. Still others feel loved only when you buy them things, when they can see what you have purchased.

The same is true with romance. Some women feel romantic only when you say certain things to them. They may need romantic poetry or sweet comments in order to feel romanced. Others need physical contact like kisses, hugs, massages, and other touch-related experiences. Still others need presents and unusual experiences like trips to new places.

Let's get into the specifics. What is a romantic situation? It is one that takes her out of her day-to-day routine and into a special world. Simon takes Molly into a new environment to achieve this. He drives her out on country roads, into areas they rarely visit. He also creates a mood by giving her gifts and planning experiences for her ahead of time. Simon successfully creates this date as an "event," not just another night out.

You don't need to create as elaborate an outing as Simon to have a memorable date. You could just as easily take her to a cultural event, exotic restaurant, or even an evening of pampering at home. The one requirement is that it is special and out of the ordinary.

Along the same lines, you could also look at romance as a celebration of being together. This celebration is that you can fully be with her, enjoying her company, and having fun in the process. If you are not enjoying yourself and having fun, what is the point of going out with a woman anyway? So much of our lives is spent working at jobs. Most of us don't even like the jobs we're at. So, why not fully have fun and celebrate being with her when you are together? Even if it is a one-night stand, why not play full out?

Romantic masters live life fully, knowing that magic happens only in the present moment. They don't waste time imagining the future or bitching about the past. Imagine how different it would be if you interacted with women as if each interaction was a celebration. We are not getting all mushy or new age-y on you; we are simply proposing a way to act and interact with women that will provide the most fun, ease, and sexually prosperous experience possible.

SECRETS OF COURTING

If you are looking for a girlfriend or a longterm relationship, to some degree you will have to court the woman. We define courting as a process in which your actions "prove" to a woman over time that you want to be with her. The term itself has links to medieval times of kings and queens, knights in shining armor defending the court. In these times courting was a long process during which the man, boy, or prince had to prove his worth not only to the girl or princess, but also to her parents and others.

Fortunately, we don't have to jump through nearly as many hoops, but these same ideas are still very much alive. Women want you to prove to them that you are worthy of having them. Sure, this is not the most feminist idea in the world, but after interviewing hundreds of women for this book about what they look for in dating partners and how they select a man, we have determined that the medieval notion of courting remains important today.

The key to courting is to prove that you are patient. You are demonstrating that you are dependable, honest, good, moral, and that you have other noble qualities. In short, you are proving that you really want her as an individual, not just a one-night stand. This means that you consistently pursue her over time. Most women, especially those worthy of having a long-term relationship with you, want to know that you like them for more than just their bodies and sex. While in a short-term relationship, sex is probably your primary objective, in a longer-term relationship, it isn't. When you court a woman over time you are getting to know her and creating an opening for her to "give herself to you" over time.

The flip side to courting is that you also get to "test her out." Is she a bitch to you, or someone you can spend hours and hours with without fighting? Is she complimentary towards you, or is she demanding? If she is nasty, mean, or doesn't fit with your picture you can stop dating her as well.

As you read this, you might think it isn't right to "prove yourself" to a woman. You may think she should just take you for who you are. Or maybe you think this idea is ridiculous and outdated. Nothing could be further from the truth. If you are naive enough to think that women don't still want you to court them and sweep them off their feet, you are dead wrong. While you *might* get a one-night-stand without courting, it is unlikely you will get much else. We will go much more in-depth about how to maintain a long-term relationship in a later chapter. For now, we just want you to understand its basic importance.

Here are a few question she will be asking herself about you. You must get over these hurdles during the courting period.

* Do I trust him?
* How much do I trust him?
* Does he have a violent temper?
* Does he want a long-term relationship?
* Is he just a player?
* How far will he go to prove himself for me?
* How demanding can I be?
* Can he stand it if I withhold sex?
* Would he be a good father?
* Is his career going well?
* Does he have drive to succeed in the world?
* Do my friends like him?
* Would my parents like him?
* Is he attractive?

Overcoming these hurdles takes time. Strangely, our experience shows that even women who say they aren't looking for a long-term relationship usually ask themselves questions like these. It's a fact of life that you will have to prove yourself to women you have sex with. Romance, it turns out, is the fastest way to do this.

HOW TO WRITE A LOVE NOTE
THAT MAKES HER MELT

The historic romancer was skilled in writing love letters. Because he rarely saw the woman before they were married, he often had to communicate through letters. This was one of the ways he created hot romance, and you must learn to do it, too. Most women love letters. We have both had wonderful success using love letters as tools for seduction and to aid the courting process. For us, these letters have taken the form of e-mails, cards, notes, and letters. Women love the thought and effort it takes you to write a note and send it off to them. It can be a few stanzas of Shakespearean poetry, or something simple like "I miss your lips touching mine." Or, "I can't wait until our next secret outing this weekend." Or, "When we left each other Friday night I forgot to tell you how beautiful your eyes are." Some women can also handle the hard stuff, like "I can't wait to get you in bed." but that's risky and to be done only after you've been having sex with her. It's up to you.

Let's look at this from a purely economic standpoint for a second. For $2.50 you can buy a great looking card from a specialty shop. Then, for the price of a stamp you can send the card. These simple actions can easily cause the woman to melt in her seat. Is it worth it, or not?

The study of romantic letters is a book in itself. What follows are tips for writing notes. The first thing to realize is that shorter is better. A few great lines that pack a punch are much better than some long cheesy diatribe that offers more opportunities for the woman to dislike the note. It is better to leave her wanting more than to overdo it and have her confused or thinking you are lying or manipulating her.

Here are the three elements of every successful love note:

1. Acknowledging how wonderful she is

The more specific you can compliment her the better. For example, commenting on how her "beautiful brown eyes reflect in a candlelit room" is much better than commenting on how nice her eyes are. Here are the top few things to comment on:

* Her hair
* Her eyes
* How sweet she is
* How you just love to stare at her
* Her lips
* The beautiful way she moves

The things to avoid are overtly sexual things about her body. Here's a few things to avoid commenting on:

* How great her breasts look in a white T-shirt
* How her lips would be great for oral sex
* How great her ass looks in tight jeans
* How you wonder what she'll look like in the morning

2. How great she makes you feel

Now you must talk about how wonderful she makes you feel. Once again, say something specific. Here are a few things to comment on:

* When we are together I lose myself
* I get that warm feeling all over when we are together
* I've never felt so comfortable with a woman before

3. You are thinking of her

The last essential component is to mention that you are thinking about her and can't wait to see her again. Here are a few possibilities:

* I can't stop thinking about you
* I am holding my breath until I see you next

* The image of you won't fade from my mind—and I never want it to
* You are special in my life beyond words

If you must enhance the letter, go through steps one and two a few more times. When you begin, however, we recommend you keep the notes short and sweet. And don't forget to sign it!

DETAILS, DETAILS, DETAILS

We can say it a million times. Details are usually the easiest actions to take, but the hardest to discipline yourself to do consistently. As men, we usually don't care about the details when we go out for a night on the town. Women are completely opposite. A good rule of thumb is that the more time you put in, or appear to have put in, to creating details, the better. If you remember this tip, everything else will go much more smoothly. In a romantic situation the details are handled. Simon, for example, had planned the outing with Molly very carefully. He thought of everything ahead of time, from the short cut down the hill to buying the wine for later in the night.

Another detail you must master is your appearance. As we discussed in Chapter Three, this means you are dressed well and have clean clothes on, smell good, and your breath is good. Further, your car and apartment are clean and ready to go. Cleanliness is good because it gives the woman one less thing to be distracted by. It also shows her that you have put thought, time, and energy into creating an event for her. One woman interviewed said, "I love going over to my boyfriend's apartment. He always has the place clean and fresh flowers ready for me. When I walk in I feel like he has prepared it for royalty. I always feel so special and appreciated when I visit him."

SENSUALITY—AWAKENING HERS AND YOURS

Sensuality is another gateway to romance, one of the key spices in your romantic recipe. Sensuality, as we define it, consists of actions that you take to awaken her senses. You must charm her mind through romantic talk and love letters. You must also turn on her body through sensual play.

We make a distinction between sexuality and sensuality. While they are similar, it is useful for you to understand the difference and how women tend to experience them differently. Sexuality is the act of sex, usually including genital contact. Sensuality refers to stimulation of the senses, which may not include genital contact or even touching at all.

Women tend to be more sensual and men tend to be more sexual. Women can cuddle all night long and kiss in front of candles while talking about "the relationship." Many guys are happy having sex for a short time, finishing, and then rolling over to sleep. Total time from start to finish—15 minutes. This is the age-old conflict between men and women. How can you get her to have sex, when she wants something different? The easiest solution is to do the sensual stuff as foreplay. After that, she will usually let you go for the sexual stuff you want.

When you are able to awaken all of her senses at once, there is a multiplier effect that creates a wonderful sexual mood. You are creating an experience for her, not just a quick and dirty thing. You are giving her what she wants, so she will give you what you want. This is usually done by touching her through back rubs and massage, baths, and cuddling. It can also include the other senses: seeing, hearing, tasting and smelling.

Calming scents

Calming scents, like sandalwood, are also good. Ask her what her favorite scents are. Burn incense or get scented oils to fill the room with her favorite odors. As we said, women have a much keener sense of smell than men do. This can work to your advantage in setting the mood. However, it can also work to your disadvantage. A woman can smell your pit sweat and crusty underwear much better than you can. She will also be more keenly aware of rotting food in the fridge and moldy beer cans under the bed. Find out the scents she enjoys and get rid of the disgusting ones to aid the seduction and romance.

Food

Food is another sensual possibility. By feeding a woman grapes, or another fruit, you will warm up her mouth and begin to shift her focus onto the world of sensuality. You will open up her taste buds and expand her erotic possibilities in the process. Chocolate is a high-ranking sensuality tool. Most women love chocolate. Correction: they don't just love chocolate—they go insane for it. The ecstatic feeling they get from chocolate is similar to how they feel during sex. For the right woman, a small piece of chocolate in her mouth at the right moment will open her up for all sorts of sensual play.

Monty was setting the mood with Janet. He began by massaging her. She quickly relaxed. He placed his hands over her eyes, kissed her cheek, and placed a very small piece of chocolate in her mouth. She chewed it sensually and pulled his mouth closer to hers. They proceeded into passionate kisses and intense sexual touching. You can do this, too.

Here's a list of the top 10 foods to use to create erotic/romantic moods.

1. Chocolate. This includes chocolate sauce.
2. Whipped cream. The classic erotic experience is to lick it off her breasts, or other forbidden places.
3. Blueberries
4. Grapes
5. Kiwi
6. Strawberries
7. Honey
8. Ice Cream
9. Maple Syrup
10. Jelly

An important note: fun as it is to do at the time, chocolate and fruit should not be put into the vagina. The sugar in these foods changes the pH of the vagina, and can cause very painful yeast infections. It's best to keep them on other parts of the body. Take it from us on this one.

Lighting

A sensual experience is greatly heightened by having appropriate *lighting*. A candlelit room in the evening, or a room that has the lights down low, will convey a softness that will create a romantic mood. Candlelight will not only set the tone of romance, but will look great on your skin. Just remember for a second how unrelaxing it is to be under fluorescent lights or bright lights or your desk lamp. When you are romancing a woman, you want her to feel comfortable, not on the spot in a police interrogation room.

After reading about the importance of lighting, Steve put a dimmer switch on his bedroom overhead light, which really created a relaxing mood. But if you are going to do this, make sure the dimmer you get has a good quality rheostat. Ask the guys at the hardware store if it will buzz. Many dimmer switches emit a very irritating sound. This will be counterproductive to the goals of your seduction.

You could also experiment with strange lighting options, like black light. This looks sexy on her naked body and may set the mood for sex. It's especially wonderful for play with fluorescent body paints. You could also try out red light, green, or even total darkness.

Another thing to play with is to have objects of different textures for her to touch such as soft fabrics like silk or a cotton blanket. The trick is to find things that you can rub on her body or that she can touch with her hands that will all retain the mood of sensuality. This includes pillows and sheets. You want to create environments where she is pampered and totally relaxed. Pillows can help arch her body in the exact position you want. Soft and sensual sheets will be just one more detail that will make the night perfect.

Jeremy went to a fabric store and purchased several small samples of soft fabrics for use on his girlfriend Wanda. He bought one-foot-square samples. They were cheap and were great to rub on her skin while in the bedroom. She was aroused and also found them fun to play with.

Music

Music also helps set a romantic mood. Have you ever noticed that, when you listen to aggressive rock music while driving down the highway, you also become more intense, aggressive, and for some reason want to just drive faster? You *entrain* with the music—that is, your heartbeat tends to go at the speed of music playing around you. A good way to create a serene, sensual place is to have soft music playing, to get you both in the mood. Some classical music is good, but check it out ahead of time: some start all quiet and romantic, then gets raucous and wild just when you finally have her in the right mood. Check out the "ambient music" of Brian Eno, Peter Gabriel's *Passion* CD, Enya, and Enigma. Or, you can play any music that she specifically mentions gets her in the mood.

Even better, you can condition a woman when you play a certain song or CD. As we've discussed before, people can be trained to have a particular reaction to a particular stimulus. Every psychology major will tell you this and back it up with all sorts of research. The upshot is, if you always play the same song in romantic moments, the song itself will start to make her feel romantic, and you can use this to your advantage. When you use a song or CD now during romantic moments, it will automatically get the woman in the mood when you play it in the future.

Talk

A woman enjoys knowing that you think that she is beautiful. Why not tell her? Put your mouth to her ear, and whisper "you are so beautiful." This will shift her mood, guaranteed. Why whispering works better than yelling, we don't know, but it does. Talking and opening up topics for discussion will also create a deeper bonding between you. Many psychologists note that communication in relationships is *the* thing that will make or break a relationship. We'll show you in Chapter 7 how to create romantic conversations that make her desire you.

THE TOP SIX SENSUAL
EXPERIENCES FOR WOMEN

You must learn how to be a sensualist. A sensual person loves feeling, touch, and experiences that come through the senses. You probably think you are a sensualist already, but you aren't. More than likely you are a *sexualist*. You love sexual experiences. You may even think that sensual and sexual experiences are the same thing. Trust us when we say that to women, sensuality and sexuality are miles apart. If you want to be sexual with a woman, you must start out by being sensual.

For a woman, "sensual" and "romantic" mean the same thing. When you are romantic, you are paying attention to every little detail in the environment. You make sure your clothes are clean, the candles are lit, the wine is good, and that everything is in place. When you are sensuous, you are paying attention to every little detail about how something feels, tastes, looks, sounds or smells to her or you. By paying attention to the senses, you are being romantic on an even more internal, intimate level.

While you won't be able to do everything we list here before the first time you have sex—most women won't let you give them a bath, for instance, until you've been sexual already—it's important for your seduction to start to understand the kind of experiences that make women feel sensual and romantic, and to begin moving toward them.

The top six sensual experiences for women are:

1. Water

Obviously, bathing with a woman is something you'll do after you have seduced her for the first time, but it's an important sensual experience for you to understand anyway. Women find baths much more sensuous and attractive than men do. If you don't believe us, ask the average guy when he last took a long, slow hot bath. Probably not recently. Ask a woman, however (and we suggest you do, as part of the seduction), and she'll probably get all dreamy-eyed, and tell you all about it. It's part of her sensual wiring.

While you can't bathe a woman on a first date, you sure can talk about bathing. You can ask her if she likes baths, and what makes up a perfect romantic bath experience for her. This will not only get her thinking sensuous, romantic thoughts and connecting them with you, it will also give you valuable information about how to set up a romantic bath for her when the time inevitably comes.

Women love baths, and it will be an added bonus to have candles, flower petals, soft music, bubble bath, and wine in the bathroom. Undress her slowly, touching all parts of her. Then, escort her into a bath at the perfect temperature. You can then get into the tub with her, or sit beside her, feeding her or pouring her wine. Be sure to dry her off as she gets out. You can then lead her directly into the bedroom, where she'll be relaxed and ready to please.

The women we interviewed while researching this book often told us that they love to be pampered by their boyfriend, lover, or husband. Pampering was equivalent to romance for them. When you include small indulgences, like baths, women will feel pampered.

2. Massage

Massage is something you can do before you actually have sex with a woman. While a long sensual bath may be more appropriate for a woman you've dated for a while, a woman you are getting to know is a perfect candidate for a massage. This can even work on a first date, if you play your cards right. Massage is good because it shows her that you enjoy her body, and can make it feel good. It also shows that you are happy just to touch her, not just to have sex with her. Paradoxically, it may be the most effective way to start the road to sex.

As with anything else you do on a date, you must begin by remembering your outcome. You are there to get her to want to have sex with you. You are not trying to give her a Japanese acupressure treatment, or create some other physically therapeutic response. You'd be a fool to do any massage that causes her pain, or exhausts her, even though such a massage-workout might be best for her physically. The point is to relax her and build intimacy, not to fix some physical problem she has. Make her feel good. Just have her sit up, or better yet lay on her stomach, and gently work on her. You are not going to grab her breasts. You are going slow.

We recommend that you get some oil and begin by getting your hands warm, putting on music she likes, and rubbing her back gently. You can trace circles or patterns on her back at first. You can then rub her neck gently, and even stroke her hair. From there you can keep working down to her butt. But stop. Don't go any further unless you are sure she's ready to get sexual. Feeling her up with massage may be fun, but if you move too fast you'll scare her. The point is to have her wanting you, while you simultaneously don't need anything from her.

After a while she can flip over on her back. At that point you can rub her stomach and maybe touch her breasts if it seems right. Remember, you are doing this to get her in the mood. If you touch her in a way she doesn't like, she isn't ready for, you will probably kill all chances of progressing any further. So, go slow with the massage.

Sometimes a massage will build a wonderful feeling of anticipation. You've got the light just right, the room is warm, the oil smells good, and you've lit candles. She's feeling absolutely safe, and you are making her feel better and better by touching her. As the feeling of anticipation builds, you both know a kiss is coming, but don't know when. If you both start feeling this, you know you are home free.

3. Cuddling

Women love cuddling. Men don't care so much about it. While cuddling may not be something you can do early on in a date—after all, she hardly knows you, yet—you can bring up the fact that you really enjoy cuddling. Don't make it a big deal, just mention it in an offhand manner.

Our student Jake gets a lot of mileage out of talking about cuddling. When he's first dating a woman, and the conversation turns to men and women, he'll say, "You know, there's something I don't understand. Perhaps you can help clear it up for me. First, let me ask you: do you like cuddling? I thought so. But it seems like lots of guys don't like it, you know what I mean?" At this point most women tell him about some jerk they knew who didn't like to cuddle and he says, "Yea, that's what I don't understand. I mean, I think there's nothing better than just holding a person that you are really feeling intimate with, you know what I mean?" By skillfully acknowledging that he loves cuddling, and that other men don't, he gets her to imagine being with him sexually, and cuddling afterwards. He gets her to think of him as sexual material.

When you have the opportunity, a great way to turn on the romance is cuddling in front of a fire, or on the beach at night with a blanket, or spooning in bed, or any other situation when you can have your body pressed tightly into hers for long stretches, without having sex. Women love this, and you can use it to your advantage.

4. Sensual food

As we said, food seems to be a romantic, sensual elixir. What's important in sensual food is that it is enjoyable and special for her to eat. If you happen to know she loves chocolate, for instance, you don't simply buy her a Hershey's bar and hope she likes it; you pay attention to details, and make it a sensuous, memorable experience, like our student Josh did.

When Josh first talked to Ellen, he found out that she adored chocolate. "Oh, I could never live without chocolate," she told him rapturously. "I love the way it feels in my mouth, and the taste! Mmm." Josh remembered this love of hers, and used it to his advantage.

On their first date he brought a chocolate bar that was the absolute best quality chocolate he could find. He pulled it out and said "I brought us a wonderful experience. Will you share it with me?" Her eyes lit up, and he asked her to unwrap it. He had her talk about everything she loved about chocolate, and slowly fed a piece to her, and she fed him another one back. It was a very sensuous and romantic experience. By the time they were done with the chocolate, Josh knew that Ellen was thinking of him romantically, and had had a wonderful, sensuous experience with him. On the next date, they had sex, largely because he was able to demonstrate that he knew how to be sensuous.

Not all women will be turned on by chocolate; many have other foods that really make them the most happy. Find out what they are for a woman and you can use that knowledge to move the seduction forward.

5. Walking in nature at sunset

Ever read personals ads written by women? Nine out of ten times, they mention loving sunsets, and long walks in nature.

Granted, these women hardly ever actually watch sunsets, or take those long walks. But to females, these two things are sensual experiences that are synonymous with romance.

Even if you aren't a lover of nature, most women are. They will usually relax, open up to you, and "get in the mood." Nature provides an opportunity for a woman to experience all of her senses and sets the stage for you to put on the charm. If you live in a huge concrete jungle of a city, this may be difficult. Even if your city has a lake to walk around or a small nature preserve this will suffice. The advantage to being in nature is that you can hold hands and use the isolation to connect.

George found that taking his dates on walks in nearby nature areas made the date much more special, more of an event. Women expect to be taken out to dinner and to a movie. Most will think it is special when you arrive near a lake. Besides, it makes you look like a sensitive guy.

6. Fire

Bringing the woman of your dreams to a place with a fireplace is the culmination of all you have learned in this section so far. When you are in front of a fire you have the dim lights, the smell, the ambiance, and all the makings for a hot love session.

Have you ever read one of the romance novels women love? Read one, and you will begin to understand what women are looking for. While men's porn magazines feature stories about hard and rough sex, or one-night stands, romance novels concentrate most on the foreplay, the chase, the seduction, and the romantic nights that lead up to sex. In many of the stories the man and woman end up in front of a blazing fire holding each other. This particular scene is depicted in movies, art, and stories. In short, this is a great way to create a wonderful night with a woman.

Ralph, for example, was house-sitting at a friend's house which had a fireplace. He took advantage of the opportunity and invited Tess over. He had purchased a nice bottle of wine and they drank glass after glass in front of the fireplace. Ralph had, of course, lit the thing before she arrived. They talked for a long time, and the music in the background created a great mood. After a while Ralph suggested he give Tess a massage. She took off her shirt and they progressed from there.

You can have such successes as well, if you become a student of sensuality. These ideas are only starters—there are many more ways that sensuality with women can lead to romance and hot sex. But if you understand the powers of water, massage, cuddling, food, walks in nature and fire, and bring them into your dates, you'll be much more the romantic kind of man women adore.

THE SIX KEYS TO ROMANCE

Now that you are beginning to get a feel for sensuality—no pun intended—you are ready to start learning about romance. There are six keys to romantic behavior with women. Here they are:

1. Romance is generous/ it's never needy

In Chapter 3 we showed you how to get over being needy by getting the validation for your life from somewhere other than from women. But how do you become generous? When you are being romantic, the focus is on her, not you. You have to put out for her, not vice-versa. This is your generosity in a dating situation.

At first it will probably be hard to put the focus on her. You may resent having to do the up-front work for the date; you may feel like she should be acknowledging you for taking all the risks you've taken to flirt with her and ask her out. Get over it. After you've practiced being generous for a while, you'll find that it's more fun than being angry. If you get resentful, remember that you are doing all this for a reason. By being sensitive, sweet, and generous, you melt her heart and open the road to sex. But don't worry—you are not just a giving machine, without needs. We would never send you into a situation to be a doormat, or be a man who gives and gives receiving nothing in return. In later chapters we will discuss how to cut off relationships with women who give you nothing back, and when to do so. For now, however, you must do the up-front work. She won't do it, and if you don't, you won't succeed.

Generosity is really a basic principles of being a powerful man. Men who command respect are not needy, groveling worms. They are men who are mature, know when to give and when to take, and who are not looking for people, especially women they desire, to take care of them.

One of the problems we observe in modern men is that many are so caught up in trying to be "nice" that they don't assert themselves in the world, or act with any "balls" whatsoever. They seem defeated, beaten down, and have an overlyintellectual approach with women. But the opposite, the "macho jerk" approach, will also fail. Besides being dangerous—in that you may be seen as abusive and end up in jail—it is also wrong to dominate women and pressure them, as macho jerks do. It is the sign of a weak man to have to force a woman to do something. A powerful man is persuasive and romantic, not overly forceful, and not overly nice.

If, for example, you seem needy, and try to get a woman to "reward" you for being good to her, she will likely and reasonably think you are a jerk who's only trying to manipulate her. If you are generous, but not a doormat, it will make all the difference.

2. Romance is patient

When you are creating the perfect romantic situation don't push her too hard. We all hate to be patient, but during a seduction, it's necessary. Nothing turns women off more quickly than a guy obviously trying to score and only hitting on her for sex. It doesn't seem romantic at all. Impatience is especially devastating after an evening of seduction. If you push too hard at the end of the date, she will probably think the whole night was just a scam, a ploy to get her to have sex with you. It will blow all the work you've put in up to that point. The solution is to be patient and learn to go with the flow.

Jason, for example, always blows dates by being too forward and intense with women. Instead of being patient he always goes for sex right away when a little bit of patience would serve him much better.

On a recent date he took Catherine out to dinner and a dance club. He immediately started "dirty dancing" with her, shoving his pelvis into her hip. He failed to notice that she didn't like it, and kept pulling away from him. In fact, he was hurting her by shoving himself into her too hard. Later, when she seemed noticeably upset, he learned the truth from her. "Why didn't you just tell me I was hurting you? I didn't know any better," he said truthfully.

Jason was what we like to call a "helpless idiot." He had no idea how to charm a woman or be seductive. He was still caught up in being an adolescent with women. He still wanted and even expected instant gratification without being sensitive or patient. We all do stupid things, like Jason, and until we realize they don't work, will continue to do them and continue to fail. Remember, be patient, and initiate sex while also going at her speed.

3. Romance is truly appreciative of her

As mentioned above, the focus of romance is on *her*. It is your job to romance her and give her the romantic feelings she wants. Start by appreciating her beauty, her eyes, her intelligence, her hair, or her apartment. You've got to understand that a woman cares deeply about her appearance. She'll spend hours teasing her hair to look just "right." She will put on an extra-special bra just to turn you on, wear perfume she thinks will attract you, and wear the perfect bracelet because it matches her shoes. If you can notice any of these easy-to-miss details and tell her so, it will certainly impress her.

You can also show your appreciation of her by focusing on the details in your own appearance. Even though you don't care if your socks match, or if your gold football medallion matches your tie, women do. Look over Chapter 3 again, and make sure you are paying attention to the romantic details of your own look.

Master romancers like Casanova understood how to really appreciate the beauty of a woman and make her feel like she is the most special person in the world. You must do this as well. By appreciating the details of her appearance, you convey to her that she is the only one in the world you would want to be with tonight, even if that isn't necessarily true. When she believes that you are totally focused on her, she will be much more likely to "reward" you with sex.

4. Romance has an air of the unexpected and unreal

Alert! Alert! This is very important, and will serve you in every step of your seduction. When we show you how to create a "seduction strategy" we will rely again and again on your understanding that romance has an air of the unexpected and unreal. Master giving women unexpected and unreal experiences, and you can have almost any woman you desire. Do this by creating surprises and doing things you normally wouldn't do.

Surprises. Unexpected and unreal romantic situations often contain wonderful suprises. We started off this chapter with the example of Simon taking Molly out for a romantic afternoon. One of the reasons why the afternoon went so well was because Molly had no idea what was going to happen next. By filling the afternoon with surprises, Simon was able to take her into another world, a world outside of their normal, day-to-day routine.

Doing things you normally wouldn't do. One woman we interviewed told us that "if a man can capture my imagination and mind, he can have the rest." When you create activities that you normally wouldn't do, you show the woman you are with that you are fun, adventuresome, and, most important, that you are willing to go out of your way to make her feel good. To plan a romantic night, add the spice of the unreal and unexpected—go to a new part of town after a movie, or to an out-of-the-way bar after a romantic walk. You want her to feel like a queen, like a princess, like a character in a movie. Creating an out-of-the-way, romantic event is a wonderful way to do this.

In the morning before they both left for work, Steve told his wife, Ruth, to be home right after work and get prepared for a wild night. That evening, he told her that for the remainder of the night they would pretend to be from another country. He gave them both new names and identities. Steve became "Ricardo," a Latin lover. Ruth became "Natasha," a Russian spy. They both dressed up in very formal clothes and "pretended" to meet at an upscale lounge in the downtown area.

"Ricardo" dropped "Natasha" off at the lounge. He then entered several minutes later. He proceeded to attempt to "pick her up." He used a fake accent and kept offering to buy her drinks. She played "hard to get." They spent hours in this type of back-and-forth flirtatious exchange. Some other guys in the bar even hit on "Natasha" because she looked so great. "Ricardo" had to compete with them for her attention. It added to the sexiness of the night. Eventually, they danced and "Ricardo" went for the kiss. "It was so hot and sexy," Natasha said later. "My husband and I tend to just watch TV in the evenings. Freshness and spontaneity often seem hard to recreate. It was easy when we first started dating, but lately it has seemed hard. When we starting using fake names and flirting all the fun and sexual tension that was there when we met came back. This was one of the most fun evenings we've ever had." After a night of pretending, "Ricardo" took her home. They proceeded to have a long night of very hot sex. By taking on false identities, they created a very romantic, memorable, and "unreal" evening.

5. Romance is confident

If you want to ruin a romantic moment, date, or conversation, be a guy who has no confidence and who isn't able to be bold. The man who has mastered romance is able to be confident in every moment with a woman. This is not being dominating or controlling. Rather, a man with confidence makes decisions, isn't wishy-washy, is able to be straight with a woman about his expectations, and not be apologetic about his sexual or other desires.

Ken, for instance, is your typical sensitive man. He rarely makes the first move and is embarrassed when women touch him in public. Though he is 35, his face looks like a 20-year-old. He has a successful job and makes a decent income, but few people respect him. Men usually think he is a wimp, with no real opinions, who is more concerned with catering to everyone's whims than to his own desires. When we told him about using romantic talk on a date, he didn't think he could tell a woman anything romantic. He was concerned that she would be offended. Needless to say, Ken had gone for the past three years without sex. To make it worse, his last girlfriend made him buy her presents, loan her his credit card, and even stole money from his house. Ken was a classic sensitive new-age guy whose inability to be confident about going for what he wanted made him a victim of his circumstances.

Isaac, on the other hand, is confident. Though it hasn't come naturally to him, he has learned to charm women and create romantic evenings that are very successful. Best yet, he has sex whenever he wants.

Isaac has studied our material and learned to be confident on dates with women. "I often feel nervous before dates and sometimes even when I'm out with my date. I just don't let it get to me. I know the Seven Habits of Highly Effective Seducers, and I've memorized them. I just keep going when I mess up and women continue to be interested in me."

Specifically, Isaac is confident when giving a woman a card, paying for the date, opening the door for her, making the first move, kissing her, being decisive, and asking for follow-up dates.

You may be saying, "Wait a minute! You just told me to be patient! Now you're telling me to be confident and bold! What's going on here?" The truth is, you must be both patient and confident. While you are waiting for her to be ready to be your lover, you must be confident and certain that everything is okay, and that you are fine, no matter what happens during the seduction. This confidence will give you the ability to be as patient as you need to be.

6. Details

We know it is totally redundant to even mention the importance of details at this point of the game, but because men are so resistant to integrating essentials into dates, we are mentioning it once again. Details will make or break the date. Use "take care of the details" as your mantra when setting up all dates.

TALK THE TALK

You can probably remember what it felt like the first time you really "got it" that someone loved you, can't you? And perhaps you can remember what it felt like the best time you experienced "love at first sight." And when you think about one of the best times you've ever had with a woman, what do you feel?

Sometimes you just feel connected to someone. Have you ever felt an overwhelming trust, even though you may not know why you felt it? Like when you met someone, it just seemed like you were connected, like you had known each other forever. Do you know what we mean?

Most people will have emotional reactions to the preceding two paragraphs. That's what makes those paragraphs examples of romantic talk. Questions and descriptions of romantic feelings will usually create those feelings in the person you are listening to. This is why you must talk the talk of romance.

As we've said before, when you describe a feeling, the person listening will automatically remember times when he or she felt the same way. So, for example, if you ask a woman what was the first time that she felt totally swept off her feet and completely enthralled with a man, she will automatically remember that experience. She will begin to re-experience that feeling in the moment.

This is a very useful tool in creating romance. By spending a little time before the date, you can memorize many romantic questions that will help to create a state of mind in the woman. You can also discuss romantic topics with her and get the same results.

Here are a few examples of romantic questions you can ask a woman:

* What is it like when you feel totally happy and carefree?
* Imagine that you have a week of vacation with the man of your dreams. What would you do next?
* What was the most romantic evening of your life?
* What was the most romantic movie you've ever seen?
* Which actor do you find most attractive and why?
* What does it feel like when you are in love?
* How do you know you are in love?
* What is your favorite thing about kissing?
* Who was your best boyfriend and why?
* Describe your favorite princess story.
* What did you think romance was like when you were a little girl?

Asking these questions will put her in a more romantic mood. We'll go into more detail about this in the next chapter.

Be warned, however: not only positive feelings can be created this way. We could get you in the mood to be scared and edgy if we asked you to recall a time when you felt threatened by another man. "What was it like?" we might ask. "Tell us all the details. What were you thinking and feeling? Did you have adrenaline pumping through your veins? How did that feel? Was the guy big or small? What did he look like? Did he have a weapon? Did you feel victimized?" Can you notice as you read this how we could psyche you up to feel scared? This is the mistake you make with women when you get into conversations about violence against women, war, and rape. When you do this, she starts imagining all that violence happening to her. Don't allow the discussion to get into descriptions of violence and horror, or you will destroy the romantic mood entirely.

This may seem like complicated stuff, but let's look at your competition. The average guy is nowhere near understanding these ideas. He treats women as he would treat really sexy men, doesn't create special occasions for them, doesn't treat them as if they are special, rarely compliments them, and is either needy or a bully to them. He's completely non-sensual, and is resentful that he has to put the focus on the woman if he wants to get sex. He is as likely to describe something violent, and make women feel scared, as he is to accidentally say something romantic. Heck, women tell us that most men don't know enough to bathe before dates, much less write romantic love notes. If you avoid the common mistakes, and even do half of the romantic things we recommend in this chapter, you'll leave women desiring you and panting for more.

chapter seven...
The
Priming Date

Wendy worked at Bruce's health club. While she wasn't glamorous, she was fit, with a small, tight body. After flirting with her a few times, Bruce realized that she was an intellectual. She was reading a book almost every time he saw her, and told him she was working on her Ph.D. in zoology. She seemed cute and sweet. He found her attractive and asked her out for coffee. She said yes, and they arranged to meet at a coffee shop near the health club at 4:00 the next Tuesday. "I'll only have about an hour," Bruce told her, "but that should be enough time for us to explore each other a little bit."

Bruce asked Wendy on what we call a *priming date* (though of course, he would never call it that to her). The purpose of a priming date is to meet with a woman for just long enough to create a romantic connection with her, to get her thinking about you in a romantic way, and to find out the best way to sweep her off her feet on the seduction date. The priming date also gives you an opportunity to decide if this really is a woman you want to pursue. It's cheap, and being only a coffee date, most women will feel more comfortable than a big dinner-and-a-movie extravaganza.

It's usually wrong to ask a woman out for a big dinner-and-a-movie extravaganza for your first date because you won't be ready. You won't know enough about her requirements in a man to arrange an efficient seduction, and thus you will be more likely to make devastating mistakes with her. If you ask her out for an evening event first, she's more likely to be put off by the intensity and intimacy of such a first date. You appear more calm and less desperate when you ask a woman out for coffee, rather than for an entire evening. You are telling her you want to see her, but aren't needy and trying to rush things. This lets a woman know that you have a life outside of seeing her, which is very important, especially with very attractive women.

On a priming date, you are priming her for your seduction. It's like preparing a camp stove before lighting it; done properly, you only need a few simple moves to create quite a hot little fire. Without proper preparation, you are always working too hard to get what you want to happen. With priming, you leave the first interaction ready to go.

THE THREE ELEMENTS OF A PRIMING DATE

1. The priming date is short

When you are seducing a woman, you want to spend as little time with her as possible before having sex because the less time you spend with her, the less time you have to make a mistake fatal to the seduction. You want to take as much time as necessary, but not an instant more. Every unnecessary interaction is just another opportunity to bungle it up.

Before the date, a woman is looking for reasons to get rid of you. Earlier we talked about how, when a woman dates someone, her orderly existence becomes shaken up. All of us resist change, even change that would make us happy. In some corner of her mind, the woman you are interested in is looking for some justification to get you out of her life. The more time you give her to find one, the more likely she is to do just that.

Once a woman has had sex with you, the rules change. Now instead of trying to justify getting rid of you, she's trying to justify why you were worth having sex with in the first place. Instead of being on the hunt for your bad points, she's more likely to be on the lookout for the good. If you spend lots and lots of time with her before sex, you spend too much time on the wrong side of the equation. Priming dates, while important, must be short.

When Bob went out with Marcella for the first time, he disobeyed this rule. He had told her that the date would last no longer than an hour. He met her for coffee. Things went so well he figured he would stretch the date out even longer. Eventually Marcella had her fill of him, and suggested that it was time for her to leave. "Oh, do you have to? Gee, when can we go out again?," Bob found himself whining. He had put himself into a powerless, one-down position, and, as a result, looked like a jerk.

When Bruce met Wendy for coffee, he knew that if things went well, that that was an even *better* reason to keep the date short. "Well, I really have to go," he said after 30 minutes. Wendy looked sad that he was leaving, because she was having such a good time. He left her wanting more rather than satisfying, or even overdoing, her interest in him. As a result, she was very receptive to his idea that they go out again.

We suggest a priming date be 30 minutes to 75 minutes long, and no longer. If you are having such a great time together, that's wonderful. Leave before you blow it, and invest her enjoyment of you into your seduction date.

2. The priming date takes place in coffee shops or another quiet public place

Having the priming date in a public place, like a coffee shop, helps her feel safe and unpressured. After all, she reasons, what can you do to her in a coffee shop? Contrast this to a first date where you invite the woman over for dinner at your house. That is a scary first date for most women. Many will find a reason to back out at the last moment. A coffee date, on the other hand, is in full view of everybody, so she knows she will be physically safe.

You want to choose a place that isn't too noisy, and where you won't run into your friends or hers. If you know that a certain coffee shop is a hang-out for her and her friends, suggest a different one. You don't want her distracted, or showing off for her friends.

You shouldn't choose a restaurant. You want her to be focused on you, not her food. If you invite her out for a meal, she is more likely to see you as just a dinner companion or, worse, a ticket to a free meal. You don't want her to be distracted by the waiter or by the taste of her food. You want the focus to be on you and the romantic possibilities between the two of you. Besides, a restaurant date will take longer, start to finish, and is more of an emotional commitment for her than a coffee date is.

When you ask her out, you must have a place in mind. Be sure the location of that place is clear. One student, Larry, asked a woman to meet him at "The Cafe Espresso on Main Street," not realizing that there were actually *two* franchises of that cafe on opposite ends of the street. His date went to one, and he went to the other, and they never did meet up. Be clear where the date is, and be able to give her simple directions if she needs them.

3. The priming date is not a time to socialize

By "socialize" we mean "hang out and talk without a purpose." That is the *last* thing you want to be doing before you've had sex with her. Hanging out and talking without a purpose is something you do with your male friends. With a woman, you must remember that dating and friendship are completely different, and cancel each other out. You can't serve both masters. You can only do one or the other. It's like drinking and driving; you either get to drink, or you get to drive. You can't do both. You must decide whether a woman is going to be a friend or a potential lover, and stick with it. Just hanging out and talking without an outcome in mind will default you into "friend" mode every time.

Your purpose for the priming date is to charm her, and to get her ready for the next level of your seduction. This chapter discusses exactly how you go about accomplishing these noble goals.

BEFORE THE PRIMING DATE

As you are well aware by now, you must do much of the work of the date before the date actually begins. In this way, dating a woman is like painting a house. When you think about painting, you probably imagine using a brush or roller or sprayer, slowly and methodically covering the surface of the building with paint.

If you've done much painting, you know that the actual painting is only the most glamorous part of the project. In advance you have to prepare the surface, which can take a lot longer than the painting itself does. You have to get off the old paint, layer by layer. You spend days scraping, or slopping on paint-removing chemicals. You have to make sure the wood itself is sound, and if it isn't, you have to repair or replace it. Only once you have everything set up properly does the painting go easily and smoothly. Even then, you have to put on a priming coat before you put on the color you really want. If you refuse or forget to do the pre-work, your painting experience will be a disaster.

Likewise, when you think about dating a woman, your mind probably tends to jump right to the actual date itself. After you've practiced our techniques, however, you'll understand that the date itself is only the most glamorous part of the project. Just as you must prepare the surface before you paint, you must prepare for the date before you go on it. The downside is, this takes some time and energy. The upside is, if you do it properly, it will make the date a thousand times more successful.

Here's what you must do to prepare yourself for a priming date:

Think about what kind of woman she might be

You probably know her well enough to make some guesses about the kind of woman she is. Is she an intellectual, a party girl, an artist, a plain Jane, a shy fawn, an overworked mom, a rebel, or another type we've left out? Making these judgments beforehand will help you in your preparations. If the woman is an intellectual, you know you'll want to prepare to be smart and funny. It might make sense to bring along some intelligent book you are reading, so she can see and comment on it. If she is more of a rebel, it might be appropriate to bring forth the more trouble-making part of yourself. This would be a time to wear your leather jacket and dark glasses. If she's an artist type, you might want to be reading a magazine on performance art when she comes in. This isn't to say that you should invent parts of yourself that don't really exist. That would be too much work, and wouldn't work well, anyway. What you should do is take dating these different types of women as opportunities to bring out and explore the different sides of yourself. This will make the date more fun for you, and make you more successful with your prospect.

Set up the date at a time and place that truly work for you

Remember, she may well not show up (more on handling this later). If you inconvenience yourself terribly to get there, and she blows you off, you're going to feel pretty stupid.

This is actually pretty simple to do. Simply make sure that the date works for you, and don't agree to anything that doesn't. This doesn't mean that you become unwilling or intractable; any coffee date with a woman is going to be less convenient than sitting at home. But canceling an important meeting or driving two hours for a date with a woman who may not show up is simply unacceptable.

Know what you will do if she doesn't show up

Bring some work to do, or a great book to read. Be ready to flirt with the other women at the coffee shop. Never, *ever*, let yourself get into a situation where you are sitting waiting for a woman to show up with nothing to do. It's humiliating and it makes you resentful. Your attitude should be that you are just as happy being there alone as you are with her showing up. Bringing things to do that will satisfy you is the best way to do this.

Remember your outcome

Before you go on the priming date, it's critical that you get clear about what you want your outcome to be. Do you want her to feel attracted to you, interested, aroused? Make sure you know how you want her to feel at the end of the date, so you'll have a target to shoot for, and a standard against which to measure possible topics of conversation.

Create a list of romantic and sensual questions you can ask her

We talked about the importance of romantic questions while flirting with a woman. Those questions are also important on the priming date. Remember, asking the proper romantic questions is one of the fastest ways to achieve your goal of getting her thinking romantically about you. This isn't just "making conversation." This is where the rubber hits the road.

Most romantic questions have three parts:

1. The excuse,
2. The description,
3. The question.

While this isn't always true, and the three parts aren't always in this order, if you follow this pattern, you'll be easily able to create romantic questions which will get women talking about romance.

The *excuse* is the part where you briefly explain why you are about to ask the question. The excuse is something like "A friend of mine and I were talking about this, and I wonder about your opinion on it..." or "I saw a TV show last night that got me thinking about the idea of attraction..." or "I've been having a lot of fun lately asking people this question about romance..."

The second part is the *description*. Before asking the romantic question, briefly describe the feeling you want her to experience. This might be "It was so romantic, the way they felt drawn together, the chemistry slowly building until they had that romantic, passionate first kiss." It might be "your heart just opened up, and you could feel your defenses dropping for that incredible man."

The third part is the *question* itself. It is "what was your first kiss like?" or "what's the most romantic thing you ever experienced?" Put it all together, and it looks like this:

* "You know, I saw a TV show last night where these two teenagers fell in love and were having their first kiss. It was so romantic, the way they felt drawn together, the chemistry

slowly building until they had that romantic, passionate first kiss. It got me thinking. . . I'd be curious, what was your first kiss like?"

* "Do you remember the first time you fell in love? Everything seemed so fresh and new and amazing, remember? It was like that first time when you really understand that someone really likes you, just the way you are. If you don't mind me asking, what was that like for you?"

* "My friend Mary was just telling me about the most romantic date she was ever on. It was amazing. Imagine this: you are out with a man you really like and find really attractive. You are sitting in this gorgeous outdoor restaurant, overlooking a lake. The autumn colors are just perfect. The air is fresh and smells so great, you feel like you don't even need to eat, just sit there and breathe that sweet air. Anyway, that's how she put it. And you have this incredible date as the sun goes down over the water, the stars come out and then the moon rises, and the two of you feel so connected, so in love, you know what I mean? What would you say is your most romantic moment ever?"

* "I was having this discussion with my friend, and I wonder what you think. Do you believe in love at first sight? Where you see someone and you just feel that 'click,' and it's like, even though you are meeting for the first time, you feel like you've known him forever? Or does that feeling of attraction just build inside of you, slowly? Have either of these ever happened to you?"

* "Do you believe in destiny, like certain things or relationships are predestined to happen? I am sure you know the feeling when you see someone and you just feel that 'click,' and even though you are meeting for the first time, you feel like you've known him forever? Has that ever happened to you?"

* "My friend Suzy is falling in love. It's so fun to watch. She was telling me about meeting this man and feeling like she'd known him all her life. Like she felt like 'Oh, it's you,' even though they had just met. Have you ever met someone and just felt like you'd known him forever?"

* "I've been thinking how great it would be to take a vacation, and asking people what they've done that they really loved.

It's been fascinating to hear about people's ideal vacation experiences. What's your absolute fantasy vacation?"

* "You know, it's interesting how different people feel special in different ways. I mean, it's like each person has his or her own code for feeling special, connected, and really loved. I'm curious; how do you know when a man really appreciates you?"

If these questions seem too personal, you can always ask questions about *women*, rather than about her. She'll tell you the same kind of answer, either way. For instance, instead of asking "how do you know when a man really appreciates you?" you can ask "how does a woman know when a man really appreciates her?" The answer will be the same.

Men tend to think the mood has to be right to ask questions like these. It's a tricky issue, because the mood that is right for these questions is created by questions precisely like these. By asking these and similar questions, you help build the romantic mood that makes this kind of talk appropriate. You've just gotta jump in and start asking them.

Also, don't be afraid to memorize these questions word for word, exactly the way we've said them here. There's a huge difference between asking about a first kiss the way we put it here and saying, "Hey, what was your first kiss like?" with no excuse or description.

You also won't want to fire these questions off in a row. It'll sound odd. You're not interrogating her. If you do ask a romantic question, and then want to ask another one later, you can simply say "I don't know why my mind seems so fixated on romance. Has that ever happened to you? Anyway, for some reason I'm wondering. . ." Be subtle and stay on task with these questions and it will greatly speed up the seduction process.

Learn from what she tells you

What she reveals about herself in these romantic conversations will be the base for the seduction date you will design for her later. If she tells you that her most romantic experience was when a man cooked for her, you'll want to make dinner for her next time. If she tells you she loves romantic walks, you'll want to set one up, complete with blankets and wine and cheese. Remember, you aren't just making random conversation. You have a job to do. The beauty of romantic questions is that they not only put her into a romantic mood, but give you the data you need to get her clothes off as efficiently as possible. Pay attention to what she says. Excuse yourself to the bathroom to take notes if it'll help you remember. Definitely take notes right after the date, while it's still fresh in your mind.

Have answers to those romantic questions prepared

As you ask your romantic questions, you'll find that, aside from answering them, your date will often also ask them back to you. Very young, attractive women will often go an entire date without asking you *anything* about yourself. This is just as well. The less she learns about you, the less she can learn that will make her decide that she shouldn't date you. Much of the time, though, she *will* ask you romantic questions back. She'll give you an answer, and then say "I don't know. What was your most romantic moment?"

The common mistake in this situation is to tell her about your most romantic moment as you experienced it. This is all well and good, but it doesn't necessarily forward the seduction. If you want to move forward, you must answer this question by describing your romantic experience, or a generic romantic experience, from her point of view. This gives you another opportunity to describe romantic feelings of attraction to her, and gets her even more into thinking about romance with you.

Here's how you do it. Suppose you asked your date "What's it like when you feel really special and appreciated?" She answers, and finishes up with, "Well, I guess that was it. What's it like when you feel special and appreciated?" Follow these guidelines, and you'll be golden:

Answer the question from her point of view. The way you do this is to say, "You know what it's like when you...?" You'd answer "It's great when I feel special and appreciated. You know what it's like when you feel like someone is seeing you as you really are. That person cares deeply about you and just thinks you are really great?" It's also useful to describe those feelings in the present tense. This makes it easier for her to have those feelings *now*, rather than simply imagine having had them, once upon a time. Say "It's like you can let go and be romantic," rather than, "It's like you felt you could let go and be romantic." Both will work, but using the present tense works better.

Describe the feeling you want her to have. Now describe the feelings you want her to have, from her point of view. You might say "It's like you feel as though you are melting, it's so great. You feel so connected, so much immediate trust, it's like you've known each other for years. Those are the most romantic moments for me."

Be general in what you reveal. If you describe a specific experience, do not describe the woman you were with, or how crazy you were about her. This will only put off your current date. Say "It was an incredible evening. You can imagine what it was like: walking under the open stars, the air, the perfect temperature, the smell of flowers. Then later, great wine and candlelight. Just perfect, you know?" Don't say "I was with Jessica. What a woman! She was so awesome, and an amazing body! The best time was when she'd go down on me for hours at a time!" This will annihilate your current seduction. Keep your descriptions general so that your date can feel included.

Turn romantic questions into romantic conversations

The seduction date focuses on creating experiences to make a woman feel sexual and romantic towards you. The priming date focuses on creating conversations that give her those feelings. If you want her to feel romantically attracted and strangely fascinated, you'll have to design conversations about those topics. You turn your romantic questions into romantic conversations by asking conversation-extending questions. For instance, if you ask a woman, "What was the most romantic experience you ever had?" she may tell you "It was at a restaurant in Italy. It was a perfect night, that's for sure." Don't let her stop there! Even though she's answered your question, you want her to elaborate, for two reasons. First, you want her to talk about her romantic experience so she'll remember how it felt, and start feeling that feeling now, with you. By explaining the memory, part of her will go back to that experience and begin to relive it. Second, you want to get data to use on the seduction date. If she's willing to tell you what worked on her before, you bet you want to listen! Here's a list of conversation-extending questions you can ask to keep romantic conversations going:

"Wow. What was it about that that made you feel best?"

"I am very impressed. Will you tell me more of the details?"

"Fascinating. Tell me more about [some part of the experience]."

"How did that make you feel?"

"That's amazing. Have you felt that way since?"

The three steps to practicing talking on the date

When faced off with a real live woman, you might be nervous. So it makes sense to practice whatever you can beforehand, so that it's easier to do. For this reason, we suggest you practice your romantic questions and answers *out loud* before the date. We know it sounds silly, but it can really make a difference in how well you lead the conversation when it really counts. By practicing you will get used to saying romantic things and begin to relax and speak with an easier flow. Use the following three steps of practice, and the romantic questions will melt any woman in sight.

First, practice the questions, as they are written above, out loud until you think you can say at least a few of them by heart. Second, imagine her responses, and practice saying the conversation-extending questions out loud as well. Third, practice answering all your romantic questions, in case she asks them back to you.

Get yourself psyched up

Use the techniques we described in Chapter 3 to get yourself ready for the date.

Prepare for success

Our students are often caught by surprise when these techniques work. At the end of his priming date with Jeanette, Morris went for the first kiss (as we'll show you how to do), and succeeded. "I was shocked, as I was kissing her," he told us. "I couldn't believe how enthusiastic her response was. I found myself walking away after the kiss, dumbfounded. I didn't realize 'til later that I could have kissed her more, and perhaps even gone somewhere and had sex with her right then!"

You prepare for success by being ready to have the outcome you ultimately want happen much faster than you anticipate. Have a condom along, and have an idea of where you could go to have sex if it turns out she is ready. If she really responds to your first kiss, go for more. You don't want to be kicking yourself later, like Morris was, for walking away from a primed and ready woman.

BEFORE THE PRIMING DATE CHECKLIST

* Bathe
* Smell good
* Shave
* Brush teeth
* Look in mirror at general appearance
* Hair looks good
* Clothes look good on your body, are cleaned, ironed if needed, not stained or dirty
* Have things to do while you wait for her
* Have a watch with you
* Have prepared at least three romantic questions/conversations
* Be psyched up
* Have car clean
* Plan to stay only 30-75 minutes
* Have money
* Have your outcomes clearly in mind
* Have a place to go if she wants sex
* Have condoms
* Have practiced romantic questions/conversations out loud
* Leave home on time to arrive early
* Have a plan for what you would like to do on a next date

USE YOUR BODY TO CONVEY THAT YOU HAVE VITALITY AND GENERATIVITY

Before you go to meet her, it's worth looking once again at that slippery beast called *attitude*. All the tools, skills, practices and checklists in this book are designed to give you a sense that you know what you are doing, which will help you have that confident attitude women respond to so well. But remember, what skill and "attitude" really convey is vitality and generativity. If you are a vital, fully alive, creative beast of a man, woman will desire you, and want to have sex with you. As you are carrying out the technology in this book, it's critical that you do it with a vital and energetic flair.

When you are feeling vital, powerful and alive, you move your body differently than you do when you are feeling depressed, unhappy, and hopeless. By changing the way you use your body, you can alter how you feel, and thus how other people relate to you. Remember, the woman is looking to you for certainty that the date is going well. If you look to her for that, you are doomed. By using your body, you can create that certain, powerful feeling that will help her feel safe.

Try this now: as you are reading this, move your body so you are sitting as though you are reading the most fascinating, exciting thing you've ever read. You may find you lean forward, and that your expression changes. Now sit as though you are an incredibly together, attractive, powerful masculine man who is on fire about his life. Breathe that way. Actually do it! This is the kind of posture you want to have when you are on the priming date. You don't have to start out feeling powerful and certain to do this. You can create the feeling any time you want by using your body.

If you do this, and don't rely on her for validation that the date is going well, you will have presence and charisma that she will notice. You will have that mysterious thing called "attitude." Add to this your romantic questions and conversations, and she'll be desiring you before the date is over.

ON THE DATE

Okay. You've done all the pre-work. You asked her out, set the time and place that was convenient for you, and committed yourself to not more than about an hour of your time. You've prepared and practiced your romantic questions and conversations. You are absolutely crystal clear about what your outcomes are. You've psyched yourself up, and are using your body to convey your vitality and generativity. To return to our painting metaphor, you've prepared the surface, and you are ready to paint!

Men often ask us if they should be late for the priming date. After all, they reason, if you make her wait, you'll have power over her, and won't be in one-down position. There are several flaws in this way of thinking. First, she will almost certainly be later than you. If you get into a little competition to see who can be latest, she will probably win. Second, if you arrive late and apologize, you don't appear especially powerful; you just look as if you have no control over your life. If you arrive late and don't apologize, it's even worse. In that case, you just look like a jerk.

We recommend that you arrive early, with something to do. When she arrives you are so involved in what you are doing, you may not even notice her until she arrives at your table. This shows that you are just as happy being there alone as you are being with her. As women routinely miss priming dates, it makes sense to be enjoying yourself anyway.

YOUR PRIMING DATE TO-DO LIST

As the priming date proceeds, you'll want to do things that convey your romantic interest, and which pique hers. Every moment of the priming date won't be taken up with romantic talk. For most women, that would appear strange. It's perfectly acceptable to ask her about her job, family, and so forth. At some point in the conversation, though, you are going to want to take a deep breath, get into a physical position of confidence, and do the following things:

Touch her at least five times

Touching a woman casually and nonintrusively establishes a precedent that will help you touch her more intimately later. It gets her used to accepting your touch, and even shows her that it can feel good.

These touches are quick, gentle, and over with before she has a chance to get uncomfortable. You may touch her arm for a moment when talking, to emphasize a particular point, or touch her back while directing her to your table.

Sometimes men get flustered, and find they have forgotten how to do this simple thing. It's easy; as you gesture with your body, there are times when your hands are far from your body. Those are the moments to push one hand a bit farther, and to touch her.

Touch her hand at least once

This touch is a bit more intimate, a bit more intrusive. You simply put your hand on hers for a moment to emphasize some point you are making, look into her eyes, then take it away.

Look into her eyes "too long"

This creates a moment of intimacy that shows her your romantic interest. You should look into her eyes when you are talking to her, at least from time to time. It's not a staring contest, and hard, long stares are commonly considered aggressive. But even if you are in the habit of never looking into a woman's eyes when you interact with her, you should at least do it occasionally. It shows her you aren't scared and, if you do it in a relaxed manner, shows her you are willing to be open and honest with her.

Once during the date, you should establish eye contact, and hold it for a fraction of a second longer than is comfortable, then look away to some other part of her face. This is especially intimate and romantic. It's a subtle way of getting her to open her "personal space" to you that prepares her for opening up even more, later.

Check out her body one time

Wait, wait! Before you ogle at her like a stripper at a bar, let us explain to you how to check out a woman's body without offending her. It's a weird dichotomy. On the one hand, women are offended if you ogle their bodies. On the other hand, they go out of their way to make their bodies attractive to look at. If you look the wrong way, she may be offended. If you don't, however, you run the risk of giving the impression that you aren't interested in her sexually. You handle this problem by looking at her body quickly. Start by looking in her eyes, then quickly, in less than a second, let your eyes sweep over her body. Then return to her eyes. By returning to her eyes, you show her that you are not ashamed of having looked at her body, and that you still want to connect with her. Do this once or twice (but not more) during your conversation with her, and it will help reinforce the romantic mood.

Make decisions easily

We've talked about this before, and will only touch on it now to remind you of its importance. Being decisive is attractive. Being indecisive is unattractive. Choose.

Wink at her one time

Winking creates a little moment of intimacy between you and someone else. Have you ever had a woman wink at you? You shared a special connection, a momentary little world just for the two of you. When you wink at a woman, you do this for her. Make the wink fast; it's not like lowering a garage door. And smile; it's not some big significant event.

Ask your romantic questions

The first step to having romantic conversations is asking your romantic questions. If you never do this, she is *much* less likely to think of you as potential romantic material, and you may find yourself in the "friend" category once again. Just open your mouth and say the lines you've memorized, even if you are uncomfortable. You can only start at the beginning and go from there.

Manage romantic conversations

Draw out her responses by asking the conversation-extending questions which you, of course, memorized before the date. You'll probably find this part easier than you think. When a person starts telling you about her peak experiences, it's easy to become genuinely interested. When she returns the questions, and asks you about *your* romantic peaks, be ready to tell her about them by describing lush romantic feelings.

Keep your body powerful

Keep sitting like you are fascinated and fascinating.

Use "seduction" words

Some words are more romantic than others. Words like "urine" or "foreclosure" are less romantic than words like "seduced," "attracted," "romance," or "love." You want to use romantic words in your conversation as much as you can, without looking like you are crazy. This means using the words more than you are comfortable with, but allowing other conversation to happen as well.

Here's a list of romantic words and phrases. You may find others to add to this partial list:

Seduced

Attracted

Falling in love

Romance

Warm and safe

Elegant

Sensual

Dreamy

Passionate

Feeling in your body

Exquisite

Exotic

Erotic

Magical

Special

Whisper or change vocal tone one time. While this isn't appropriate on all priming dates, if things are going well, it can help push the romantic interaction to the next level.

Whispering to her is powerful for a number of reasons. First, when you whisper, you command her attention more fully. If she doesn't pay attention, she'll miss what you are saying. Second, when you whisper, you create a little world that is for the two of you only. Third, you have to get closer to her to whisper. If you lean across the table to whisper, your mouth can get perilously close to her ear. It's intimate, yet easy for her to accept. This makes it easier for her to accept your romantic approaches later.

Compliment her three times

In the film *An American President*, the President, played by Michael Douglas, was about to go on his first date since his wife died. His daughter advised him to "compliment her shoes. Girls like that." Mystified, he complied, much to the pleasure of his date. Women love to have their looks noticed and complimented. They work hard and long to look good for us. Why not notice it?

Obviously, your compliments won't be too sexual in nature. "Your breasts look so great in that outfit, I can hardly keep my hands off them" is only one step above professing a fascination with serial killers in terms of destroying any possible romance. Try complimenting her shoes, if they are at all nice. Tell her she has a wonderful sense of style, or a beautiful smile. Find *something* and praise it.

The only exception to this rule: if a woman is extremely beautiful, and knows it, a man complimenting her is nothing unusual. In fact, some such women may hold it against you if you do. One woman told us, "A guy compliments my body. Great. Another guy who wants me. How original. Who cares?" If you must compliment them, find something unusual to focus on. Oscar met Sheila at a global warming lecture. She was staggeringly beautiful. He didn't want to just be another guy groveling before her good looks. On their priming date he told her, "You know, you're real pretty and everything, but when I knew I had to meet you was when you asked that question at the lecture. I said to myself, 'I've got to know this woman.'" He managed to compliment her on something unusual—her intelligence—while still acknowledging her good looks. She was impressed, rather than simply throwing his compliment on the pile with all the others.

Have fun

Like "have a good attitude," "have fun" is one of those commands that people give you without ever telling you how to do it. We suggest that, on the priming date, you remember that one of the purposes of going is to have fun, and that if the opportunity arises to actually enjoy yourself, you should take it. Study all these guidelines before the date, but on the date, let yourself relax and forget them from time to time. If you've studied first, your brain will be able to keep you on track. While this is work, it shouldn't be laborious. Remembering to have fun can help.

10 POSSIBLE PROBLEMS ON THE PRIMING DATE

Not all priming dates go hitch-free. Lots of things can, and do, go wrong. However, everything doesn't have to go right for the date to be a success. The moment a problem happens on a date, most men panic and think the whole thing is ruined; this simply is not true. But you do have to be able to handle problems as they arise. Fortunately, you have our watchful guidance to help you solve whatever they might be.

1. She doesn't show up

The most common problem is that she doesn't even bother to show up. Astonishingly, women "forget" coffee dates very, very often. Attractive women in their early twenties are especially susceptible to this. As you begin dating a variety of women, it is inevitable that some will stand you up.

Actually, having a woman stand you up is a good experience. It teaches you not to take dating so personally. It teaches you not to rely on women to make you feel good, or to solve your problems.

When a woman stands you up, you remain responsible for your feelings, your beliefs about yourself in the face of rejection, and your life. Here's how to make a "stand-up" work for you.

Don't take it personally. Of course your date is late. Of course she's standing you up. This doesn't mean she doesn't like you, or won't eventually end up sleeping with you. She just got scared, or involved in something else that seemed more important, or just didn't feel like coming to the date. She may even have forgotten. Don't worry about it. We'll show you in a bit how to turn the entire scenario around on her, and actually use her standing you up to forward your seduction.

Don't jump to conclusions. Amazingly, she still might be very interested in you. She just didn't feel like showing up. We know this is astounding, but you must get used to it. Some extremely attractive women would literally never think to lift a finger to pursue, or even keep their word with, men they want to be with. Denise was one of these women. When she met Steve, she was very interested in him. She told her friends "He seems so cute, and smart, and fun." But she never did anything to pursue him. In fact, she did quite the reverse. She didn't return his two phone calls, and when he finally did set up a priming date, she didn't show up. But she was still interested. You must understand that this kind of thing really does happen.

And, of course, there may be a legitimate reason for her absence besides she "forgot," or didn't feel like coming. People do get lost or have emergencies. When Sunshine didn't show up for her priming date with Alvin, it turned out that two of her friends had died in a car accident. His anger disappeared pretty quickly when he found this out, and he offered his shoulder for her to cry on instead.

How to handle a no-show. First, you wait only 15 minutes for her to arrive. If you are still there when she arrives 20, 30, or 40 minutes later, all you are doing is showing her that you are a worm who will still be there for her, no matter how she treats you. If she shows up 30 minutes late and you are gone, it shows her that she has to treat your time as respectfully as she'd like her own treated. If a woman isn't there by 15 minutes after you've scheduled the date, there is only a small chance she will show up anyhow.

Check if she's left you a message. Sometimes when a woman is running late, or can't make it, she'll call your answering machine or voice mail to let you know. After waiting 15 minutes, check your machine. If there's no message from her, leave. If you don't have an answering machine you can check remotely, you should get one if you are going to date a lot of women. It will save you a lot of wondering time.

If she's running late and tells you, it is permissible to wait, but you should still cut the date off quickly. For instance, if your date is scheduled for noon, and at 12:15 you receive a message that she'll be a few minutes late, and she finally arrives at 12:35, it is critical that you still leave the date at a time you would have if she hadn't been late. At five to one you would warn her, "Boy, it's fun to be with you, but I have to go in a few minutes." Hopefully the shortness of the date will inspire her to be more punctual next time. If you stay extralong, and rearrange your day to accommodate her lateness, there's no reason for her to change her behavior, and she will continue to be late in the future. This will result in a pattern of inconvenience for you and will reinforce her taking advantage of you.

Call the next day and apologize for not showing up. If a woman stands you up, your call the next day is where you turn the entire humiliating experience around. Usually, we don't advocate being dishonest with women in any way. But when she stands you up, in our opinion she needs some correction. Here's how you do it.

Don't call her the day she missed the date. This is for two reasons. One, calling her that same day makes you look more desperate than you are. You want her to understand that you have a busy life, and her missing the appointment didn't throw you into a tizzy. Two, she might call you and apologize, though in our experience and that of our students, this has never happened.

Call her the next day, and *apologize for missing the date.* Even though you were there, you say "I'm so sorry I missed our date yesterday. Things just got wild at work, and I just spaced it out. I really apologize. I hope you'll let me take you out again, and make it up to you." At this point, she has two choices. One, she can say, "Oh, that's okay, I didn't show up either," which shows that she is at least honest. Two, she can lie, and say, "Yea, I waited twenty minutes, and you never came!" Either way, your response is the same. You do not call her on her lie—remember, your purpose is to seduce her, not to be right. (You do notice, however, that she is a woman who both didn't show up and lied to you about it, neither of which is a good sign.) What you do is you say, "I'm so sorry. I promise I'll make it up to you on our next date." You can then either push the program and ask her out to a more romantic date, or bring her flowers on the next priming date and more thoroughly seal your romantic interest. Set up another date and, in the guise of "making it up to her," hit on her even harder.

2. She doesn't show up repeatedly

We suggest you adopt a "three strikes and you're out" rule in your dating. If a woman doesn't show up to the *third* priming date (assuming that you told her you missed the first one, but not the second), you must tell her that it isn't personal, but if she doesn't show up to the next date, you won't be able to talk to her for a long time. If she doesn't show up again, don't call her or talk to her. If you see her on the street, ignore her to her face. While this may seem harsh, you are more likely to end up in bed with this woman if you pull the plug on her and make her work to get you back. The bottom line, forget about her and move on.

3. She brings a friend or girlfriend

If she brings a female friend she's probably bringing a chaperone to check you out. Be charming, but less pushy with the romantic questions. You can still show your interest, of course. You may even ask the other woman how she met your prospect, and talk about how you felt when you first saw her. You can say to her, "Isn't Sheila beautiful?" as a way of complimenting your date. When you call your date later (if you decide to), joke with her about hoping that you passed the test with the chaperone. She'll deny she brought the friend to help her check you out. Accept this by saying, "Of course. I was just kidding," and set up your next date.

If she brings a guy friend, your problem is more serious. Why has she brought competition? Is she so popular that she has to date in groups? It could just be that she is extremely thoughtless. Or, it could be that she is psycho. Use your psycho-spotting skills, and scale back the seduction significantly. Leave after 20 or so minutes; you won't get much done with that guy there, anyway. If you decide to call her later, again joke about hoping you passed the chaperone test. When you ask her out again, humorously request that this time she come alone.

4. She is boring or weird, but you still want to have sex with her

You will have the occasional woman who seems strange and you are completely uninterested in her intellectually, while still being hot for her body. In these situations you must move faster, take more risks, and either push the romance to its conclusion, or offend her and get her out of your life. The most common mistake men make in this situation is that they decide that making the romance move faster means not doing all the little things that make her desire you in the first place.

When Bob decided to push his seduction of Maria forward because he found her boring, he stopped touching casually, looking into her eyes, winking at her, or doing anything to make her feel special. It's as if he decided that because she wasn't special to him, he could seduce her by treating her the same way. Needless to say, when Bob lunged at Maria to plant an awkward, unprepared-for kiss, she recoiled.

A top seducer understands that, in these situations, you don't stop the romance. You stop everything else. From there it can go either way. She may well reject you, saying that though she is attracted to you, she "wants to know you better first," or she may have sex with you. You can decide from there if you want to keep seeing her.

5. Your romantic questions and talk seem to make her uncomfortable

Sometimes women squirm or get quiet when you are romancing them because they are attracted, but scared. Sometimes they do exactly the same things because they are repelled, and scared. It's hard to know the difference.

You'll learn the nuances of handling this as you practice your dating skills. As we've said before, every woman will resist dating you at first because they are resisting change. You have to push forward and keep being romantic, and wait for her to get over it. If she is profoundly uncomfortable with your romantic talk and not attracted, you'll naturally slow down. She may even tell you she's not comfortable. If she never lightens up, then don't date her again.

6. You push too hard and too fast

When you first use these tools, you are basically practicing. Because you are awkward and inexperienced, your new set of behavior, discussion, and dress styles may seem unnatural and strange to you. However, that doesn't mean that it will seem strange to her. After all, she doesn't know how you normally behave. She doesn't know that you don't usually wink, or check women out, or make romantic talk. Only you know that. Most of the time, you will be the only one feeling weird about it. That huge risk you take when you ask her about her most romantic moment doesn't seem risky to her; it is only in your head. Don't mistake your own tension for hers.

Especially at first, she may feel that you are coming on too hard and fast. She'll seem offended or pull back when you touch her. She may even ask something like "Are you doing some weird thing to seduce me?" Tell her that you like her and are interested in her, and apologize (briefly) if you are coming on too strong. Have neutral conversation about her job for a while, then start bringing the seduction back in.

7. You are intimidated by her beauty

When you first go out with a very attractive woman, it's easy to get overwhelmed with your concerns about things going wrong. After all, she's so beautiful, you'd better get it right. More than likely your fear will drive you to do things your old, unsuccessful way. This will only leave you with another beautiful female "friend." Don't default into your old ways; they won't serve you.

The best solution is to go into dates with beautiful women as if they were an experiment. When Russ first set up a date with Tina, an actress, he was overwhelmed by her beauty. And she was a real looker. She had been on the beauty pageant circuit before becoming an actress. He came to us for help preparing for the date. "I can hardly talk to her, she's so damn hot," he told us. "What can I do?"

First and foremost, we counseled Russ to look at this date as an experiment. Because this was his first truly beautiful date in his entire life, he was likely to screw up since he'd never had any practice before. We advised him not to worry about it. "The idea isn't to bed her in this case," we said. "The idea is to see how far you can get without screwing up, and to learn as much as you can from any screw-up that you make. The more you learn from this beautiful woman, the farther you'll get with the next one you find." We also told him to make sure to use his body powerfully, and to do all the confidence-building things we teach in Chapter 3.

He took our advice, and approached dating her as an experiment, rather than as a task at which he had to "succeed." As a result he learned a lot from his interactions with her, and actually got to the point of kissing her before she rejected him. Russ was thrilled he got that far, rather than depressed, and the next very hot woman he pursued, he had sex with.

8. She offends you, or you disagree strongly

Sometimes a woman is so unpleasant to be with that you change your goal. You quickly decide that it would be more enjoyable to give her a piece of your mind than it would be to sleep with her. If that is the decision you make, then by all means fight with her. Have a ball. But don't kid yourself, and think that you'll ever have sex with her or change her mind. You won't. But fighting with her is your right, if you want to do it.

If you disagree with her strongly, or she offends you, but not enough to put you off entirely, you simply must sacrifice your point of view for the seduction. But remember, if you don't like her, you don't have to sleep with her. If you are constantly pursuing and talking to women, you'll have plenty of others to choose from. You'll simply have to experiment and decide what works for you with women who offend you.

9. You don't do the little things

Because so many of the steps in romancing a woman seem so small, many men think that they can get away without doing them. They don't wink, or smile, or compliment. They decide it's okay to skip the romantic conversations. These men believe that they will get away with putting out the least amount of effort, and will start doing the little things when the woman proves her worth. This is just plain silly. If you don't do the little things, she won't be interested. Don't fall into this trap. Do the little things.

10. She wants to cry on your shoulder, but doesn't want to have sex

This is the worse-case scenario, and sometimes it does happen. Reggie liked Wanda, but when they went out she confessed that she was very confused about her sexual identity. "I really wish I wanted men, but I only desire women," she told him. "But I want to get married and be a normal person!" She went on in this vein for their entire priming date, continually re-routing all romantic conversations back into laments about her problems. At first Reggie thought she might be worth the effort. He instantly fantasized about sleeping with Wanda and one of her sexy friends, every man's fantasy. Sadly, when he asked her "Have you tried being with a man and a woman at the same time?" she was deeply offended, saying "Why do men always say that?" If you desire a woman who won't stop using you as a therapist, you should accelerate your seduction, and either get her into bed or get rid of her. When Reggie tried to kiss Wanda at the end of the date, she refused, and he never called her again.

Remember your purpose. Most of the time, a woman who wants to cry on your shoulder but doesn't want sex will continue to not want sex with you. You don't have time for this.

ENDING THE DATE AND DANGLING THE BAIT

You are leaving the priming date. How do you know if you should make a pass at her, or wait until the next time?

In terms of the seduction, you are better off kissing her quickly if you can. If you kiss her, she's left having to give herself reasons why she did the right thing by allowing it. If you don't kiss, it leaves her more easily able to think of you as a friend. The downside of kissing her at the end of the priming date is that, if she's not ready, you risk blowing what you've worked for.

There are logistical considerations as well. If she decides to stay behind at the coffee shop, it's harder to kiss her. If you are walking her to her car, however, the relative privacy of a parking garage might be more conducive to the first kiss. We'll discuss how you go for the first kiss (and more) in Chapter 10.

Even if she refuses your kiss, she may simply be telling you she's not ready yet, but will be. Ken tried to kiss Mindy after their priming date, standing next to her car. Realizing he was rushing things, and not sure how it would be received, he warned her first. "Oh my," he said. "I don't know if I can resist kissing you." "Please don't," she said, smiling. "It's just too soon. But you call me, how about that?" "Oh, so you want to be pursued more," Ken laughed. "I can do that. I have a feeling you are worth every minute." She laughed, and got into her car, and he walked away. A success, even though he didn't get what he was after. Mindy made it clear that all he had to do was more work, and he could have her. Ken didn't object to doing the work, so he left feeling happy and confident about the seduction.

If you have a clear idea in mind for the seduction date, it's perfectly fine to ask her out and make the plans at the end of the priming date. Simply say, "This has been great, and I'd like to see you again." It's better to nail things down when you are with her. In this age of phone tag and people who can't make plans without their three-ring filo-fax binders, it can be a lot easier to just set up the next date right then. It is also good to ask her out while she is right in front of you, feeling the joy that you created on the date, rather than later when she's had lots of time to think about why you are a jerk. Be general, unless you have a seduction date strategy already in mind. Set a date, and ask her when the best time is to call her to set up the details. Your next stop is to design your seduction date strategy.

AFTER THE DATE "DID" CHECKLIST

* Asked the romantic questions you memorized
* Conducted the romantic conversations you prepared
* Touched her hand
* Looked into her eyes, a little too long
* Cut the date short (75 minutes tops)
* Touched her nonintrusively and casually
* Made decisions quickly and easily
* Made her smile and/or laugh at least one time
* Pursued your goals
* Made your romantic interest known
* Were early and absorbed in something else when she arrived
* Gathered information about her romantic needs
* Complimented her five times
* Had fun at least 40 seconds
* Checked out her body in the way specified
* Used seductive language (seduce, attraction, falling in love, romance, etc.) seven times
* Used interested body language
* Whispered at least once
* Took notes about what makes her feel romantic afterwards.

AFTER THE DATE "DIDN'T" CHECKLIST

(The nine date-killers)

* Didn't treat her like a friend
* Didn't insult her
* Didn't complain
* Didn't complain about other women
* Didn't check out other women
* Didn't grab her ass

* Didn't rely on her for certainty that the date was going well
* Didn't allow yourself to get upset when you forgot your lines, etc.
* Didn't take anything she said or did personally.

AFTER THE PRIMING DATE STUDY QUESTIONS

We recommend that you sit yourself down and ask yourself a few questions after the priming date. Whether or not it went the way you wanted, you can learn from the experience and be a more skillful seducer in the future.

* Is she worth the work she will probably be? How much do you want her? How much work are you willing to put in?
* What did you learn about what is important to her in relationships and dating?
* What worked, and made her feel especially connected to you?
* What didn't work, and seemed to make her feel more separate from you?
* What did she like about you?
* How responsive was she to romantic and sexual talk?
* How was the date a success?
* What did you learn about seduction?
* What does your intuition tell you about seducing this woman?
* How psycho is she?
* Does she live with her parents, or in some other arrangement where it might be hard to have sex with her?
* Does she seem to prefer me acting dominant or submissive?
* What topics should I avoid and/or pursue?
* What seductive conversation worked best?
* What is the cost/benefit ratio?
* Which of the four kinds of women is she?

PASSING THE PRIMING DATE
WITH FLYING COLORS

When Bruce went out with Wendy, he passed the priming date with flying colors. When she arrived, he was absorbed in his book, an intellectual work called *Sex and the Brain*. Her "hello" popped him back to reality, and he greeted her. "Wow, hi. I was so absorbed in this book, I didn't see you come in." Wendy, an intellectual type, was immediately impressed and interested in his book. This led to conversation about sex and how men and women become attracted to one another. Bruce took the opportunity to use seduction words, like "romance," "attracted," "chemistry," and so on.

He also used the conversation as an opening to ask her about her romantic experiences, and how those experiences felt to her. After telling him about her most romantic date ever, Wendy laughed and said "I feel like I'm telling you everything about me! Now you'll know everything about romancing me!" "Well, that's just great," Bruce responded. He leaned forward, whispering more intimately. "But trust me, I have a few romantic surprises for a beautiful woman like you that you haven't seen before." He smiled conspiratorially. "You'll see," Bruce said, as he leaned back, and winked. For the duration of the date he made decisions easily, and used his body to convey his vitality and interest in her. He touched Wendy's arm several times, and then placed his hand on hers.

At one point, while Bruce was describing a romantic experience of his in response to her "what about you?" question, he said "it felt so beautiful to connect, you know what I mean?" and reached out to lightly touch her cheek for a moment. She blushed, and they went on with their conversation. He held her eye contact a fraction too long, and, as he was getting up to leave, checked out her body one time.

Wendy was awed by and attracted to Bruce's confidence. She was surprised by how naturally she found herself thinking romantically about him. She didn't realize that he'd left her little alternative. He was obviously not going to be a friend; all of his behaviors told her that. Bruce showed his interest in her romantically and skillfully. She either had to think of him as possible romantic material, or as a pushy jerk. Either way was fine with Bruce, because either option moved him closer to his goal. If she thought of him romantically, she was more likely to go to bed with him. If she thought of him as a pushy jerk, she'd get out of his life and he'd have more time to pursue other women.

After 40 minutes Bruce got up to leave. "Well, it's been great seeing you," he told her. "How about we get together again?" "That'd be great," she said. "Please call me!" At that moment, he could either set up the date then, go for an early kiss, or leave and call her later. He had choices, power, and the date was cheap and didn't take too long. By following our directions, Bruce put himself on the road to romance. If you follow them, so will you.

chapter eight...
The Seduction Date

After a successful "priming" date, Bruce knew Wendy was interested in him. She seemed sad that the last date ended, and kept staring and smiling at him throughout the time they were together. When he winked and checked out her body, she still smiled. Bruce knew that if he had made the first move, they definitely would have been making out near the coffee shop, but he didn't want to push things too hard, too early. Bruce looked forward to turning up the romance on a seduction date. He found her attractive, intelligent, and sweet. They had been on the priming date only a week before, but Bruce wanted to move quickly. His next step was to create an afternoon adventure, a date that would provide fond memories. A magical afternoon.

Bruce waited until Thursday to call Wendy. She sounded happy on the phone. After a few minutes of chitchat, he asked her out for Saturday. "I can hardly wait to see you," she said. "We will be going on a secret adventure," Bruce warned. "I love secret adventures," she responded. Bruce's only instructions were that she dress like a sexy female FBI agent who was going on a bust. She laughed and said "OK." Bruce hung up the phone excited about the date. He couldn't wait.

The purpose of a seduction date is to create romantic experiences which lead to sex. Priming dates create rapport through conversations; seduction dates do this through experiences. A seduction date assumes that she knows you are interested in her romantically, and she is still interested in dating you. On priming dates you research the qualities she looks for in a man, and the experiences she considers romantic. All this information comes together on a seduction date.

After four priming dates with Kathy, Bob decided to take her on a seduction date. Even though she didn't seem that interested in him, and they never came close to kissing, Bob wanted to move things to the next level. He failed to notice that Kathy had ended all the dates first. On one date, she asked to borrow money, and kept asking him to pay for dinner at expensive restaurants. At no point did she exude any interest in him at all. Not only was Bob a sucker, but he was nowhere near ready to be on a seduction date with her. Bob didn't generate any romantic feelings with Kathy on the date, nor did he create much of a connection. He rarely asked her romantic questions and gave off a weird vibe. Bob did not come across as boyfriend material. He would have been better off going out with any other woman, rather than trying to force Kathy to be on a date with him.

On his 30-minute priming date, Bruce left Wendy wanting more. They constantly talked about romantic topics. He found out her favorite type of movies (science fiction), food (Chinese), that she loved nature and animals. Her ideal Sunday morning was to wake up with her lover, have him go out and get *The New York Times* and bagels, and have them cuddle in bed, drinking coffee, reading for hours. He frequently touched her and kissed her hand. By the end of the date, they were laughing, having a great time.

THE EIGHT COMPONENTS OF A TRIUMPHANT SEDUCTION DATE

1. The seduction date takes place over many hours.

On a priming date, you focused on *not* spending too much time with the woman, because there was a good chance you would blow it by saying something stupid. The purpose of these dates is to leave the woman wanting more. On a seduction date, it is useful to you spend at least four hours together. Romance and feelings of sexiness usually take several hours to build. They are a series of progressive successes stacked on top of one another. One reason why the seduction date takes longer is that women usually love the courting process. For them it is like a cat-and-mouse game. They get to be the cat, and you the mouse. They get to be in charge, and have you running all over the place trying to impress them and prove that you are patient in a game that requires many hours to play.

Another reason why seduction dates take longer is that it gives the woman a justification to sleep with you. Most women feel bad about themselves when and if they meet a guy at a bar and go home with him. They often regret the experience and avoid the guy. When you spend many hours with them, it is easier for them to justify being sexual.

Jim took Sandy on a seduction date. It was winter in Colorado and snowy. On a priming date he found out that they both loved winter sports, especially skiing. He had been an avid skier for the past 15 years, and she, too, loved to be on the slopes.

As a result of their shared interests, Jim set up a day-long ski trip for the two of them. He found a remote resort few people visited. It was very out-of-the-way, and only the most devoted ski bums knew of it. Though it wasn't as high quality as the more popular sights, it would be a better place, he figured, to create a romantic outing. They arrived around 1:00 pm on a warm Sunday. It was a perfect day to be out, and there was hardly anyone else skiing. Jim flirted with Sandy all day. On a break, they held hands, talked, and laughed. It not only took them away from her normal circumstances, but it gave Jim hours to flirt and connect with her. Later that night, after a wonderful meal. They went to her apartment, watched movies on her couch, and kissed for hours. They did everything short of making love. The date ended perfectly.

2. Seduction dates make the woman feel special

Priming dates focus on deepening the connection between the two of you. How you relate to one another changes, from acquaintances to possible dating partners. The date invokes romantic feelings between the two of you by making her feel special and appreciated. Priming dates address her concern about whether or not you are safe to date. Seduction dates address her questions about whether you are a potential boyfriend or not.

If you are like most men, you would sleep with a woman regardless of whether or not she seems like a potential girlfriend. Women, on the other hand, often search for a potential mate. Single women over 30 tend to focus on men who are "marriage material." Your job is to come across as the type of man who can fit her desires, no matter what they are. When you spend hours together it helps you seem like the boyfriend she has always wanted. You are not only spending quality time with her, but courting her in the ways she wants.

A woman—any woman—wants to feel special. It is your job to make her feel that way. For most women, the man of their dreams appreciates how they dress, the topics they discuss, their interests, and much more. Given that you are striving to be viewed as a potential boyfriend, it would help the situation for you to also take an interest in these subjects. Their ideal boyfriend would most likely give them long back rubs, hold them close, pay for dates, and enjoy kissing softly in the moonlight. If that is what they desire, do those actions. You'll probably find you even enjoy them. Seduction dates work best if you go into them looking at giving her what she wants, rather than expecting her to give you what you want.

One way to make a woman feel special is to make the seduction date a celebration for her. This means you do things she would like to do. As a rule of thumb, stay focused on her and her desires throughout the date, making her feel special, but find a way to have a good time for you, too. Do this when you plan the date, are on the date, and afterwards when you evaluate the date. Later in the chapter we will cover the specific techniques you can use to acknowledge her and make her melt.

If a woman feels as though you are just using her for sex, she probably won't sleep with you. Even if she is the type to have one-night stands, she will want to know that you appreciate something about her personality. She wants to know you think of her more than just a woman to have sex with. The most efficient way to accomplish this is to imagine you are her, and imagine what you would like to do, and how you would want to be treated. Chances are that you won't be able to fully understand where she is coming from, but it will be a good way to guide your behavior nonetheless.

If you can pour on the charm, women will often feel appreciated. Charm is based on respect. You must respect her likes and dislikes. Even if you don't think of yourself as a sensitive guy, it is important to respect her wishes and her boundaries during the date. If not, you will blow your chances.

FROM TRASH TO TREASURE: THE ROMANTIC POWER OF LITTLE GIFTS PROPERLY GIVEN

Another way to show your appreciation is through little gifts. Women love gifts; who doesn't? The great part of "little gifts" is that you can give her a very inexpensive gift and it will melt her heart almost as much as an expensive one. We highly recommend that you do this on seduction dates to increase the feelings of romance and affiliation.

Little gifts serve many purposes. First, their "surprise factor" can be used to get her attention. By giving her something she doesn't expect, it shows you are interested and thoughtful. Second, it shows you are generous. Third, she will feel appreciated and cared for because you went through the trouble of purchasing something for her. Fourth, little gifts give something tangible from the date to remind her of you after she goes home. If it is a gift she enjoys, she will probably stare at it or use it long after the date is over. Even something silly like a Wonder Woman key chain can help remind her of how fun and crazy the date was. She will probably look at the chain and laugh, thinking about a joke you told, or how surprised she was to see a plastic statue of her childhood cartoon super hero. The gift will actually anchor more romantic and good feelings to you, even when you are not around.

As important as the gift itself is how well it is wrapped. This is critical. The act of unwrapping a present is an exciting ritual for her, and you will enjoy watching her do it. If the gift is inexpensive, as it should be, wrapping it well makes it ten times more special than it would be unwrapped. Remember, you want to give her a good experience. Unwrapping a gift is an experience she'll remember for a long time to come.

The Five Rules for Gift Giving

1. It must be wrapped nicely
2. It must be in good taste (nothing like a huge vibrating hand or a deck of cards from Hooters)
3. It must be inexpensive
4. It must be either fun, funny (to her), or romantic
5. It must be given at random times. You don't want a woman to start expecting and demanding gifts on every date.

Examples of cheap gifts women love:

* Stuffed animals
* Chocolate
* Cute cards
* Funny pens
* A memento you buy while on the date
* Flowers
* A cheap license plate with her name on it from a travel store
* A CD of good romantic music
* A funny toy
* Bath soap
* Food
* Massage oil
* A goofy hat
* A shell from the ocean
* A book

3. The seduction date takes place in an out-of-the-ordinary place

You must take a woman out of her ordinary surroundings on a seduction date. Remember, you want to create a memorable experience. One way to create such an experience is to break out of the normal routine and go places you've never been—different scenery, smells, sights, vibes, everything. By doing so, the experience will seem exciting, bold, and adventurous.

The date can take place at a museum, a shop across town, a sporting event (only if she has mentioned her love of sports), a concert, a special restaurant, or any other place she is likely to enjoy. The only condition is that you don't go to places she tends go to in her normal routine. So, if she goes to the museum every week to observe Egyptian artifacts, don't go there. If, however, there is a helium balloon show nearby, or an art show she wants to attend, it's perfect. These experiences are new for her, and more likely to be an "event."

Jason racked his brain for hours thinking of where to take Shannah. At age 40, he thought of himself as successful, attractive, but very shy. He wanted to date Shannah, a woman he met at a neighborhood coffee shop they both frequented. Jason flirted with her over a few weeks, and slowly found out details of her life. After nearly a month, he finally mustered up the courage to ask her out for coffee. Since he had been to one of our seminars, he knew enough to take her to a *different* coffee shop than the one they both enjoyed.

After the priming date, he felt he was ready to seduce her. Though he had lived in New York for the past ten years, every place that came to mind seemed cliché and silly. He wracked his brain thinking of places she would like. Finally, Jason decided to take her to the Statue of Liberty. He reasoned that it would be romantic to be on a boat, and he knew she had always wanted to go. Shannah had said so a month ago when he first started flirting with her and finding out about her life.

The date turned out wonderfully. The boat ride was fun and the tour of the statue was more interesting than he imagined it would be. Afterwards, they walked around neighborhoods she had wanted to visit. They looked at architecture, churches, and other points of interest. Jason and Shannah walked, holding hands, occasionally stopping for coffee, donuts, or just to rest. At the end of the date, they went back to her house and kissed passionately. It was the first of many dates for them.

One reason the date worked so well was that Jason took her to a place she wanted to go. Second, the date took them both out of their normal routines and into "foreign" territory. Third, by being together over hours and hours, they were forced to bond with one another. In the coffee shop they could talk to other people, and retreat into their books or newspapers. On the boat ride and while walking, they had to be together. They could either enjoy one another or suffer. Being out of their normal routine forced them to bond, which moved the seduction forward.

4. The seduction date includes the element of surprise

When we interviewed women about where their most romantic date took place, most said that the place was less important than how the date was structured. What made it romantic was that the man had taken care of all the details and that she felt like she was in another world. One woman commented that on the best dates, she felt "transported into a romantic world." Surprises are a wonderful way to create such feelings.

Since childhood, most of us have loved surprises. We've been conditioned to appreciate them. Why, for example, do kids love scary movies? Why do kids love roller coasters and hide-and-seek? The element of surprise makes a mundane activity into an event. It transforms the ordinary into the extraordinary. The element of surprise creates a quickened bonding process and invokes fun, ecstasy, and romance.

Creating a wonderful surprise for a woman also brings out the playful parts in you, which is always a good idea while getting to know a woman. Most women want a man who is sensitive and fierce, fun and playful, and at least somewhat unpredictable, all at the same time. When the date is full of surprise you are unpredictable, exciting, and it is difficult *not* to have fun. We highly recommend experimenting with surprise on seduction dates and keep it going while in a committed relationship. It adds spice and freshness.

During our interviews we also asked what made the best dates go well. Part of the magic, women told us, was doing things they didn't normally do. "I want to be taken out of my environment," one woman said. "I want a guy to bring me somewhere I'd probably not go alone or with my girlfriends. Even if it is just a funky coffee shop on the other side of town, or to a ballet, what impresses me is when a guy treats me like I'm worth putting in effort for." Secrets, surprises, and mystery all drive women crazy.

When Bruce asked Wendy out and told her only to dress like an FBI agent, she was instantly interested. Even though it seemed strange, she was deeply intrigued. In fact, she couldn't wait to see what kind of date he would concoct for her. Being asked out on an exciting adventure made her feel special and appreciated. It also sounded like a lot of fun. Wendy looked forward to flirting with Bruce, while pretending to be a sultry agent. Her response was exactly what Bruce hoped for.

5. You pay for the date

Some men aren't so skillful. Along with being a bumbling idiot, Bob is a cheapskate. He doesn't like to spend money on himself, on a woman, or on anybody. "I don't want to blow any money if sex isn't going to happen," he says. "Why should I spend my hard-earned money on a woman?" One reason Bob is such a failure with women is because he is unwilling to put out for them. He expects them to just throw themselves at him, and beg him for sex, even though he isn't willing to do much of anything for them. We're not talking about spending lots of money on a woman. That would be stupid and naive. But we are talking about providing for them on some level. A seduction date is about supplying the women fun and excitement, romance and appreciation. Part of how you create this is by taking financial responsibility for the date.

By refusing to spend even $20 on a movie date, Bob shoots himself in the foot and ruins his chances of success. By being overly paranoid and stingy, he turns women off. Many men fall into this trap. When you pay for a woman, you are demonstrating your ability to be generative. You are showing her that you are willing to do your part. Most women expect you to pay for them and will think less of you if you don't. You are welcome to argue about the fairness of this all day long if you want. You can be right about it until the cows come home. We don't care. The bottom line is, all the women we interviewed mentioned that this is what they expect.

If you have little money, don't fret. Spending lots of cash isn't necessary. Creating a memorable experience for her and taking charge of managing the date are more important than spending money. It would be a fine, memorable and *free* date if you took her to a free museum and then on a walk around a lake. If you know her better, you can rent movies and make her a wonderful dinner. Another option is to visit a nearby town and window shop down Main Street. These are all cheap options. The important part is that *you* are creating experiences for *her* and taking responsibility for the date rather than expecting her to do so.

Murray was quite knowledgeable about plants, majoring in horticulture in college. He had researched forest ecology and could identify nearly every tree, shrub, and plant in the botanical gardens nearby. He decided to take Beth on a visit to the gardens. In an earlier conversation she had mentioned her love of exotic birds, plants, and trees. Murray saw the botanical gardens as a perfect place to walk and bond. From there he planned to take her to a lunch spot, and then to a chocolate factory. The whole date, he figured, would cost around $15. It would give them an opportunity to be together in a romantic spot and have the date be memorable.

Howard is a dating master. He always has a steady stream of women to date. He meets them everywhere he goes. Over the years, Howard has developed a long list of dating laws that he strictly follows. One is the $40 rule: he never spends more than $40 on a seduction date. He simply decides ahead of time his spending maximum, and never spends more. This rule has served him well, and never leaves him broke or resentful.

We recommend you do take Howard's lead and do the same thing. Set aside a fixed amount and design a date that won't go over it. People who go gambling, and decide how much money they will lose ahead of time, and never exceed that amount, leave casinos happy. They live within their means and don't injure themselves chasing something that is improbable, like beating the odds at the blackjack table. The same is true on seduction dates. If you are not winning, and a connection is not being made, don't force the issue. If a date begins going badly, don't fall into the trap of spending more money in an attempt to fix it. That's desperation, not confidence, and it doesn't work. Spending more money won't help things. You will probably leave feeling even worse, and no closer to your goal.

Even though paying for the seduction date is recommended, don't foolishly believe that paying for dates negates the importance of creating and maintaining the romantic mood. Money is never a substitute for the other work required. You must still touch her, charm her, create bonding, and much more. If you take a woman to a very expensive restaurant, she may be impressed, but if you fail to create any romance, she will only view you as a sucker whom she can manipulate into buying things for her. There must be a balance, and the work on the date must be done in tandem with paying.

6. The seduction date is not a time to socialize

Just as the priming date wasn't a time to socialize, neither is the seduction date. Sure, having fun is part of the date, but you are still "at work." You are still focused on your goal of created sexual tension between the two of you that you can have fun resolving later. The other task you are working on is creating romantic feelings. As a rule of thumb, be clear about your goal every time you interact with your date. When you stray from this focus, get back on track. If you forget your goals, you will likely fail.

7. Seduction dates are on a flexible schedule

Priming dates have a definite format. They are short, usually 40-75 minutes. Discovering the woman's likes and dislikes is the focus. Seduction dates follow a completely different format. While they are goal-driven, the pace is slower and less intense. The goal of the seduction date is sex, and there are many paths to it. The easiest one is to let go of having to make your plans work perfectly, while at the same time pursuing your goal. Does this seem confusing? It should. We are telling you two completely opposite things at the same time.

Most guys have a hard time just "going with the flow." They prefer to know ahead of time how every moment is going to be spent. Then they fret when things don't go as planned. The likelihood of your success will be greatly improved if you can let the ambiguity and uncertainty be there, while still following the other principles. Otherwise, you'll turn into a control-freak. After a few seduction dates, this formula will make much more sense.

When Danny took Amy to an art opening, he never expected that they would be invited to the artist's hotel room for a private show. While he was a bit worried that the artist would hit on Amy, he went anyway. They ended up talking to the artist for the next few hours, drinking wine, and getting to know him. Afterward, Danny took her home and they ended up having sex. Because he was open to changing his plans, while still remaining focused on the outcome, he gave her a very special experience, and was successful.

Most people go through life busy and hurried, not allowing much time to be relaxed and to enjoy what is going on in front of them. When you allow for the date to unfold in its own time, you create a relaxed environment for her and this will greatly aid you. This in no way means you don't plan out the date meticulously and have an abundance of options at your fingertips. You must allow for both a tightly structured outing and one that is flexible.

Remember also: no woman wants to be with a man who is constantly trying to rush the sexual mood. If you try to hurry things, a woman won't respect you, and certainly won't put you into the category of "boyfriend material." Men who are unsuccessful with women lack the ability to be tactful. When you relax and let the date unfold and go at her pace, and still follow your plan, she will respect you and eventually give you sex.

8. Seduction dates plan for success

While planning a date, you must assume that sex will happen and do the steps necessary to get ready. This means that you prepare mentally, physically, practically, and emotionally. You also prepare your environment to lend itself to a sexual experience. Most important, you end up someplace you can "do it."

Calvin, a successful student, reported that one of his first seduction dates failed because he didn't plan properly. The date had been going well and he and a delightful young woman wound up at her home. So far, so good, he thought. They began by kissing passionately on her couch, and after a while they moved things to the bedroom. Calvin took off her top and played with her breasts. The kissed more, and she pulled off his pants and underwear. They continued and she took off her blouse and bra. Calvin was in heaven. After another half hour of foreplay, she begged him to have intercourse.

At that exact moment, Calvin realized that he didn't have any condoms. "I felt like a total idiot," he recalls. "I had no idea things would go so far on the date. If I had, I would have planned. I still kick myself when I think of my blunder." Calvin's lack of planning cost him a great night and the respect of the woman.

Most men are so used to failing with women that they expect the worst. After many rejections, they expect to strike out. They don't plan for success and are surprised when it happens. Like Calvin, they don't bring condoms on a date because they don't even think they could possibly score. They don't bother cleaning their bedroom because they don't think the date will lead to the woman coming home with them. They don't dress well because the woman probably won't like them anyway. We could go on and on.

In our experience, holding onto negative beliefs and pessimistic attitudes will give you what you've always gotten: poor results and lukewarm-to-cold responses from women. We recommend that as of this moment every date you go on from now on, you plan for success. It is crucial that you be ready for things to go your way. If you aren't, you will end up a chump and the only one you will be able to blame is yourself.

BEFORE THE SEDUCTION DATE

We always stress the importance of preparation for a date; you should know this by now. Planning, after all, is 90 percent of the work. Imagine all the work set designers do before a movie shoot.

They are on site weeks before the actors even show up. They spend weeks constructing buildings from scratch, parking lots from corn fields, saloons from barns, anything needed to match the movie script. After all the preparation is done, the actors stroll onto the set and shoot the scenes. Filming usually takes place for less than a month. The designers are there before, during, and after, making sure everything works as planned.

Successful dating works in much the same way. It requires hours of pre-work to set the scene. The work is constant. The demands are great. But the hard work pays off when the actors (you and her) seem to create magic from thin air. Here are guidelines of things you must cover before the date.

Assess the attraction level between the two of you

In earlier examples, you saw how effectively Bruce prepared Wendy for the seduction date. He moved the relationship from mild interest to having her attracted to him and excited about the next date. Bob's date wasn't prepared at all. In fact, she seemed *uninterested* in him. It seemed likely that she was only dating him out of politeness, and as a way to get free meals. The different levels of attraction Bob and Bruce are experiencing shows how they are in completely different stages of the seduction process. By being brutally honest with yourself about how much attraction is present, you can custom design a date that will work effectively.

Here is a short quiz for you to take. Your answers will help you measure her level of interest in you. If you answer "yes" to three or more of these questions, she is likely to be quite interested. If you answer "no" to three or more, there is a minimal connection and more bonding is necessary.

1. Did she seem interested when you asked her romantic questions?
2. Did she seem excited about the idea of another date, or was she just being polite?
3. Does she seem willing to alter her schedule to see you?
4. Does she seem happy when you touch her nonintrusively, or does she squirm to get away from you?

5. Has she complimented you on your looks or behavior?
6. Have she welcomed discussions of anything sexual?
7. Has she mentioned that she talked about you with her friends?

By realistically assessing her current level of attraction, you allow yourself to prepare intelligently for the date. You are likely, however, to fall into one of two traps. First, you might think that if you are really attracted to her, she must be really attracted to you. Remember, you want to assess the amount of attraction *between* you, which will probably be mediated by her, not by you. Second, you may let your fear do the assessing for you, and decide that there's no way she could be attracted to you. That's not realistic, either. Look at the situation as if you were an outsider observing a budding relationship, and make your assessment from there.

Create a sexual goal for the date

Now that you have measured the degree of attraction between the two of you, it will be easier to create a sexual goal for the date. Remember that, by definition, all seduction dates aim to create an opening for sex.

You want to pick goals that are attainable. It is okay to push yourself to a new plateau, to stretch and reach beyond where you've been in the past. But the goal must be doable and realistic. Many men choose goals that are out of reach, beyond their skill level. They would rather live in a dreamworld than face up to gritty reality. By choosing something beyond your skill level, you will hurt your self-confidence. By not being honest with yourself, you perpetuate boyish delusional ways of thinking that will prevent you from the life you want. If Bob, for instance, really thinks his date will sleep with him, he is nuts. It would be miraculous for him to even kiss her, given the way things are going.

While Bob has zero chance with his date, Bruce is likely to bed Wendy on their seduction date. She has already shown signs of sexual interest in him, and the chemistry is right. They already have a strong attraction to one another and both seem to like each other. If he creates and executes a date that she enjoys, sex will probably happen. Whether you are in a situation similar to Bruce or Bob, you must decide how far you think things can go, and plan from there. Each seduction must be custom designed to match the individual woman and circumstances.

Make sure the time and place work for you

Do you really have enough free time to devote to a date? If not, either create the time, or don't have the date. In planning, it is crucial to make sure you have the free time required to make the date a success. If you have a demanding job, like most of us, it is likely that you occasionally are expected to work on weekends, or extra hours during crunch times. We strongly recommend that you never mess up your work schedule for a date.

At all times, you must remember that your work is more important than a woman—especially during the beginning stages of a relationship. It is lunacy to put your job in jeopardy to date a woman, no matter how attractive she is. Out of desperation, men often harm themselves to get women. In the end, acting from desperation will cause more problems down the road. If you skip work to be with a woman, you will probably be preoccupied anyhow, and the date won't work. The solution is to set up a seduction at a time and place that truly works for you.

Decide how much money you are going to spend on the date

As we discussed earlier, you must decide ahead of time how much you are willing to spend on the date. Budgeting is important because it acts as a safety measure to insure that you don't feel taken advantage of by a woman. Some men tell us that they tend to feel used by women; they report that women often only seem interested in dating them so they can get their money. In these situations, the men end up paying more for the date than expected. At the same time, they don't get any sex. If you are to avoid falling into this trap, you decide ahead of time how much you are willing to spend, and stick to it.

*Use the information from the priming date to guide how
you plan the seduction date*

Priming dates function as fact-finding missions. By asking a
woman romantic questions, you find out what she looks for in a
man, and what turns her off. You also learn about her likes and dislikes, interests, and topics to avoid. All of this information, including
your intuitive sense about her, helps you plan the seduction date.
Begin by looking over your notes about the priming date. Go over
everything you know about her. Recall her likes and dislikes, everything that seemed interesting about her, anything that seemed
wacko, and any other details that stand out. This data will help you
decide where to take her and what the most effective strategy with
her will be.

THE SEVEN STEPS TO A KNOCK-OUT
SEDUCTION DATE

Your success depends upon how you construct the entire date.
Merely taking her to a wonderful park or getting great tickets to an
opera is not enough. You must create the romantic and sexual mood.
Remember, sexual tension is the goal. If you take her to grandiose
places, but don't create the mood of attraction and sexual attention,
everything you do will be pointless. Just as spending money doesn't
insure success, having one great place to go, in a vacuum, doesn't
ensure success either. It must work from start to finish. Here's how
you create a knock-out seduction date.

1. Recall insights you have had about the woman and things she
   seems interested in.
2. Make a list of potential places she may enjoy.
3. Pretend that you are her and pick the two that seem the most
   romantic and fun.
4. Write down a basic time-line for the date.
5. Find creative ways to string the two activities together.
6. While on the date and while planning, constantly ask yourself
   what could make the experience more romantic and sensual.

When you come up with an answer, figure out how to include it.

7. Ask yourself what you could do to turn up the fun to the next level, and add that into your dating structure.

Part of the planning process is to call ahead of time and make sure the place where the date will happen is actually open. Find out the hours they are open and if there are places nearby that might interest you and your date. Also, find out if reservations are needed, and what the cost will be. If you accomplish all seven steps, but don't call ahead and make sure the place is even available, you may be creating another failed date.

Here are two lists; one offers possible places to go on the date, and one of places to avoid. If you read these lists and still feel stuck, call her and get her opinions. Most women will be honest with you about where they'd like to go, and it will help ensure that the date goes well.

Potential places to take her

* A movie in an out-of-the-way or artistic theater
* Nature (only if she is a nature lover)
* A road trip to a nearby quaint little town or exciting city
* A part of town, that is safe, that neither of you frequents
* Museums
* Concerts
* Wonderful restaurants
* Beaches
* Parks where you can feed bread to birds
* Out for ice cream
* Amusement parks
* Botanical gardens
* A drive in the country
* A planetarium
* A wonderful dance club

* Drive-in movies
* Plays
* Zoo
* Aquariums
* Cooking together
* Wine-tasting parties
* Tourists' spots
* Bike rides
* Comedy clubs

Places to avoid taking her

* Anywhere dangerous
* Martial art demonstrations and professional wrestling matches
* To a sporting event, unless she specifically mentioned she loves sports
* Anyplace where there will lots of guys who will hit on her
* Gory movies
* Strip clubs
* An enrollment event for your multilevel marketing company
* A baseball card convention or Star Trek convention
* Any place your buddies hang out
* A concert where you aren't sure if she'll like the music
* On an overnight trip
* Any lecture that could lead to a political argument between the two of you
* A sports bar
* A nudist colony
* Anyplace too private if you think she still might be afraid of you

These lists are only partial, and are here to get your imagination going. You will be able to best come up with something that suits her perfectly by listening to her and using your imagination. Remember, each woman is different, and the ultimate seduction date might be a total turn-off for another. These lists, however, should get you started.

The importance of a backup plan

Seth had created the ultimate date for Stephanie. He made reservations to go on a hot-air balloon ride, after which they would have a picnic in a nature preserve. After that, he planned that they would attend a performance of *Romeo and Juliet* at a nearby outdoor Shakespeare festival. He knew Stephanie would enjoy everything. It all looked perfect.

On the day before the date, he grinned to himself, thinking he was so cool for planning such an awesome date. He daydreamed about having sex with Stephanie outside. He imagined pulling into a country motel because they would both be so full of lust that they couldn't wait to make it home.

On Saturday Seth woke up to shocking and upsetting news. It was raining outside. In fact, the sky was dark and thunderstorms loomed overhead. He panicked, not knowing where else to take Stephanie. In the end, he canceled the date because he had no other options. By being overly cocky, and not having a backup plan, Seth created a losing situation. The same thing can happen to you if you don't have a backup plan in place because any plan can be ruined at the last moment. We recommend that you pick three or four places to take a woman for a date and have them planned out, just in case any problems occur.

Purchase at least one surprise gift for her

When Bruce went out with Wendy, he arranged the theme of the date with her in advance. They both would pretend to be FBI agents on a bust. Every stop on their road-trip was part of an imaginary afternoon-long chase. This was off-the-wall enough be memorable and fun. Assigning Wendy the position of FBI agent provided her a fun type of power from the start. Bruce was able to flirt with her as though she was Agent Scully and he was Agent Mulder of the

TV show "The X-Files." This opened the door for comments about handcuffs, seducing an officer to get out of trouble, and much more.

Bruce surprised her with several gifts along the same lines. He bought toy handcuffs for her. These were funny, and also invoked an erotic, sexual mood. To go with the cuffs, he also bought toy squirt guns and police badges. He even created on his computer a silly version of a search warrant for her to carry. In the document, he included a stipulation that she could strip search anyone she met, including her FBI partner. He had them all gift wrapped. She laughed and was thrilled to receive them.

Bruce also purchased a few gifts that were more traditionally romantic. For example, he got a small box of chocolates for her. He told her this was for their "celebration" when they caught their criminal. He also purchased a bookmark, with quotes from her favorite author. All totaled, he spent about $10 on the gifts. In her mind it seemed as though he went to great lengths to create a perfect date for her. These gave him many "brownie points." It was also fun for Bruce. He got a kick out of pretending to be an agent and seeing her happy. Creating fun for both of you is a great way to ignite the magic of romance.

Be prepared

Like any Boy Scout, you must be prepared for every circumstance. For those of you who have been paying even the slightest amount of attention, the following list of things will be old hat. By the time you are done reading this book, they will hopefully be second nature. For those of you not paying attention, let's go through it again. Remember to:

* Clean your car
* Bring condoms
* Clean your bedroom
* Put clean sheets on your bed
* Have candles in the bedroom ready to use
* Make sure your roommate won't barge in on you
* Dress for success

Generate romantic questions to ask her

The priming date chapter covered how to create romantic questions. We recommend that you memorize them and practice them often. On the priming date, you peppered them into the conversations throughout the date, created romantic feelings, and gathered information about her. You may have had some full-blown romantic conversations, but because the date was short, they were short. The seduction date is different. We suggest you get into longer and deeper conversations about romantic topics. Your romantic and exciting settings will make this easy.

During the first hour of his seduction date with Jodi, Shane began asking her about her most passionate kiss. At first he jokingly asked her these questions. He was surprised at her detailed answers. Jodi described how good the man's tongue felt in her mouth, and how much she enjoyed being close to a man. She went on and on, leaving Shane shocked. Finally, after discussing various kissing techniques, he went for the kiss. That began a long and hot make-out session.

The success that Shane experienced stemmed from his ability and willingness to use romantic questions on seduction dates. It is important that they be used to open up longer conversations. Many of the questions can be used as foreplay throughout the date.

Memorize her phone number

During our interviews, several women noted that they were impressed when a man memorized their phone number. Though it may sound trivial to you, they found it to be a sign that the guy was thinking of them often, and it made them feel special. It is an easy feat to accomplish, and will help shed a better light on you in the future.

Get psyched up

Use the techniques we described in Chapter 3 to get yourself ready for the date.

MASTERING THE SEDUCTION DATE

It is a major accomplishment to get this far. You should congratulate yourself and be proud. By getting this far you are way ahead of 90 percent of other single men and you are certainly on the right course.

Look at some of the hoops you've already jumped through: you asked her out; survived at least one priming date; prepared your clothing, car and apartment; created a great seduction date plan; prepared for sexual success; practiced romantic questions; created a time-line and a budget; created a back-up plan, and much more. She will never know all the things you did to make the date go, but we do, and we salute you. You are very close to being a true Seducer.

If you have laid the foundation properly, the date should go well. If you haven't, problems are inevitable. Whether you have done the pre-work or not, it is important that you put it all behind you once the date starts. On the date, focus your attention on her. It will go much more smoothly if you tune all the expectations, thoughts, opinions, and regrets out of your head. We know this is very difficult, and something few people can do perfectly. But if you can do it, every seduction will go better.

Be punctual

Though a seduction date goes at a different pace than a priming date, it is still important for you to be on time. Based on our research and personal experiences, dates flow best when they start on time. Women tend to respect men who are punctual compared to men who tend to be late. Which man would you count on in a pinch? Who would you want as a husband? One who is on time, or one who is late? Punctuality is a wonderful habit to have. It gives you breathing time and helps you concentrate on the date, rather than on how you are going to explain to her why you are tardy.

Be exceptionally polite

A great number of men have a hard time understanding modern day dating norms. In a time of extreme political correctness and dramatic change, they repeatedly comment on being confused about how to treat women. "I've been on dates over the past year where the women got mad when I opened the door for them," one guy said. We know it can be puzzling to know how to act around women. As a rule of thumb, we highly recommend you conduct yourself as a man with exceptional manners. For example, open doors for her, take her coat when you go out, help her with her coat when she puts it back on, make sure she sits at a table before you do, and don't start eating a meal before she does.

You can't please every woman all the time. All you can do is behave consistent with your beliefs. If a woman is offended that you open a door for her, just listen to her complaint and use the nine-step process for handling complaints that we'll show you at the end of this chapter. Get past it, and move on with the date.

Treat a woman differently from the way you treat your buddies

It is important that you watch how often you use "vulgar" language, and that you act as "civilized" as possible. The hackneyed cliché, "there is a time and place for everything," is useful in this situation. When you are with your buddies, it's great to eat with your hands, swear, burp, fart loudly and laugh about it, drink beer from a can, and slap the guy next to you on the back. These behaviors don't cut it on a date. Most of us know this intuitively, but often fail to manage ourselves properly on a date itself.

In our research for this book, numerous women told us that men show up for dates smelly, and dressed like slobs. They also told us that many men do stupid things to "ruin" the date, The man might burp loudly and then laugh to himself, or maybe he talks about how all his co-workers are stupid, and may even indulge in "colorful" language. When you do these things, the woman will disqualify you for "lover material" and start planning how to cut the date short. By being clear about which behaviors are appropriate around women and which aren't, you will avoid these dating pitfalls.

Focus on your date, not other women

You probably don't even realize it, but if you are like most men, you constantly look at women on the street, in bars, in restaurants, everywhere. For a single man, the world is his shopping mall. Why not ogle at the attractive woman? Most men stare and wonder what women are like in bed, if their breasts are real, and what the chances are of dating them. These are perfectly natural reactions.

While it is all right to look at women on the street, when you are on a date it is totally unacceptable. Do you want to blow the date and lose the respect of the woman you are with? Of course not. When you stare incessantly at other women, she will probably feel angry, jealous, and sad. When she feels upset, it is more work for you, and delays creating the sexual mood.

The first step is to realize that you habitually check out women. The next step is to decrease the frequency with which you do it. Third, when you find yourself doing it on a date, stop instantly. After a while you will have a handle on this habit.

Darrell was on a seduction date with Betsy. They were having a fun time at the zoo. It was summer, and they sat on a park bench in the shade eating snow cones. Sitting on a nearby bench were two amazing looking 20-year-old women who, frankly, were much more attractive than Betsy. They both wore very short skirts and tight shirts. Their breasts were nearly popping out, and their nipples were clearly visible. Darrell couldn't stop staring at them.

After a few minutes, it became obvious to both Betsy and the young women that he was checking them out. Betsy became upset and threatened to leave if he didn't stop. "Why did you even ask me out if all you are going to do is look at other women?" she asked. "Don't you think I'm attractive? I thought we were having a romantic time and I was starting to like you, but now I am not so sure." It took hours for Darrell to regain the mood he had lost in the park. He learned the hard way that while it is natural to look, you must restrain yourself from checking out other women when you are on a date.

Be affectionate

Most men have a difficult time being affectionate. They reserve affectionate words and touching for the bedroom. In day-to-day life, men are apt to worry about being viewed as "soft" or wimpy. Women, however, love it. You can speed up your seduction and begin to "sweep a woman off her feet" by being affectionate.

Affection can take the form of compliments. Here are a few examples:

"Joyce, I really enjoy spending time with you. I am amazed at how close I feel to you after such a short time."

"I must tell you that you look even more beautiful on this date than I've ever seen you look before. It is a delight to be able to look at you."

"I am having such a fun time being with you. I want to thank you for being such a great date and being so easy-going about the plans today."

"Joyce, you are the type of woman I've been waiting to meet for a long, long time. You are a very special woman and I really appreciate being with you."

What links all the above examples together is that the woman is thanked, complimented, and acknowledged. You must do this in your own way, in your own unique style. If you use our words, and they are contrary to your own, your affectionate words will sound awkward and insincere.

More frequently, affection is expressed through actions. These can be soft and gentle touching, notes, a quick phone call, or a surprise gift. The same rules apply, as we discussed earlier. The action must acknowledge, compliment, and thank her in some way.

Ben took Erin to the movies. They saw the latest "chick flick." Toward the end of the movie one of the main characters was on her deathbed in the hospital. The character was explaining to her granddaughter all the hardships of growing up on a farm in the 1930s. Erin began crying during the scene. Ben thought the scene was silly and unrealistic. However, he reached for Erin's hand when she began to cry, and offered her a tissue. In that moment, he displayed affection and caring for her. She was impressed at his level of sensitivity.

Later, when they sat drinking coffee, Erin complained about her stiff neck. Ben offered to rub it, and proceeded to do so for several minutes. He also wrote a short romantic note to her, and made sure to put it in her jacket during the movie. She found it later in the date. All of his actions were examples of being affectionate toward her. They are all small actions that yield large results down the road.

Touch her at least six times

During the priming date you began touching the woman non-intrusively. You did this to set the stage for more affectionate touching. On the seduction date more deliberate touch is required. You want her to be frequently reminded that you are interested in her. By setting a precedent of touching her, you build a mood of sensuality for later.

You may wish to hold her hand, touch her face lightly, touch her hair, run your fingers on her neck, or touch her back and waist. We highly discourage you from touching her breasts, butt, lips, or thighs. It is important that you kiss her before touching any of these "private" areas. You must start small and build from there.

Warning: some women will be uncomfortable with you touching them so often. While they may even like you, and want to sleep with you, they may feel freaked out. Always pay attention to a woman's response. It is crucial that you be respectful and don't upset her. Realize that religion, culture, and family norms all play a part in how she responds to you. A highly religious woman may feel uncomfortable no matter how you touch her, while another might enjoy holding hands and passionate kissing in public. It all depends on the woman. It is your job to note her reactions, and act accordingly.

Compliment her often

One of the best ways to make a woman feel special is through compliments. It is important, however, that you be truthful when you compliment her. Women are highly skilled in their ability to spot insincerity, and can usually spot a lie a mile away. If they think you are lying, they will undoubtedly hold it against you.

Women are likely to be flattered if you compliment them on something most guys wouldn't notice. We've explained how important it is for you to set yourself apart from other men. When you compliment a woman in a sincere manner about something most people don't notice, she is likely to be impressed. For example, noticing an interesting barrette in her hair or a necklace will show her that you are aware of more than her breasts or her butt.

Here are a few examples of things to compliment her on: the clothes she is wearing, her eyes, an article of jewelry, her smile, her hands, an intelligent remark she makes, her presence, or her sense of humor.

While on a canoe ride, Zach and Chris had a deep conversation about Eastern religions. He was surprised at how much she knew about the subject and immediately complimented her. Later on, he told her how cute she looked with a canoe paddle in hand and a life preserver around her neck. He also commented on how good her hair looked in the sun. By paying attention to Chris, Zach had an easy time coming up with several ways to compliment her.

Talk about upbeat topics

It is important to discuss upbeat topics. We don't mean that you come across as some Pollyanna type of guy, who is always smiling and happy-go-lucky. We do say that being negative and criticizing everyone and everything will not work either. If you frequently discuss harsh topics, complain, talk about things you hate, insult your date, and seem preoccupied with sex, the date won't go well. Remember, the purpose of the date is for her to have fun and enjoy being with you. If you create a negative mood through your conversations, she will likely find you creepy and look for ways to avoid you. After all, most of us avoid being around people who scare us, or who seem nuts. Your date is not any different.

Some men also tend to be overly serious. This works just as badly as discussing death or war or how much you hate your job. You create fun by talking about upbeat topics, and this helps he woman relax.

Bob was a strong believer in recycling. He shared his views with Carla on a seduction date. He admitted that he hated the mayor of their city for being so lax in his recycling campaign. "The mayor is such a jerk," he said. "I think politicians are mostly morons. Many of them would be better shot than serving our communities. Don't you agree?" Carla became nervous with Bob's violent comments. Though she too believed in recycling, his intensity scared her. If he had said the same thing in a milder manner, Carla could have discussed the topic with him, and even agreed. Instead, he looked like a freak.

On his date with Wendy, Bruce told her about many of the international trips he had taken in his life. He shared his experiences visiting the rainforest in Brazil and climbing in the Swiss Alps. While he was forthright about a few political issues that came up on the date, he made sure Wendy always felt like she was part of the conversation. Bruce frequently asked Wendy about her opinions. He made sure not to say things that would be construed as too intense or harsh, and often brought the conversation back to upbeat topics when it threatened to get glum.

Topics to avoid discussing

* Controversial topics that could offend her
* Anything too overtly sexual
* Violence
* Death
* Children being harmed or abducted
* How much you hate your boss or job
* The IRS
* How much you hate marriage
* Your fascination with serial killers
* How you collect cigars
* Past girlfriends
* How often you like to have sex
* Cruelty to animals, especially cats and dogs
* Topics she is not interested in, like cars, math, Star Trek, Babylon-5, Doctor Who, computers, sports, or others.
* Your bad habits that you really need to overcome

Make decisions

On a seduction date it is important that you come across as confident. Women want to know that you are comfortable with yourself and not apologetic for who you are. We've said it before and we'll say it again: one easy way to demonstrate confidence is to be decisive: in planning the date, when talking to her about where to go next, what restaurant you desire, what table to sit at in the restaurant, what music to listen to in the car, and what section of the museum to check out first.

At the same time, you don't want to come across as a control freak, or a condescending jerk. Just remember this: a man kills a date when he constantly responds with "I don't care what we do next. What do you want to do?" or, "I don't know," in the face of a decision. Being wishy-washy shows that you lack confidence and lack direction. Make decisions on the date and you will increase her level of respect for you. If you haven't learned this yet, learn it now.

Listen to her opinions

As we mentioned before, it is important that you take her opinions seriously and always include her in the decision making process. Many women complain that men don't listen to them, don't care about what they think or feel. When women express their opinions, men tend to view them as nagging, or as a demand. It is natural to feel this way. However, it is still important, whether you think she is being a nag or not, to listen to her opinion and to let her talk.

When a woman begins opening up to you, it means that she has begun to view you as a potential mate. She trusts you enough to tell you her thoughts, opinions, and ideas. One of the hidden costs of dating is that you will have to put up with things you don't want to. Our advice is to notice when you are upset or annoyed when the woman talks too much or is overly demanding, and simply keep listening anyway.

Cheryl loved to talk. Talk, talk, talk. She spouted off her opinions to anyone who would listen. Dean was attracted to her, but occasionally could not stand to listen to her nonstop talking and unfounded opinions.

Dean's tendency was to argue with women. He would meet a woman, they would date for a few weeks and he would finally tell her what he really thought about her and her opinions. She would, of course, promptly dump him. After a few years of repeating this pattern over and over again, he realized that the way he interacted with women fundamentally didn't work. Soon after, he became one our students and his problems soon vanished. He realized that women mostly want someone to just listen and take their opinions seriously, so he stopped getting upset. He found out that he could be bored when Cheryl talked, while still listening to her. He also noticed that after a few minutes Cheryl would usually be done giving her opinions, and the date could continue. Because he listened to her, Cheryl felt very close to him, and wanted to be sexual.

FROM RAGING BULL TO PURRING KITTEN IN NINE EASY STEPS

As you've seen, seduction dates are dramatically different from priming dates. But problems do occur on seduction dates. Given how much time you are spending together and the fact that romantic feelings will likely be in the air, you both may be more tense than usual. She will be off in her own world thinking of reasons why or why not you could be a couple. You will probably be off in your world thinking of the stupid things you've said, worrying about whether she is having fun, and wondering when you'll get to see her naked. All this can create trouble.

Another thing that makes seduction dates even more volatile than priming dates is that by this time you both have more of an investment in each other than you did before. This creates expectation and tension, which can create problems.

You'll know you have a problem if she gets upset about anything. You may say or do something that offends her, or that goes against her values. The two of you together might have an upsetting experience, and she may need to talk about it. No matter what happens to upset her, the solution is the same. This model is effective on any date, with any woman, at any step along the way. If you modify some of the steps, you can use them in long-term relationship conflicts as well.

1. Listen to her

When they are upset, most women just want someone (you) to listen to them. If your date can express her problem, concern, or misunderstanding early enough, it will likely go away easily. We recommend that you just listen without interrupting her, or trying to fix it. When you listen to her, she is likely to calm down quickly.

2. Repeat back what you heard

A woman not only wants to know you listened to her, but she also wants to make sure you completely understand everything she said. When you repeat back what you heard her say, it gives you an opportunity to clarify anything you may have misunderstood, and an opportunity to demonstrate that you really are listening, which will also help calm her down.

3. Thank her

Even if you feel angry that she is telling you all her thoughts and opinions, and you really couldn't possibly care less, thank her for taking the time and the risk to talk to you. In her world, she is taking a risk by telling you her problems or concerns. By getting it off her chest, so to speak, she is likely to feel more relaxed and more connected to you.

She may also be testing to see how you respond. When you thank her, she can see that you are caring and sensitive. It also foreshadows, for her, how you might respond during a future conflict. When you behave like a gentleman and respond like a caring guy, she will trust you more, and want to be sexual with you.

4. Continue to listen to her

It is likely that after she has one problem, another will surface in conjunction with the first. Once again, let her tell you any other problem she feels is necessary. Your job is to listen, repeat it back to her, and to thank her.

5. Make promises and apologies

If you follow the previous four steps, she will calm down. When she stops talking for a minute, we advise you to promise to do or not to do whatever the action or behavior was that got her upset in the first place. It is also important to apologize for anything you did to cause her to be upset.

If, for instance, you made the mistake of criticizing dogs because they tend to urinate all over the place, and she was upset because she loves dogs, you would promise not to criticize them again. Next, you would apologize for hurting her feelings with your insensitivity.

6. If you really, truly don't care

If she has a huge problem with something you think is insignificant, determine if you want to end the date or not. Determine if you think sex will happen. If you are attracted to her and foresee future dates with her, and if you can honestly do so, apologize. If she doesn't seem worth the hassle, end the date then and there. Quit wasting your time and hers. If she does seem worth it, let all your frustrations go, and move on to the next step.

7. Let it all go

Given that she was upset, you are likely to be also. We strongly recommend that you don't fan the fire by telling her your opinions or showing her your anger. You have to keep yourself focused on your long-term goals. If you tell her all your opinions, show her how much she upsets you, and logically prove how very wrong she is, the date will likely fail. If you want success, you must let it go.

8. Compliment her

Not only do you have to apologize and thank her, we also recommend that you compliment her again to end the whole thing. Most guys who make it through these steps fail to leave the conversation on a good note. Complimenting her leaves the whole conflict clean and complete. Then you can move on to something easier and more fun. She will likely be impressed if you compliment her on her ability to be straight with you and on her communication skills.

9. Repeat this process as many times as it takes

Then get on with the date.

AFTER-THE-DATE "DID" CHECKLIST

* Made sure the date lasted at least four hours
* Made her feel special
* Gave her at least one small gift
* Took her outside her normal environment
* Had surprises on the date
* Paid for the date
* Were flexible with time
* Made her smile and/or laugh at least one time
* Planned for success
* Assessed the attraction level
* Created a sexual goal for the date
* Scheduled the date at times that work for you
* Decided ahead of time how much money you were willing to spend and stuck to that amount
* Used information from the priming date to guide the date
* Took her to a romantic spot during the date
* Used seductive language (seduce, attraction, falling in love, romance, etc.,) seven times
* Used interested body language
* Whispered at least once
* Constructed the date using the method we recommend
* Created a backup plan
* Prepared yourself and your surroundings
* Memorized her phone number
* Got psyched up before the date
* Were punctual for the date
* Acted with exceptional manners
* Treated the woman differently from your buddies
* Focused on your date, not other women.
* Were affectionate
* Touched her at least six times

* Kissed her at least two times
* Complimented her often
* Were easy and fun to be around
* Talked about upbeat topics
* Made decisions
* Listened to her opinions.

AFTER-THE-DATE "DIDN'T" CHECKLIST

* Didn't treat her like a friend
* Didn't insult her
* Didn't complain
* Didn't complain about other women
* Didn't check out other women
* Didn't grab her ass
* Didn't rely on her for certainty that the date was going well
* Didn't allow yourself to get upset when you forgot your lines, etc.
* Didn't take anything she said or did personally.

HOW TO END THE SEDUCTION DATE

If you've done all the steps we recommend, the date should end with you both feeling romantic and sexy. Since you have planned for success, you will end the date near someplace where you can explore each other's bodies. As the date nears an end, timing becomes even more significant. We recommend that you be romantic and sexy during the entire date so that you will "naturally" end up in one of your bedrooms, or any other place that seems right to kiss and do more. If there is sexual chemistry and the mood is right when you get to the end of the seduction date, go for it. In the next two chapters, we will show you how to get the first kiss, get her into bed, and be the lover of her dreams.

chapter nine...
Closing the Deal: The First Kiss and More

On the rare occasions that Bob has actually attempted to kiss a woman, everything has gone wrong. Having decided that he was sick of being alone and that it was time he "made his move" on his friend Sherry, he invited her to see an artistic, x-rated film at the local foreign film theater.

During the film, which showed many people having sex, Bob noticed that Sherry was sitting as far from him as possible without actually moving to a different seat. In view of that, he decided not to put his arm around her. After all, he reasoned, why make her uncomfortable? They were both watching people have sex: of course she would just naturally want him the way he wanted her.

After the film, Bob was almost shaking with nervousness, but figured that they had just seen a (sort of) romantic movie, so it was now or never. While still in the lobby, he took Sherry by the shoulders and tried to kiss her. She recoiled, pulling away from him and turning her face aside. "Please!" she said. "Bob, I like you as a friend! As a friend!" He was crushed, and when Sherry said "I must leave now," he didn't even walk her back to her car. His first kiss had failed, and he was alone again.

Paul had been dating a therapist named Annie. It was their third date, and he noticed, once again, that she seemed cold and distant. "She's boring," he told himself. For the rest of the evening, Paul didn't touch her, didn't wink at her, and did nothing to make her feel romantic. "After all," Paul told himself, "I don't really care about her, anyway. Why put out all the effort?" They went to a poetry reading, where he told her, "I'm tired. Let's go." He took her back to her house, no longer concealing his boredom with her. As they sat in his car, just in front of her house, he said to her, "How about a kiss?" Of course, she said no. Why should she kiss a guy who was trying to ditch her? She got out of the car, and Paul went home.

Men often ask us why getting the first kiss is hard for them. They find themselves ready for it, but the right time never seems to come. Or they wait for the woman to make the first move, which she almost never does. They find themselves waiting for that one woman who is so obviously attracted to them, with whom the chemistry is so overwhelmingly great, that the first kiss seems to "just happen." While such chemistry does exist in the world, and most men have experienced at least one time when getting sexually involved with a woman seemed easy and effortless, if you wait for "magic" to happen, you will have a long, long wait.

If you learn nothing else from this book, learn this: waiting for magic, and hoping that something good happens, will never get you the life you want. It won't give you the sex-life you want with women, and it won't give you the results you want in the rest of your life either. Besides, being a man who waits and hopes for magic will actually make you less attractive to women, who tend to go for men who actively create the lives they want. You must commit yourself to learn what it takes to create the life you want, and follow through until you achieve that result. When it comes to the first kiss (and more), you can't wait for magic. You have to learn and apply the necessary technology. Waiting for magic will leave you lonely once again.

THE SECRET OF GETTING THE FIRST KISS

The secret of getting the first kiss is so simple that, once you understand it, getting it will be a trivial risk rather than a huge event for the rest of your life. The secret is the pre-work. By the time you go for that kiss you must have her so ready, so prepared, and so desiring that kiss that she is more than ready to go. Once again, it's like lighting a camp stove. If you just lunge at the stove with a lit match, of course it won't light. If the stove doesn't light, the problem isn't with the match you are using, how you are holding it, or the way you struck the match on the box. It's not a defective camp stove and it doesn't hate you. You just haven't primed it properly. If you focus on thinking that you are doing something wrong during the lighting stage, when the problem is that you haven't primed the stove properly, nothing you do will work.

The first kiss—and the first time having sex—is the same. If you prime the woman properly, the kiss is easy and seems natural. Men believe that getting the first kiss is difficult, or that there must be some complicated move or line that they are missing. They tend to focus on the wrong side of the problem. Understand this: the end of the date is *too late* to start preparing her for your kiss. Rather than focusing on the moment of the first kiss, you need to focus on taking the proper steps leading up to it.

When Bob goes for his first kiss with Sherry, he's done none of the necessary pre-work. First, Sherry sees him as a friend, and he's never given her any reason not to. He hasn't shown any romantic interest before his attempted kiss. If he had, he would have found out that she wasn't interested. Knowing this ahead of time would have pre-qualified her out of the running before he wasted time dating her. He even ignored our advice to ask romantic questions on the date as a way to set the mood. By taking her to an erotic film, without any romantic prelude, Bob created a situation which made her scared of him. Then he had the nerve to wonder why the first kiss seemed hard to get!

Paul makes similar bonehead mistakes. Once he decides that Annie isn't worth the trouble, he stops doing anything romantic. He treats her like a woman he wants to get rid of, then is surprised when she doesn't want to kiss him! Both these men wonder what they did wrong at the moment they went for the kiss. They couldn't possibly be looking in a worse place for the answer to their problem.

Bob and Paul need to be more like Bruce. Bruce realizes that the first kiss is simply a result of properly making romantic moves earlier in the date. When he first kisses Wendy, she is ready for it. He pre-qualified her as an interested woman immediately, and showed his romantic interest consistently. He asked romantic questions, and engaged her in romantic conversations. He did everything we describe in this chapter. By the time he went for the first kiss, she was ready and willing, and responded passionately. Bruce knows that the first kiss is not difficult. It's the work that leads up to it that he knows he must pay attention to.

REVIEW OF THE PRE-WORK

By this time, you already know most of what you must do to get a woman thinking romantically about you. If you need more information about these things, re-read this book! The preceding chapters have covered everything you need to know to prime a woman for physical involvement with you.

Before going for the first kiss, you must have:

* Asked the romantic questions
* Conducted the romantic conversations
* Touched her hand
* Looked into her eyes, a little too long
* Touched her nonintrusively and casually
* Made decisions quickly and easily
* Made her smile and/or laugh
* Been clear about your goals
* Made your romantic interest known
* Gathered information about her romantic needs
* Fulfilled her romantic needs on the Seduction Date
* Complimented her five times
* Checked out her body in the way specified
* Used seductive language (seduce, attraction, falling in love, romance, etc.) seven times
* Used interested body language
* Whispered to her

These are the bare-bones basics. If you haven't done most of these things, don't even consider the first kiss. Go back and do them more. Create more romantic conversations. Put her into more romantic situations. Get the basics handled, then move on.

After you've done the pre-work, there are only two steps left for you: testing her readiness, and going for the kiss.

TESTING HER READINESS

When you are going for the first kiss, certain conditions must be met, or your attempted kiss will fail. Until all of these conditions are met, you might as well not go for it; she's only going to say no. If, on the other hand, you have fulfilled these conditions, feel free to try! She's ready. You should know, however, that these conditions may be met faster than they are in the examples in this book. If the chemistry is there and if it "feels right," no matter when it comes, go for the kiss. This may be at the end of, or even during, the priming date. It may even be *before* the priming date, when you notice that her stove is primed and ready to be lit. It can even be when you first meet a woman, if she's attracted to you and the energy is right.

The conditions you must meet before going for the first kiss are:

* She is not surprised by the kiss.
* She is thinking of the kiss, and more.
* She knows that you want her, and likes the idea.

But how can you know if these conditions are met? We've developed a series of tests for our students to use before they go for the first kiss. These tests will tell you if your date is ready, and help continue to prepare her at the same time. We suggest you perform these tests, and check out her responses, before you try for it.

Touching Tests

You can test her readiness by gauging her responses to casual and romantic touching. Casual touching is simple and fast. It's when your fingers touch her when you give her a cup of coffee, or when you touch her arm or back to guide her to the table you've selected. Casual touching is ambiguous; you might be touching her as a friend, or you might be touching her as a potential lover. Romantic touching is more intrusive. If you are touching and holding her hand, or rubbing her arm, or keeping your hand on any part of her body for more than a few seconds, you are touching her romantically.

You want her to welcome longer and longer periods of touch from you. First, touch her casually, and see how she responds. More than likely, she will have no visible response at all. If she pulls away, keep your touching extremely brief, and keep up your romantic conversations. If she continuously shrugs away from your touch, consider getting rid of her and moving on. There's no reason to stay with a woman who is cold, unresponsive, and doesn't want to be romantic with you.

If she does respond positively, touch her for longer periods of time. If she gets more relaxed and animated, if her skin flushes, or if her eyes get shiny and reflective, these are all signs of positive response. In this scenario, move to putting your hand on hers for longer periods. Don't make a big deal of this, just let it seem to happen.

The hug test

One way to find out how a woman feels about you is to see how she responds to being hugged. Like casual touching, hugging is something you can usually get a woman to accept just by doing it. When you hug a woman and don't make a big deal out of it, much of the time she'll just assume that you are a guy who hugs, and not make a big deal out of it either.

We usually recommend that you avoid hugging a woman much before you are having sex with her. Hugging is a friendly thing to do, rather than a lover-ly thing to do. If she gets use to being in your arms without kissing you, it's easy for her to resolve the apparent incongruity by telling herself that you are simply a friend. Also, hugging is a time when men who are starved for touch accidentally show some desperation. They grab hold, get caught up in how good it feels to them (rather than to her), squeeze too hard, and don't let go. One woman told us about a guy she met at a party who hugged her when she was leaving, after knowing her for less than an hour. "He hugged me, then put his hands on my hips, and held me close while he said good-bye to me. It seemed really weird to be held there. I felt like I couldn't get away." The hug is a chance to screw up, so if you do it, you want to be sure to do it properly.

The first rule of hugging a woman that you are dating is that you keep it short. Short, short, short. Use it as a test of her readiness, not as a chance to get your sexual or touch needs met. You'll get enough of that later on. When saying hello or good-bye to her, you can often simply take her in your arms and hug her. If you keep it short, it won't scare her, and you'll be able to gauge her response. Does she press into you? Does she seem to want to really hang on? That's a good sign, and you might want to move to kissing her right then. If she seems to want to get away, then you know you have more work to do in making her feel romantic feelings.

The face kiss test

Along with hugging, you can try face-kissing. This is when you kiss her cheek, to see how she responds. If she leans into the kiss, and smiles, she's into it, and will be receptive to your lip-kiss later. If she pulls back, or winces, then it's back to the drawing board again. She most certainly won't be receptive to a lip-kiss if she won't take one on the cheek willingly.

Enthusiasm test

You can also gauge a woman's level of interest by her level of enthusiasm. This will be shown in her overall demeanor, but it's best shown in the time between one activity and the next. It's *between* the activities that you do together, rather than *during* them, that she has the best opportunity to claim she is tired and needs to go home. Watch her level of interest. After the movie, is she eager to go out for coffee or a drink, or does she seem reluctant? Does she seem to be looking for a juncture at which she can end the date, or is she up for partying with you all night long? It's these "between spaces" that will tell you her level of interest.

When Mike went out with Kary, he was careful to notice how she behaved between events. He took her to the local botanical gardens for their seduction date, and afterwards, invited her to get some ice cream with him. "Great!" she said. He knew that she was enthusiastic, and would probably be interested and responsive when he tried to kiss her later.

A few weeks earlier, when he had taken Kelly to that same botanical gardens, she had said "Well, I really have to get going. I've got a lot of work to do, so…well…" At this point he knew she wasn't interested, and that she probably wouldn't be responsive to a kiss. He let her leave at once, and didn't ask her to stay, whine, or, most important, try to kiss her.

Pretend kiss test

This test also primes the woman for your kiss. You begin by moving towards her, as if to kiss her, at some point "change your mind," and back off again. If, as you move toward her, she backs away, she probably doesn't want to kiss you. If she stays still, or moves slightly forward, she's probably interested. The pretend kiss can "seal the deal" for the real kiss later. If she hasn't moved away, then you both have acknowledged that a kiss in inevitable, and it's only a matter of time.

When Bruce seduces Wendy, he does all the pre-work. As the date progresses, he also tests her readiness by touching her, hugging her and kissing her face, noticing her level of enthusiasm moving from one activity to another, her responsiveness to compliments, and her response to his "pretend kiss." All these actions also improve her readiness for the kiss. Anytime he gets a response he doesn't like, he returns to building their sense of connection by doing more of the pre-work. By the time he goes for the kiss, her response is passionate and displays obvious interest.

TEST CHECKLIST

For your convenience, here is a list of the tests.

* Touching Test

* Hug Test
* Face Kiss Test
* Enthusiasm Test
* Compliment Test
* Pretend Kiss Test

GOING FOR THE FIRST KISS

If you've done the pre-work, and she's responded well to the tests, you are ready to move ahead, and kiss her for the first time. She's well-primed, ready, and all will almost certainly go smoothly. We have to cover only a few elements of technique to finish your preparation.

Timing

In every sexual and romantic interaction, timing is everything. When you go to kiss a woman, you have to be in a romantic moment *right now*. Not yesterday, not a few minutes ago, not last week on the phone. In time and with practice, you'll learn to feel romantic moments as you create them. When the romantic moment is present, make your move. Don't wait to kiss her outside her door, like men do on TV and in the movies. When the mood is there, go for it. You never know how long the mood will last, and it may not come back for hours.

Timing is one of the most difficult skills to teach. Learning this art requires practice, and a willingness to mess up. We believe that good timing is natural to all men—we just do things that destroy it. With that in mind, we can tell you the basic blocks that destroy it in romantic interactions with women:

1. Lack of confidence kills timing. By now, this should sound like a broken record to you, but we keep repeating it so it will become ingrained in your brain. Managing your confidence level with women is one of the most important things you can do. The biggest way men destroy their confidence is to look to the woman for assurance from her that the date is going well. Don't do it. Go with your gut, and move when you feel certain the time is right.

2. Being attached to the outcome kills timing. When you are acting with complete confidence, you are fully present in the moment, paying attention to what is going on around you. If you are worrying that your desired outcome won't happen, you won't be paying attention to the woman in front of you. Because you won't be paying attention, you'll mess up. Let go of your outcome—she's either going to respond, or she isn't. When you are relaxed and are goal-focused, while knowing that anything that happens is fine, you will have much better timing.

3. The wrong attitude kills timing. Just like for the rest of the date, your attitude should be one of confidence, caring, yet a bit distant, knowing that if this woman won't kiss you, another will. You must show her that she is special and you enjoy her company, but have many other loves as well.

The biggest way to destroy your attitude is to think that having success with this woman, today, will be the thing that validates your life. How many times must we say it? Nice as it is to be successful with women, you shouldn't base your self-image on whether or not the woman you are dating wants to have sex with you. Keeping that in mind will help create the proper attitude for that first kiss, and make you more attractive to her.

HOW TO GO FOR THE FIRST KISS

So you've done your pre-work, run some tests, and think she is ready for the kiss. You feel confident, have given up your outcome, and you are both feeling the romantic mood. How do you go for that first kiss?

There are four ways. They are: the "just do it" method, the "ask" method, the "announce" method, and the "she kisses you" method. Let's go over these methods one at a time.

The "just do it" method

When the feeling is right, you simply kiss her. This can happen in many different ways, depending on the circumstances. It may work best to take her in your arms; it may work best to simply lean over and kiss her lightly. The details will change depending on the situation, but the foundation of this method is consistent. You kiss her, you just do it, and don't worry.

The "ask" method

In this politically correct world of ours, this is the most legally appropriate approach to getting the first kiss. After all, kissing a woman without her permission can be considered assault. Of course, if you've used the techniques in this book, you are very unlikely to be trying to kiss a woman who would be so offended by it that she presses charges.

The problem with the "ask" method is that it works worst of all, and some women, who are interested, are turned off by this approach. Many women have told us that they are offended by men who ask if they can kiss them. Natalie, one of our interviewees, commented, "I hate it when a man asks if he can kiss me. One guy did that a few months ago, and I told him to bug off! If a guy wants to kiss me, the least he can do is be man enough to do it without asking!" It's a hard quandary for men. On the one hand, some women are telling us that we must get absolute, crystal-clear consent from men every time we touch them. On the other hand, women tell us that they are turned off by men who ask before the first kiss! We suggest that, most of the time, you not ask before kissing a woman. It simply creates more problems than it solves.

The "announce" method

This method can work quite well, and gives the woman an out if she doesn't want you to kiss her. By making some sort of announcement about what you are going to do, you aren't actually asking permission—which, as we have said, puts some women off—but you are still giving her a chance to tell you to bug off if she doesn't want a kiss. You might say "Oh, my. You are so beautiful. . .try not to panic, I'm about to kiss you," and then go for it. The "announce" method works well, and keeps you on "the right side of the law."

The "she kisses you" method

This method is just what it says: she gets so aroused and romantically inclined that she kisses you. You're probably saying to yourself "boy, that would be so great if that ever happened," but as you begin to master the material in this book, you'll start to understand that the first kiss is no big deal, however you get it. It doesn't make a huge difference if she kisses you, or if you kiss her. It's just another step in her inevitable seduction.

IF SHE SAYS NO

Congratulations! A woman rejected your kiss! While this probably won't happen often, it may well happen. Welcome! Join the club! Here's what you should and shouldn't do when a woman spurns your attempted kiss:

Decide what you are going to make it mean

Your first action, when this happens, is to decide what you are going to make it mean to you. Left to your own devices, you would probably make it mean that you are a loser and a jerk, some Saturday-Night-Live quality "Wild and Crazy Guy." Don't leave yourself to your own devices. *Decide*, in advance if possible, how you are going to handle it.

We suggest that you interpret her rejection to mean that she isn't ready yet to kiss you. It is as though she was saying, "Not now, but some other time." You may also want to take it as a sign that you have more pre-work to do. We strongly advise you to avoid making it mean that you are a loser. If you want success with women, you must make a more empowering decision about what rejection means. From our experience, no man ever has constant success without first having to face many rejections.

Never ask "why not?"

Asking "why not?" is a typical rookie mistake men make. First, it will make you look like a wimp. It calls to mind a little kid, whining "why not?" to his mother. She may view this question as a form of begging. This will make her want to kiss you even less. Second, when you ask her "why not?" she'll tell you, and that's the last thing you want. It forces her to come up with justifications for not kissing you. The more she comes up with, the less likely she will *ever* kiss you. Asking this question is virtual suicide.

Never argue with her about it

Arguing is the other rookie mistake men make in the face of women's sexual rejection. It does the same thing as asking "why not?" because it makes her dig into her position more completely. We know of no instance in which a woman has changed her mind and wholeheartedly kissed a man because he argued with her rejection. All it does is insure that she will never kiss you, ever. She will think of negative thoughts when she thinks of you, and avoid you in the future. By arguing with a woman's decision, you are saying that you don't respect her opinion and her boundaries, which will likely turn her off more.

Never beg her

Some men make this horrid mistake. Begging is a more popular move once they are in bed with a woman. Don't beg, don't cajole, don't "Aw, c'mon, you don't know how it hurts a guy." Begging a woman shows her that you are a wimpy, powerless man, who can't handle waiting for what he wants. It shows her you have no resolution to make your life what you want, and demonstrates to her that you go groveling through life. Don't do it. You will definitely lose your self-respect by lowering yourself to her whims.

Try again later

She's only rejecting you *now*, not later. While you don't want to badger her, it's a good idea to remember that some women will just want to see how you handle them saying "no." Others just aren't in the mood for it today, but they would be another time. Still others will be willing to kiss you, but only after you've done more work to show you really like them, not just their bodies. Some women simply don't want you, and never will. Remember that each "no" is a stepping stone to an eventual "yes," if not with this woman, then with some other.

THE TEN CRUCIAL MISTAKES THAT BLOW THE FIRST KISS

By now you realize that most of your dating problems have come from the dumb things you've done to wreck seduction situations. You've been "a friend," or treating a woman as you would a guy, or you've been indecisive. Let's look at the top mistakes men make going for the first kiss, and show you how to avoid them.

Mistake #1. You announce your intention to seduce her

Here's a very dumb thing that you may be tempted to do: tell your date that you have a seduction book, are studying it, and intend to use the techniques on her! You may think no one would be this dumb, but we've known plenty of men who've done it. Needless to say, she won't want to kiss you after that.

Mistake #2. You offend her by saying or doing something stupid

There's no shortage of ways to offend a woman you are dating. A *Cosmopolitan* magazine article gives a few examples of stupid things men have said or done on first dates:

* The man who asked his date, "Why is it that all the good women are taken?"

* The man who said, "I'm so intrigued by the mind of a serial killer. The rage and passion he must feel while actually killing someone is fascinating to me."

* The man who offended (and mystified) his date by saying "I shower four times a day. I have to."

* The man who felt compelled to admit that "When I have sex with a woman, I always have to imagine I'm with someone else."

* The man who said about marriage, "I'm not a big fan of the institution myself."
* The man who said about his ex-girlfriend, "Some people just *need* hitting."
* The man who invited a woman for dinner at his house and, at the end of the date, said, "To keep this relationship devoid of any sense of anyone owing anyone anything, why don't you pay your half?" He then presented her with an itemized bill of what he spent.

You can also alienate a woman by discussing your love of pornography, commenting on other women's bodies, or taking a position on a political or gender issue that she profoundly disagrees with.

You can further offend her by lighting a cigar (unless she lights one first), or engaging in a prolonged scratching session. If you do something that insults her deeply, back off at once, apologize briefly if you think it will help, and go on with the date as if nothing happened. Sadly, you often won't know what she feels. She won't tell you; she'll simply write you off, and get away from you as quickly as she can. She certainly won't kiss you.

Mistake #3. You approach the kiss as though it was a business transaction

This is a common problem for men who want to get to the bottom line, and "get down to business." You may have this problem if you are used to the business world, or are just very practical.

Men who fall into this trap have a harder time than others accepting that they must go out of their way to make a woman feel special. They see all the work involved as false, manipulative, and dishonest. They don't like it one bit, and seem set on proving us wrong. Sadly for them, we aren't wrong, and when the practical-minded man approaches a woman for a kiss, she inevitably ends up rejecting him. She tells him that he seems too "cold and calculating," which he is. You want to be warm and kind and this is achieved by being romantic, doing the little things, and following the guidelines laid out in this book.

Mistake #4. You are indecisive

When you decide to go for the kiss, go for it! Whatever method you use, this is the time when "he who hesitates is lost." Women want a strong, decisive man, and that is never more evident than on the first kiss. This does *not* mean that you become overly forceful, or that you ignore her if she protests. If she doesn't want to be kissed, of course don't kiss her. But you shouldn't weasel around about it. If you've done the pre-work, and she's passed the tests, go for it!

Mistake #5. You act like she is doing you a favor by kissing you

When Bob eventually gets that first kiss, he thanks his date! This is a mistake. You can say, "that was very nice," but don't act like she's doing you a favor that is any bigger than the one you are doing her.

Mistake #6. You get flustered by minor problems on the date, and give up

Giving up is almost always worse for the seduction than any mistake you made. Men often get flustered if a conversation doesn't go well, if she becomes offended, or if she seems suspicious of their romantic questions. Remember, she's either going to respond to you, or she isn't. It doesn't mean anything about you. If you get flustered, you can often pretend nothing happened, and move on. She may be looking to you for verification that the date is still okay, even if there was an awkward moment of odd exchange. If you don't give up, she'll see that things are fine, and probably relax.

Mistake #7. You push too hard, too quickly

Every seduction has its own pace. You can destroy the effectiveness of any of the technology in this book by doing it too hard, too fast, and too inexpertly. We know this may be hard to hear, coming as it does after hundreds of pages telling you how important it is that you take action in the seduction, but it's still true. You must take action, and you must also move at her pace.

Practically speaking, you must learn to pay attention to her responses. If she is consistently resistant and unresponsive, you may be scaring her or making her angry by pushing too hard, too quickly. Slow down and back off a bit.

If she says that you are coming on too strong, don't worry. It's great that she gave you the feedback. Remember that she's not necessarily telling you to stop seducing her, she's probably just telling you to slow down. Just say something like "Am I coming on too strong? Sorry," and compliment her. "It's just that you seem like a great woman. I'll slow things down." By saying this type of thing, you've shown her that you were only moving so fast because she's so great. By reassuring her that you will slow down, you also acknowledge that you are seducing her, and will continue. If she accepts this, the entire interaction will move the seduction forward.

Mistake #8. You surprise her by trying to kiss her "out of the blue"

Women like subtlety. They don't like aggressive surprises that seem to come out of nowhere. Your first kiss should be the culmination of a long sequence of demonstrations of your sensitivity to her. If your kiss surprises her and seems "out of the blue," she'll conclude that you are insensitive and she will not desire you.

The solution is to distinguish between your desire and your romantic-feeling moments, which will come and go. Make sure you kiss her in a romantic moment, not just because you are horny. Using the "announce" method will give her at least a few moments to prepare herself for kissing you.

Mistake #9. You ram your tongue into her mouth

Many women have told us about men who wrecked kisses they would have succeeded with by tongue-kissing too hard, too soon. The first kiss is a gentle peck, not a long French kiss. The gentle kiss acts as a prelude to a longer, more intense one. After Bruce first kissed Wendy, she said "that was the most gentle kiss I've ever had." That's the kind of response you also want.

Mistake #10. You taste like garlic, have bad breath, or taste bad

It's no use doing all the pre-work, passing all the tests, and really establishing a connection with a woman if you are just going to ruin it by having bad breath or tasting bad. A number of women have told us that men who have tried to kiss them have disgusted them by bad breath. You must not let this happen to you.

The solution is to make good breath a priority on a date. But—this is important—*never* squirt a breath spray into your mouth in front of a woman. For reasons we don't understand, women find this a total turn-off. If you have to secretly bring a toothbrush and toothpaste to the date, and excuse yourself to use them after dinner, do so (though don't tell her you brought them). Most of the time, using some kind of breath-freshener, gum, or breath mint will suffice.

TAKING THE KISS FARTHER

If she allows the first kiss, you should consider going for more right then. Ideally, you will push your kissing to the point *right before* she stops you for "going too fast." Gauging when a woman is about to stop your kisses is about as easy as cooking a soufflé until just before it burns. You can do it, but it's likely that you will end up burning it no matter how careful you are.

Allowing the kiss is not the same as enthusiastically responding to it. If she presses her breasts into you and kisses you hard, stay with it. If you are in a place conducive to more intense kissing, do it. When Josh first kissed Lynn, she responded enthusiastically. He had walked her to her car after their priming date. They both had to go to appointments. At Lynn's car, Josh kissed her. She responded well, pressing her body into his and wrapping her arms around him. He kissed her more, and they started French kissing. "Why don't we get into the car?" he asked. They got into the front seat together, kissing more and more passionately. Josh started touching her body as she panted enthusiastically. Finally he said, "The heck with my meeting. Let's go to my house." She agreed and drove him there, where they had sex.

While this will rarely happen, on occasion it will. You've got to be ready to take a first kiss as far as it can go. You must be gauging her response and continuously taking your interaction to the next level if you can. If she seems uncomfortable, slow down or back up. If she seems to be into kissing, take it farther. If you aren't paying attention, you will either take things too far, or not far enough.

Keep in mind, this is not a race. If you've done all the pre-work she will actually desire you. As a result, you can go back for more later. In many ways you are better off leaving her wanting more. Women aren't used to men who can walk away from an offer of sex, and it impresses them. After all, you may really have something else to do. You must make it work for your schedule, as we've said so many times. You want to tell her something like, "This is great, but I really do have to go. You are really something special. Can I come over later tonight, say around 10 pm after my evening commitment is over?" Get directions, set it up, and finish making love to her, at your leisure, later that night.

PASSIONATE KISSES!

You now have no excuse for wondering what you are doing wrong at the moment of the first kiss. You now understand that that moment is comparatively trivial when compared to all the important steps that come before it. You understand that there is little work that needs to be done to improve the moment of the first kiss; the real work is during every single moment leading up to it.

You start preparing a woman for the first kiss when you first meet her, when you start setting yourself apart from men who end up being "friends." You also prepare for the kiss when you show your romantic interest and flirt like a man who is interested in her. After you have her feeling good, after one or more interactions, you either ask her for her phone number, or you ask her out. If she says yes, you proceed to the priming date. If she says no, you move on to the next woman, or keep working on her and ask her out again later.

On the priming date, you prepare for the first kiss by being decisive, looking into her eyes, touching her, continuing to make your romantic interest known, making her smile and laugh, using interested body language, checking out her body, whispering something romantic to her, asking romantic questions, and conducting romantic conversations.

If you don't kiss her on the priming date, you continue to prepare her for the first kiss on the seduction date. This is done by repeating much of the priming date, plus setting up experiences that create romantic feelings in her. These experiences leave her feeling special, attracted, and cared for. You test her readiness, which also prepares her further. Finally, when you kiss her, she is not surprised, is totally ready, and is thinking about it, too. You are finally ready to proceed easily onto the next step—being the man of her dreams in bed.

chapter ten...
Being the Man of Her Dreams in Bed

After months of work, Bob finally brought home a woman. Barb was in her late 30s, fairly attractive, a cute face and tall, but overweight. Earlier in the night they had watched football at a sports bar. Bob kissed and held her as they stood in the crowd. As soon as the game ended, he suggested that they move the date to his home. She agreed.

Minutes later, they entered his dark and gloomy house. Dirty clothes were strewn around the room, as were empty pizza boxes and dishes with moldy food stuck to them. To make things worse, there were the stacks and stacks of paper all over the floor.

Bob shoved the garbage away to create a path to the couch. The hot and sensual feeling had been lost among the mess. Barb sat on the couch and Bob immediately began stroking her hair and kissing her. He then tried to touch her breasts. She pushed his hands away. Once again they kissed, and he attempted to grab her. When she pushed him away a second time he felt embarrassed and angry.

Bob stopped touching her, crossed his arms, and sat looking angry for several minutes. Luckily, Barb said, "This isn't working. Let's start over again." She made the move and kissed him gently. Again he grabbed one of her breasts. She pushed him away again.

"Bob, that hurts. Be gentle with me, or I'm leaving," she said. "Pam, my ex-girlfriend always liked it when I pinched her nipples," Bob argued. She responded "Look, either be gentle with my body or I'm leaving."

Bob made a greater effort and touched her gently. Barb calmed down and the mood intensified. She then took off her shirt, slowly undid her bra, and placed Bob's left hand on her right breast. "Touch it gently, like this," she explained. He enjoyed himself, rubbing circles around her nipples with his fingertips. She moaned, and asked him if they could cuddle in his bed.

"Now I am going to get some," Bob thought to himself. "All the months of waiting are about to pay off." They walked hand-in-hand into his bedroom. "Let's get naked," he exclaimed, as he began throwing off his clothes. "No, please hold me. I just want to snuggle next to you and feel how much we like each other," Barb replied. Once again, he felt upset, but did it anyway. They held each other in his bed. He softly stroked her hair and kissed her all over. Barb laughed when he kissed her neck. He immediately responded in a defensive manner, "What are you laughing at? What did I do this time?" She told him, "I like how you are touching me. My neck is just ticklish, that's all." He seemed so inexperienced to Barb. She found it kind of cute, and decided to continue. Just then, the phone rang and he stopped to answer it. Barb stared at him in disbelief. She couldn't believe that he would stop a romantic moment to talk on the phone.

Once he got off the phone, she kissed him and pushed him onto his back. She pretended to ride him like a horse, and he enjoyed this position immensely. Bob began unbuttoning her jeans and running his fingers over her underwear. He pinched her thigh very roughly and it hurt her. Once again, she asked him to be more gentle. As she told him this, he looked at his watch. "Do you have an appointment sometime soon?" she asked him.

Bob continued to make every mistake in the book. Even so, Barb was ready for intercourse. She asked him where he kept the condoms. "Gosh, I didn't think we would get this far tonight. I don't have any. If you want to wait, I can drive down to a nearby all-night grocery store." Barb stared at him in disbelief and shrugged her shoulders. "I have one in my purse." She ran into the living room and returned with one in hand.

"Why do you have condoms in your purse? Is this something you do often?" he asked her. "Shut up, Bob! If you offend me one more time I'm leaving. What I do in my life is none of your business. You're lucky I am letting you touch me at all. Besides, *you* didn't have any condoms. I would say that beggars can't be choosers." Bob felt humiliated, but wanted to have sex so badly he didn't dare respond.

He ripped open the condom package and quickly put it on. He immediately tried to enter her. "Not so fast. Slow down, cowboy. Kiss me first," Barb said. He kissed her insensitively, jamming his tongue into her mouth, and then attempted to enter her again.

By this time Barb could not believe how strangely and uncomfortably Bob was acting. Even so, she continued to have sex with him. Throughout the experience, he refused to look at her. She kept looking into his eyes and smiling. The more it happened, the more uncomfortable he felt. He even interrupted the process to turn off the lights to avoid seeing her face. When they finally did have sex, he tried to be fast and furious, ignoring her desires. Never did he attempt to see if she was enjoying herself, or if he could do anything to improve her experience. Bob went on, only concerned with his own pleasure.

After he was satisfied, Bob turned over, without saying a word, and instantly fell asleep. Moments later, Barb got dressed, and stormed out of the house. She felt angry, and vowed never to see Bob again.

We know you're not Bob, but you think you're Casanova, and you're not. You think you satisfy a woman every time, and are the opposite of Bob, but it's not true. You assume your sexual communication skills are wonderful, but they aren't. You know that you are easy to get along with, but it's a lie. No matter how great you are in bed, there is always more to learn.

This chapter focuses on how to be a great lover. We will cover the common problems and concerns men go through when having sex for the first time with a woman, and during relationships. We'll also discuss strategies to use before, during, and after sex.

THE TRIANGLE OFFENSE: THE THREE KEYS TO IMPROVING ANY MAN'S SEX LIFE

Bob is a horrid lover because he hasn't mastered three critical areas in the bedroom: communication, technique and attitude. This chapter will give you hands-on (no pun intended) skills in these three areas. As you increase your degree of mastery, your sex life will also inevitably improve. Better yet, each of these three solutions supports the others. So, for example, if you better your technique, your attitude will improve. When your attitude improves, so does your technique. Besides, spending time perfecting these areas can be a lot of fun.

We know you have a busy life and you don't need yet another set of things to do. There are hundreds of other books that describe sexual etiquette and women's hottest fantasies, including the wonderful *Sexpectations* by Ron Louis. By routinely spending time increasing your knowledge and skill level in each of the following three areas, you will become a master in the bedroom.

Communication

Any problem can be resolved through communication. Any concern, fear, mood, or thought can be transformed by opening your mouth and talking. We are always communicating. Body language, listening skills, vocal tone, word choice, and volume all play a part in communication. In the bedroom, communication skills are particularly essential if you want to be a hot and memorable lover. They can make or break the mood. If a woman feels afraid during sex, a good communicator can quickly calm her down and comfort her. Someone like Bob, however, will make the problem worse.

A chronic complaint among women is that men just don't communicate and talk enough. For our purposes, let's bring communication into the bedroom. Given that all women's bodies are so different, you will have to ask questions during sex.

The sexual master asks questions, not the amateur. The master knows that talking will intensify things, not interrupt them. Rod, for example, was in bed with Patricia. He began licking her left breast and she moaned. He continued, and began touching her other breast with his hand. She moaned even more. This continued on for several minutes. Rod took a short break, and asked her how hard she liked to be touched. "Because my breasts are so large, they also need a lot of stimulation," she said. When Bob touched her again he used more force. Patricia moaned even louder. By asking a simple question, he turned her on even more.

Technique

By technique, we are referring to a man's knowledge of female anatomy, and his familiarity with sexual interactions. To be specific, different positions, fantasies, products, methods, foreplay, afterplay, kissing, and much more. These are all forms of sexual interaction that, when combined, create a body of distinctions called technique.

Bob treats Barb so roughly, he fails to keep the mood. He has no idea how to be gentle when touching her vagina. He has no idea what or where a clitoris is. His technique is nonexistent. To learn more, he should start studying and understanding what women want in a lover. This information is readily available.

This chapter is not going to tell you all the secret sex positions in one easy lesson. We recommend that you go into a bookstore and pick up books on how to satisfy a woman, a detailed position book, a massage book, and one that tells you how to keep yourself going all night long. These are the techniques needed to be a world-class lover. When you feel comfortable with your skill level, you will have an easier time relaxing. And the sex will be even hotter.

Attitude

Attitude is everything! If you have a good attitude in the bedroom, sex will be fun, easy and ecstatic. A bad attitude will leave the woman thinking you are hard-headed, nasty, cocky, worried and a womanizer. Bob has a bad attitude and it is the first thing people see when they meet him. He is unpleasant to be around, and most women won't even give him the time of day. It is his attitude, not his technique, that makes women react this way.

We recommend that you adopt a fun, outrageous, confident, playful, and easygoing attitude in the bedroom. If you want to be a memorable lover, you will have to leave her feeling special, full of passion and fun. Besides feeling totally unsatisfied, Barb left Bob's house vowing to never see him again. In fact, the sex was so bad that she kept hoping it would end so she could finally go home. If Bob had talked to her, and had been open to having fun, they both would have had a better time. She may have instructed him on how to please her. Instead, Bob was so caught up in trying to look like he knew what he was doing, and pleasing himself, that he missed the opportunity.

One attitude killer that affects many men is the classic dose of guilt. This feeling arises when a man thinks he is pulling one over on a woman, and manipulating her for sex. If he is doing something that violates his integrity, or that he feels is wrong, it will bleed into every interaction with her. Worse yet, he fails to realize that women are fully aware that men do this. Women are smarter than you think. They know that all you want to do is get them into bed, and they know that you will do anything to accomplish this. When you interact with a woman fully aware that she knows what you want, it will boost your confidence. It will open up many nights of hot sex and a freedom for you to let go of expectations.

To improve your attitude, study men who interact with women in ways you respect. Sean Connery, Clint Eastwood, John Travolta, and Jack Nicholson all tend to play strong male figures who have no problem meeting women and going to bed with them. They do this on screen and off. They display a playful, yet very strong male presence that drives women wild. Study their attitudes, and they will rub off on you. Before you go into bed with a woman, decide what attitude you want to convey. Use the exercises to psych yourself up, and then create the ultimate experience for the woman you are with.

PREPARING FOR THE MOMENT
WHEN IT TURNS SEXUAL

There is a moment when the date turns sexual. It may occur while you are kissing and turned on, when you both want more. Or, when you are watching a movie on the couch and passion erupts. Whatever the details of the situation, there is always a distinct moment when the kissing moves into more. Pay attention to this time. Savor it! Begin to notice what led up to it. There are several things you can do to create this moment. By doing the pre-work, once again, and preparing yourself and the environment, the likelihood greatly improves.

Creating the romantic space

You don't have to be a genius to realize that a romantic mood can be created. We've told you this in every way we know how. What follows is a basic list of qualities to make a room romantic. Just as you've been preparing yourself mentally for dates, by psyching yourself up and practicing romantic questions, we also recommend you prepare the physical space and get it ready for hot and heavy fun.

Soft lighting

No one in their right mind feels sensual in a brightly lit room. In fact, studies have shown that people tend to relax in a dimly lit room, and become tense in brightly lit ones. This phenomenon can be used to your advantage. When kissing a woman, it works best to dim the lights. Do it discreetly. A woman won't be impressed if she thinks you are a playboy trying to be smooth and are trying to seduce her. Be subtle. Lower the lights and let the mood shift slowly. Let her relax over several minutes and then prepare for romance 101.

Music

The same geniuses who spent time finding out that dim lighting mellows people out also realized that music alters the mood. We bet you aren't too surprised to find out that blaring Led Zeppelin at full volume has a different effect than playing gentle classical music in the background. Good music can become your friend. It not only blocks out background noise, but creates an atmosphere conducive for your sex. It is important, however, to play music she enjoys. If you get the chance, find out which artists she likes before the date. Better yet, let her browse your CD collection and pick the ones she

likes. The mood will be ruined if she dislikes the music you are playing. Make sure the music fits the purpose of creating the magical
mood and you will be that much closer to a memorable night for
everyone.

Incense

Women are much more sensitive to smell than men. As a result,
we recommend *not* burning incense unless you are sure she enjoys
it. Since smells are very personal, there is a high likelihood of burning something she will dislike, which may then actually turn her *off*.
The same is true for air fresheners, aromatherapy, aftershaves, and
potpourri. If she picks a scent and associates it with sex, it will be
wonderful. You can create the association between sex and a scent
early on if you go to a perfume store, or health food shop, and have
her pick a vial of aromatherapy essence, incense, or aftershave.

Candles

After dating Wendy for a few weeks, Bruce set up a hedonistic
picnic in his bedroom. He had researched her ideal foods and music
ahead of time. Everything was set up to her specifications. She
arrived at his home promptly at 11:00 pm. After talking for a few
moments, Bruce told her to close her eyes, he had a surprise for her.
He held Wendy's hand and guided her into his bedroom. The entire
place was perfectly clean, and lit candles were placed along the window sills and on the nightstand. When Wendy opened her eyes she
was amazed at the room. Everything was perfect. The candles were
the added extra that made everything work.

Candles are part of the traditional romantic scene. A candlelit
bedroom full of pillows and great music will be irresistible. Minimal
light is much better than total darkness. Women want to keep an eye
on you. Candles truly set the mood, and leave everyone happy.

Fireplace

If you look back at the past decades of *Playboy* magazine, you
will find many of the models posing in front of a fireplace. If you
wanted to bore yourself to tears and read through hundreds of the

romance novels women read, you would again find dozens of scenes where women are making love with broad-chested men in front of a fire. We found this striking. While men and women are different in thousands of ways, one shared appreciation is to make love in front of a blazing fire. You and the woman will be in heaven if you can find a way to have a romantic evening doing the same.

Just imagine for a moment that you are out on a date, and it has been going great. You took a wonderful woman out to dinner and a walk. Now you and she are lying on a carpeted floor. Seconds ago, you fed her pieces of fruit, and gently kissed her lips. You then ran your fingers down her naked body. The room is dark, except for light from the fire. It crackles as she touches you. Do anything you can, pull any strings, pay money if necessary, to find a room with a fireplace to take your date.

SETTING THE MOOD
WITH SENSUAL TALK

Having the room ready to go will greatly aid the creation and maintenance of the mood. The next step is that the discussion also switch to romance and sex. Romantic conversation is a form of foreplay. In fact, it's nearly as important as touching and caressing her. Most women, in a romantic situation, will melt when you compliment their body, answer romantic questions, and describe what it feels like when they feel really attracted to someone.

In our interviews, most women mentioned feeling nervous the first time having sex with a man. Each woman feared that her sex partner wouldn't like her body. From this information we saw the importance of complimenting a woman's body during sex. Compliments create and maintain an atmosphere in which she feels safe and alleviates her fears. Compliments can be a wonderful turn on and make her want you even more.

What to compliment her on

1. Her Body. Compliment specific body parts. Compliment her on the sparkle in her eyes, or the way her skin glows in the candlelight. Be careful, however, not to be crude. Saying something like "you have great tits" won't seem like a compliment. "Your breasts are beautiful" will. Go through her body and compliment the different areas. This can also make her laugh, which will also add to the fun.

2. Beauty. An important aspect in being a memorable lover is that the woman leaves the experience feeling like you had an outstanding experience with her. She wants to be noticed as an individual, not just as any woman. One way to accomplish this is by frequently complimenting her beauty. Let her know that you are attracted to her. Let her know that she is special and that you are thrilled she is with you. By telling her she is beautiful, gorgeous, pretty, lovely, hot, sexy, vivacious, radiant, splendid, and the hundreds of other forms of beauty, she will likely melt in your arms.

3. Technique. Along with compliments about their looks and specific body parts, all women want to know you enjoy being in bed with them. Most guys don't realize that women want to be complimented for their sexual performance. Once again, women want to know that they please you. They know that sex is one of the most important things to guys; if they can be hot looking and be good in bed, a man will more interested in them than if they aren't. By complimenting a woman on her sexual technique, you will make her feel closer to you, and the chances of a repeat performance are greatly increased.

THE MOTIONS THAT CONVEY EMOTION

During both sex and foreplay it is important that you maintain eye contact. This simple rapport greatly aids in the connection between the two of you. Bob, for example, refuses to look at Barb while they make love. Avoiding eye contact makes it seem like he doesn't care about her, and puts distance between them. When you smile at a woman, for example, during love making, it bonds the two of you, and makes her feel appreciated.

The same is true for kissing her in loving ways. A gentle kiss on the cheek during sex, will reassure her, and let her know that you care. These small signs add up for women. They will experience them as forms of nurturing, affection, and appreciation.

When Bruce has sex, he frequently smiles and usually retains eye contact. Chara recently stripped for him. He stared hungrily into her eyes. At the end of the dance, Chara walked to him and they kissed long and hard. As they took each other's clothes off Bruce smiled while looking into her eyes. He kissed her cheek and undid her bra. Chara smiled back, and even giggled a little. Even though Bruce wanted to close his eyes and go off into his own world, he kept occasional eye contact to hold the mood. He realized that eye contact and gentle kisses would keep Chara calm and connected. Bruce has mastered doing these small things, and the women usually come back wanting more.

TOPICS TO AVOID IN BED

Compliments will aid the mood, but there are numerous topics that can kill it. Read these over carefully to insure you don't screw up a hot moment. We also recommend that you pre-screen her for offensive talk by asking questions during the foreplay time, such as "Do you think women like guys who talk dirty during sex?" You will then get the lowdown if she likes that sort of thing. Any other questions you have, do it during the seduction date, or during foreplay.

Avoid:

* Talking about other women
* Your love of pornography
* Admitting that you don't understand her, or any woman's, body
* How long it has been since you've had sex
* Using vulgar words, unless she starts
* Telling her when you are about to have an orgasm
* Insulting her body
* The future status of your relationship with her
* Talking about topics not related to sex, like sports scores or work.

THE ART OF FOREPLAY

If you had to pick one sexual position or act that the majority of women report as essential to satisfying them, what would it be? Is it having an orgasm? No. Is it being bitten on the nape of the neck? No. Is it penetration? No. Is it having their breasts touched? No. If you responded yes to any of the above questions, you are wrong!

Since the earliest sex surveys, women have reported that foreplay is their favorite and most satisfying part of sex. They also reported that men consistently don't spend enough time on it. Most of us avoid it. Instead, we go right for intercourse. Your new job is to satisfy her, and blow her away with your skills in the bedroom. We strongly advise you to alter your routine from focusing on yourself and your needs, to her and what makes her hot.

We first want to make sure you understand what foreplay is. We define it as all the kissing, touching, and talking that comes before intercourse. Remember all the steps and preparation that went into the first kiss (flirting, casual touching, romantic talk, tests for readiness, etc.)? Foreplay is the pre-work for having sex. It is the necessary activity that insures a memorable experience. All master seducers spend time on foreplay. Even if they just want to cut to intercourse, they spend time doing the pre-work because they want to please the woman and increase the chances of a repeat sexual experience.

We recommend that you change your sexual habits and stretch out the amount of time you spend on foreplay. It is important that you become a woman's favorite lover. We hope this book has taught you, if nothing else, that being confident and powerful as a man will get you a woman. If you blunder your way through sex, however, and don't turn her on, or create and maintain the mood, all your progress is flushed down the drain. She probably won't be too impressed if you are ignorant about the basics, and she'll probably avoid going back to bed with you.

We also recommend that you go from five minutes of foreplay and three minutes of sex, to at least 15 minutes on foreplay and 30 minutes of sex. Remember, all women are different. What one loves, another hates, and so on. So begin touching and caressing her, exploring what she enjoys. The same goes true for kissing. Does she like short kisses, or long sloppy ones? Find out immediately, and continue in that vein. Go with the flow. The sexual world is a spontaneous one. You never know what will happen. Maybe you'll end up on the floor of her apartment, having intense sex. Or on the couch kissing and having oral sex. Let it happen.

THE MAIN EVENT

Now that the foreplay is done, let's move on to the main event. Many women require at least 15 minutes of foreplay to get turned on enough for sex. After that, they need at least 15 minutes of attention to have an orgasm. Most women can't orgasm solely from intercourse. Usually, spending time touching, rubbing, or licking her clitoris is required. If you aren't sure where the clitoris is, and how to touch it, rush out and buy a sex book today. This knowledge isn't secret, and you should avail yourself of it before you get into bed with a woman again.

During sex, we recommend that you make her come first. Most guys have no problem achieving orgasm quickly. In fact, there are millions of men who suffer from premature ejaculation. If you get her off first, you can justify coming quickly. Your job is nearly done.

A good lover is also generous in the bedroom. When Bob, for instance, only focuses on himself, Barb thinks he is a jerk and is not satisfied. We have found that most men are more satisfied knowing that the woman had a good time. Men often report feeling a sense of confidence knowing that they brought her to orgasm. We recommend you spend whatever time is necessary learning how to bring a woman over the edge.

If sex is working the way you hoped, you will both be pleasured by the experience. We recommend that you study up on sex positions to make sex even greater. No one wants to fall into a monotonous sexual trap. Books like the *Kama Sutra* and dozens of others, available at most bookstores, will help broaden your sexual horizons. The woman will appreciate your knowledge of sex, and respect you for it. It will also be worth your time to learn ways to control your orgasm and increase your sensitivity.

ENJOYING AFTERPLAY

Most men fail to realize that afterplay is essential each and every time you have sex. Now that the action is over, you probably just want to turn over and go to bed. Yes, you did go through the laborious process of pleasuring yourself. It is still essential, however, that you hold and cuddle with her before sleep. The sexual masters know that cuddling and talking after sex must become habitual. While all you want to do is fall asleep, she, most likely, wants to be held, kissed, and shown that you still appreciate her. If you don't, she'll probably think you're a jerk. Besides, while you are holding her, it is also the perfect time to deepen the bonding between the two of you. Afterplay doesn't require hours and hours of time; even 5-10 minutes should suffice. Spoon with her, give her a few kisses and compliments, and you can be on your way to a night of relaxing sleep.

Another key reason to spend time cuddling is that the first time you make love with a woman, she usually decides if it will happen again. If you hold her, compliment her, and follow the other steps mentioned, sex will probably be repeated. If not, she probably won't want to see you again.

POSSIBLE PROBLEMS
AND HOW TO SOLVE THEM

Whether they come at convenient times or not, problems in the bedroom are inevitable. Sex is a topic that causess more controversy, upset, and problems than nearly anything else. Sex will frequently trigger emotional responses for you and for your erotic partner. As a rule of thumb, all problems are an opportunity for you to handle and create a deeper connection between the two of you. Sex has the power to ruin or strengthen any relationship. A relationship can quickly be destroyed if you fail to take a woman's problems seriously while having sex. This is a cardinal sin of any master seducer.

We offer a list of potential problems, so you won't be caught off guard when they inevitably happen. Refer to the conflict resolution techniques explained in the Seduction Date chapter to guide you through most conflicts.

"I am not comfortable with the speed we are going at."

In sexual situations women usually think that the man is going too far, too fast. The solution is simple: Slow down! Perhaps it was so simple that you missed it, so we'll say it again: Slow down! A wonderful lover never pushes a woman. He respects her wishes and immediately slows down. Someone like Bob gets angry at the woman when she makes any comments or requests in bed. Bruce realizes that if a woman feels that things are going too far, respecting her wishes is crucial. He wants the date to go well, for her to be happy, and to stop the sexual process at any time she wishes. In these sensitive times, he knows that if you don't stop, or slow down, when a woman asks, she may consider it harassment, and put him at legal risk. He never wants to be in this position.

Think about it this way: if you and a woman are kissing and heavy petting, she obviously likes you. It is also likely that she is interested in spending more time with you. Even if you end up spending a half-hour touching and kissing and she wants to stop, do it. It will make the next time that much better. Most men find it useful to take the long-term view towards sex. By stopping, you insure that you will probably see her again. If you feel that she has required you to stop prematurely, go on to someone else and come back to this one later.

"I'm sort of seeing someone."

The classic moral dilemma: Do you date a woman who has a boyfriend or not? The first question to answer is whether or not you feel comfortable having sex with someone in a relationship. We've had students who care and those who don't. We refuse to make this moral decision for you. The most important factor is to always act consistent with your beliefs. If you care, don't date her again. If you have no moral dilemma, go for it.

If you decide to go through with it, and start seeing her regularly, console her, and comfort her. Be understanding of her predicament. She probably feels guilty for cheating on a guy she's dating. At the same time, make sure to leave the commitment loose. After all, unless her relationship is on the rocks, or the verge of breakup, she will likely see you as only a diversion from her normally bleak existence. In other words, you will be her sex buddy. This arrangement may work perfectly. The larger strategy is to *not* make her comments a big deal. Stay calm, cool, and collected, and then move forward.

"I really care about you and I want more than a one-night thing."

Many women date in hopes of meeting a special man for a committed relationship. Men often date in hopes of pure sex. The solution to this problem is to assure her that you too are looking for more than a one-night thing. It's true. Whether the sex is good or not, you want to keep her around for more than one night. Once again, be sympathetic and comfort her while still being honest.

Bob and Sharon had been out a few times. On the fourth date they wound up in bed together. Sharon mentioned to him that she wanted a boyfriend, and not just a one-night sexual experience. Bob commented, "I think we should skip all the chitchat and get down to business." He made the mistake of trying to ignore her concern, without providing her with a satisfactory solution. This common concern can't be ignored. It must be dealt with.

Here are some suggestions:

"I am unsure about my long-term goals. Eventually I want a serious girlfriend, but now I'm not so sure. However, I like you a lot and hope we can continue getting to know each other."

"It is okay if you want to stop. I know that if we continue it will intensify for both of us. I know that I care about you very much and it will change things. However, I am willing to take the risk if you are."

"I have some disease, herpes, or VD."

Hopefully the woman will mention this fact *before* you sleep with her. If she admits this to you *after* sex, leave and break up with her immediately. A woman who lies to you and puts your health in jeopardy is trouble and has already put you in great risk.

If she tells you about her diseases *before* sex, stay calm and don't get upset. Don't jump to conclusions. First, find out what she has and if it will *definitely* interfere with your sexual relationship. Getting the information will help you make an informed decision about things. Talk to a doctor or pharmacist about it. Diseases are far from an exact science. It is likely that even if she thinks the disease has been cured, or isn't contagious, you still have a good chance of catching it. Be smart.

If you see a future with the woman, purchase the necessary protective gear for sex. A dental dam, for example, allows you to explore her vagina, without getting the secretions in your mouth. Look at a guide to safe sex for other pointers.

If she has a more serious disease, like crabs, chlamydia, gonorrhea, stop seeing her until it is cured. All three can be knocked out with prescription drugs.

HIV is a much more serious problem. Definitely don't have sex with her, even with condoms. The risks are too great. You might want to touch and fondle each other, and stop there. But for most men this won't be satisfying for long. If you fall in love and foresee a long-term relationship, however, there are always methods to make it work.

Unfortunately, if she has diseases, you shouldn't see her until you understand them better. We are not doctors and cannot give you advice. As ministers of sex, however, we know that many STDs are treatable and do go away. We recommend that you spend time at the library, on the computer, or in a bookstore, finding out the facts. Always talk to a doctor if you have any concerns. In this day of such dangerous diseases prepare yourself.

"If I were to get pregnant, I'd keep the baby."

No matter on what end of the abortion issue you stand, when a woman tells you she would keep a baby, it is reason to worry. Why is she telling you this? She has already decided what to do if, and when, someone impregnates her. You should be fully aware, too, of these risks. We recommend that you proceed with great caution. Don't depend on her to provide the contraception. Even if she uses an IUD, is on the pill, uses a diaphragm, or anything else, always use condoms religiously and use caution. Stop often to make sure that the condom is still on, and hasn't broken. If you ignore our advice and have unprotected sex with a woman who is committed to keeping a baby, you can easily get stuck with child support payments for the next 18 years. This does happen. Don't let it happen to you.

"I hate condoms; we don't need to use them."

When a woman tells you that condoms aren't necessary, an alarm should go off in your head instantly. You can be sure that the woman is incredibly stupid, dangerously so. If you follow her moronic advice you not only are risking your future health, but future finances if she gets pregnant.

Even though she may be dumb, you can still sleep with her if you have a condom. She may just really like you, and feel swept up with the heat of the moment. Once again, proceed with caution and make sure to wear a condom. Generally, in cases like this, we would advise you to avoid this woman. She will probably cause trouble down the road.

She complains about her body

The date went great, just as planned. Now you are finally in bed with her. After 15 minutes of foreplay, you are in a frenzy, grunting, eyes closed, teeth clenched, feeling like a million bucks. You are having sex and loving every second. Out of the blue, you are brought back to reality when the woman starts to whine about her body. "Do you think I'm pretty?" she asks. Or, "Do you think my butt is too large?" The last thing you want to do is talk, let alone discuss one of her pet problems. Unfortunately, to insure that the experience continues, you must stop and handle her momentary problem.

The solution is to always compliment her. Say something like, "I love your body as it is. I wouldn't change a thing. The way you look totally turns me on. Your (body part that she is complaining about) is perfect. In fact, I love it. I want it." This type of response should calm her down and allow you to continue with sex, until satisfied. Repeat the above process as many times as needed until she is happy.

"I am still healing from old relationships and I can't risk getting hurt again. My heart just can't take it."

All of us are vulnerable after ending a relationship. Women going through the healing process are particularly sensitive because they are acutely aware of the potential pain that comes from breaking up. Women in this position are usually looking for an informal relationship, not another serious one. They are on the mend and are looking for a transitional fling to get their feet back into the dating world. They probably want a man who is fun, easy to be around, and not demanding.

When a woman tells you she is still healing from a breakup, she wants to make sure you are not going to fall in love with her or become dependent on her. She wants to avoid the hassle of taking care of you and worrying about yet another man's feelings. We recommend you talk to her and tell her that while you are open to a relationship, you are more focused on having something fun that's *not* serious. Ironically, most of the time, mentioning to a woman that you are interested in a serious relationship is good. It is what they want to hear and it's a credibility booster. A woman on the mend, however, wants to avoid a serious relationship. If she thinks you are looking only for something serious, it will be another strike against you.

She cries during sex

It is a natural occurrence that some women cry during sex. They cry for many reasons such as the emotion of it all, the intimacy, because they care so deeply for you, as a release after an orgasm, because they remember a traumatic sexual experience or host of other reasons. Most of the time, just staying calm and continuing will make everything fine.

When the woman reacts to sex with all-out sobbing, stop having sex immediately. Hold her and find out what is going on. If you continue with sex, it will be trouble later. By continuing, she'll think you are insensitive. After holding her and talking for a few moments, the majority of women will calm down. You can then move back in for more action. If not, be patient and weigh whether or not sex will happen again that night.

STAYING ALIVE: SAFE SEX IN THE '90s

If you want to be a scholar of romance, you have to learn to use your big head rather than the little one. There are two things to worry about: sexual diseases and pregnancy. Whether you care to admit it or not both problems effect you. While each can cause massive problems, they can also be easily avoided.

Most men blame the heat of the moment for not using condoms. Or they dish off responsibility to women for such things. The immature man fails to use condoms because he doesn't stay aware of the dangers. He will ultimately be full of regret for not taking a long-term view of things and only going for momentary pleasure with a woman. Using condoms 100 percent of the time is the only sensible solution.

The most common sexually transmitted diseases (STDs) are chlamydia, crabs, genital warts, gonorrhea, and herpes. Consult with your local Planned Parenthood Organization or bookstore to receive brochures on these topics. We will cover the most simple basics, and strongly recommend you do more reading on the subject to fully understand the dangers.

If you have an STD, we advise you to tell all the women you might have infected. While it may be embarrassing, it simply is the right thing to do. Many of the diseases can be a serious problem if not treated soon after infection.

We always advise you to see a doctor the moment there are any problems. There are free clinics all over the US that can help if you don't have money. STDs are nothing to mess around with. They are very serious, can cause you and your partner horrible health risks, including death. We are in no position to advise you on any medication or cure; only doctors can help with this. We mention these signs and symptoms as another way to advise you to take the potential risks seriously.

Chlamydia

Chlamydia is the most common STD. The Centers for Disease Control and Prevention report that approximately 4 million people are infected with this disease every year.

It is particularly prevalent among those 25 and under. Most symptoms have a delayed reaction and lie dormant in men for three weeks or more. The reactions are simply minor irritations of the penis. In women, symptoms stay dormant until they appear as a serious problem. If it goes undetected, chlamydia can damage their reproductive anatomy and even cause infertility. The cure is antibiotics, which usually get rid of the disease and symptoms in one week.

Genital warts

Few things seem worse than having a wart-covered penis. However, up to 3 million new cases are reported every year, and 24 million Americans may already be infected. This bad news comes from the National Institute of Allergy and Infectious Diseases. If you are dating many women at once, your likelihood of getting warts is greatly increased.

Warts are small, painless bumps. Most commonly, they are found on the penis, scrotum, anus, or mouth. In women, they are usually spread deep inside the vagina, or on the cervix. If they go untreated, they can grow into huge fleshy bumps.

Warts are very serious and require the help of a doctor. The standard treatment is to remove them with lasers or by freezing. Even after they are removed, repeat visits to a doctor are advisable.

Crabs

Crabs are similar to lice. They have short lives, yet lay eggs all over the area they happen to be in. Unlike most of the other diseases, you can get crabs not only from intercourse, but also through close physical contact. You can even get them from bed sheets and clothing. Most commonly, they go for hair: armpit, public, and on the top of your head. From there they spread onto eyelashes, and any place else they can get to.

The main symptom of Crabs is itching. The most irritating spots might look like a rash or zits. You might also notice little white bumps. These are eggs laid by the crabs. The solution is to purchase an over-the-counter shampoo and use it, as directed, to kill the suckers. Also, wash all sheets and clothing that could have come into contact with them. Eventually, the problem will be solved and things will get back to normal.

Herpes

Perhaps you've teased friends who have the obvious herpe canker sores on their mouth. There was a swell of the disease during the 1980s. The Centers for Disease Control and Prevention now estimate that approximately 16 percent of all Americans over the age of 15 are infected. That amounts to 30 million people, with 200,000 new cases per year.

There are two kinds of herpes. The first type is spread through cold sores on and around the mouth. The second type is spread through the genital area, usually through sex. Once you have herpes, it will stay in your body indefinitely. The good news is that it only flares up occasionally. Some people have appearances often, as in weekly or monthly, and others only a few times per year.

The first time they appear is the worst. Most people get flu-like symptoms which usually return before each outbreak. This is followed by skin discomfort. Herpes looks like a blister, and eventually scabs and heals. Most people have it for short periods of time, usually no longer than ten days.

The bad news is that it never goes away. There is no cure. Once infected, you are always contagious, sometimes more than others. The closest thing to a remedy is Acyclovir, a prescription drug. Currently, it is the only prescription for herpes approved by the FDA. While it won't keep herpes away permanently, it seems to greatly reduce both the severity and frequency. Talk to a doctor for a prescription. We also recommend that you call the Herpes Hotline at (919) 361-8488; it is a wonderful source of information on how to live with the disease.

Gonorrhea

Nicknamed "the clap," gonorrhea continues to be a huge problem. Approximately 1 million cases are reported each year with an equal number unreported. If left untreated, men can expect to have painful urination permanently. The symptoms can also spread to the brain, heart, and joints. For men, the first symptoms will appear ten days after contact or later. Experiencing pain in the penis and burning during urination are the first signs. The next step is for a greenish, grayish liquid to drip from the tip of the penis. Many men, however, don't experience any symptoms.

The good news is that antibiotics get rid of gonorrhea easily and painlessly. Your doctor can conduct a urination test to make sure.

AIDS & HIV

The myth that HIV is only in the gay community is completely false. In 1992, AIDS (acquired immune deficiency syndrome) became the leading cause of death among American men aged 25–44. By 1995, it was the leading cause among *all* Americans in the same age group. We are talking about a problem so horrid and scary that you don't want to be stupid enough to ignore its far-reaching effects. There is, as of yet, no cure. All other venereal diseases are a cakewalk in comparison.

However, even if a person is infected with HIV, it doesn't mean that he or she has AIDS. HIV can live dormant in the body for many years. Eventually, however, most cases turn into AIDS. All of a sudden the disease paralyzes its victim's immune system.

HIV is transmitted through blood and sexual fluids. This usually means through needles and unprotected sex. If you use condoms, you should stay safe. The other solution, is to avoid sharing needles. If you have herpes, for example, you have a higher risk of contracting HIV because the sores on your genitals or mouth are an open target for transmission.

We recommend that every man reading this book get tested to insure you don't have the disease. It is a cheap and quick test and can reassure both you and your partner that you *don't* have HIV. If you do contract HIV a doctor will be required. You can also call the national AIDS Hotline at (800) 342-AIDS for help and information.

CONDOMS:
EVERY MAN'S NECESSARY WEAPON

Birth control and prevention against STDs is *your* responsibility. The days of unprotected sex are gone. So are the days of depending on women to provide the protection during sex. Here are the facts: If you don't use condoms, and you aren't in a monogamous relationship, you have a huge chance of contracting VD.

No forms of birth control are 100 percent effective, even when used in conjunction with condoms. This includes Norplant, diaphragm, IUD, cervical cap, and the rhythm method. They are all risky. No forms of birth control, except condoms, prevent the spread of STDs. This is why condoms are required for every man.

The only kind of condom that is effective at blocking the spread of disease is latex; the lamb skin condoms feel better, but they don't prevent the spread of diseases. We recommend that you purchase a box of condoms tonight, and keep them handy. They are your required weapon against diseases and pregnancy. Every successful seducer has made peace with the fact that condoms must be worn during every sexual experience.

There are many ways to botch up a sexual experience. If you are like Bob, you forget to treat a lady like a lady, don't spend time on foreplay, fail to prepare a room romantically, are overly rough with a woman, fail to understand her body, don't talk during sex, fail to retain eye contact, try to rush things, don't hold her or cuddle after sex, answer the phone, look at your watch, don't have condoms on hand, insult the woman, and do many other stupid things.

All of these mistakes boil down to three main areas of sex in which you must become proficient if you are to be a master man in the bedroom: communication, technique, and attitude. This chapter has covered how to learn, study, and master all three techniques. We recommend that you be rigorous in your studies and you will soon see progress. It may take months or years to become familiar with them, but it will be well worth it.

From there we discussed the importance of foreplay. We even provided you with an easy-to-use check list. Along with foreplay we discussed the pre-work required. Creating the mood, for example, is a major task. Focusing on the lighting, incense, candles, fireplace, and music are all important parts.

From there we gave you the basics about her orgasm. Most women need at least 15 minutes of foreplay to get turned on, and from there at least 15 minutes to achieve orgasm. There will be many women who require more time, and some who will require less. We advised you to get her off before you get off. This will ensure she has a good time, and you will be more likely to get a second date.

After intercourse, the next step is afterplay. We mentioned that, just as it is esential to get her turned on during the experience (fore-play), it is equally as important to have her calm down and relax afterwards. We call this afterplay, which includes holding, cuddling, talking, and the other forms of touch that come after sex. If you fail to do this, like Bob, she will most likely think you are a jerk.

Then we covered some of the possible problems and how to handle them. We discussed safe sex and examined the different forms of STDs and the possible cures. The STDs include: chlamydia, crabs, genital warts, gonorrhea, herpes, and HIV. The only way to reduce your risk is to wear condoms during sex. If you want to be a master seducer, condoms are essential.

If you follow our advice in this chapter and master communi-cation, technique, attitude, safe sex, and always wear condoms, you will soon become a sexual master and have many nights of mind-blowing sex.

chapter eleven...
When Babes Attack: Handling Problems Women Cause

BAD DATES FROM HELL

Date #1

When Jacob went to meet Zoe for their first date, he was expecting her to be a little nervous. She was a girl who worked at the health food store where he shopped. She was tiny, punky, and cute, and responded well to his flirting and romantic overtures. After a few weeks of romantic banter, she'd come running out of the storeroom to see him if she heard his voice. He set up a coffee date with her at a nearby coffee shop. The shop was convenient. The plan seemed foolproof.

He arrived at the coffee shop, armed with an interesting book in case she didn't show up. But she did show up, shortly after the agreed-upon time...with a guy.

"This is my roommate, Tony," she told him. "I figured you wouldn't mind if I brought him along."

"Of course not," Jacob responded, realizing instantly that his seduction of Zoe wasn't going to move very far that day. The three of them sat down. Jacob immediately noticed that Tony was not a stable person. His eyes and face looked wild and very unattractive.

He seemed preoccupied by conspiracy theories. After making polite conversation for about 20 minutes, Jacob concluded that if he pursued Zoe further, this psycho guy would probably cause him plenty of trouble. Two days later, when he called Zoe, she told him "Tony and I are moving out of town tomorrow. He thinks you're stalking me." To his relief, Jacob never saw Zoe again.

Date #2

Dennis was new to dating. In his early twenties, he'd always been too scared to ask women out. The few women he'd dated had pursued him, and he had always let them have all the power in the relationships. They decided everything. He passively hoped the relationship would go the way he wanted, though it never did.

The one woman he did ask out was Daria. She was 19, elegant looking, and for reasons he couldn't explain, seemed to really like him. On their first date they sat on a park bench and talked, and she kept leaning forward, "accidentally" making it easy for him to look down her shirt. He asked her out again, she said "yes," and he figured he had it made. Not having read this book, he took Daria to dinner and a movie for their first date.

Trouble first started when he met her for dinner. "We had our whole meal, and I guess I made kind of a slip," he told us. "I said 'you are paying for yourself, aren't you?' and she said, 'I don't have any money.' From there it went downhill."

It turned out Daria was completely unable to take care of herself in any way. She had no money, and then when they got to the movie—an "R" rated one—she didn't have any ID, and they had to go to a children's movie instead. "She just got madder and madder with me," he says now. "Each time I paid for something, even though I tried not to make it a big deal, even though it was." After the movie, he dumped her off at her house, and left behind the most uncomfortable date of his life.

Date #3

"We went to see the movie *Schindler's List*," Fritz told us. "I had no idea she'd be so upset by it. She started crying about 10 minutes into the movie, and was still crying in the car all the way back to her apartment. She couldn't stop, she was really freaked out by it. Needless to say, my seduction plans were destroyed for that night."

Date #4

Anna had the punk look down cold. Amazingly beautiful to start with, she had bright orange hair, leather clothing, torn-up T-shirts, chains, and combat boots. She was also extremely sexually attractive, going through life looking like some sort of dressed-up fetish dolly. Brett was thrilled to be going out with such a hot woman, but there was one problem.

"Of course people stared at her, because she was so hot," Brett says. "And she hated it. If guys looked at her, she'd glare at them, and say things like 'what are you looking at, jerk face? Wanna make something of it?'" Then I had to deal with these huge angry guys. After I got punched trying to defend her, I finally broke up with her."

Date #5

Thirty-six, tall and tan, Rebecca had taken care of her body, and was often mistaken for a woman in her 20s. The first time Sal had sex with her they were at his house, and she was incredibly aroused. "Oh God, I'm so turned on," she told him. "Do me without a condom! I hate those things! Don't worry, I won't get pregnant! Even if I do, I don't care, I don't mind having your baby! Just do me without a condom!" Needless to say, Sal used a condom anyway, but found himself worrying about Rebecca's attitude even as he was having sex with her. "How psycho is this?" he asked us later. "To want me, a virtual stranger, to possibly get her pregnant or give her a disease? What is going on here?"

Date #6

Rich and Roger were housemates. Roger had been dating Jill, an unstable, neurotic, highly sexual woman. "I love crazy women," Roger told Rich when he started dating Jill. But soon her crazy behavior was driving them both mad. One day Rich was sitting home when the front door opened and in stalked Jill. "Where is he?!" she screeched. "Where are you, Roger, you jerk! I've let you have my body ten times, and now you are going to give me what I want! Where are you?" Roger had to call the police to have Jill removed, screaming, from their house.

Date #7

Bob and Yolanda were on their third date, when she flipped out. They were talking about gender issues, and how women and men are different, and she, as he put it later, "just went nuts on me." She started ranting about all the bad things men do to women, about females being used as sex slaves, and female circumcision. "I started realizing that she was nuts, and I asked her to change the subject. That's when she hit me!"

Date #8

Dwayne and Emmie were friends. She often came to him with her emotional problems, of which she had plenty. She seemed almost like the "trauma of the week." One week it was "my dad abused me," the next "I think my mother killed my twin brother." He had no way of knowing if these traumas really happened to her, or not. He assumed they must have, or she wouldn't have been so unstable.

One night she came over late, talked to him for a while, then slept on his couch. Four days later, she called him. "You sexually abused me while I was asleep the other night." She told him, "I'm calling the police." Fortunately, he had saved many of her crazy, ranting, self-contradictory phone messages, which gave him a good chance in court, so she decided not to press charges. If she had, he might be in jail today for a crime he did not commit.

Date #9

Henry picked up Jean in a bar. He couldn't believe his luck. She was sexy, slutty, and had amazing breasts and a completely flat stomach. It was a dream come true. They went to his house, had drunken sex, and when he woke up in the morning, she was gone.

And so was his wallet, his checkbook, and some of the more valuable knickknacks around his apartment. He never saw her, nor his money, again.

Date #10

Albert went out with Wendy, a chiropractor who lived in his town. They had several dates, and were checking out the possibility of being romantic with each other. They'd had some long phone conversations, and generally felt pretty connected. One day when he called her, she said, "I'm gonna stay in alone tonight, and watch a movie. What do you recommend?" He told her about a film he'd seen recently, *The Addams Family*. She rented it, watched part of it, and called him up the next day. "I just had to tell you," she said, "that I can't date anyone who would like that movie. I can't see you anymore."

SO HOW DO YOU HANDLE PROBLEMS?

Has anything like this ever happened to you, or to a man you know? If it hasn't, it probably will. We don't say this to curse you, but simply to warn you. Not every woman you get to know will be stable, mentally healthy, and sincere when she interacts with you. Some will be difficult, strange, unpleasant, scary, or even possibly dangerous. This chapter is about how to handle difficult women.

The best way to handle a problem is before it becomes a problem. If Henry had seen the warning signs in Jean, he might not have been so quick to fall asleep before getting her out of his apartment, and could have saved his wallet and his valuables. If Roger had known how dangerous Jill could be, he would have thought twice before dating her often, or letting her know where he lived. If Dwayne had seen the warning signs in Emmie, he would never have let himself get into situations where she could accuse him of sexual impropriety. By taking simple precautions in advance, these men could have easily made their lives much simpler and safer.

Men tend to be extremely naive when it comes to women. They think that nothing bad could possibly happen to them in a dating situation. Nowhere is this naivete seen more clearly than in sex. Many men idiotically—and incorrectly—think that they are exempt from needing to wear a condom, for instance. They won't get a woman pregnant. They won't catch HIV, or some other STD. This sort of "everything will be fine" thinking permeates men's relationships with women, and makes them unable to see, in advance, the problems women are setting up for them. This chapter will help you give up your naivete around women once and for all. After you read this chapter, you'll see the problems coming, and be able to get out of the way easily.

GAUGING THE MAINTENANCE SPECTRUM

All relationships require some maintenance. Each person, man or woman, needs certain things to happen in order to feel as if someone cares about them, and to feel attracted. These needs in a woman are the maintenance you must do to keep her happy.

Women need varying degrees of maintenance in order to feel appreciated. Some women's needs are fairly simple. If you are considerate, or don't treat them like dirt, they feel appreciated and attracted to you. Other women only feel attracted to you if you treat them poorly. Still others require constant compliments, gifts, and attention. Some even need to fight with you and have regular conflict in order to feel that the relationship is right for them.

You've probably heard men talk about women as "low maintenance" or "high maintenance." This is a very useful distinction to make. Here's how you tell the difference, early on, between low maintenance women, high maintenance, and women who need too much to be worth it.

LOW MAINTENANCE WOMEN

The low maintenance woman is a gift to men. She doesn't require elaborate rituals to feel okay about you, and about dating you. Her needs will be simple, and easy to figure out. She'll even help you, by telling you exactly what she needs, and meaning it.

Here's what you need to know about her:

* She takes very little in life personally. The low-maintenance woman won't jump on your every slip or bonehead remark. When she is upset, she lets it go easily and is therefore easy to be with.

* She contains her feelings well. If she's upset, she doesn't show it, or doesn't take it out on you. She's responsible for her feelings.

* She is not unreasonable. She really tries to be reasonable at all times, thus making your life easier.

* She doesn't "flip out." If she feels anxious, upset, or stressed, she handles it responsibly, and often you never even know about it.

* She feels she has more to learn about everything, and doesn't jump to conclusions. She isn't overly attached to her own opinions.

* Her feelings in the moment are not too important to her. She listens to her feelings, but makes decisions in life from a rational and logical base.

* She consistently desires sex. She either wants it most of the time, or gives you sex because she wants to please you.

* She doesn't expect you to know what she needs; she is happy to tell you.

* She is emotionally consistent, and doesn't have massive mood swings.

* She is not overly concerned about what other people think of her.

* She likes you, and likes men.

* She is generative and creative and amuses herself well.

* She rarely complains.

MEDIUM MAINTENANCE WOMEN

You are more likely to encounter medium maintenance women than low maintenance. The medium maintenance woman has more needs and takes more things you say and do personally than does the low maintenance woman. At the same time, she isn't so wrapped up in her own feelings that she's impossible to deal with, like the high maintenance woman. The medium maintenance woman:

* Takes some things in life personally. There are some topics you'd better just avoid, like pornography, or other women's larger breasts. Fortunately, this isn't too difficult.

* Takes her feelings out on you occasionally. If she's in a bad mood she sometimes takes it out on you, and will be bitchy and start a fight. She'll usually apologize for it afterwards, though, and perhaps even apologize with sex.

* Is sometimes unreasonable.

* "Flips out," but feels bad about it later. When she has emotional scenes, she apologizes later.

* Can be sensitive about her weight or looks.

* Is moderately creative, is moderately whiny.

* Likes sex, but sometimes says "no," and has some gripes about your performance.

* Has moods, but is mostly stable. One day she may be happy, the next, sad, crying, or furious.

* Worries sometimes about how she looks to other people, and what other people think about *you*.

* Dates men, but sometimes likes them, sometimes doesn't.

TOO HOT TO HANDLE
(HIGH MAINTENANCE)

The high maintenance woman is out of control. She has little control over her moods and behaviors, and has constant problems with everything, most especially you.

The high maintenance woman believes that she has the right to be as difficult to be with as she likes. She is incredibly impulsive, and you have to deal with it. If she feels like yelling at a dangerous looking stranger, she does it, and you have to handle the consequences. If she feels like screaming, or crying, or pouting, or generally acting like a baby, she would never dream of containing herself. She thinks nothing of yelling loudly at you during dinner at a nice restaurant and creating a scene. After all, she reasons, if she doesn't completely express her feelings at every moment, you are trying to repress her. The high maintenance woman:

* Takes everything in life personally. If it rains out when she wants to go on a walk, she's angry at the weather.

* Takes her feelings out on you. If she's in a bad mood—and she is—she takes it out on you.

* Feels she has the right to be unreasonable. She never makes any attempt to be reasonable, and you have to just live with it.

* Feels she has the right to "flip out." If she feels anxious, upset, or stressed, she cries, or screams, or does whatever she feels like, wherever you might be, and you have to handle it.

* Feels she understands "God's opinion" about everything, and is happy to set you straight at all times about what you are doing wrong.

* Is insulted by everything you do.

* Believes that her feelings in the moment are the most important thing in the universe. She can never just "get off it," and get on with life. Has to process or fight about everything right now.

* Is impossible to give feedback to. If you tell her anything about her behavior, she flips out, screams, and cries, which she feels she has the right to do.

* Generates nothing, is not creative, complains constantly about being bored.

* Is incredibly sensitive. Will think you think she's fat, or not attractive, at the slightest provocation. You don't dare look at another woman while she's around.

* Is on or off sexually, and you never know which you are going to get. One night she'll be an incredibly hot vixen, the next she'll become furious at some little remark you make, and kick you out of her house.

* Becomes furious if you don't instantly and automatically know what she needs at all times. Your inability to be psychic with her is proof, in her mind, of your insensitivity.

* Is incredibly inconsistent. One minute she may be happy, the next, sad, crying, or yelling.
* Believes there's only one right way to do things, and you are doing it wrong.
* Worries continuously about how she looks to other people, and what other people think about *you*.
* Is very picky about your behavior.
* Dates men, but doesn't really like them. Sees men as a necessary evil.

Which type of woman do you tend to date? Is she the ultra-demanding high maintenance type. Or is she the medium maintenance, fairly demanding type? Understanding which degree of maintenance a potential date will pose is wonderful because it allows you to determine if it will be worth it to date her or not. Also, you can expect her to behave in the ways we've outlined. We are now going to cover how to handle many of the problems women will cause.

THE 8 SECRETS OF HANDLING THE PROBLEMS WOMEN CAUSE

The biggest trap men fall into with women is they handle the problems women cause incorrectly. Instead of diffusing the problem, they often make things worse. You've surely had this experience: you are with a woman, and she seems upset. You try to help, and end up fighting with her. She then complains that you are an insensitive bastard who's incapable of understanding her. This happened because you probably violated one or more of the following eight secrets of handling the problems women cause. Follow these rules, and your fighting days are over.

1. Never solve a woman's problem, or you will become her problem

Men who don't understand this get themselves into unending trouble with women. Solving a woman's problem is a big mistake, because if you do, she'll make *you* her problem. Here's how it works.

Women live with problems differently than men do. When men have problems, we want to solve them, pure and simple. And, by and large, we don't have a lot of tolerance for men who just want to complain about problems, but not try to solve them. If a man is designing a computer program, for instance, and can't get it to work, other men won't ask him, "Wow, how do you feel about that?" They won't spend time sharing how it felt when they had a similar problem with a program they were writing. They roll up their sleeves, and get in there and try to fix it.

Similarly, men don't indulge each other complaining much about relationships. If two guys are at the gym, and one says "I met this hot woman, but she hasn't called me!" the other won't commiserate much about how bad that must feel. He'll more likely say, "What's the matter, forget how to use a phone? Call her up, you idiot!" Problem solved, and on to other topics of conversation.

Women, on the other hand, treat problems differently. Strange as it seems, women *like* problems more than men do. They use problems as opportunities to share their feelings with one another, and to bond with each other. Women in the locker room will routinely complain about men they desire who don't call, and would rarely dream of solving each other's problems by saying "call him, you idiot!" *Simply having the problem, together*, is a way of bonding for women that men must learn to understand.

This difference between men and women is shown clearly in a recent *Cathy* comic strip. Cathy's car had broken down on a winter morning, and she couldn't leave the house to get to work. She called her boyfriend, Irving, and he said he'd come over to help her. As she waited for him, a fantasy formed in her mind. "He'll come over, and we'll be so happy to see each other. We'll drink coffee, and eat morning buns, and be brought together by this car problem. Everything else will disappear, and we'll be laughing and happy and in love on this cold winter morning."

At that moment, Irving entered. "I called a tow truck, it'll be here in ten minutes," he tells her. "I also called a cab, so you'll be able to get to work. I must go, big meeting this morning." Whoosh, he was gone, and Cathy was left sulking in the final frame, "Men have no idea how to handle problems."

When a woman comes to you with a problem, you must not solve it. Let us repeat that, because it seems so strange: when a woman comes to you with a problem, you must not solve it. We feel odd even saying it. But it's true. If a woman presents you with a problem, and you try to solve it, she'll almost certainly be angry with you. She'll accuse you of not listening to her, or not being sensitive, and that's the thanks you'll get.

When a woman comes to you with a problem, be grateful. As long as she has that problem, she won't be making *you* her problem, and you are in the clear. Instead of fixing, we advise you to listen to her, be with her, and help her believe that you understand her feelings.

When Leo first started dating Karen, everything seemed to be going well. One day everything changed. He went to her house for a date, and found her crying. "I didn't know what to say," he told us, "but I remembered not to solve her problem. Without saying a word, I just took her into my arms, and allowed her to cry." This went on for five or ten minutes, and eventually she stopped. "Later she said to me, 'I can't believe how wonderful you were! You were just so perfect when I was so upset!' That blew me away, because I didn't actually do anything!" If he'd tried to "solve" her problem, she wouldn't have thought he was so wonderful, and perhaps would even have been angry.

You must try to be like Leo and comfort her by just being with her, not fixing. If you must speak, here are some possible things to say:

* "Wow, tell me how that feels."
* "Sounds pretty intense. Tell me more, if you want to."
* "I just want to support you."
* "I really admire how you're handling this."
* "Is there anything I can say or do that would help?"

Don't worry if you find yourself repeating these phrases over and over. She simply wants to be heard. Your mind will be busy anyway, reminding yourself to not try to fix her problem. If you find yourself about to say any of the following things, stop yourself, and say instead one of the platitudes listed above:

* ✳ "I think you should..."
* ✳ "Why don't you just..."
* ✳ "I don't see why it's such a big deal."
* ✳ "Have you tried..."

These statements will have you starting to fix her, and will get you into big trouble. Some men think that if they solve a woman's problems, she'll sleep with him. We discussed this thoroughly in Chapter 2, and will just remind you now that if you solve a woman's problem, she won't reward you with sex. All she'll do is think of the problem every time she sees you, and think of you as a "friend."

2. Remember that fighting with a woman is like defusing a bomb

One of our students was a military demolitions expert. He told us about working with bombs. "Most of the time, you handle a bomb by sending in some sort of robot to just blow it up. No problem if you're not nearby. The real problem comes when you have to get in there and do it yourself. You really want to be patient, not jump to conclusions, and remember what you are up to when you defusing a bomb."

It occurred to us that he was not only describing defusing a bomb—he was also describing fighting with a woman. If you can get someone else to take the blast, so much the better, but most of the time, you'll have to do it yourself.

Fighting with a woman is a delicate procedure. As in the bomb analogy, you can't let your mind wander from the most important thing. In dating, with a woman, the most important thing about a fight is to end it, quickly, and with the minimum stress. If you get caught up in some detail of the fight, or let your anger take over, you'll lose the fight, even if you "win" it technically. You might be able to badger her into admitting that you are right and she is wrong, but you will not have created harmony, and you won't be having sex later.

3. Keep asking yourself, "What's most important to me?"

It's easy to lose your head in a fight with a woman. She says things that hook you, and make you want to defend yourself. This is almost as big a mistake as trying to solve a woman's problem. Consistently remember what your outcome is. If it is early on in your relationship, and you haven't even had sex with her, we strongly urge you to avoid fighting with women altogether. If you must fight, remember what's most important to you: is it more important to make her see that you are right, or is it more important that she desire you? Your answer to this question will guide your behavior in any fight you might encounter.

When Bob fights with a woman, he destroys any chance of being sexual with her. On his first date with Annette, he started telling her about his favorite television program, "Babylon-5." "Geez," she responded. "My one wish in life is that people would stop telling me about Babylon-5. I don't care about that science fiction stuff!" At this point, Bob needed to ask himself, "What's most important to me, sleeping with her, or arguing?" Had he done this, he might not have made the mistake of responding, "I don't know what you're so huffy about. It's only the best show ever made—everybody thinks so." Naturally, she took offense at this. "Oh, everybody does, do they? Well, *I* don't." They started having a little fight, which irritated Annette, and made her less attracted to Bob. "What am I doing with this jerk?" she asked herself. It was a good question.

It's important to realize that taking offense at what someone says is a choice. Have you ever been insulted by someone, and simply let it roll off your back? Perhaps you thought to yourself, "It isn't worth it," and simply went on with your life. At that moment, your commitment to something else—having the life you want, perhaps—was more important than proving to someone that you wouldn't accept an insult.

If you haven't ever allowed yourself to not take offense at a potential insult, you had better learn if you want romantic success with women. Women will give you plenty of opportunities to get angry. You must choose to not take the bait, and choose to not get offended by anything they say. . If a six-year-old kid told you the same thing, it might seem obnoxious and annoying, but it wouldn't have the same impact as coming from a woman you are interested in dating. If you can "pretend" she is that kid being silly, it will help you keep your mind on the seduction.

Our student Ivan made such a choice with Bonnie. He met Bonnie through a mutual friend, who was taking them both sailing on his boat. She was in her late twenties, and looked good in her one-piece bathing suit. "She was cute enough," he told us, "and so I decided she'd be worth some effort." Their mutual friend mentioned that Ivan had self-published a book, and since he happened to have it with him, he showed it to her. "Women usually respond positively to it," he told us. "But Bonnie started finding all these errors in how it was typeset, and talking about how it wasn't put together properly. It really started pissing me off—after all, what had she ever done that she could talk about? But I kept asking myself, 'What's most important to me,' and I realized that I didn't care what she thought of the book. I just wanted to get that suit off." He changed the subject, without fighting, and went on to other topics. He got her e-mail address, seduced her first by e-mail, then in person, and eventually had sex with her. "If I'd fought with her about the book, I would never have made it anywhere with her," he told us. "It really made a difference to ask myself what was most important."

4. Never reason with an upset woman

In the film *As Good As It Gets*, Jack Nicholson plays a writer who is asked, "How do you write female characters?" He answers, "I think of a man, and I remove the reason and the accountability." While this is by no means always true, you will be far more successful in fights with women if you act like it is.

If you are with a woman and she is upset, this is also the time she is likely to be unreasonable and difficult to be around. But this also holds true for everyone. When *you* are most upset, *you* are most likely to be unreasonable, too. Have you ever tried pointing out the lack of logic in an upset woman's thinking? How well has it worked for you? Our guess is, not at all. Reason and logic will only make her more upset.

At a time like this, your job is *not* to influence her. Your job is to influence yourself. You must not get hooked, not try to fix it, and not try to make her see reason. Keep asking yourself what you are committed to, and go for that.

5. Don't take anything personally

Geena and Tony were on their seduction date. Their conversations were going fine until Geena said, "It must be hard not really being in the real world. I mean, since you only work at the university and around eggheads all the time, it must make it hard to relate to real people." Not in the real world? Only work at the university? This might be an insult, or it might not be. Unfortunately, Tony decides to take it as one. "Well, what's that supposed to mean? I'm in the real world!" he says to her. He has taken something she said personally, and allowed a possible fight to begin.

Think back to a fight you've had with a woman. Most of the time, the conversation was going along fine. You two were talking and there was no problem. Suddenly, someone said something stupid that could be considered insulting. The other person took it personally, and a fight ensued. Sometimes the woman you are with will say bone-headed things that sound like insults to you. Sometimes you will do the same thing to her. As the man and the seducer, it's your responsibility to make sure the date goes well. If you take something a woman says or does personally, you lose sight of your outcome, and the seduction will be ruined.

You must remember what your outcome is with a woman, especially in any stressful interaction. It's incredibly easy to take personally something she says or does, and to let yourself become insulted and start a fight. Here's a list of things women will do that you shouldn't take personally. As you date, you'll no doubt find other things to add to this list.

* Not calling you back
* Showing up late, or not showing up at all
* Canceling or changing dates at the last minute
* Not appreciating all the nice things you do for her
* Being cold, distant, insulted, or difficult to talk to
* Not responding to your seduction
* Ignoring you when you say hello

6. Handle female rudeness gracefully

So how should you handle these difficult behaviors if you can't take them personally? Little things, like not calling you back, you don't really have to deal with if you simply take it on that you will always do the calling. Ditto with a woman you've just met seeming cold, or difficult to talk to. Handling that is your job as a man. But truly rude behavior, like missing several dates in a row, must be dealt with. If you let a woman seriously inconvenience you without responding, she will simply do it again, and worse.

The secret is to know how to handle female rudeness without getting into a fight, and the key to that is not taking what she did personally. Yes, you want to handle it, but just so she knows what's okay to do with you, and what isn't. You aren't mad, you aren't out of control; women won't respect men who act like this. It only scares them. But to set a boundary for a woman, you must be firm. If you don't take it personally, you'll be able to say what needs to be said, and to let it go. You'll be much more effective, and she'll respect you more for it.

Cindy missed two priming dates with Lyle. He didn't take it personally. He reasoned that Cindy was pushing him, to see what she could get away with. Because he kept his mind clear, he was able to talk to her on the phone without starting a fight or making her feel bad. Instead, he said, "Listen, I like you and everything, but you've missed two dates. I have a rule you need to know about: if you miss another date, I can never talk to you again. So if you want to go out with me, you've gotta show up." His voice was firm but not yelling, and he was unapologetic. He set a boundary, and instead of whining about how rude she was, he gave her a simple choice: show up, or get lost. She showed up for their next priming date, which went directly into seduction, and then sex. "She was pushing to see how far she could go," he told us. "I wouldn't have talked to her again if she missed another date, but I'm glad she showed up." By not taking it personally, Lyle was able to handle the situation without getting caught up in his feelings.

7. Listen actively

Some guys think that listening is what you do when you are waiting for an opportunity to speak your piece. Other guys seem to think that listening is what happens in between her opening her mouth to talk, and when you tell her how to fix her problem. If you are one of these men, have no fear. We're now going to show you exactly how to listen in the way that makes women feel the best.

Women we interviewed complained about not "feeling heard" by the men they talked with. You can overcome this if you follow the simple steps of active listening.

Look interested. Remember when your teachers in school would ask "are you paying attention?" and you'd snap into focus? Think about what your body was doing before she spoke to you. She thought you were bored because you looked bored. You were leaning back, slumped over, your eyes were unfocused, and you weren't looking at her. Now think about how you held your body when you wanted to look interested. You were leaning slightly forward, looking at the teacher; you were nodding, breathing deeply, and acting alert.

Many men allow themselves to look bored when listening to women they want to seduce. Even if you *are* listening, you won't look it if you are in a bored posture.

Repeat back what she said. If you are in a conflict with a woman, it can be incredibly helpful to repeat back what she said. You don't want to be a parrot, like some annoying comedian who mimics everything everybody says. That would be bad. By repeating key parts back, however, you show her that what came out of her mouth actually went into your ears and is still in your brain. Believe us, she'll be impressed, and it will make anything she has to say to you easier and faster.

When Chuck's girlfriend Stacey was mad at him for flirting with other women, he used this very effectively. First he got himself into a posture that conveyed that he was interested in what she was saying, even though the truth was that he'd rather have been just about anywhere than listening to her complain. "I don't like it when you flirt with other women at parties," she said. "It really makes me feel bad, like you don't love me." "Let me see if I'm getting what you're saying," he told her, "because it's important to me to really hear you. You don't like it when I flirt with other women at parties, and it makes you feel bad, like I don't love you. Is that right?" "Yea," she responded, calming down. "I really want to feel like I'm there with you, as a couple." "Oh, I get it," he said back. "It's important to you that you feel like we're a couple when we are at parties. I didn't know you felt that way." By this time Stacey was calm enough to talk normally, and they were able to resolve the problem, all because Chuck was willing to employ active listening. You don't have to solve the problem, or even agree with her. A woman will calm down if she feels like you are listening, and repeating back is an excellent way to seem like you are.

8. Don't explain yourself

When you are in a conflict with a woman, you will be tempted to explain yourself, and to justify who you are, and why you do things the way you do. Don't do it. A good rule of thumb is to only answer questions. If she asks you why you did something, tell her, but don't feel as though you owe her an explanation for every aspect of your behavior just because she is upset with you.

Remember, you are not out to get your validation in life from women. You are getting that other places, remember? Women are an addition to your life that makes you feel good about yourself, not the central validating factor. If you violate this principle, you are more likely to be explaining yourself to women in conflicts. Simply remember what is most important to you, answer relevant questions, and get through the conflict.

THE THREE WAYS WOMEN FIGHT AND HOW TO HANDLE THEM

People fight in different ways, and each person tends to be consistent in his or her way of fighting. There are three basic modes that people default to. They either cry, yell, or manipulate. Let's discuss each one of these in detail, and show you how to handle women in each situation.

1. Crying

Some women love to cry. They default into crying at movies, weddings, even at long-distance phone service commercials. They get hurt easily, have tender feelings, and tend to cry right away when you have a conflict, rather than get angry, or solve the problem.

How to spot her early on: The crier gets moved easily. A wounded bird on the street causes her to rush out to save it. She seems to get upset at the slightest thing. If she is extremely emotional about anything, she is probably a crier. You can ask her how she feels about starvation, or the plight of Native Americans, and see how intense she gets about it. If she gets wide-eyed, and her voice gets urgent, she's probably a crier.

How to fight with her.

Don't get hooked. The crier hooks you with her tears; she gets you upset and manipulates you. If you'll do anything she wants to stop her crying, you lose, while she wins. Ultimately, this can be a loss for her, too. Many of our students have made promises to a woman, which were so outrageous they couldn't be kept, only to stop her crying. When they broke their promises, even bigger fights ensued. Getting hooked by a woman's tears, and saying anything to get her to stop just causes trouble down the road.

Don't be difficult by acting guilty. Men who act guilty and ashamed when women cry often think they are being compassionate. Our interviews show the contrary. Women think men who act like this are the difficult ones. All of a sudden the women feel responsible for your pain and suffering. It makes things worse for her and you. If a man acts guilty when a woman cries, he isn't paying attention to the woman. He's all wrapped up in himself, and seems selfish and self-absorbed. He needs the woman to tell him he's not guilty, and is generally very "me-centered." Women have told us time and again that they prefer men who aren't guilty. As one woman said, "If a guy's not going to do what it takes to make me happy, he might as well not feel guilty about it. That just makes him seem like an immature baby."

Understand this, because it is important: your suffering and feeling guilty doesn't substitute for giving a woman what she wants from you. It only makes you harder to deal with. If you aren't going to give a woman what she wants, that's fine. But don't think that feeling guilty will make any positive difference in her experience.

Here's what you should do:

Keep asking yourself "What's most important to me?"   There's not much more for us to say about this that hasn't already been said. Simply keep your outcome firmly in mind.

Don't try to fix the problem.   We don't need to go over this again in depth, but we do need to note that it is especially important with the crier. She doesn't so much need you to fix her problem, as she needs to think you are willing to hear about it. She wants you to be with her while she cries. This is not a time for solutions. Don't give them.

Say the right things.   It helps to know what to say to a crying woman. If you aren't going to suggest solutions, what can you say? Try these statements:

* "I didn't know you felt that way."
* "I can see why that would be rough for you."
* "I can see this is very upsetting for you."

You can repeat these as often as you need to. They help a crying woman feel understood, without getting in the way of her feelings.

Silence is Golden!   The best thing you can say is nothing. If she's not upset about you, you can even hold her, silently, while she cries. It's amazing how often a man can be with a crying woman, saying nothing but feeling like a world-class dork, only to have her say later, "You were so perfect when I was upset! How did you know not to say anything?" Silence is your best friend when you are with a crying woman.

If you don't allow yourself to be manipulated by them, the criers are the easiest to deal with. They eventually calm down and are clear about what they want and need. While they are crying, you must simply remember what's important to you, show her compassion for her suffering, and hold your position. Eventually she'll stop crying, and you can go on with your date.

2. Yelling

Women who default to yelling don't cry—they get *angry*. Subconsciously, they figure they can control you if they can scare you with their anger. If they can't, they will either respect you more, or get out of your life. Either way you win, so it's worth learning how to handle women who act this way.

How to spot her early on. The yeller is a warrior by nature. She often likes to fight, looks tough, and is willing to take offense at the slightest thing you say. If you find that you have to tip-toe to keep her from getting angry, you are with a yeller. You can also spot one by her willingness to complain about service in restaurants, or by the stories she tells of conflicts she's been in.

How to fight with her. The yeller wants to scare you into submission. Subconsciously, she figures that if she is unreasonable enough, she can get her way. Besides, it's worked for her in the past. The solution is to avoid fighting and leave immediately. Later, after she has calmed down, you can talk and resolve the conflict, if it seems worth it. But when she yells, or throws a fit, do not tolerate the abuse. Leave immediately.

3. Manipulating

You've probably heard the saying, "Don't get mad, get even." The manipulator lives by this code, taking control of you indirectly and evening the score. Manipulators are the control-freaks in life. They don't feel safe unless they are able to control everything around them. This tendency gets much worse when they are in conflict, because a conflict is a direct challenge to their control.

While the crier attempts to control you with tears, and the yeller tries to control you with anger, the manipulator tries to control you with mind games. She is especially preoccupied with being "right," and having "logical" arguments that prove her correctness. She will have justifications and arguments for why she is right, but will drive you crazy in a fight because her "logical" arguments won't be logical. She'll irrationally insist that they do make sense, all the while questioning your sanity as you get angrier and angrier about her inconsistency. She will portray herself as the soul of sanity, a civilized woman sadly drawn into having to defend herself from your unreasoning, brutish attack. This will make you even crazier, proving even more in her mind that you are unreasonable and therefore wrong. When she points out to you how crazy, and therefore wrong, you are acting, you're liable to lose your mind entirely. This is not a pretty sight.

How to spot her early on. The woman who is a manipulator is often very intelligent, and may be in a field that requires a lot of "civilized" conflict, like law or administration. She may well be highly educated. These signs alone, however, are not enough; many women who aren't manipulators share these characteristics, and many woman who are manipulators don't.

When you are on a date with a manipulator, you'll find that she needs everything to be "just so." She is very particular about her needs and her comfort. It is often important for her to reject your idea, just so she is sure she has the power to do so. Her "reasons" occur to you as incredibly lame. You may ask her out to a Chinese restaurant, for instance, only to have her reject your choice by saying, "I had Chinese food last week." She's practicing her control. Watch out.

The manipulator is hard to please. There's always something just a little wrong with everything. Complaining, for her, is a way of establishing her control. She may send back her food at a restaurant, or want a drink with a particular brand of gin. If that brand is not available, she will, with a heavy sigh, have nothing at all. She may complain about details of the way you dress. You'll notice that you feel as if she is particularly controlling and persnickety. That's because she is.

How to fight with her.

Don't argue with her. Watch out, this kind of woman can drive you crazy. The only way to keep from going insane with a manipulator is to not fall into the trap of arguing with her about the nonsense she is spewing forth. This will never work, and will only drive you insane. Your rebuttals will only perpetuate the fight. What the manipulator wants is control, not logic. She is afraid that if she loses control, something bad will happen to her. Pretending to care about logic and reason is her way of getting that control. She gets to drive you crazy, then demonize you as an illogical, wrong, out-of-control nut case. If you argue with her about her logic, she has won immediately, and it's all over for you.

Tell her she's right. Tell the manipulator that she is right as much as you can stomach doing it. If there is some small point that she is correct about, tell her, and emphasize that she is right about it. "You are right that this relationship is very important to us both," you might say. "That's very, very right." Try not to sound sarcastic. You are trying to give her as much control as you can, so she'll calm down, without letting her control *you*.

Apologize for not being logical. It's also very powerful to tell the manipulator that you are sorry that your feelings aren't logical. She can insist that your feelings should be logical, but you can always come back with, "I guess that's not the way I am." As long as you don't get drawn into an argument about whether or not you should be more logical, you are safe. "It's just important to me to be able to go out with my ex-girlfriend as a friend," you might say. "I'm sorry it doesn't make any sense. I know how frustrating that must be. But it really is how I feel, and I don't think that's going to change."

Tell her how important she is to you. Keep in mind, she's not a bad person, she's just scared of being out of control. It can help her calm down if she hears how important she is to you. If she's not important to you, you can find something about your relationship that is. You can almost always truthfully say that "I hope you know, it's important to me that you feel good and happy." Of course it's important—she's much easier to be with, and you get more of what you want when she's happy. Just hearing that will often calm the manipulator down.

Change the scene. You probably aren't going to get anywhere useful in argument with a manipulator, so you might as well get it over with as quickly as possible. See if you can leave, or get the two of you doing something else that doesn't allow you to argue, like seeing a movie or being with other people.

These are the three defaults of conflict for a woman. But don't think that only women fall into these categories. Men do, too, even *you*. Most men are yellers or manipulators, few are criers. You might want to look over this section again, and see which kind of fighter you are, and see if that's really the way you want to be.

THE FOUR CLASSIC WOMEN TO AVOID

While all women cause problems, certain types cause more than they are worth, and you are better off avoiding them. For example, there are four classic psycho-types: The Flipped Out, the Paranoid Police-Caller, the Street Fighter, and the Bitch Goddess. You must know about them so you can spot them, and avoid having them mess up your life.

Craziness in women is on a continuum, and it's not always easy to tell when a woman is so crazy that you should avoid her. Here are the general warning signs that should alert you to the presence of a possible psycho woman:

She had an abusive childhood. Psycho women were often abused, sometimes more severely than you can imagine. Severe physical and sexual childhood abuse is tragically common, and psycho women are often the outcomes of such childhoods. If she tells you she was beaten and raped as a child, she may very well be worth avoiding.

She tells you intimate details right away. This often comes along with an abusive childhood. If a woman was abused, and she tells you about it the first time you meet her, that's an especially bad sign. It means she probably has very weak boundaries. The good side of this is that she might therefore be easy to get in bed. The bad side is that it won't be worth it when she flips out.

She's been in a lot of abusive relationships. Same as above. Avoid her.

She seems like a hypochondriac. If she seems to have a lot wrong with her physically, that can also be a sign of a mental problem, though this is by no means always true. It's our experience and that of our students that a woman with lots of allergies, for instance, or food sensitivities, can be trouble. A woman who needs to never be around perfume or in a room where someone once smoked a cigarette can be impossible and unstable in relationships. We don't know why, but it's true.

She is obsessive/compulsive. Often such women will tell you right away. "I'm a really obsessive person," she might say, or "I've never let go of anything that didn't have claw marks from me holding on." It may seem strange that someone would show you such a disturbing part of her psyche right away, and it is. It's a warning sign to stay away, unless you want her obsessed with *you*.

A "red flag" goes off inside of you. This is the most important guideline of all. Men's good sense disappears when it looks like they might have an opportunity to have sex. They pursue sex even when it's with crazy women who they *know* will cause them unending problems. Don't be a jerk. If a "red flag" goes off inside of you, and you have a bad feeling about a woman, be a powerful, confident man and *stay away from her*. If you are smart enough to apply the technology in this book consistently, you *will* be having sex. You don't need to humiliate yourself by making trouble with psychos. We say it again: if you have a bad feeling about a woman, *stay away from her*. Listen to yourself, and trust your instincts.

The four types of women to avoid have these characteristics in abundance. Let's look at them more closely, one type at a time:

1. The Flipped Out

The Flipped Out is like the crier, only much more so. When she "flips out" and cries, it is often in the context of a sexual abuse flashback. She tends to hyperventilate as she cries, saying one word with each breath, so her speaking sounds like "I (gasp) am (gasp) feeling (gasp) very (gasp) scared (gasp)..." By hyperventilating, she unconsciously assures that her brain chemistry will stay messed up, and she will stay flipped out.

2. The Paranoid Police-Caller

This woman will tell you about men she's been stalked by, men she's called the police about, and men she has restraining orders against. It is critical for your future life out of jail that you stay away from this woman. She often has an abusive and crazy ex-husband or lover who she says still torments her. She changes her unlisted phone number every few months. This woman has been traumatized and learned that men are going to hurt her, and that the law is her only recourse. Eventually she will inevitably see you as a perpetrator, too. Stay away from her, no matter how hot her body is.

3. The Bitch Goddess

This woman is like the manipulator, only much more so. One such woman was in the film *L.A. Story*, playing Steve Martin's girlfriend. At one point he says to her, "I don't think you understand how unattractive hate is." The Bitch Goddess never does.

You are only likely to pursue such a critical, difficult woman because she's very physically attractive, and you think you can get her into bed. You ignore how negative and hate-filled she is, because you hope to have sex with her. Of all the types to avoid, this one is the most benign. If you can have sex with her a few times, then get rid of her, your suffering will be minimal. If you get into a relationship with her, however, you might as well castrate yourself now, because she's going to do it eventually.

It's good to start to notice such women and practice keeping away from them. By avoiding the most psycho of women, you will save yourself from much suffering.

4. The Street Fighter

The street fighter is the type who loves conflict. She can turn a wonderfully fun evening into an all-out crappy time. The fighter will constantly try to get you to argue with her, and the moment you fall for her ploys, you are in deep trouble. She tends to be mean-spirited, dramatic, and highly passionate.

Some signs of the street fighter are that she loves to criticize others and basks in being opinionated, asserting her opinion, and generally turning people off. She tends to be highly political, righteous, bitchy, and difficult to be around.

If you stay with a fighter, you will get burned badly. She will eventually test your patience, and you will try to get out of the relationship. It will end in a huge blowout. The other threat is that this type will become violent with you, and attack you. If a woman shows signs of being a conflict-lover early on, take it as a sign to get rid of her.

THE TWENTY-THREE PROBLEM WOMEN

All women are problems. (Don't get too smug about that, though. You are a problem, too, as we'll see later.) The faster you can recognize what kind of problem a woman is most likely to present, the faster you'll be able to deal with that problem, and the more likely the two of you will be to have a happy relationship. Here's a list of problem women. How many of them do you know?

The rich bitch

The alcoholic/druggie

The therapist

The princess

The "I hate you for loving me"

The bar-fighter/cat-fighter

The depressed

The angry feminist

The arguer

The complainer

The religious moralist

The drama queen

The nag

The wounded bird

The stalker

The anorexic

The hypochondriac

The enabler/rescuer

The performance artist
The control freak
The know-it-all
The look-gooder
The earth mother

SIXTEEN PROBLEMS CAUSED BY YOUR TENDENCIES

As we've mentioned, women are not the only source of problems in relationships. You cause problems, too. So it is just as wise to prepare for the problems you'll cause as it is to prepare for the ones she'll cause. Here's the list of problem men—which one are you?

The Sensitive New-Age Guy

The Sensitive New-Age Guy, or SNAG, tries to seduce women by being forever nice, helpful, artistic, and sensitive to women's issues. He wears crystals and lets his hair grow long. He may pretend to be a peaceful musician and play the drum, or may enjoy practicing guitar in the woods. The main problem he causes is that he pretends, even to himself, that he's not a rutting sex-crazed beast, like other men. He's all full of light and goodness. When he does something mean to a woman—and he does—it is totally unconscious. Further, he never takes responsibility for all the people he offends. He also has no vitality or masculine presence. If you are this guy, get more guy friends and start eating meat. Go see some strippers. Admit you have a dark side. Be more like other men, and you'll get more sex.

The Special Boy

Like the Sensitive New-Age Guy, the Special Boy prides himself on not being like other men. He often has one or two "special" relationships, usually platonically with women. He often dresses in an unusual way, or wears very "special" items of clothing. Most women avoid him because he sends an immature message about himself. They say that there's something weird about him. Those women who don't avoid him like him, but only as a friend. If you are a Special Boy, you'll be happier and get more sex if you concentrate more on how you are like other men than on how you are different.

The Feminist Man

This well-meaning man has taken on women's freedom struggle as his own, but there's a subtext to his behavior that is disturbing to most women. He is able to talk easily about how men are the problem in the world, and how "all men" hurt women in various ways. It's as if he doesn't think of himself as a man. He may even say that he doesn't, preferring the term "person." The Feminist Man is deeply ashamed of his maleness, sexual fantasies and masculinity. On top of all this, he secretly thinks he can get sex by apologizing for being male.

If you are one of these men and you want to be successful with women, you have a problem. You must stop aligning yourself with a movement (feminism) whose leaders say, as Andrea Dworkin did, that "all men are rapists, and that's all they are." Practice saying, "I support equal rights and responsibilities for women, and I am not a feminist." You'll start to feel better about yourself immediately.

The Woman's Friend

As we've said before, you must limit your number of female friendships, because they get you in the habit of not being women's lovers. If you must be friends with women, at least *try* to seduce them, even if only in a joking, flirty way. Never let it be forgotten that you are a man and she is a woman.

The Woman's Friend thinks he can get sex from women by being friends with them. This ploy rarely works. If you use this method, and want sex, stop being their friends. It really is that simple.

The Beaten Down by Life/No Vitality

The fundamental message of this book can be boiled down to one statement: Be a generative, vital man, and women will want to give you more sex than you can handle. Everything else in this book is just telling you how to do that with women. The Beaten Down Man has given up on life. He has no energy, no vitality, and barely makes it through the day. He seems slumped, stressed, and depressed. Life is too hard for him. The Beaten Down Man is not attractive to women because he's not generative and vital. Who wants to be around someone who isn't fun, energetic, and who is overly serious?

If you are Beaten Down, you can overcome it. Taking on the practices in this book will increase your vitality and generativity. You may also need to look at your physical health, to change your diet, or exercise regularly, or get massage, or do *something* to bring more energy into your body. As you become more vital, women will desire you more.

The Beer-Drinking Jerk

The success of the drink-beer-be-jerk-get-girl strategy is almost directly related to age and physical attractiveness. If you are an attractive 22-year-old weightlifter, being a drunken jerk in a bar can get you sex. If you are 40 with a beer gut, however, this strategy is out of date. You not only have to study the techniques in this book, but also to un-learn your old ways of getting drunk, burping, and belching to get women. It won't work for you anymore.

The Know-It-Alls

These are the guys who have an answer for everything. Women hate it when men lecture them or talk down to them, all things the classic know-it-all loves to do. He often works with computers, or in another technical field. He believes that the more knowledge he can share, the better person he is. The more technical language and examples he uses in conversation, the more people will like him. He often uses his knowledge as a way of one-upping himself over some-one else. This helps him feel good about himself. When you show off your knowledge as a source of self-esteem, you are actually only showing off your level of insecurity. You are much better off developing your self-esteem from how you live your life, not from how much data you've absorbed.

If you think you might be a know-it-all, practice saying "I don't know" at least once a day, even if you think you do know. Stick with your assertion that you don't know. If people around you seem more relaxed and friendly when you do this, you are probably a know-it-all. Give it up.

The Control Freak

Did you think only women can be control freaks? Guess again, you too might also be one. The Control Freak has to control every little detail of everything. It's very hard for him to go with the flow, or follow someone else's leadership without criticizing. An insecure woman who has no self-esteem might be attracted to a man who provides so much structure, but eventually she'll rebel. If you notice that everybody always seems to end up doing what you say, you might be a Control Freak. Try doing what other people want occasionally. You'll be more attractive to women.

The Androgynous Boy

"Androgynous" means "appearing both male and female." Some men favor this feminized, non-masculine look. If this describes you, it will actually cause more problems with other men than it will with women. Some men are infuriated by men who seem "too feminine." One androgynous man we know is constantly hassled and harassed by men even though he is straight.

If the Androgynous Boy is cute in a boyish sort of way, some women will be attracted to him, while others will be repelled. Sadly, though, few will take him seriously as a fully mature, adult man. If he is not particularly attractive, however, it will be very hard for him to get sex. If you are androgynous and not attracting the women you desire, try wearing more masculine clothing and eating more meat.

The Comedian

The comedian performs for women. He thinks that if he's funny enough, and entertaining enough, women will sleep with him. It is true that women tend to value a sense of humor over almost anything else in men they are attracted to, but alone it is not enough. Women will end up thinking of you as an entertainment machine, and expect you to perform, rather than as a man they could get romantic with.

Comedian men also show a certain level of insecurity through their constant need to make people laugh. It's as if they are always asking for some sort of validation from others that they should be getting from themselves. Women sense this, and relegate the comedian to the status of "friend." If you find you are a comedian with women, joke less, and see what happens. They might find you more interesting.

The Geek Boy

It's more fashionable to be a geek now than it used to be, but it is still a horrid seduction strategy. The Geek Boy's main problem is that he is more comfortable with machines than he is with people, especially women. He retreats into the world of computers or machines, where he feels he understands what's going on.

This book is perfect for the Geek, because it presents a manual about seducing women. The Geek can become a good seducer because once he understands a system can be mastered, he masters it. Geeks do especially well with our system, and if you are a geek, you are reading the right book. Read the damn manual, as technical support often says, and do what it says.

The Therapist

The therapist breaks the cardinal habit of Highly Effective Seducers— never be a prospect's therapist. The Therapist thinks that if he can only solve a woman's problems, she'll want to make love to him. As we said in Chapter Two, what happens in fact is that she wants to get away from him, and will then come to him about problems she's having with the jerk men she's having sex with. If you find yourself in this category, you have a choice to make. Do you want to be a woman's therapist, or do you want sex? If you want sex, make the right choice today. If she brings up her problems, change the subject, and start seducing her.

The 12-Stepper

The 12-step program is a wonderful fellowship that has saved many lives, and we're not here to put it down. But it is worth mentioning that men deeply involved in the "program" create predictable problems seducing women. If you are such a man, it's a good idea to know what to watch out for.

The 12-stepper tends to take life a little too seriously. He screws up seduction by needing to talk too much about his emotional pain, and by his need to appear "vulnerable" by sharing his childhood traumas. He also turns women off with his need to think of everything in terms of addiction. If she wants a drink, he asks if there is a history of alcoholism in her family; if she lights a cigarette, he lectures her on the perils of nicotine. Pleasure, it seems, is inherently suspect to him, and a woman notices this. Not wanting to hear him describe his sex addiction, she doesn't get sexual with him. Worrying about addiction and the free spirit of seduction don't necessarily go well together.

If you are in a 12-step program, more power to you. Stay with it; it can make a huge difference in your life. And when you try to seduce a woman, remember you are not at a 12-step meeting. She doesn't want to hear about your emotional pain, or about what an addict you are. Keep your outcome in mind, and focus on the seduction.

The Slave

The Slave thinks that any positive attention from women is a sign that he's on his way to having sex with them. To this end he does everything for a woman that she could possibly want. If she's hungry, he makes her dinner. If she needs his help moving furniture, he makes an elaborate show of canceling going to a party so he can be at her beck and call. He figures that her occasional compliments about how "sweet" he is, along with the obvious sacrifices he makes for her, will eventually and inevitably add up to sex for him. He keeps being her servant as he awaits that day.

The truth is that women hate Slave men, even as they use them mercilessly as handymen, cash machines, and secretaries. The day of sexual reward will always remain in the future, and the Slave will never get what he wants. It's like the *Dilbert* cartoon where he has a date with a woman to "grout the tile in her bathroom." That's not a date, it's being an idiot. If you find yourself being women's slave, you must stop right now, as you are destroying your chances with her sexually. Realize that every Slave action you take only builds her contempt for you, even as she praises you for your "sweetness." Take the actions we recommend in this book instead.

The Whiner

The Whiner is like the Beaten Down By Life guy, only louder. Rather than suffer in silence about what the world has done to him, the Whiner makes sure everybody knows about it. He sends a loud and clear message to women that says "I am immature and you want to stay away from me." Women get the message, and want nothing to do with him.

You may have every right to whine. You may have an especially rough life, and everybody may well be out to get you. We don't argue with that. Our point is that you'll get more women by dealing maturely with your problems than you will by whining about them. Like the Slave, the Whiner thinks that, if he gets a positive, compassionate response from a woman, he *must* be on the road to sleeping with her. Like the Slave, he mistakes any positive reaction for arousal. The only difference is that, while the Slave seeks a "you're so sweet, you make me so happy" reaction, the Whiner seeks a "I feel so sorry for you" compassionate reaction. Neither approach works with women.

If you find yourself complaining to women about the difficulties of your life, stop it right now. They may appear compassionate about all you've suffered, but compassionate and aroused are completely different emotional states. Deal with your life, and seduce women. Don't complain to them.

The Desperate

We've talked a lot about the dangers of desperation to your seduction, so we'll only touch on it briefly here. The Desperate man needs women to validate him; this results in a constant inability to relax around them. He is more like a puppy dog waiting for a treat. He seems heavy and awkward to women because he is so afraid that he won't get the validation that he needs so desperately from them. If you are Desperate, you must learn to get your validation from your life, rather than from women. It is especially important that you pursue many, many women, so that any one woman's response to your seduction is not particularly meaningful. As you do this, your desperation will decrease, and you will have more success.

We've seen that women don't cause all the problems, after all. Too bad; it's much more satisfying to pin the blame on someone else, rather than on ourselves. A powerful man, however, is accountable for every area of his life, and takes responsibility for how things turn out. As you figure out the kinds of problems you are likely to cause when seducing women, you can take responsibility for those problems, solve them, and be a much better seducer.

HOW TO HANDLE THE TOP PROBLEMS WOMEN CAUSE

You no longer have the excuses you once did for getting into relationships with extremely difficult, demanding, unstable women. If you apply yourself to mastering the techniques in this book, you will be able to date as many women as you like. You'll be able to pick one that works best for you.

But trouble rears its ugly head even in the most "together" of women. To help you handle those inevitable breakdowns on the road to utter sexual fulfillment, we are providing this emergency tool kit of ways to handle the common problems women cause.

Q: What should I do when she cries?

A: If a woman cries on a priming or seduction date, it's a very bad sign about her stability. There may be some extenuating circumstance—she just dropped an anvil on her foot, or her mother just died. But most of the time, she'll be crying because she's emotionally unstable and unable to contain her feelings. You may be able to have sex with her, but proceed with extreme caution. Keep an ear open for any indications that she's had to involve the police in any of her relationships. If she has, she might be unstable enough to mistakenly interpret something you do and call the police on *you*. If she has called the police, stay away from her. If you do decide to go ahead with her, be aware that you will probably want to have sex with her only a few times because she's likely to be too unstable for anything long-term.

If she cries *after* you've been having sex with her for a while, it may simply be an isolated emotional episode, and you can follow the advice from earlier in this chapter, and let it go. If a woman cries *while* you are having sex with her, you have to give up on the sex and deal with it. The bad news is, if she does this once, she's likely to do it again. If she hyperventilates while she cries, and gasps a lot and can't stop, she may be having a flashback, and is re-experiencing some earlier sexual trauma. If this happens, you need to know that it probably is not going to stop happening any time soon.

Q: What should I do when she's inconsistent?

A: Inconsistency and illogical behavior are commonalities shared by all humans, including you. She's probably marveling at how inconsistent *you* are. You've got to expect a woman to be inconsistent, and not worry about it. One minute she might like chocolate, the next, hate it. Fine. One day she may think your new leather jacket looks great, the next, bad. Okay. One date she may want to get away from you, the next, have sex with you. Whatever. Don't take it personally.

Q: What should I do when she is moody?

A: Many women think that they have a perfect right to be moody, and a right to be as difficult as they want to be when they are in a mood. As one woman we interviewed told us, "I don't care if I am difficult to men!"

As usual, you must ask yourself what's most important to you, and not take her behavior personally. The most critical thing to know when dealing with a moody woman is how to not reward her for being in a bad mood. You may not think you reward women for being in bad moods, but you probably do. If you tiptoe around her, cow-tow to her every demand, and are extra-nice to her, all you are doing is training her that being in a bad mood is a great way to get you to treat her better. Guess what? She'll be faster to get back into a bad mood, and stay there longer, because of you.

The key for handling a woman's bad mood is to:

1. Acknowledge it.
2. Show some compassion for her problems.
3. Stay upbeat and happy.
4. Get away from her as soon as you can. Let her work through her mood, and get together with you later when she's feeling better.

Here are some things you can say to take you through each of these steps:

1. Acknowledge the mood. "Had a bad day, eh?" "Not feeling so good today, eh?" "Having a rough time, eh?"
2. Show a little compassion for her mood. The key here is to *never* try to solve her problem. Just listen to her, and show a little compassion. You might say: "Sounds rough. I know how bad a bad mood can be." "Wow, I'm sorry you are having a hard time."
3. Stay up-beat. This is critical. You must go on with your life, little affected by her bad mood. Otherwise, you are simply indulging her and rewarding her for being down. You shouldn't do this in a sarcastic or overly enthusiastic manner; just make it clear that her mood is not going to change yours.
4. Get away from her as soon as you can. If she's really down, she'll either want to sort it out with your help, sort it out alone, or take it out on you. If she wants your help, don't offer solutions: just ask her clarifying questions so she can get clear on what she's upset about. Hopefully, it won't be *you*. If she wants to sort it out alone, or take it out on you, get away from her. You'll be happier later that you did.

Q: What should I do when she has PMS?

A: Premenstrual Syndrome is real, and has a profound effect on women's physiological and emotional states. If you don't believe such a thing is possible, remember back to a time when you felt so horny that you were about to lose your mind. Perhaps you hadn't had sex in a while, and felt particularly teased by all the lovely young women around you. Some men get so riled up that they start bar-fights and get into trouble, just to deal with the hormonal mess that is going on in their bodies. PMS is equally real. The main difference is that a woman who behaves badly because of PMS has a medical excuse. When you behave badly because you are horny, you are still just a jerk. Oh well.

A woman who has constant problems with PMS may make a good short-term lover, but, sadly, is very difficult to be in a long-term relationship with. If she gets angry or weird or difficult, then apologizes by explaining she has PMS, seriously consider dating someone else. This is not going to get better, only worse. If she is committed to handling it responsibly, and is treating it medically, she may be a good relationship partner. But if she handles it by taking it out on you, even once, consider looking elsewhere. If you are in a relationship with a woman who has PMS, stay away from her when she is at her worst.

Q: What should I do when she has a flashback?

A: A "flashback" occurs when a person, male or female, relives the emotions of a past trauma, as if it were happening right now. Flashbacks are part of a syndrome called Post-traumatic Stress Disorder, and you are probably not qualified to handle it if the woman you are with has one. Flashbacks can involve hyperventilating, crying, touch-aversion and even talking to people who aren't there. A woman in a flashback might scream "He's coming to get me!" or "It's happening again!" If a woman was severely sexually abused, she may have a flashback while you are having sex. This is not fun for either of you, and a good reason to avoid having sex with any such person. Staying out of these situations is the best thing you can do.

While we are not putting ourselves in the position of giving you medical or therapeutic advice (which we are not qualified to do) we can tell you our anecdotal experience, which indicates that if you stay with her, the flashback will usually end in an hour or two. But sometimes it won't, and some people have to be hospitalized. If she starts to freak out in any way during sex, stop at once, and see if you can change her focus off the feelings in her body. Take her out for ice cream, or take her into a different room. Get her involved in a TV program. Ask her questions about her work. If you can get her mind involved in something else, she may not flashback. Then stop pursuing her romantically, and find a more stable woman.

Q: What should I do when she criticizes me?

A: There are different levels of criticism. You have to balance the criticism against how attractive the woman is, and how fun you think she'll be in bed. If the criticism is small and her breasts are large, you may want to let it go. The best way to let it go is to not defend yourself. Simply say something like, "Oh, that's interesting that you feel that way," or "I didn't know you felt that way." *Never* justify what she is criticizing, or explain yourself. That will get you into a conversation, or even an argument. Remember your outcome. You are there to seduce her, not prove how right you are, and how much you are above her criticism. If you acknowledge it, and let it go, her criticism can go away as fast as it arrived.

It sometimes works best to nip criticism in the bud. She may not even know she is doing it, and may need you to call her attention to it. You might calmly but firmly say "Hey, you've never spoken to me like that before, and I didn't like it. Please don't talk to me like that again." If she is very critical, this will only start a fight, but you shouldn't be spending much time with very critical women anyway. As Madonna says, "Respect yourself." Have sex with her a few times, and when her critical nature gets unbearable, move on.

Q: What should I do if she hits me?

A: Leave instantly. Get your hat and coat and *go*. Say nothing. Ignore everything she says. Be out of her house or apartment within thirty seconds. We mean it. You want her to learn that striking you ends all interactions immediately. For a woman, that is a big punishment. You also want to leave her with the knowledge that she just hit you. When she thinks of you, you want her to remember that the last interaction the two of you had was her hitting you. That is more likely to change her future behavior than anything else.

It goes without saying that the stupidest thing you could possibly do is hit her back. You must *never* hit a woman, under any circumstances, do you understand? In the eyes of the law, when a woman hits you, even if she hits you first, it is almost always self-defense. If you hit her, no matter what she did to you, you are *always* domestically abusing her. Your pathetic whining that "she hit me first" will not keep you out of jail, especially if she denies it, which she will. Don't hit her back, and don't stay and argue. Leave at once. It's the best way.

Q: What should I do when she doesn't want sex?

A: Having an ample sex life means that you can pretty much have sex whenever you want it. There are plenty of women out there who love sex as much as you do, and who will almost never say "no" to you, once you have become lovers. This is the kind of woman you are looking for.

If a woman doesn't want sex the first time you are in bed together, that may be a sign of a problem. If she simply wants to wait a date or two for the "big event," go ahead and wait. If she says that she simply doesn't feel like it, however, you may well be left wondering why she got into bed with you in the first place. She may have a very on-again, off-again relationship with her desire, one moment wanting sex, the next hating it. Such a woman will destroy your sense of sexual confidence, and you must get rid of her and sleep with somebody else.

If you are sleeping with a woman on a regular basis and she occasionally doesn't want sex, lighten up. It's not a big deal. If she consistently withholds sex, you aren't lovers anymore, and you should stop dating her.

Q: What should I do when she criticizes my sexual performance?

A: Not all people are sexually compatible. One of our students dated a woman who accused him of being sexually violent when he thought he was being gentle. One woman we interviewed told us she was "riding" a lover, thinking she was displaying enthusiasm and passion, and he told her dryly that her movement up and down reminded him of a sewing machine. The point is, the message you think you are conveying sexually may not be what she is getting.

Some women simply can't be dealt with once they've started criticizing a lover. One man told us about a woman he dated who would cry during sex because "you are doing it all wrong." When he asked what she wanted different, she said "You have to just know! Oh, someday I hope I have a lover who knows how to do it right!" He had a choice between this difficult woman and his sexual self-esteem. He broke up with her, and moved on.

Other times a woman's criticisms are worth listening to, and can improve her responsiveness. If she doesn't like her nipples pinched, and you pinch them, she'll be a happier and better lover if you listen when she tells you to stop. The best way to avoid a woman's sexual criticism is to ask her questions about what she likes during the first time you have sex, and afterwards. If you integrate these suggestions into your sexual play, she'll have less to criticize.

You can also find out a woman's lovemaking preferences before you first have sex with her by asking "What do you think is important to women in a lover?" She'll then tell you what *she* likes, as if she was speaking about all women.

Q: What should I do when she hates my porn collection?

A: When you are seducing a woman for the first few times, she simply shouldn't be allowed to find out that you have pornography. The only exception is if she asks to see some while you are having sex, and this is rare. Put it away where she won't find it when she's looking for a shirt to wear while she makes coffee the next morning.

As you get to know her better, continue to keep your porn where she won't see it, until you can figure out how she feels about it. The main thing you need to know is that if she hates porn, you must never argue with her about it. Simply listen to what she has to say, then change the subject. Arguing about pornography will *never* change a woman's mind on the subject. Don't even try. And keep it away from her.

Q: What should I do when she doesn't like my friends?

A: When you are first seducing a woman, she shouldn't meet your friends. Your friends represent an unnecessary variable in the seduction equation. You don't know what kind of idiotic things they may say or do to screw up your seduction. They may even try to steal her from you! If you run into a friend when you are out with her, get rid of him as quickly as you can.

After you've been sleeping with a woman for a while, she may begin to get to know your friends. The thing to know is that you must never abandon a friend because a woman doesn't like him. Don't hang out with them at the same time, but don't write him off, either. Some men abandon their male friends when they get into a relationship with women, and they pay the price in loneliness later. Don't make this mistake.

Q: What should I do if she hates sports?

A: Ah, sports, the great divide between men and women! First and foremost, you don't indulge her desire to argue with her about sports. This is another instance where you can be as right as the day is long, and discussing it with a woman will still do nothing but cause trouble in your relationship. If you are in the process of seducing a woman, don't share the sports-loving part of yourself. No positive purpose is served by telling her that your idea of a great Sunday afternoon is to watch two football games and both of the pre-game and post-game shows. She'll find that out about you soon enough. If you are sleeping with her regularly the rule is the same: don't argue about it. If she wants to, acknowledge that she doesn't like it, and change the subject.

Q: What should I do when she is jealous?

A: The first question to ask is, why is she jealous? Is it because you flirted with and tried to seduce another woman, right in front of her face? Remember, when you are out with a woman, she is the only woman who exists. You must not check out or flirt with other women, or you will irritate your date, and the seduction will be ruined.

Q: What should I do if I find unpleasant surprises under her clothes?

A: This can happen. Henry was a rock musician and, after a performance in a bar, picked up an extremely hot woman and took her home. "When I reached under her skirt, I discovered she was a 'he!'" Henry told us. "Needless to say, I told him to get the hell out of my apartment." This is an extreme example of the kinds of surprises you can get when you finally get a woman's clothes off.

One of our students took an attractive woman back to his apartment, only to discover that all of her body was covered by fine black hair. "It was an incredible turn-off," he told us. "I felt bad about it, but what could I do?" Another man told us about a date whose bustline turned out to be entirely padding. "I was so looking forward to getting my hands onto her breasts," he said. "I might as well have saved myself the time I spent seducing her, and grabbed a box of tissues!" Another man told us of a woman who had a pungent, unpleasant smell once he got her in bed. It's tragic, but sometimes it happens that you want to get rid of a woman because you discover she just doesn't turn you on. What should you do?

Most of the time, it doesn't pay to tell her your specific gripe about her body. All you'll do is upset her about something she may have little or no control over. Why devastate her? Why be mean? Try saying something like "I know! Let's go get some ice cream!" Then jump up and start putting on your clothes. You can also say "I really want to know you better before we take this any farther," to tactfully slow down unenjoyable sexual play. It's no fun to have to bail out on a sexual experience, but if you do, try to do it as gently as possible.

Q: What do I do if she wants to talk about marriage on the first date?

A: Sometimes relationship and marriage conversations can show up on the first date. Women who are over thirty years old often suddenly decide that it's time to get married. They will sometimes tell you this on the first date, or even before accepting your invitation to go out at all. "I have to tell you," she might say, "that in my twenties I was really into just dating around. Now I want a serious relationship. What do you think about that?" If you don't answer that you want a serious relationship, too, she probably won't go out with you.

The proper way to handle this is to be honest, but not to put her off. If you aren't really looking for a long-term relationship, remember that this doesn't mean you wouldn't get involved in one if you met the right woman. She might actually be that woman; you simply don't know. So you don't say "I'm just looking to date around and have lots of unattached sex." She'll disappear instantly. Instead, try "I'm not really sure. I know that if I met the right woman, I'd be interested in the long term. I just don't know if I've met her yet." She'll stay interested, and you'll be able to go out.

You are now ready to handle the problems women cause. You can spot the women you should avoid, and understand the three modes of female fighting. Also, you've looked at the problems you cause in dating, and seen some steps you can take to stop creating the problems you have been having with women. You have a list of pro tips for handling specific problems. You are ready to roll.

More important, you now understand that no matter how skillful you are with women, problems are inevitable. You can let go of worrying that there is something wrong with you if the woman you are dating goes wacko on you. It's not personal, it's just part of dating.

chapter twelve...
After the Date—
Keeping
Up the Pursuits

So you've been flirting like crazy with every woman you meet, and asking out the most responsive ones for priming dates. Of those, some have shown up for the dates, and some have not. With some of those who showed up, you did a good job making the proper romantic moves, asking the romantic questions, and leading romantic conversations. With others you got scared, lazy, or intimidated. With some you winked, smiled, touched, held eye contact, and even went for that first kiss. Some may have been put off by you, and others were entranced. You set up seduction dates with those that were entranced, those who liked you, and prepared for the next move.

On the seduction dates, you created romantic experiences that excited and entranced both of you. You spent time together doing things that were extraordinary and wondrous for her. You gave her little gifts. You paid attention to the little details, and those details made the experience seem like magic. You ended up near a bed, and had condoms with you. When the time was right and she was thinking of the first kiss and more, you went for it.

You got her into bed, and were an attentive, creative lover. Now it's the next day, she's left your home or you've left hers, and you are looking back on the date, feeling satisfied, powerful, and happy. You succeeded in the best way possible. Congratulations!

Or perhaps something else happened. You had a seduction date, but didn't make it all the way into the bedroom. Perhaps you created romantic feelings, and kissed her until she told you to slow things down. Or perhaps she rejected you completely, and couldn't wait to get away from you. Or perhaps you didn't even try, and let the seduction date deteriorate into mere socializing.

Under any of these circumstances, what should you do next? No matter how far the date went, your course afterwards is clear: you must make it a success in your own mind, decide where you want the interaction to go next, maintain your investment, and create the next seduction date. This chapter will tell you how to do all of this, and keep all your seductions alive and moving forward.

MAKE IT A SUCCESS IN YOUR OWN MIND

When Bob goes out with a woman and doesn't end up having sex with her—which is most of the time—he beats himself up. "Why can't I ever get a woman to want me?," he moans. "After all the work I do, I never end up with anything. I bet I'll never have sex with a woman again." His catastrophizing and pessimism make it impossible for him to think he's succeeded at any aspect of the date unless he's had sex with a woman. At the beginning of your training to become a seduction master, such a way of thinking is impractical. You must learn to make *every* interaction with a woman into a success, whether you had sex with her or not.

You have to decide what your definition of a successful date will be. If you are like Bob, and you see a date as successful only if you had sex, you are making it more difficult for yourself. The bottom line is that your definition should leave you feeling good after any interaction with a woman. Your definition must help you learn whatever you can from the date, and leave you charged up for your next encounter.

The average guy seems to think that to be a success with a woman he has to be able to go from first seeing her on the street to having sex with her in twenty minutes or less. Alternatively, he thinks that he must be able to always be perfectly smooth, never alienating or blowing it with any woman. This is too stringent a definition of success, and will not get you the kind of life you want.

Besides, these goals are unrealistic, even for the best seducers. Even they can blow it, and are occasionally rejected. What they do know is how to make all interactions with women, even the "failures," into successes.

We suggest that you adopt this definition: if you learned something from your interaction with a woman, it was a success. This isn't just "fancy footwork" thinking, either. If you've learned *anything* from the experience, you'll be able to handle that situation better the next time it comes up with another woman. And it almost certainly *will* come up again, you can be sure of that. You should be able to find a way to learn something from every interaction; therefore, you should always be successful.

No matter what kind of a date Bruce has, he finds a way to make it into a success. If he goes out with a woman who turns out to be a screaming angry feminist, he may learn some new ways to notice such women earlier, or he may use the date as an opportunity to try a new approach. If he goes for the first kiss and the woman says "no," he may learn some new warning signs of sexual rejection. Or, looking back over the experience, he may discover some crucial step in the seduction he's been skipping. If, after making out with him, a woman refuses sex at the last minute, he may notice something he was doing that was offensive that he never noticed before. By changing this, he may be able to get sex more reliably in the future.

We suggest that you make every learning experience with a woman a success, and that you not rest after any interaction until you've discovered what you have learned. Just keep asking yourself, "What did I learn from this?" and eventually you will figure it out. This way you insure your future. You keep yourself moving forward, rather than allowing yourself to become dejected and to give up. You drive yourself relentlessly toward inevitably having the sex life you desire.

DECIDE WHERE YOU WANT
THE INTERACTION TO GO

Now that you know the woman a little better, you must ask yourself: where do you want this interaction to go? Do you want this woman to be a short-term sex partner, or do you think she'd be good relationship material? Are you excited about seeing her again really soon, or are you burning her phone number and hoping she'll never find out where you live? You must assess your reaction to the date, and decide where you want your interaction to go next.

While you usually won't be able to tell right away if a woman would be a good relationship partner, you can often tell if she *wouldn't* be. There may very well be something about her that you know you could handle for the short term, but that will inevitably destroy any chance of you having a long-term relationship with her. You are better off acknowledging this to yourself right away, and living with that reality. If you don't, you are in denial and allowing yourself to get sucked into a relationship that will cause you constant suffering. If a woman is too unstable for you, or too fat, has political beliefs you find repugnant, has an annoying personality, or is simply not good enough in bed, you need to recognize it right away. With such a woman, plan to have a short-term relationship.

MAINTAIN YOUR INVESTMENT

By the time you've gone on a seduction date, you've done a lot of work to move things this far. She feels good about you, and you feel good about her. There's a sense of chemistry and connection between you. Now you must keep those feelings alive. Whether you had sex with her or not, if you don't maintain the feelings that you've created, they will go away, and you'll have to start all over again. Remember, a woman likes it when you are attentive, and when she thinks that you are thinking about her. If you disappear after a date, she'll assume that you aren't thinking about her, that you have lost interest, and don't like her. Worse, she may decide that you only wanted her for sex. If she had sex with you, she'll assume you used her and are now tossing her aside. Thinking this will make her angry. If she didn't have sex with you, she may assume that you only wanted her for sex, and are now dumping her because she didn't put out right away. This will make her angry, too. The next time you approach her, you may have to overcome this anger to even get back to the level of connection you were feeling before you disappeared. Sometimes this is easy, sometimes it's hard. If you maintain your investment in the first place, you'll have less re-work to do.

As you date more and more women, you'll find that sometimes you stop doing the things that are necessary to maintain a connection with some of them. This may be a sign that you are not interested, and you may want to let them go. It may also be a sign that you are getting lazy, and sloppy. If you want success with women and an abundant sex life, you must, as we've said so many times, be working on many women at once. This means that there will be a number of women who you are maintaining and deepening your connection with at the same time. If you find one has slipped out, and you still desire her, simply start maintaining the connection again. There's a very good chance that, with work, you'll be able to rebuild the good feelings she has for you.

It's important to understand maintenance because it is an important key to all kinds of success. It's not only important in short-term, but also in long-term relationships, and in every other area of your life. Consider: the parts of your life you maintain are the parts of your life that you focus on improving daily, or almost daily, in some small way. Your constant attention maintains those parts of your life, and allows them to continue to expand and grow. For instance, if you are committed to making more money, and maintain that commitment by taking action on it every single day, you will make more money. If you are committed to improving your health, and you maintain that commitment by taking action on it every single day, your health will improve. If you are committed to improving your long-term relationship, and you maintain that commitment by taking action on it every single day, your relationship will improve. And if you are committed to building romantic connections with women, and you maintain that commitment by taking action on it every single day (or at least consistently), you will build romantic connections. *Maintenance* is the way you keep these connections growing once you are dating or having sex with a woman.

It's the sad truth that dating is like everything else in life: you are either moving forward on it, or you are moving backward. Your connection with a woman is either getting better, or it's getting worse. There is no standing still, no middle ground. Life moves on; you are either keeping up with it, or falling behind. You must use maintenance to keep things moving forward with the women you are dating.

THE ART OF MAINTENANCE

Maintenance is anything you do to keep the good feelings going in any connection you are building with a woman. Bob doesn't practice it. After Bob goes out with a woman, he is usually so depressed that he can't bring himself to do any follow-up work. After one date, a woman Bob is interested in never hears from him again. "I'd call her, but I'm really busy right now," he tells himself. "Things are swamped at work, and geez! I really need to get organized in my life before I get into pursuing women. Besides, if she's interested, let her call me up!" Of course, all of this is just excuses. The truth is, Bob is too busy wallowing in his self-pity about being such a failure to take the consistent actions that would lead to his success. Two months later, he thinks longingly of that woman again. "But I can't call her now," he tells himself. "I haven't talked to her for months!"

Let's compare Bob to Tom. When Tom first started dating Lisa, he understood the power of maintenance. "We went out for a priming date, and at the end of it I kissed her. We then went on a seduction date, where I took her to the zoo, and gave her some nicely wrapped little animal trinkets I'd bought earlier at the zoo store. We kissed at the end of that date, but it didn't feel right to take it any farther. But I knew it was important to maintain the feelings that we had built. Between the first seduction date and the second one, I made sure to drop by her work and leave a little love note for her with a single rose. On the next date, we had sex." After having sex with her, Tom decided that he liked her enough to continue seeing her, and so he continued to maintain their connection. "I called her, we had sex, and I sent her another note," he says. "She was overjoyed to go out with me again."

You mustn't do what Bob does. You must maintain your romantic connections by taking simple maintenance steps so that you can keep the romance alive and growing.

What maintenance does

Maintenance accomplishes three key tasks in keeping a romantic connection vital. It makes a woman feel special and attracted to you because:

Maintenance shows you are thinking of her. Even if you aren't thinking of a woman all the time, it's worth taking the time and energy to do some things that make her think that you are. Women love to know that a man they like is thinking of them, and they hate it when you are not. Therefore, showing you are thinking of them is a key female need that maintenance fulfills.

Maintenance shows you are putting in time and effort. Maintenance shows a woman that you are putting time and effort into your connection with her. Note that we said "time and effort," not "money." Most women are far more impressed by a card you made yourself or a brief love note with a rose, than they are by something you spent lots of money on but much less time and effort. As we've said before, spending lots of money to seduce a woman is not necessary, and, by itself, can be counter-productive. If on your date she longs for the days when Coca-Cola came in bottles rather than cans, listen to her. If you find her a six-pack of bottles of Coke, wrap them nicely and give them to her with a humorous note. We guarantee you'll get farther than you would with a more expensive, but impersonal gift.

Maintenance shows her you are a generative man Women are attracted to men who are able to create the kind of lives they want. They are usually *not* attracted to men who are victims in their lives, and to whom life seems to "just happen." When you maintain your connection to a woman, you show her that you are a man who is committed to and capable of generating, in a sustained way, the kind of life that you want. You show her that you are creative, and action-oriented. You set yourself apart from other whiny, complaining, victim men, and become more desirable to her.

The secret of good maintenance

Maintenance will probably not come naturally to you, and you'll have to make yourself do it. It's like doing your taxes, or getting the oil changed in your car. Like Bob, you'll find excuses for not maintaining romantic connections. In truth, you'll just be too scared to try something new with a woman, and will tell yourself you are too busy or give yourself some other lame excuse. You'll want to have a romantic relationship "just happen" rather than put in the effort to generate it yourself. Because of this tendency, you must *use your date-book to schedule time to work on maintaining your romantic connections*. This means you schedule time in, just as you would a meeting or an appointment.

Tom does this for the women he's working on. He currently has five women he's in various stages of dating; two he's flirting with on a regular basis but hasn't asked out yet, two he's had priming dates with, and one he's had sex with several times. He has 15 minutes scheduled three times a week to work on things that will maintain these relationships. "Sometimes the time goes over, but I know that in fifteen minutes I can at least put together a game plan," he says. "With Stacey, the woman I'm having sex with, I put in enough time to figure out something special to do on our next date. I also see if I can figure out any new ways to make her feel special. For the two girls I've had priming dates with, I spend time devising our seduction dates, perhaps calling museums to find out hours or preparing fun little gifts I can give them. One of them has e-mail, so I spend some time sending her romantic poetry that way. With the two I'm flirting with, I try to figure out when I can conveniently drop by their work."

By scheduling the time to do these things, he's able to create the impression that he's naturally spending time coming up with ways to make each woman feel special. He's not doing it naturally, though, and neither will you. He's scheduling time to do it, the way he would any other appointment or task. Maintaining connections with women is surprisingly fun to do, but only comes naturally in relationships where there is "magically" intense chemistry and strong feelings. By making yourself do this kind of maintenance, you create and build those "magic" feelings.

Frequency of maintenance

When you take maintenance actions in a relationship with a woman, you are applying what behaviorists call "reinforcement." A "reinforcement" is a reward—something that feels good—that the subject gets for performing a certain behavior or for having a certain feeling. For instance, giving a dog a treat when he comes when you call his name reinforces the behavior of coming when you call. In time, the dog will look forward to coming when you call, because he knows that obeying you will mean he'll get a reinforcement that he likes.

The thing to notice is that if you give the dog a treat every single time he comes when you call, he'll start to get lazy. He'll figure, "Eh, why should I hurry? I can get over there in my own good time, and take the treat." Constant reinforcement stops being effective after a while.

You may have noticed this in your own relationships. Have you ever had someone who consistently goes out of his or her way to make you feel special? Suppose that one morning, out of the blue, someone at your work place brought you a cup of excellent coffee when you first sat down at your desk. You'd probably feel pretty special, and you'd be happy to see that person later in the day. You would have associated seeing that person with the good feelings you got from the gift.

But now imagine if that person brought you coffee every single day, like clockwork, and never missed a day. At first you'd probably appreciate it, then you'd notice it less, then you'd hardly notice it at all. You might even start complaining when the coffee wasn't exactly the way you liked it, or get angry if he or she missed a day. You'd naturally go from being delighted by the constant gifts to seeing them as a regular part of life, or even as something you intrinsically deserve. This is a natural reaction to constant, unvarying reinforcement.

If you constantly shower a woman with gifts and attention, you run the risk of the same thing happening. At first, it's important to reinforce a woman constantly; it gets her in the habit of being happy about seeing you. But after a while, if your gifts and attention are going to stay effective, you must start bestowing them a little more irregularly. This is what behavior experts call a "variable schedule of reinforcement." You don't give her flowers every week, or every date. You don't always have a little gift for her. You don't always show up to flirt with her at the same time, or on the same day. You vary your schedule of making her feel extra-good, and thus keep the interaction exciting and fresh for her.

Tom puts a variable schedule of reinforcement to good use. "When I first start dating a woman, I go out of my way to make her feel good a lot," he says. "But in time, I know I can start scaling back. As long as I keep making her feel good often, I get better results if I don't reinforce her with special gifts or presents every single time I see her." The classic trap to watch out for is any reinforcing behavior that begins to look like a habit to you. Keep an eye open for things you *always* do to make her feel special. Don't always bring her gifts, don't *always* visit her work place once every three days. Vary your schedule of reinforcement, and you'll have a lot more success.

THE FOUR MAINTENANCE KEYS THAT KEEP HER WARMED UP AND WAITING FOR MORE

We've helped you understand what maintenance is, why it's important, and how often to do it. Now let's give you some specific things you can do to maintain your budding romantic relationships.

Each of these activities is easier to do if you actually like the woman you are maintaining. In fact, all of your interactions with women will be much more successful if you select women that you like. All these activities are the things you would naturally do if you were falling in love, and had chemistry driving you both crazy with attraction and lust. But beware—these actions will likely not only make her feel attracted to you, they will also increase your attraction to her. Don't be surprised when you start to really like her as you do these.

1. Love notes and poetry

We discussed love notes in Chapter 6, so we'll review them here only briefly. Before you have sex with a woman, love notes should be brief. After you are having sex with her, they can be longer, but only if you are sure what you saying to her will be well-received. A quick note with a single rose, delivered to her work place a few days after a priming date, can do wonders for your seduction.

2. E-mail

Always ask women you are interested in if they have an e-mail address. E-mail is the perfect medium in which to write romantic letters that will flatter and arouse her, but not seem too overwhelming.

You can conduct romantic conversations via e-mail, and have the "home-court advantage" of being able to carefully pick your words and review them thoroughly before she ever sees them. Simply pose one of your romantic questions as we describe in Chapter 7. Then answer it, as if she had asked it back to you. Say something like this:

"My friend Mary was just telling me about the most romantic date she was ever on. It was amazing. Imagine this: you are out with a man you really like and find really attractive. You are sitting in this gorgeous outdoor restaurant, overlooking a lake. The autumn colors are just perfect. The air is fresh and smells so great, you feel like you don't even need to eat, you just want to sit there and breathe that sweet air and look into each other's eyes. Anyway, that's how she put it. And you have this incredible date as the sun goes down over the water, the stars come out and then the moon rises, and the two of you feel so connected, so in love; you know what I mean? I'd be curious to know, if you'd care to share with me—what would you say was your most romantic moment ever?

"Mine was seeing a Celtic music concert in a beautiful outdoor theater in Boulder, Colorado. You can imagine how it felt: there you are on a cool summer night, listening to this amazing music with a person you are so attracted to. And I love the way great music gets into your body, you know what I mean? It's like you can get lost in the rhythm of it together; it's incredible. Afterwards, walking under the mountains on the grounds near the performance, that warm, safe feeling of holding hands...just spectacular.

"Anyway, I seem to be getting carried away here. I just wanted to tell you I had a great time on our date, and am looking forward to seeing you again."

By describing these romantic experiences, you cause her to visualize them, experience the feelings of them, and to link those feelings to you. If you go into great detail, it's a good idea to add a closing paragraph that says something like "Anyway, I seem to be getting carried away here," or "I see I'm rambling on; I guess I'll close this note now." Such statements seem to soften any odd feelings she might get from what you wrote, and help her feel comfortable e-mailing you back.

3. Flowers

Sending or bringing her flowers is a powerful romantic move. While you would probably like it if a woman sent you flowers, women *really* like it. Flowers are an enduring (at least for a while) reminder of you to her. They go well at any stage of a relationship.

There's no need to spend lots of money of flowers if you don't want to. A simple $10 bouquet or a single rose with a note and a handful of chocolate candies will go as far as $60 worth of roses, and cost a lot less.

Buying flowers is simple. Go to a flower store, and tell the salesperson, "I want to spend ten dollars on romantic flowers. Set me up." Buy or make a card, write a few romantic lines on it, and you're done!

Having flowers delivered is more expensive, and is most appropriate after you've had great sex with a woman. If you get a woman into bed and the sex blows your mind, you might want to send her flowers at work, along with a card that says "Words fail me. That was wonderful. Thank you for last night." If you do this, more sex with her is virtually assured.

If you drop flowers off for her at her work, be sure not to stay very long. We suggest that you pop in, leave her with a great feeling, and get out. If you hang around, you just get in the way of her work and risk saying or doing something that messes up the seduction. If you hang around, you are also more likely to start thinking of yourself and your needs, and to begin ignoring hers. You are likely to start wanting her to acknowledge what a great guy you are. Keep the focus on her, and leave her alone with her flowers.

4. Gifts

We taught you about the power of little gifts, properly given, in Chapter 8. Let's review the basics.

First, when you give a woman a gift, it can be cheap as long as it is clever, funny, or meaningful. Second, the gift must be well-wrapped. If you don't have time to wrap it, don't give it to her. Giving a woman a wrapped little gift is like giving someone a gift certificate to a favorite store. It shows thought and feeling, and makes her feel good. Giving a woman an unwrapped little gift is like giving someone your pocket change, and saying "buy something with it." It gives the impression that you aren't really putting any effort into the present.

If you take a gift to a woman's work place, treat it as you would flowers. Give her the gift and get the heck out. It's no use risking messing up a good feeling by hanging around and getting in the way of her work.

DESIGN THE NEXT SEDUCTION DATE

Along with handling the maintenance, you need to start designing the next step of the seduction. If she's not yet an utterly willing sex partner, panting for you to come to her house and have sex with her at any time day or night, there's still work to be done.

Not all seduction dates end in sex, so it's important that we look at all of the possible outcomes, and show you how to generate the next step. Our diagnostic benchmark will be the kiss. Did you kiss her? Did you kiss her and make out with her? How much? Did you have sex with her? Did you try to kiss her and were rejected? Did you not even try? Depending on how far you got, you'll have varying options for your next seduction step. You must assess what you accomplished or didn't accomplish, and plan your next moves accordingly. Let's look at these outcomes one at a time, and help you generate the next step in where you go from here.

You kissed her

Congratulations! You achieved an outcome you were after. If you kissed her and didn't take things any farther, the question to ask yourself is, why did you stop? It may well have been the right thing to do: it might be very important to her that the two of you move slowly. She may not be feeling enough connection with you yet to take things farther. You may have decided to slow things down, or you may have decided that you don't really desire her after all. If you want to take things farther, you must plan. Ask yourself what's it going to take to get her into the mood to have sex with you. Another seduction date? Calling her late in the evening and asking if you can come over? Cooking for her at your house? Answer these questions as part of your planning.

You kissed her and made out with her

Good work! You've gotten that first kiss and more. You made out with her, possibly felt her body, and taken some of her clothes off. The questions for you to ponder as you design your next seduction date are these: do you still want to have sex with her? What will it take to accomplish that? If you got significantly more than a kiss, but less than sex, you probably will get sex the next time you go out with her, provided you don't screw things up. You might ask yourself what you can do to keep the romantic feeling alive, while still getting her in bed quickly. Plan another seduction date, and keep things moving along.

This time, you can start it, rather than end it, near a bed. On Franklin's first seduction date with Petra, they took a walk at a zoo, went out for a nice dinner, and ended up making out for more than an hour on his living room floor. He removed most of her clothes, and she removed most of his, but her panties and his underwear remained on.

For the next date, he wisely invited her to his home for dinner. He touched her romantically the moment she arrived, and she was responsive. They had drinks and hors d'oeuvres before the meal, and, in his candlelit living room, began to kiss. It got more and more intense, and they ended up having sex right there on his living room floor, before they even had dinner. "Total elapsed time from coming into my house to having sex with me: one hour," he told us. "If we'd gone out, it would have taken much longer." If you kissed and made out, having a bed—or some other private area—nearby is a good idea for the start of your next seduction date.

Your first kiss led to sex

If you had sex with her, congratulations! You are "the man"—for now, anyway. You now have some fun things to decide:

First, decide if you want to have sex with her again.   Some connections with women are best kept to one-night stands. She may tell you this, directly or indirectly. If she jumps up to leave right after you've had sex, it's a sign that you just had a one-time sexual experience. Ditto if she suddenly gets cold and distant. She may be afraid of getting "too close," and be withdrawing emotionally to keep that from happening. Let her go, be grateful you had sex at all, and realize that it may be harder to get her in bed the second time.

You may decide that, much as she might like to see you more, having sex with her again wouldn't be right for you. You might not have liked sex with her very much; perhaps she cried, or just wasn't a good lover. Perhaps you found her personality so aversive that you aren't willing to risk that seeing her again might lead to some sort of relationship. She might also seem overly unstable to you.

Whatever the reason, if you are certain you don't want to have sex with her again, there isn't much to do. You may decide to call her the next day (see below), but if you leave her alone, she'll probably leave you alone. If you do want to have sex with her again, read on.

Decide if you want to call the next day.   It's really important to women that you call the day after having sex with them. Really, really important. They tell us that it upsets them when men don't call. Once again, it's a double-standard: while they would never dream of calling you the next day, they absolutely expect you to.

This doesn't mean you *have to* call, of course. You only *have to* call if your top priority in life is never upsetting a woman. We believe that women aren't delicate flowers. They are tough, and they know that dating can be tough. While she does want you to call, she probably won't be sobbing on her couch, surrounded by attendant girlfriends giving her Kleenex and cartons of Rocky Road ice cream if you don't. You probably don't have the power to upset her that much. The problem is if you don't call the next day she'll be angry, and she won't want to give you sex again anytime soon. For this reason, as much as any other, it's best to call if you think you'll ever want another sex session with her.

The call doesn't have to be any big deal. Sometime during the next day, call her at work or at home, and say something like "I just wanted to call and thank you for last night. It was great. I keep thinking about what a great time I had, and what a great woman you are. Thanks." In this case, communication by answering machine is permissible. The important thing is that you call, and that she know you called.

If you do talk to her in person, keep it short. You can set up the next date at this time (if you have planned it out!), or simply set a date and not make specific plans for what you will do. You can also tell her you want to see her again, but don't have your calendar in front of you, and will call her. But don't tell her you'll call her if you don't intend to. Simply thank her for a great time, and end the call.

You tried and were rejected

Perhaps you tried to kiss her, and she said "no" to you. That's fine; a little rejection helps remind you to not take what happens with a woman personally or too seriously. How should you handle it?

The first thing to do is assess the duration of the rejection. Was she rejecting you forever, or was she rejecting you "just for now"? If it was a "just for now" rejection, she may still be interested, but want you to first do more pre-work. She may simply need another romantic date, some flowers, and a little more time. If she says something like "not now," or "I'm not ready yet," or "I don't know you well enough," that's a good sign, even if she's turning down the kiss. It means you are on the right track, and with enough work you will get what you want.

She may also just be testing you. Some women want to see how you respond when they say "no." They want to make sure you are taking them seriously and will respect their opinions and wishes.

If her rejection is more permanent in nature, you have a bigger problem. If she slapped you and stalked off, or if she pulled away from your attempted kiss and winced, it may be more permanent.

Women who are rejecting you for the long term are more likely to tell you so: they'll say "I don't feel that way about you," or "I just see you as a friend." If it's a permanent rejection, don't waste any more time on her; it's bad for your self-respect to chase after a woman who has zero interest in you. Why bother wasting time? Get away from her and keep working on the other women you are pursuing.

It's not always easy to figure out if a rejection is temporary or permanent. We've seen a woman angrily reject a man's advances, only to go over to his house later that evening, uninvited, for sex. We've also seen a woman tell a man "I don't know you well enough to kiss you yet," only to reject him later because she knows him too well and doesn't want to "spoil the friendship." The best indicator of whether a rejection was temporary or permanent is in her reaction to an invitation for another date. Most women who are repelled by you will tell you they are busy. Women who are interested, or at least neutral, will say "okay."

The second thing to do is ask yourself why she said "no." Put yourself in her shoes, and pretend that "you" are out with "you." Don't make things better than they were, and also don't make them worse. Be "dirt honest" with yourself. Did you do something that turned her off? Did you say something or spout off some opinion that offended her? Did you treat her like one of your buddies, instead of like a lady? Was it something you didn't do, like open a door for her or take care of all the details of the date? See if you can remember a moment where she might have decided to write you off. Review, on paper if necessary, the pre-work that you did. Look at the checklists in Chapters 7 and 8 and see if there were any steps that you missed. Figure out the high points and the low points of the date, and devise a new date that is more like the high points, and less like the low. Back up and redo some of the pre-work from Chapter 7, then give the kiss another go.

It's important to note that you should never ask her what you did wrong, or how to correct it. Most women want a man who is assertive enough and brave enough to figure out what happened, and try something new. If she has to lead you by the hand through the seduction, what will you be like in a relationship? Figure out a new strategy yourself and try again.

You didn't even try

If you didn't even try to kiss her, the question is, why? There are lots of possible reasons why. You must first get absolutely crystal clear the reasons you didn't try, then clarify how to overcome those problems. Next you must do what it takes to be able to kiss her on your next seduction date.

Here are some of the possible reasons:

She did something that changed your mind about her. It's entirely possible that she did something on the seduction date that you disliked so much that you decided that you didn't want her after all. Alternatively, she may have told you something about herself that made you stop desiring her. She may have confessed to having a venereal disease, or told you that she doesn't believe in contraception. She may have frightened you with tales of men she's called the police on, or with talk about a jealous ex-lover who attacked the last man she dated. If she puts you off, you have every reason to not kiss her.

You got scared, lazy, or sloppy. This is more likely. In this case, you didn't kiss her because you blew off doing any of the pre-work. Or perhaps you asked a romantic question, she seemed surprised or suspicious, and you gave up. One thing is certain: if you don't actually use the technology in this book, it won't do you a bit of good. If you got scared or lazy, you need to look at why that is. Is she the only woman you are pursuing, so you have all your eggs in one basket? If so, you must work on other women, and have more than one prospect before you go out with this woman again. Did you not practice romantic questions and conversations out loud before the date? If you didn't, you won't know what to say on the date, and won't be able to build romantic feelings. You must practice, and review the checklist of things to do on the date, so you'll be ready for whatever happens. Did you forget to treat a lady like a lady, and decide that you'd just hang out with her like one of the guys? If you did, notice the result you got—nothing at all—and resolve to not make that mistake again. Did you feel lost about what to do when? Keep studying the book, and keep practicing and making yourself ready.

You also have to notice if there was a specific problem on the date you need to learn to overcome. Did you do something that offended her? Figure out what it was. Does she have some criteria you haven't met yet? If she does, think about how you might be able to meet it. Does she view you as a friend only? It may take more time and more dates to change her mind.

Your natural tendency will be to make excuses for why you didn't go for it. We don't want to hear about it. Don't beat up on yourself, just learn from the experience. Read this book again, and give it another go. Have another seduction date or another priming date with her, and this time follow through.

She wasn't ready. If you ran the "first kiss" tests on her and she didn't seem ready, and if you didn't feel the romantic feelings, or think you generated any romantic moments, then you were right in not trying to kiss her. If you were doing everything "by the book," she simply might not have been ready, or might not have been into you at that exact moment. Sometimes a woman is just having a bad day, or is simply wrapped up in her own world, and is not feeling sexual or like connecting with you. She may be looking for a boyfriend, and not want to go too fast. It's okay if this happens. Simply learn what you can from the date, and either arrange another seduction date or go back to another priming date.

She told you she has a boyfriend. Many men stop their seductions when a woman tells them she has a boyfriend or is seeing someone. This is not always the wisest response, or even the response she wants.

It's legitimate to wonder, "If she has a boyfriend, why is she out with me?" There are several possible answers. One is that a lot of women are just staying with the guy they are dating until something better comes along. If you can show that you are "something better," you can easily be her lover. Other women are in relationships that are open, or are women who cheat regularly on their boyfriends. Still other women will tell you they have a boyfriend because they are scared to get involved with you, or have decided they don't like you and need an excuse to get away.

You are the only one who can decide if having sex with such a woman is okay with your integrity. Some men feel they must have a clear indication that the woman is single and available before they feel okay about having sex with her. Others think any woman is fair game. Todd, for instance, sleeps with any willing woman he desires, whether she has a boyfriend or not. "If he can't keep track of his girlfriend, it's not my problem," he reasons. You have to decide if sleeping with an "attached" woman is a moral or immoral thing for you to do.

If you are considering sleeping with a woman who is already involved, we suggest that you assess the risks carefully. What is her boyfriend like? Is he likely to hurt you if he finds out what you are up to? Is he on the police force, or in a gang? Does he have a history of violence? Your primary concern is your physical health; no matter how hot she is, and how much you like her, an evening of sex is not worth being attacked over.

If a woman tells you she is involved or that she has a boyfriend, don't dwell on it or question her directly about him. Simply acknowledge it, and move on with your seduction. A little bit later, ask her if she's ever been with a really jealous guy, or had an ex-boyfriend be upset about her new relationships. If you can find out what he does or what he is like from a mutual friend, by all means do so. If he doesn't pose any direct danger, then go with your conscience.

You didn't follow the Seven Habits of Highly Effective Seducers. This is a lot like getting sloppy or lazy, and it's so easy to do that it's worth going over the habits again. For the sake of review, remember that a Highly Effective Seducer:

* Constantly pursues what he wants
* Knows that rejection is the key to sexual prosperity
* Always dates more than one woman
* Is always prospecting
* Always acts with an outcome in mind
* Always makes life work for him
* Never grovels for sex
* Is not a woman's therapist, confidant or buddy
* Is always willing to walk away from a seduction or a woman
* Makes it look like he's not working on the romance.

If you are violating any of these habits, you are getting lazy, and you make it much more likely that your date won't desire you or want to kiss you. You also make it more likely that you won't even try to kiss her, because it just won't "feel right." If you find you are dropping any of these habits, the solution is to re-read Chapter 2, and recommit yourself to making these principles and practices central to your life.

AFTER THE SEDUCTION DATE

After the seduction date, your course is clear. First, you must make the date a success in your own mind. By finding something that you learned from it, you assure that every experience you have with a women is successful, and that every experience drives you on towards your ultimate goal of abundant sex.

Next, you must decide where you want to steer your next interaction with this woman. Do you want to pursue her more, think of her as a potential short-term relationship, or get rid of her completely? While it's often hard to tell if a woman is long-term material, it's often easy to tell if she isn't. If she has some flaw or problem that really puts you off, face that fact now so you won't get overly involved with a woman who will cause you nothing but trouble and pain later. The information covered in the next chapter about diagnosing if a woman is worth keeping or not, will be helpful.

Next, you must maintain your investment in her, or all the good feelings you've created are in danger of slipping away. Maintenance shows her that you are thinking of her, that you are putting time and effort into your relationship, and that you are a generative, creative man. The secret of good maintenance is to schedule time, in your date book, to do little things for her that maintain your connection. You can spend this time creating your next date with her, writing her love notes and poetry, composing romantic e-mails to her, buying her flowers, or selecting and wrapping fun little gifts. Just remember to vary how often you give her presents and surprises. If you do it too regularly she'll come to expect it, and it won't make her feel special anymore.

Next you must generate the next step in your seduction, and design the next seduction date. The first step in doing this is to assess how far you got in the seduction date you already had. Did you kiss her, kiss her and make out, have sex with her, try to kiss her and get rejected, or not try to kiss her at all? After assessing your outcome, design your next date to overcome any obstacles, and to move your seduction forward. If you follow these steps you are sure to keep your connection with the woman you are dating alive and growing.

chapter thirteen...
Breaking Up Is Easy to Do

Bruce decided that after six dates and a few hot sex sessions with Belinda, he was ready to move on. Though they got along well, and he was attracted to her, he knew there was no way he was ready for a committed relationship. After deciding, Bruce waited a few days before calling her. During that time he went through the gamut of emotions: guilt, sadness, regret, everything.

Eventually, he decided to call her and break up. "Did I do something wrong?" she asked. "No, not at all," he said. I really like you. Since the beginning, I told you that I wasn't looking for anything serious. If we keep going, I know it will probably develop into more. I thought it would be easier to break up now, rather than save us both the heartache later." Belinda began to cry.

Bruce tried to comfort her, and then began to feel guilty. He started to regret his decision, and question his reasons. But then he remembered why it wouldn't work, and how if he continued to put off breaking up, it would end up being even more painful. "You have been a treasure to date, Belinda. I appreciate the time we've spent together. I've learned a lot from you and I think you are very special. I just can't keep going," Bruce said. They talked for a few more minutes, and finally Bruce ended the call. "I am sorry, Belinda, but I must go. Is there someone else you can talk to about how upset you are?" Belinda decided to sleep at her sister's home, and they agreed to talk again soon.

Meanwhile, Bob had been dating Shirley for three months. They spent two or three nights per week together, and more time on weekends. He was never that interested in her, but continued dating as something to do until a *better* woman came along. Bob figured it was better to spend time with *some* woman, rather than to be alone.

One night, after they got into a fight, Bob decided it was finally time to call it quits. The next night, while hanging out at her apartment, Bob told Shirley that the relationship was through. She was very upset. His announcement came out of the blue, and caught her off guard.

"What isn't working in our relationship?" she asked.

"The whole damn thing just sucks," Bob responded.

"Can't we work things out, Bob? I really like you, and want to keep building our relationship."

Bob responded, "We never *had* a relationship, Shirley. What we had were a few good times, and some hot sex."

She began to cry. He did nothing to comfort her. "Quit crying, it isn't the end of the world. You are so damn emotional. Why do you always cry when it gets tough? That's part of why I want to break up," he told her.

"Maybe this is easy for you, Bob, but I am really hurt. I care very deeply for you. I thought we had something, something special. I counted on you. But now you are throwing that all away."

"Why are you arguing with me, Shirley? You are just too demanding. I need my space. We are through, and that's all there is to it." Bob got up, grabbed his coat and left without saying another word.

One of the hardest parts of being a successful seducer is the break-up process. The more successful you get at seduction, the more frequently you'll be in this position. Cutting off a relationship is rarely easy, no matter how gently it's done. Unless you are a heartless jerk, both of you usually leave feeling upset. Breakups are a reminder that you are dealing with a live, breathing, feeling woman. It is important to learn how to end a relationship in the least painful manner, while still retaining a sense of integrity for yourself.

As usual, Bob makes dozens of mistakes in his split with Shirley. Primary, he is unnecessarily cruel. Next, out of ignorance, he is unable to deal with her being upset by the split-up, and makes things worse by ignoring her cries for help. He also storms out of her apartment, leaving her in tears, and leaving their interaction incomplete. This will only come back to haunt him soon. Last, but not least, he fails to do the proper pre-work to make the break up easier for her.

In a larger scope, Bob is oblivious to the fact that most women *will* take a relationship seriously and be hurt if a man suddenly, without mutual agreement, breaks up with them. In fact, dating for three months implies you are in a relationship, and requires more than simple conversation to break up.

Shirley has assumed that Bob spent so much time with her because he was interested in pursuing a relationship. She figured that he wanted to be her boyfriend, and create a future together. In her mind, why else would a man spend so much time with a woman? In the end, she is left feeling heartbroken and confused.

Even though Belinda is upset when Bruce calls it quits, she isn't surprised. In fact, she knew it was coming a few weeks prior. Bruce had told her all along that he didn't want a girlfriend. He only wanted to casually date. When Bruce finally initiates breaking up, he makes sure to compliment her, and show his appreciation for what they had. He reassures Belinda, and makes sure she knows she did nothing wrong. At the same time, he doesn't argue with her, or feel intimidated when she begins to cry.

Bruce has thought out a strategy to break up in the least painful manner possible. Yet he doesn't fool himself into believing that it will be easy for her. He is willing to take any heat that may come his way, and deal with the consequences of his actions. Though he has pangs of guilt, he stays true to his purpose and is able to ignore the disempowering thoughts about not breaking up and the regret inside his head.

While talking to Belinda, he constantly asks himself what he could do to make the conversation and the breakup easier for her. By asking her if there is anyone else she could talk to, for example, Bruce makes sure she won't be alone while feeling so upset. He is, once again, taking care of her.

A few weeks after the breakup, Bruce still has his connection with Belinda. They agree not to date, or be sexual, but to be friends.

Bruce figures that it is better to have another friend or acquaintance than it is to have an enemy. By allowing her the space to be upset, cry, and emote, Bruce makes sure that they would remain friends. In fact, because he is so skilled, Bruce rarely creates enemies when he breaks up with women.

Once you've moved through all the stages of dating—from meeting her and flirting to getting the date and seducing her—you will probably be left wondering if you should stick with the woman you've seduced, or whether you should move on. This chapter will show you how to decide if the relationship you are developing works for you or not. From there, you can plan a break up that is the most sensitive, yet easiest to accomplish.

TO COMMIT OR NOT TO COMMIT: THAT IS THE QUESTION

We have found that, eventually, most men want a long-term relationship. Contrary to popular belief, however, such a desire cannot be forced. It can only occur naturally and when the time is right. Wherever you are, wanting a relationship or a one-night stand, we support you, and are committed through the information in this book to give you exactly what you want.

Bruce is clear that he is not ready to be in a relationship. He is content dating and flirting. He has moved from feeling intimidated by women, and afraid to flirt, to being on his way to mastery. Bruce has gone from being lonely on the weekends to having more dates than he can keep up with. He is living his dream life, and only wants to bask in his success with women.

In the past, Daniel also was only looking for women to date. He wanted nothing to do with commitment. Since learning our material over the past two years, he has changed from being shy and sloppy to being a stud, always dating several women at once. Eventually, Daniel got tired of dating and decided to settle down with one woman. He credited his changes to first mastering short-term relationships. "It was only after I knew I could sleep with many women that a relationship seemed like a good idea. If I hadn't waited, and had just committed to the first woman who seemed interesting, it just would have been another unsuccessful relationship. I would have been making decisions from a state of desperation rather than choice," he said.

Bruce and Daniel are each clear about what they specifically want from a woman. Bruce wants to continue dating. Daniel is happy being in a committed relationship. If you are in Daniel's position, ready and eager to commit for the long term, move on to the next chapter. That chapter focuses on how to keep a relationship going. If you are ready to break up with a woman, or foresee a breakup in your future, keep reading.

SO YOU THINK YOU WANT TO BE A STUD...

No matter how many times we mention it, some men will remain unclear about what they want in a relationship. If you are one of the foggy ones, you are that way because you haven't yet chosen between dating or being in a committed relationship. Indecisiveness is debilitating. If you can't decide what you want, you will probably end up bouncing from woman to woman, unwilling to do the work of a seducer while simultaneously unwilling to do the work required for a committed relationship. Being unsure creates failure in either circumstance.

So, we ask you again, what do you want? A committed, happy erotic relationship, or a harem of young nymphs?

Before giving your promise to a woman, we recommend that you first make sure that she has the qualities and characteristics you desire. We require all of our students to develop a list of their conditions for choosing a woman. Making this list is crucial for several reasons. For starters, if you don't know exactly what you are looking for, you will likely end up with someone who isn't right for you. Hence, the relationship will fail. Worse, you will likely end up with someone with whom you do not essentially connect. This will result in a constantly strained relationship.

Most men aren't clear about what they want and expect from a woman. They get into relationships, but act as if they didn't really choose to do so. You would think the relationship just mysteriously happened one day. Contrast this to how these men behave when buying a car. Our bet is that most men bring a much higher degree of rigor to the process of selecting and purchasing a car than they do to finding the right woman to settle down with. In fact, most men know *exactly* what they want and expect from a car. Here are Simon's conditions:

1. It must cost no more than $22,000.
2. It must be at least a six cylinder or a V-8.
3. It must be a stick shift.
4. It must have 4-wheel drive.
5. It must have air-bags.
6. It must be black.
7. It must be domestically made.
8. It must have anti-lock brakes.

There are also a few conditions that he feels are not necessary, but would be great added extras.

1. It would be great if it had a sun roof.
2. It would be great if it had an awesome stereo.
3. It would be great if it had power windows.
4. It would be great if it had cruise control.

If you are like most men, you have never sat down and given yourself the time to really think about what you want in a woman. Perhaps you have flirted and dated women who caught your eye, or kept dating women because you felt too scared and guilty to break up with them. Making a list of conditions for choosing will greatly aid you in clarifying what you want. Note, however: it will likely be harder to decide, and figure out, conditions you require from a woman than it will for what you require in a car. But it's worth the effort, and the difference it can make in your life can be huge.

Follow the steps described here to make your list.

1. Set aside at least 15 minutes.
2. Begin by listing qualities you require in a woman for a potential committed relationship. Don't censor yourself. Start writ-

ing and let the ideas flow. If you get stuck, jot down the qualities you *don't* want in a woman. This will get you looking in the right direction.

Here is an example to help guide you.

Joe's list

I must feel attracted to her.

She must be shorter than me.

She must enjoy science fiction movies.

She must be punctual.

She must want kids.

She must have long blonde hair.

She must be a football fan.

She must be emotionally stable.

She must be willing to talk and resolve disagreements.

She must have a sense of spirituality in her life.

She must love me and act kindly.

She must cook.

She must have cool friends.

She must be willing to have sex at least twice a week.

She must love giving oral sex.

She must not be offended when I burp.

She must enjoy travel.

She must have a stable job.

She must enjoy the music of REM and jazz.

We must agree on political issues.

She must be intelligent.

She must love beer.

3. Now that you have the list, prioritize the requirements. Actually go through the list and mark which ones are flexible and which aren't. Remember, you are looking at qualities and conditions for a long-term relationship. The emphasis is on

long-term. When you take a long view of things, it usually decreases the significance of superficial qualities, like enjoying the same music or beer. As a rule of thumb, the shorter the duration of dating, the more significant the superficial things seem.

Here is Joe's revised list. He separated the qualities into three categories: things he was unwilling to be flexible about, qualities he was somewhat willing to be flexible about, and those that would be great if she had them, but are not necessary.

Unwilling to be flexible/must have

I must be attracted to her.
She must want children sometime.
She must be fairly emotionally stable.
She must be intelligent.
She must be willing to have sex at least twice a week.
She must be willing to talk and resolve disagreements.
She must have a sense of spirituality in her life.
She must love me and act kindly.

Somewhat flexible/it would be great if she had these

She must cook.
She must have cool friends.
We must agree on political issues.
She must not be offended when I burp.
She must enjoy travel.
She must be shorter than me.
She must be punctual.
She must enjoy science fiction movies.
She must have a stable job.
She must enjoy giving oral sex.

Even less important/won't effect the relationship either way

She must enjoy the music of REM and jazz.

She must have long blonde hair.

She must be a football fan.

She must love beer.

Now that Joe has a list, he can then choose a woman based on it. He can instantly measure if he and a potential mate are compatible based on his required qualities. If you are like Joe, you have a tendency to avoid commitment at any cost, and actually make up, out of thin air, reasons *not* to commit. By clarifying what you want, it will be easier to overcome feelings of ambivalence. You will finally have something concrete to measure a woman against, rather than your moment-to-moment feelings, thoughts, and opinions.

WHY BREAK UP

"You've got to know when to hold 'em, when to fold 'em, when to walk away and when to run." These dorky song lyrics describe more than gambling strategies; they also give clear instructions for dating. It is important to know when to keep a woman, when to break up, and how to do so. Cutting off relationships can be complicated. Even a cowboy like Kenny Rogers knows that relationships sometimes don't work out.

Bad relationships are similar to broken down cars. They get worse and worse, and constantly need more repair. At a certain point it makes more sense to junk the vehicle and get a new one. The other option is to maintain the car over the long haul, and never let it get junky in the first place. If you are willing to do the work necessary to keep the car running over time, and put in the necessary money and time, you can keep it going indefinitely.

Diagnosing where you in the commitment game

As a rule of thumb, the longer you date a woman, the harder and more painful it will be to break up. The more extensively you get to know one another, the higher the investment and the greater the loss when it ends. We've developed a method to diagnose your level of existing commitment. This eight-type method shows the degree of commitment and the predicted level of difficulty in breaking up. Begin with where you are on the commitment scale.

THE EIGHT DEGREES OF COMMITMENT

1. One-night stand

One-night stands are eternally popular. Most women interested in only one night aren't looking for much else. There is no investment in a relationship on either side. The experience was probably purely sexual for both of you. A one-night stand requires no explanation. The best way to "end it" is to simply not call her again, or to call the next day to thank her, and then not call her again. Most women expect you to call after you've had sex. If you don't, the possibility of any relationship will not just be cut; it will be annihilated. A one-night-stand-woman probably likes you somewhat, but won't be crushed if she never sees you again.

2. An acquaintance

By acquaintance, we are referring to a woman you just met, or have dated a few times. While a one-night stand is primarily sexual, an acquaintance is someone you've probably spent more time talking to and getting to know. After dating once or twice, there is a minimal investment in a relationship between the two of you. Not enough time has elapsed for her to become crazy about you. We recommend using the same strategy as for a one-night stand. Simply not calling her back will probably suffice. If not, having a short conversation will be all that is necessary to cut things off. As with any break-up discussion, sensitivity and gentleness are required. Harshness will only hurt her, and actually prolong the situation.

3. Dated three or four times over the past few weeks

If you've been on three or four dates with a woman, she definitely likes you. Otherwise, why would she bother spending the time? After a few dates, your level of attraction is probably somewhere between finding each other sweet and interesting, and wanting to rip each other's clothes off and jump into bed.

Breaking up in person will be best. By this time, she has begun thinking of you as a potential boyfriend. If you've been having sex, it will be that much harder to cut off from her. Being honest about why you don't want to be with her will be the easiest. At the same time, being diplomatic and not telling her details that will be interpreted as cruel is also suggested.

4. Slept with her a few times and realized it was going to become a problem

We discussed problem women in the When Babes Attack chapter. These are the classic "psychos" who are potential stalkers, violent, cruel, hyper-emotional, and all-around trouble. Maybe you didn't notice her psycho qualities at first, but it soon came up during conversation or during sex. Maybe you were so swept up with her beauty that you ignored our warnings. In any case, it is important to get away from such a woman quickly. The longer you are with a problem woman, the harder it is to break up, and the more trouble it will cause down the road.

Breaking up with a troubled woman will probably be difficult. She will most likely have a strong emotional reaction. It is important that you watch your safety; psychos can react violently. It is best to simply say that you are not ready to be in a relationship, or that you realize you can't give her what she wants from a man. You certainly can't tell her that she is psycho, or anything that will be construed as nasty. Be careful and try to be as gentle as possible.

5. She is an occasional sex partner

A woman who is having sex with you, and not requiring a commitment, is a wonderful find. First, examine why you are dismantling the relationship. If you are looking to date many women at once, this is the perfect one to keep. She is a perfect addition to your harem. If she is the type who is fine with only occasional dating, first ask yourself why you are considering getting rid of her. What could be better than a woman who is willing to let you sleep with her on an irregular basis, without demanding you be in a formal relationship?

One reason to break up is that, after informal dating, she begins to want more. At first, being occasional sex partners worked, but now she has fallen for you, and wants it to be serious. Meanwhile, you want it to remain informal. The other reason to call it quits is if you meet another woman and begin a committed relationship. In this case, the occasional sex partner will have to go. A simple phone call or in-person conversation will likely do. Just be honest, and the breakup will probably be easy. She'll likely understand, and may perhaps even congratulate you.

6. Dated for a month or less

A month is right around the time when things start to get serious. First, why do you want to break up? What in particular isn't working? Get clear about the specifics before you have a break-up conversation.

We recommend you use the break-up strategy employed in type #3, in which you have a face-to-face conversation, and break up in the manner suggested. The best way to avoid this situation is to be clear from the start that you aren't looking for a girlfriend.

7. Dated for over a month

If you've been going out for over a month, you are getting into the troubled waters of commitment. She obviously likes you; otherwise she wouldn't have dated you for so long. After being together this long, breaking up is best done over a few weeks. First, do the pre-work items, as suggested later in this chapter. Second, plan to discuss breaking up with her over several conversations, not simply during a one-shot thing. Be honest, tactful, and responsible for her reaction. You will likely have to have a few conversations with her for everything to be straightened out, and the breakup to be done.

8. Dated for over three months

For all practical purposes, after three months you *are* in a relationship, and you *are* her boyfriend. Even if you don't think so, she most certainly does. A break-up at this stage must be well planned out. She will likely be hurt, and it will be best to break up over a few weeks.

Pre-work for the breakup

As with anything else in the dating game, there is always pre-work. Ceasing to date will be easier and less painful for both of you when it's planned out ahead of time. By creating a step-by-step plan it will make everything go that much more smoothly. Find a way to be as compassionate as possible; being impulsive won't do.

Don't date a woman for more than a month

We know it sounds harsh, but after a month things will begin to get serious. If you want to make sure you don't hurt a woman by dragging things out, cease dating after a month. If you continue longer she'll consider you her boyfriend. If, on the other hand, she is enjoying the informal nature of the relationship, and doesn't appear to want more, initiate a "relationship discussion" after a month and tell her your future intentions. The clearer you are, the easier it will be. Remember that no matter what either of you says, you always run the risk after a month that she will become more and more attached to you.

Get all your things out of her apartment first

At least a week before the cut-off date, make sure to get all your stuff out of her apartment. This includes CDs, clothes, books, everything that you care about. Once you split up, your stuff is in jeopardy of being destroyed or thrown out. By taking your valuables out ahead of time, you have one less thing to worry about.

Make sure she doesn't view you as a long-term man

If you are not interested in having a serious relationship, never lie and say that you are. Be honest with her from the start. If you string a woman along, telling her that you want a girlfriend when you don't, the breakup will be horrid, and she will likely end up hurt.

If you lie, it is likely that you will feel guilty and worry if she'll find out the truth at a later time. Lying simply isn't worth it. If you are straight from the start, the woman won't be shocked when you stop dating. She will be aware of the risks ahead of time. It is cruel and unnecessary to put a woman through more crap in the dating arena than necessary.

Don't plan events with her far in advance

Naive men often make plans with women far into the future. The problem is that planning so far ahead deceives the woman into thinking a guy also plans to be with her, and she begins to think of him as a longer-term mate. Given that most men have tunnel vision in relationships, and only focus on the near future, if you start planning vacations six months later to France, or an end-of-the-year cruise, the woman will likely interpret this to mean that you plan to be with her for a long time. Hence, you are *de facto* in a committed relationship. The solution is simple: only make plans in the near future, and make sure to avoid commenting on anything that could be interpreted to imply long-term plans.

Scott and Donna dated for a few months. From the start, he only wanted a sexual relationship. They both enjoyed international travel and frequently discussed exotic countries they both were interested in visiting sometime. In Donna's mind, he discussed these things because he wanted to visit those places with her. Scott even mentioned, informally, that they should visit Jakarta and New Zealand within the next 15 months. She began telling her friends that Scott wanted to take her on a year-long world trip. When he initiated the breakup, Donna had a very hard time. All along, she assumed that they were planning a long trip together, and a relationship would bloom from there. If Scott had watched himself more carefully and had avoided mentioning long-term plans, it would have been much easier.

Avoid talking about long-term plans to a short-term woman.

Don't be the perfect boyfriend

When we say "don't be the perfect boyfriend," we are *not*, in any shape or form, suggesting that you ever be mean, nasty, cruel, or hurtful. Instead, we are saying that if you act "perfect," i.e., buying her flowers before every date, always being sweet, dressing well, calling her all the time, and generally taking care of her, you will come across as *the* perfect boyfriend, and she'll probably fall in love with you. On the other hand, treating her with respect, being kind and gentle, paying for dates, and doing everything else to charm her is important. In fact, we've stressed them all through the book.

If you are not committed to being with her for the long term, however, you must realize that the more perfect you are, the more she will want a serious relationship. As a result, it will be harder to break up. We suggest that in this case you occasionally do things that are less than perfect, are obnoxious, or are annoying. If you want to break up, start increasing the frequency and number of behaviors and habits that she probably dislikes. By acting in ways she *doesn't* like, it will be easier for her to let you go. It may even prompt her to get rid of you and initiate the breakup.

You can start to get more into sports. This will likely put her off, without hurting her. A healthy love for cigars is also a turn-off. Dressing sloppy can help, as will a new love of avoiding deodorant, and occasional swearing. We're sure you can find other things to do that will turn her off. More than anything, be aware that if you act perfectly, it will make breaking up harder. . . But in no way do we recommend that you insult her, or are mean in any way. You can stop being the perfect boyfriend by reducing the number of wonderful things you do, rather than by acting like a jerk.

THE THREE TYPES OF BREAKUPS

1. Mutual

A mutual breakup is the best kind. You both agree that things are not working, neither of you is getting what you need, and neither sees a future together. These types of breakups have the highest potential for remaining friends.

After dating for a month, neither Andrew nor Pauline was satisfied. They had begun fighting, the spark was gone, sex turned boring, and they both only called out of obligation. During a walk, they both admitted that they weren't interested in dating any more; it simply wasn't working. By mutually agreeing to break up, neither party felt responsible or guilty.

2. She breaks up with you

There are two forms of her breaking up with you. The obvious one is that you are interested in staying together, and she isn't. She cuts you off. She finds something wrong with you, or the relationship, and she's done.

The second type is when you do things to get her to break up with you. For example, Heather told Robert that if he ever slept with another woman, she would break up with him. Several months later, Robert did just that and it prompted her to break up with him. There are many other examples of men crossing a line that leads to the woman officially doing the breaking up. When examined, the man was the one who caused the breakup to occur.

3. You break up with her

Need we even explain this one? You decide that you don't want to go out with her, for whatever reason. You then do the pre-work necessary. Next, you break up, and deal with the fallout of your actions.

As mentioned earlier, some men break up out of fear. Deep down, they want to stay together, but are scared of commitment. If you break up out of fear, we recommend you rethink your decision and do what it takes to make it work.

If you are breaking up because it isn't working well, or is going in a direction you are not committed to, go ahead and break up. Use all the information in this chapter to help you.

THE EIGHT WARNING SIGNS
THAT IT'S TIME TO END IT

We all have blind spots—things, or issues, that we can't see. Before reading this book, Bob, for example, never realized that dressing sloppy would repel women. He simply had no idea that it made a difference, that he dressed in ways that kept women at bay.

Men have many blind spots in relationships. They are issues they simply don't want to admit are problems, or potential problems. It is common for a man to ignore warning signs that a relationship is failing and that a woman he is involved with is dangerous and is psycho. Men don't register the warning signs as significant. They downplay the possibility of the dangers and hazards involved.

What follows are warning signs. If you are currently experiencing one or more of these signs, you should seriously consider ending the relationship. We have had too many students report horrible consequences of staying in dangerous and abusive situations. Getting out quickly and avoid the inevitable headaches and heartaches.

1. You stop having the sex life with her that you want

A short-term relationship should be chock-full of sex. If it isn't, why are you in it? If the sex stops, the relationship is in a crisis. Women usually stop being interested in sex because of a problem in the relationship. Usually it is because the man stops doing the little things for her, and all the maintenance items we've discussed throughout the book. If she has a problem with you, and you are unwilling to deal with it, the relationship will continue to decay until you either deal with it or get out. In a long-term relationship, you must deal with any problems that arise; that is part and parcel for the relationship.

2. You don't like yourself when you are with her

There are women in this world who probably bring out the worst in you. The worst temper, qualities, thoughts, feelings, everything. A man usually doesn't take responsibility for his anger. Instead, he blames the woman, claiming she is doing something to bring out his bad feelings. Though you may dislike her, she probably isn't doing anything. You simply react to her. The bottom line is that you don't like yourself when you are with her. Take responsibility for your part.

Jim, for instance, was dating a political activist named Hara. About half of the time they got along well. It always seemed as if he had to hold back his thoughts and opinions from her, afraid they might get into a heated argument. Hara could share her opinions with him, however—she did this all the time. Jim acted meek and timid around her, and hated himself for it. He felt as if he was groveling for sex and approval, and as if he was subservient to her whims and desires.

As you can guess, the relationship quickly failed. If Jim had paid attention to his fear and dislike of how he felt around her, and had remembered that there are plenty of other women to date, he would have saved himself a lot of hassle and would have broken up more quickly.

If you don't like how you act around a particular woman, either change your behavioral patterns, or get out of the relationship. The cost is simply too high to stay in a messed up situation. Remember, if you feel bad around her, it is your responsibility to get out, not hers.

3. She doesn't like you

It may sound funny, but many men report dating, or marrying, women who dislike them. Women have reported the same thing, being in relationships with men who seem to dislike them. In these situations, the couple stays together because there are qualities about the other that each likes and enjoys, but on the whole one party dislikes the other. The disdain comes across in the form of constant criticizing, complaining, and general nastiness.

Unbelievably, some men stay in relationships like these, usually sidestepping the pain it causes them, or the constant blows to their self-esteem. There is no reason to continue dating someone who doesn't treat you in the way you want.

One of the fundamental values we teach in this book is that your self-esteem and confidence as a man are essential to success in any area of your life. If a woman, or a job, or anything else hurts you, cease the activity or relationship immediately. If you are not empowered by the relationship, get out.

4. She has constant emotional problems

Darlene was usually lovable. She was sweet, sincere, beautiful, and had a great job. At the same time, she was highly emotional and had constant emotional outbursts. It was nearly impossible to predict what would set her off. When she was angry, she would swear and throw things at anyone within firing range. When she was sad, she would hyperventilate and sob. Her full range of emotional outbursts scared David. He really liked her, but felt that her emotional problems prevented him from getting to know her, and ever feeling comfortable.

Darlene belongs in a group of women who are lovable, yet are so out of control emotionally that they are hard to date. Even though David liked Darlene, we still advised him to break up with her. She simply was too wild and too unpredictable. In a short-term relationship, someone like Darlene is unacceptable simply because she is too much work to date and maintain. While it may sound harsh, the best way to protect yourself, if you are dating an overly emotional woman, is to break up. Be gentle in the process, and do everything you can to stay friends.

5. She is too demanding

Some women act as if you have no other purpose in life than to serve them. Perhaps they frequently call you at work, and ask you to spend inordinate amounts of time talking when you should be doing something else. Maybe they stop by your home at all hours of the night, and bang on the door, wanting to cuddle. Or, they call and want you to pick up a huge grocery list of "female supplies" for them. Women who do these things all of the time can be too demanding.

Some men have an easy time setting hard-core limits with demanding women. When a woman tries to interfere with their work schedule, comes over at odd hours of the night, and makes other demands, they simply tell her "no." End of story. The majority of men, however, mess up their schedules and their lives to cater to such a woman.

The problems start when your schedule is thrown off because you are spending time doing things for her that should be spent on your own life. The first solution is to start religiously using the magic word "no" in all your conversations with her. It may take a while to get your life back in order, but if you are strong-willed and can make friends with "no," it is imaginable that you could keep things going. If this doesn't work, or if she becomes even *more* demanding in the face of your refusals, then it's time to split up.

6. She tries to make you feel guilty about male things

Some of the ways men and women flirt are by teasing each other about "male" and "female" things. You tease her about how long it takes her to put on her makeup, and she teases you about loving sports. That is a fun-natured banter. There are other women, however, who will try their hardest to hit you where it hurts. They will insult your masculinity and try to make you feel guilty about anything that can be construed to be manly. She might insult you for looking forward to your weekly ritual of watching Monday night football with your buddies. She might comment on how stupid the game is, and how you are supporting a violent sport. She might also complain about your trips with the guys to auto shows, sporting events, violent movies, or anything you find to be "male." Finally, she might constantly blame the problems of the country or the world on men and their "fragile male egos." She may claim that if the country was run only by women, everything would be fine. If you are with a woman who spouts off similar comments, a troubled relationship is in your near future.

Some of these women are the angry feminist type. They will constantly harass you simply for being a man, and they will not let up. They will verbally hit you in every way possible with the unalterable fact (in her opinion) that being a man means living a life of privilege, ease and power, while being a woman means living a life of unremitting degradation and enslavement. While you might agree with some of her assertions, she is attacking *you*, nonetheless. It is important for your self-esteem and sanity to cease being around a woman who dislikes you for being a man.

The fact that you have a penis is nothing to ever apologize for, or feel ashamed of. If you respect her as a woman, you should expect the same in return. If not, go on to another woman.

7. You don't respect her

Why are you with a woman you don't respect? Is it that she is beautiful, rich, a stepping stone for your career, or what? You are in for real trouble if you date women you don't respect. There is nothing that will harm your self-esteem more. If you don't respect someone you sleep with once, that is fine. Other than that, you are hurting both of you in the process, and it will eventually weigh on you and chip away at your confidence. What does it say about you, that you have to date women you don't respect? This question will probably come back to haunt you.

8. She wants to come between you and your buddies

As we've said many times, close male friends are very important. The "lone rangers" in life, who only spend time alone or with their woman, will eventually bottom out. The nurturing, teasing, obnoxious, straight-with-one-another type of camaraderie and support men give each other is completely different from relationships between men and women. A good seducer has men he can talk to, support, and confide in.

When a woman tries to come between you and your buddies, she is trying to control your life. She is trying to cut off your contact with others; in essence, she is cutting off your mainline of masculine energy. Why is she doing this? What threat do your buddies pose to the relationship?

The bottom line is that no woman is worth cutting off your friends for. The women may come and go, but close male friendships will usually last forever.

THINGS TO WATCH OUT FOR DURING THE BREAK-UP CONVERSATION

She may try to entice you with sex

If a woman is upset about the breakup, she will likely go to extreme measures. A woman will frequently offer sex as a way to get a man back. She thinks that if she offers him her body, he will remember how much he loves her and call off the breakup.

When Bob initiated the cut off from Veronica, she began crying. Her next move was to unbutton her shirt and tell him that he would be missing out on a lot. "Don't you just want to make love one last time, for old times sake?" she asked. Bob stupidly fell for it, and made love with her. The whole time he felt guilty. "How can I make love with her and then just leave?" he thought to himself. After making love, Bob decided he should stay with her a few more weeks. Then he initiated the breakup again. She again tried to seduce him into staying; he fell for it again. After three cycles of breaking up and seduction, Bob finally learned to not have sex or let himself be seduced into staying.

While the possibility of sex is very tempting, it is rarely worth going for in a break-up situation. Stay strong and focused on the long-term happiness of both of you, rather than the one-time sex experience, and it will be easier to break up.

She may argue with you

Most women will argue when you break up. It helps them understand and cope with the split. They want to know if there is anything they can do to avoid having you leave. Out of their sense of loss arguing and extreme emotional outbursts can be expected. The answer is to simply avoid long conversations or arguments with her. Our research shows that the more you argue, the harder it is to break up, and the more upset each of you becomes. Be kind, gentle, and honest; arguing won't work. If she won't stop arguing, leave the situation and set a later date to talk again.

Physical violence and threats

Rob had been dating Karen for a few months before he realized it wasn't working. She wanted to spend more and more time with him. When they were together, however, it constantly felt like work. Rob knew it was time to break up. He was scared, however, because during previous arguments, she had slammed doors, screamed and cried. It turned out that Rob's fears were correct. During their break-up talk, Karen screamed at him. She then threatened to call his job and tell Rob's boss that he abused her. She grabbed a metal bowl and warned him that if he tried to leave, she would throw it at his head.

While it may sound unbelievable, these things do happen, and can be quite scary. If you are ever in a similar situation, we recommend that you leave immediately (and watch your head). You never want to endanger your own safety. Get out, and stay away from her forever. If you see the violent potential in a woman you are dating, avoid her, and break up—in public, so there will be the calming influence of witnesses—as soon as you realize it.

She will promise to change

During the break-up process, many women, out of desperation, beg the man to stay. They promise to change. They promise to eradicate any part of their personality he has ever complained about. They beg for one more chance. In response, the man who initiated the breakup gets drawn into all the drama, and stops. Soon after, he will want to break up again and will, once again, be faced with her promises of changing. The problem, however, isn't whether or not the women will change. Unfortunately, this will only prolong the inevitable breakup, and ultimately hurt her more. It is best to stay on course with why you are breaking up, and never waiver. Never be cruel, but don't fall into the trap of feeling guilty and let it back you down from the breakup. You are walking a thin line. Stay on course and everything will work out.

EXAMPLES OF CLEAN BREAKUPS

Craig thought he loved Bonnie. From the moment he laid eyes on her, she seemed perfect for him. They loved the same rock groups, the same food, and always had a great time when they partied. They saw each other all the time. After a few weeks, the "glow" wore off. They started fighting frequently. One night Bonnie attacked him. She threw a plate at his head, it nearly hit him. She then jumped on him and slapped and kicked him where no man wants to be kicked! Craig was in pain for a few days, and vowed never to see her again. She apologized, and begged him to come back. He couldn't help himself. Craig thought that he really did *love* her.

They got back together and things went smoothly for a few weeks. But then they fought again. This time she tried to shove him down a flight of stairs. Craig protected himself and avoided a potentially dangerous situation. The next day he knew they had to break up. He was scared, however, to initiate it. "What if she goes nuts again?" he asked himself. He spent the next few weeks gathering his things from her apartment while he planned the breakup. Craig also reasoned that if they were in a public spot, she would be less likely to attack him. He waited until they were sitting in a coffee shop to finally tell her that he didn't want to date anymore. She was upset, but accepted the breakup.

Ken met Mary Lou at a party. They drank, danced, and talked until 4 am, at which point he asked her to come home with him. She agreed. From the start, Ken had no desire for a girlfriend. Indeed, at the same time, he was dating three other women. Mary Lou went to his apartment, and they made love. In the morning, he took her out for breakfast. Over the meal, she confessed that she was looking for a boyfriend, and thought that he might have potential. Ken told her that he would like to see her again, but she should know that he was dating others. She seemed mildly upset, but gave Ken her phone number and asked him to call for a date. They had a good time continuing the talking and flirting during the meal. After breakfast, he drove Mary Lou home.

After dropping her off Ken threw her phone number out the window. While he enjoyed both sleeping with and talking to her, it seemed as though her desire for a serious relationship would taint future interactions. Rather than having to constantly tell her that he didn't want a girlfriend, he decided to simply not call her again.

The sex was always intense, passionate, and wild between Kay and Alan. It was as if there were some magical chemistry between them. They saw each other three or four times per month, and sex was always a main part of the date. Both actively dated other people, and saw each other as only part-time lovers. After a few months, however, Kay wanted more. She was interested in being in a relationship with Alan.

One night, after a sensual experience, Kay confessed that she was falling in love with him. Rather than avoid discussing the topic, Alan said that he didn't feel the same way about her. He enjoyed the sex and closeness they shared, but didn't want to go further. She was upset. At the same time, she knew it was unlikely that he would feel the same way about her. They went their separate ways, and while Alan missed the sex, he knew that if he had continued, the breakup would have been much more difficult.

Bob and Diane had been dating for two months. They liked each other, but both were honest that they didn't see any long-term potential, and that they were dating other people. One evening, Bob noticed that Diane seemed more distant than normal, and he asked her if there was anything wrong. "Well," she told him, "I'm dating someone else, and it's starting to get serious. I really like you, but I have to stop seeing you, and just be with him."

"I understand," he told her. He was sad, but he also knew it was for the best. They became friends, even though they didn't have sex again.

As you can see, breaking up is often painful, difficult, and problematic. The master seducer, however, prepares himself for an easier breakup. This chapter began by exploring what type of relationship you want to be in. We asked, do you want a long-term, or a short-term erotic relationship? From there we discussed how many men avoid long-term relationships because of fear.

We then walked you through a step-by-step process to discover what you must have in a woman you commit to. We then showed you how to refine the process and come up with the qualities you require, you desire, and would be great, but aren't necessary.

We talked about the eight types of commitment, and basic strategies to break up in each stage. To refresh your memory, the stages included the one-night stand, the acquaintance, a woman you've slept with a few times and realize that it is becoming a problem to be together, an occasional sex partner, a woman you've dated for a month or less, a woman you've dated for between one and three months, and finally a woman you've dated for over three months.

From there we discussed the pre-work we recommend you do before breaking up. This includes doing things like making sure all your things are out of her home, not being a perfect boyfriend to begin with, making sure she doesn't view you as long-term man, and never dating a woman for more than a month and then being surprised when she considers it serious.

Now that you have done the pre-work, the next step is determining what are reasons to stay or break up. The eight warning signs give you a diagnostic tool to determine if a woman is acting in ways that will lead to trouble down the road, or just behaving normally. Some of the warning signs: a sudden reduction in how frequently you have sex; you don't like yourself when you are with her; you don't like each other; she has constant emotional problems; she is too demanding; you don't respect her; she wants to come between you and your male friends; and she has constant emotional problems.

Once you decide to break up, there are several possible problems that may occur during the actual break-up discussion. Some things to watch out for: her possibly enticing you with sex to avoid breaking up; arguing with you, point for point, on why you are breaking up; threatening you with physical violence and scaring you into not breaking up; promising to change and become your ideal girlfriend. All of these problems have simple solutions: break up quickly and be respectful in the process. The pre-work is also crucial to all split-up scenarios.

You've now seen how the masters break up, and how the novices blunder their way through painful and laborious breakups. No matter what your skill level, breakups are often full of pain. The master seducer deals with the pain, and takes responsibility for himself, the woman, and the situation. He places her comfort above his own desires to be right and makes things easy. The wimp-man blames all the problems on the woman, and is cruel in his approach. He insults her, or screams in her face. The more successful you are in seduction, the more you will be in the break-up mode and will have to face the common problems involved. If you are a man of integrity and sincerity, you will steer your way through possibly difficult situations, and come out with exactly the relationships you desire.

chapter fourteen...
From Casual
to Committed

For years Daniel heard the same thing from women. Date after date he'd try to seduce them, only to have them say, "Sex isn't that important. I want something more." It drove him crazy, because he couldn't even get sex, much less the "something more" women were talking about. It seemed to him as though the women he dated wanted "something more" because they could already get sex in abundance. After all, lots of men desired the women he desired, too. "I tell you," he said to his friends. "Someday I'd like to be able to ask for 'something more' from a woman. That'll be great."

After working with us and attending our workshops, Daniel's success with women skyrocketed. He found that if he was willing to do the work, he could seduce as many women as his heart (and other body parts) desired. Daniel dated a lot, and had sex with many women.

Finally, a time came when he knew with absolute certainty that he had no sexual deficit. He knew he could get sex anytime, and that, in his life, there would never again be a shortage of sexually available women. Suddenly sex, which had seemed so important to him his entire adult life, started to seem trivial. He knew he could get it, so what was the big deal? Daniel got tired of dating women for short periods of time, then moving on. He found himself wanting "something more." Daniel was ready for a long-term relationship.

"SOMETHING MORE"

Early in this book we introduced you to the idea of short-term relationships, which is one in which you have sex with a woman for a few weeks or months and then you both move on. This may have been your first exposure to the idea that you could consciously decide to have a short-term relationship, or that it could be an okay thing to do. Many men we've known have wished they could get short-term sex, but never knew it was possible, or that it was something they could pursue. We've spent most of this book showing you how to do exactly that.

After you master these, what happened to Daniel is likely to happen to you. You'll stop feeling any sense of sexual desperation in your life, and your backlog of need for sexual variety will be fulfilled. You'll know you can get sex, and you'll start wanting "something more." You'll start being ready for a long-term relationship.

It is critical that you know how to make this transition from short-term to long-term dating work for you. If you do, a long-term relationship is something that can support you in your life, give you a sense of security, and be a constant source of excitement and pleasure. If you don't know how to make long-term relationships work, then they can become the worst of all possible worlds: suffering and boredom, no access to sex or supportive companionship, topped off with a commitment to not pursue someone better.

This chapter will show you how to make a long-term relationship work. This information is absolutely crucial if you want to take a short-term girlfriend and turn her into the long-term woman in your life.

When you commit to a woman, you are giving your word that you are going to be romantically involved only with her, and with no other woman. She is no longer "one of your women"; she is the one and only. She's your girlfriend. You make long-term plans together, and don't cheat on her. You have a current intention of lifetime involvement with her.

In a long-term relationship, most of the rules change. Most men have a part of their brains that thinks of long-term relationships as suffering, as giving up any last shred of freedom or happiness, or as accepting a ball and chain for life. It is true that, when you go into a long-term relationship with a woman, there are things that you are giving up. There is also a lot for you to gain: the support and intimacy you can experience can't easily be duplicated by anything else.

Whether or not your long-term relationship is drudgery and suffering or ecstasy and fun is entirely up to you. If you know how to select the right woman, and how to keep a relationship alive and growing for the long-term, you can create one that gives you more than you ever dreamed possible. If you don't know what you are doing, you can screw up a relationship with the best woman imaginable, and turn all your interactions with her into boredom and pain. Yes, it is all in your hands.

Because this chapter is so critical to your maintaining long-term happiness in a relationship, it is one of the most important in this book. Pay attention: it's the rest of your life we are talking about here. When you do settle on a woman for a long-term relationship, you'll be quizzed on the material in this chapter every day for the rest of your life.

LOVE HER FOR WHO SHE IS
AND FOR WHO SHE IS NOT

This entire chapter could be summed up with two sentences of advice: love her for who she is, and love her for who she isn't. The rest of the chapter will cover how to maintain the relationship, and keep it fresh and alive. Knowing this is crucial. But behind it all, underneath the tips and strategies, you must stay aware of why you love her. You must stay aware of what qualities she possesses that you adore, all the humor you share, the great discussions you enjoy together, the similar interests, shared experiences, and the connection you feel. The good in her is what we recommend you constantly focus on.

The other half of the picture is to love her for who she isn't. In other words, finding ways to make peace with the qualities she doesn't have, her quirks that irritate you, the reasons you fight with one another, everything that seems less than perfect. If, and when, you can accept her for not being perfect, and for all the ways she "isn't," you can then deepen your relationship and real intimacy can develop.

When you stop having conditions for your love and accept that she has personality quirks like the rest of the world, intimacy will also develop. When you shift from the boyish notions that the world is out to serve you, and women's role in life is to give you everything you want on a silver platter, with you giving nothing in return, everything will go much smoother.

THE SIX KEYS TO KEEPING A LONG-TERM RELATIONSHIP HAPPY, EXCITING AND HOT

Great long-term relationships rarely "just happen," just as great short-term seductions rarely "just happen." You have to do things to create them, keep them growing and remaining fun. If you are keeping your body healthy, one workout a month will hardly suffice. Nor will following your diet for one day a month. Relationship maintenance, like physical maintenance, demands constant focus and attention.

1. You keep doing the "little things"

Most men start taking the woman they are with for granted after they've been together for a while. One woman tells us this story: "Before we got married, Rich always made me dinner one night a week. It was so wonderful to come home to hot food, music on the stereo, candles, and a glass of wine all waiting for me. It always made me feel so loved.

"After we got married, all that suddenly changed. He stopped doing any cooking at all, except for unfreezing the occasional pizza to eat while he watched football. When I finally asked him why he stopped cooking for me, he said 'Oh, that was courting. We're married now.' Five years later, we were divorced."

Much of the time, your change in behavior isn't that dramatic. The change is gradual as you stop doing the "little things" because you stop feeling like it. Early on in the relationship, you were so wrapped up in love with her, that you didn't even have to think about going out of your way to make her happy. You just did it. You seemed to have infinite energy to do the little things that pleased her because you were so in love. And that's how you fell into the trap.

When a man is solely motivated to keep doing all the little things in a relationship because he feels passionate about them, and the woman, he unknowingly sets himself up for eventually destroying the relationship. The problem is this: at the beginning, you are naturally enthusiastic about the woman you are with. That natural enthusiasm gives you plenty of energy to please her. You feel like doing the "little things" that keep a relationship going. You do them, and continue to make her happy.

Sadly and inevitably, you will begin to lose your desire as time goes on. Here's how it works:

As you get to know her better, and begin to see some of her flaws, you'll naturally tend to become just a little complacent. As that happens, you'll not feel so much like doing the little things, so more and more often you won't. As you slacken, your sense of her being special will diminish, and you'll feel like doing the little things even less. In time you'll stop doing them entirely. After all, you no longer feel like it! Congratulations. You have killed your relationship, and soon will be complaining that the spark has died. Before you know it, you'll be looking for another woman to take your girlfriend's place.

You have fallen into the relationship complacency trap. Because you relied on your feelings to guide how much you did the "little things," you inevitably did them less and less. The less you did them, the more tepid the relationship became. The more tepid it became, the less doing the "little things" appealed to you.

The solution is to not let your feelings be your guide for when you do the "little things" that please her. If you want the relationship to stay alive and continue to be exciting, energizing and fun, you must commit yourself to doing them whether you feel like it or not. Once again, schedule time in your date-book if you must (but don't tell her you are doing so—it won't seem romantic). Just get those little things done.

Men who are in successful long-term relationships understand that the good feelings are created by doing the little things, not vice-versa. As a result, these men commit themselves to continuously finding ways to delight their partners, as if the relationship was new and fresh.

Deb and Kevin have been married for nine years. They are the wonder of all of their friends, most of whom have been married and divorced at least once in that time period. For some reason, their relationship seems alive and growing, while those of their friends are failing. The reason the relationship is doing so well is because Kevin always does the little things.

For instance, we were at their house when Kevin decided to run out to get some tapioca for dessert, to go along with the meal Deb was making. We went along. He first went to one store, where he bought a package of single-serving tapioca desserts. "Y'know," he said to us, "I think I'll run across town to the other food store and see if they have another brand. Then we'll have Deb do a little taste-test, and tell us which one she likes better. She loves little events like that."

Deb was delighted to have the selection, and tried them both, pronouncing one much better than the other. She felt loved because Kevin did the little things to keep the relationship alive. She, in turn, looked for ways to make him happy. Why shouldn't she? After all, he consistently takes the time to make her happy. She wants to respond in kind.

The number one key to maintaining long-term relationships is the understanding that the seduction is *never* over. You must *always* continue doing the little things. We can't possibly emphasize this enough. If you want your relationship to last, you must keep courting her, keep seducing her, and keep doing the little things.

2. You support her fully

You must be a constant source of support for her, or your relationship will die. She must know and trust that you will stand by her side, no matter what. It is that type of trust and support that keeps the bond between you strong.

Over the course of your relationship, you will both be discovering, on a deeper and deeper level, who you really are and what you are really like. To the extent that all of life is a process of self-discovery, relationships are a process of self-discovery as well. We don't mean to get too psychological on you here, but this is important to understand if you want to have a long-term relationship that lasts.

Another way to put this is to say that both you and your girlfriend will always be growing, learning, and becoming different people from who you were when you first met. In the face of this fact, you have a choice. You can either support her as she grows and develops, or you can resist her. If you support her fully, she'll support you fully. If you don't support her fully, she will eventually break up with you. It's your choice.

This is how Bob lost his last girlfriend. Cathy was always interested in changing and growing. She had a full-time job, but took classes at night. After they'd been dating for about a year, she started taking art and dance classes that really excited her. "I feel like I'm finally starting to find myself," she confided in Bob. "I think I might be an artist, deep inside. It's really fulfilling something in me that nothing else ever has."

Instead of supporting her in these new interests, Bob got scared. "More fulfilling than me?" he immediately—and stupidly—asked. "How about that. Well, I hope you won't be too disappointed when this doesn't pan out for you, either. Besides, I don't trust those artist types, especially the dancers. They're all gonna try to get into your pants, anyway. Promise me that you won't cheat on me, okay? Promise me right now!"

For the next two months, every time Cathy brought up anything about her newfound passion, Bob responded in the same unsupportive way. It finally all ended when Cathy told him that she was sleeping with a guy from her art class. "He understands me, and is supportive of what I'm doing," she told him. She explained the breakup to her girlfriends this way: "I guess we just grew apart."

Of course it can be scary when someone you love becomes enthusiastic about something you know nothing about. Certainly you might get tense if your girlfriend is suddenly around people different from those you hang around with, or pursuing something that seems silly to you. In spite of all that, you must be supportive of her self-discovery if you want to maintain the relationship. If she gets into art, take an interest, whether it's convenient for you to do so or not. If she becomes a modern dancer, go to watch practices, be there for every performance, and be the all-around most supportive partner you can be. This will cause your relationship to get better, rather than allow it to "grow apart."

When Susan got a puppy and became passionately interested in dog training, Daniel became interested, too. While he knew it was really her hobby, he made himself get involved and found ways to enjoy it. The truth was he didn't naturally like dogs much, and would rather have been hanging out at home than go with Susan to dog training classes. He made himself be interested in it because he knew that becoming interested was the best way he could keep their relationship alive and growing. He also knew that her interests were a wonderful way for him to get outside of his normal routine. He knew that if he were left to his own devices he'd probably watch football and drink beer, only spicing up his routine with the occasional porn video. By sharing her interests he kept himself growing and got out of his normal routine. It assured that he would continue to grow as well.

Being supportive of the woman you are in a relationship with is critically important to the long-term success of your romance. If you start trying to block her growth, rather than support it, you will end up alone.

3. You listen to her

We went over communication basics in Chapter 8, when we talked about the nine steps for turning a roaring lioness into a purring kitten. You may want to review that communication process, and really get yourself to the point where you can really use it in a relationship. As a brief reminder, the nine steps are:

1. Listen to her
2. Repeat back what you heard
3. Thank her
4. Continue to listen to her
5. Make promises and apologies
6. Handle it if you really, truly don't care about what she's telling you
7. Let it all go

8. Compliment her
9. Repeat this process as many times as it takes.

In Chapter 11, we also talked about "active listening." We gave you pointers for looking interested, and how to repeat back what she said to you. A man who follows these techniques will be miles ahead of 95 percent of other men, who don't follow any discipline when talking to women they care about, and who don't have the slightest clue about how to listen so women feel heard.

4. Maintain your own sanity

Many men make the mistake of thinking that their relationship will see to all their emotional needs. While it will take care of many, it will *never* see to all of them. When you try to make a single relationship meet all of your needs, you place an unfair burden on both the relationship and the woman. It creates stress, which you only make worse because your needs are not being met. Certain things that men tend to let slide once they have a girlfriend are actually more important in long-term relationships. Here are the things you must do to maintain your sanity in a relationship:

Have male friends. You must continue to have male friends if you want your long-term relationship to work. It's easy, especially at the beginning of a romantic relationship, to lose track of your other friends. You can get away with this for a while, but once the relationship becomes more settled, it is essential that you re-establish contact with your male friends, and keep them in your life. Ideally, you'd never lose touch with them at any stage.

Friendships with other men give you a space, away from the woman in your life, to kick back and get into all the parts of yourself that you normally don't let out around your girlfriend. You can swear more, burp with impunity, and talk about how much you'd like to have sex with other women. You can complain about your girlfriend without getting into trouble.

If you don't have these friendships, you run the risk of starting to treat your girlfriend the way you would a buddy. This will show up in two ways. One is that you will start checking out other women when your girlfriend is present. This is still a no-no, even once you are in a long-term relationship. That's just one of the sacrifices that you have to make. Second, you'll start joking with your girlfriend the way you would with guys, giving her grief and teasing her. You should know by now that it's important for you to treat your girlfriend differently than you do your pals. Men give you a release valve, so you can "let it all hang out."

Male friends will give you feedback in a way that your girlfriend can't; they can also give you great guidance about your relationship that you or your girlfriend would never think of. When Jacob was having hard times with his girlfriend, Molly, he counted on his male friends to give him clear, "straight from the hip" feedback about how he looked from the outside. This feedback made all the difference in Jacob's ability to restore life to his otherwise failing relationship.

Becoming a man who only hangs out with his girlfriend is natural. It's also juvenile. Do what it takes to keep your friendships with men alive.

Don't share everything with her. Many of the thoughts you have don't help a long-term relationship. Your longing for a woman who has larger breasts or your occasional thoughts about leaving her are not always smart to share. Ditto some of the conversations you have with your men friends. There's no need to tell her things that will upset her that have no bearing on the relationship. Some things you just have to let go of.

When Bob has a girlfriend, he feels it is absolutely necessary to share every thought, feeling or sensation he has with her. He doesn't understand that many of the thoughts and feelings he has are basically insignificant to their relationship. He strongly believes he's being dishonest if he doesn't tell her every little thing that pops into his head.

For instance, once he was out having dinner with a girlfriend when a stunningly beautiful, sexy woman walked right past their table. Bob gawked openly, not realizing that he should ignore the woman, and concentrate on his girlfriend. She immediately asked him, "So, do you think she's more attractive than I am?" Bound by his idea of "honesty," he answered, "Of course." He should have known, as a master seducer would, to say something like, "Sure, she's attractive, but you have everything it takes to enthrall me completely. I love looking into your eyes, kissing your lips...and I'm so grateful to be with you." Bob allows himself to get drawn into a conversation about his girlfriend's merits, relative to those of the supermodel who had walked by them. Because of his need to be "honest" and share everything, he tells her about how much he'd like to have sex with a woman who had such a great body. He ends up in a fight that he stupidly started by sharing his every thought.

No matter what woman you commit yourself to, she is going to have qualities that bug you. Listing them to her is not honest, it is stupid. Her little flaws in personality are probably not going to change, and sharing your feelings about them probably won't make a positive difference. Complain to your men friends about these flaws, and let go of them when you are with her. Tell her what is important, but don't go generating trouble when you don't have to.

Keep building a life you love. Just because you have a girlfriend doesn't mean that you can now start getting your sense of validation from her. The same rule applies to you now that applied to you when you were dating: get your sense of validation from your life, not from women. The way you do this is by continuing to build a life you love.

Remember, you want her to be a wonderful part of your life, not its centerpiece. You must continue to have goals, and you must continue pursuing them. You must continue to do the things that make your life the way you want it to be. You must continue to explore your personal style, and continue to pursue what you love. Look at it this way: your passion about your life is probably part of the reason your girlfriend fell in love with you in the first place. If you let that go after you are in a committed relationship, you won't be the man she fell in love with. In time, that simple fact will destroy your relationship.

5. You sacrifice for the relationship

Most men hear word "sacrifice" and think it means more suffering, or doing more housework, or letting a woman dictate their behavior. Whatever it means, it is something they don't like. In fact, sacrifice means none of those things; it means that you consistently put what is necessary for the relationship ahead of your own personal needs. This doesn't mean that you sleep less, or miss work, or stop enjoying sports. What it means is that you do whatever is necessary to make the relationship work. So if, for example, your girlfriend feels that you disagree about important issues, and need to go to therapy, you do it, even if you think it sucks and is ridiculous. You do it as a way to sacrifice for her happiness, and to make the relationship work better.

Women learn to sacrifice for men early on. They put up with our obnoxious nature, offer us their bodies, cook food we like, dress the way we fantasize about, compliment us when they don't want to, and do dozens of other things to keep us happy, and to keep relationships going.

If you are unwilling to do the same, then grow up, or get out of the relationship immediately. Without some ability to sacrifice, the relationship will fail. If you are unwilling to do so, stick to short-term dating.

Think of sacrifice as getting a shot when you were a kid. Remember how much it hurt, and seemed horrid? Even though it was scary and it hurt, someone forced you to do it because that person knew it would help for the long term. Sacrificing for a relationship is the same way. You do it, even if you don't like it at first, for long-term benefits.

If you look closely, you probably are already doing it, but don't realize you are. When you do "the little things" for her, you sacrifice. Buying little gifts for her, when you don't have money is sacrifice. Listening to her cry, or complain when you want to watch TV is also sacrifice. Anytime you "give up" something to make her happy, or to make the relationship work, it is sacrifice. If you constantly keep thinking about ways to do this, you will keep the whole thing alive and flowing.

6. You keep your sex life happening

You can't afford to let your sex life die. Once again, keeping it lively is dependent on your choices, not your feelings. If you stick with your feelings, after a few years your desire will start to wane, even with the hottest of women. You must take the consistent actions that keep your sex life lively. Review the sex chapter, and commit yourself to staying interested sexually. This may mean that sometimes you make yourself have sex with her, even if you initially don't feel like it. Men we know tell us that the desire starts, once you do. We recommend that you always and forever experiment with new types of sexual play and always strive to keep your sex life fresh.

You must not let your sexual relationship die; your sex life is the thing that separates your relationship with your girlfriend from the others in your life. If you are not having sex with her, she might as well just be a friend. Sex is the heart and blood of a passionate relationship. Fortunately, simply committing yourself to continuously expanding your sexlife is often enough to keep it vital.

THE SIX STUMBLING BLOCKS TO HAPPY, HEALTHY AND HOT LONG-TERM RELATIONSHIPS

Just as there are things you must do to keep a long-term relationship happy, there are things you must not do as well. You must keep your eyes open for the stumbling blocks to healthy, happy and hot long-term relationships. They are the main reasons for relationship degradation that we've seen, and the problem is, each one of them is completely natural. If you are not vigilant, you will slip into any or all of them. If you are, your relationship will prosper; if you aren't, it will wither away and die.

1. Treating her like a guy friend

If you get nothing else from this chapter, get this: the best way to degrade your romantic relationship with a woman is to treat her like one of your guy friends. The way this shows up for most men is joking with and teasing a girlfriend or wife the way you would a buddy. Don't do it.

Harold made this mistake constantly with his wife, Collette. They were out with another couple, Stan and Jody, when Collette brought up a book about gender issues that had helped her understand Harold better. She recommended the book to Jody. Thinking he was being clever, Harold told Stan, "It'll probably make Jody more appreciative of you, just as it made Collette finally appreciate me." Collette was immediately hurt. "What's that supposed to mean?" she asked him. "I do appreciate you!" Harold hurt Collette's feelings by making a teasing joke that would be much more appropriate with a guy friend than it would be with a woman.

This may not seem like a very big deal to you, but it is. If you make even one insulting/teasing joke to your girlfriend per week, you are unnecessarily insulting her more than 50 times a year. Don't think she doesn't notice, because she does. And don't think she won't get you back for it, because she will do that, too. She won't do this because she is a mean or vindictive person; she'll do it because you drove her to it.

Here's another way to think about this: It's as if you have a bank account in a romantic relationship. The more "little things" you do, and the more you are romantic and make a woman feel good about herself, the more you have in that account. The greater your balance in the account, the more she'll want to do things to make you happy.

On the other hand, the more you hurt her feelings, the more you take out of this account. Making little teasing jokes at her expense costs more than you think. When the account gets negative, she'll start extracting revenge, and will find ways to hurt you back. This isn't because she's a bad person; she's just trying to balance the books.

As a man, it is your job to make sure that the balance in this account is always positive, and greater than it's ever been in any relationship she's ever been in before. You want to constantly overwhelm her with the abundance of generosity, love and appreciation you have toward her. If you do this, she'll always be forgiving and loving. If you don't, you can turn the nicest woman into a shrew.

Save your teasing for your buddies. Don't do it with the woman you love.

2. Belittling her

This is truly one of the stupidest things men do, and *lots* of men fall into it. Belittling the woman you are in a long-term relationship with, especially in public, will drive the love out without fail. Don't do it.

Belittling her often takes the form of teasing (see above) and "pet names" that insult her intelligence. Some men actually call their girlfriends or wives "my little idiot," or "stupid." The tragedy is, men tell us, that once they get used to belittling the woman they are with, it starts to seem natural. They just get into the habit of remarking caustically upon their wife or girlfriend's lack of intelligence. They find that saying "Geez, how can you be so dumb?" just seems to fall out of their mouths.

We shouldn't have to tell you by now that the cost of doing this will be your happiness. Obviously, if you ever catch yourself doing this, you will apologize at once, and commit yourself to *never* doing it again.

3. Fighting

Speaking of stupid, getting into a screaming fight with the woman you love is a stupid thing to do, too. Angry fighting tends to feed upon itself and, worse, feeds upon the relationship.

To understand why this is, think back to what we taught you about flirting with a woman you want to seduce. We showed you that you need to teach her to associate your presence with good feelings, so that when she sees you or even thinks about you, she feels good. You do this by always providing good feelings while she is looking at you. In time, seeing you and feeling good become linked.

When you fight with a woman this same dynamic works against you. If you have lots of angry, unpleasant fights with a woman, you teach her to associate your presence with angry, bad feelings. When she sees you, or even thinks about you, she'll feel angry and bad. She'll learn to associate you with those feelings, and that's not good.

To make matters worse, the same thing will happen to you. After a number of fights, you will have learned to associate her with fighting, anger, and bad feelings. Seeing her, or even just thinking about her, will make you angry.

For this reason, it's important that you don't get into out-of-control fights. People often think that they have the right to treat poorly the people who are close to them —remember the saying, "You always hurt the one you love"? If you find yourself starting to fight, make an effort to stay civil. Of course you will have disagreements, and of course you will get angry. Just moderate it. If you think that you are going to get out of control, get away from her, and deal with the problem when you are feeling calmer.

Allen and Lisa do all their fighting via e-mail. "It just works so much better for us to be able to pick and choose what we say, and to really think about what is going on between us," Allen says. "Besides, then I don't associate all those bad feelings with her. It just works better." If you have a real problem with anger—and many men do—it may make sense for you to get professional help. A good therapist can help you let go of anger and be more successful in relationships. Our point here is that all-out fighting is bad for relationships, and you shouldn't do it.

4. Lying to her

Some lying is "white lying," or is on the order of "not sharing everything." This is okay; it's actually a form of being polite. If she asks you how you like her new shoes, for instance, and you couldn't care less about them, you certainly do want to say "I think they are very nice." If she asks you what you are thinking, she really wants to know the good things you've been thinking about her lately. Don't tell her that you are thinking about how hot Mira Sorvina looked playing a prostitute in the movie you saw together the previous night, and how great it would be to have sex with her. Tell your girlfriend something truthful about how special she is to you. If you are doing the things we are teaching you in this chapter you'll always be aware of something special about her, anyway.

Destructive lying is different. Destructive lying to your girlfriend or wife starts you down a slippery slope that will eventually destroy your relationship. Lying often starts after you decide, on some subconscious level, to wreck your relationship. It starts at that moment when you decide that doing the "little things" for this woman is too much work, and that you aren't getting enough back to make it worth your while. It starts when you decide subconsciously that she isn't worth the effort anymore, and that someone else would be. You start looking for that someone else, and you start to lie.

A woman who is close to you will "just know" when you are lying to her. Psychologists often say that 80 percent of communication is nonverbal. If you don't think she'll pick up on your duplicity, you are mistaken. When you try to hide the truth your face will change, your way of moving will change, and your vocal tone will change. She'll know something is wrong, and you will eventually pay the price.

Here's a true story about how this happened to Lonny, a friend of ours. He was dating Joy who, a year into their relationship, moved to another city in order to go to school. They got together about once every two months, talked on the phone, and sent e-mail to keep the relationship alive.

One day Lonny met Dee Dee, and was overwhelmed by their mutual attraction. In short order he went to bed with her, even though cheating on Joy was something he had sworn he'd never do. The next morning, Joy called him up. A few moments into their conversation she asked him, "Did you have sex with another woman last night?" He compounded his error by lying to her about it, and within two months they had a horrible breakup. Dee Dee was disturbed by the fact that Lonny lied to Joy, and broke up with him as well. He was left alone and hurting, largely because of his lying.

Though perhaps more painful initially, honesty would have been his best policy. His first lie was promising Joy he wouldn't cheat on her. He didn't know it was a lie, but it was. If he'd kept his word to not cheat on Joy, he wouldn't have had to tell her other lies as well.

When Joy asked him the next day if he'd slept with another woman, it would have gone better if he'd told the truth and faced the music right then. She would have been upset, but it would have put him in a situation where he had to decide which relationship was most important. It would have given him an opportunity to really acknowledge the problems the long-distance relationship was causing, and to take definite actions to solve them.

Instead he lied, pretended everything was fine, and created a situation in which he had to continue to lie to keep up the facade.

Ultimately she found out the truth, and it led to their breakup. There was no way she could trust him after he had lied to her, repeatedly, about his sex with another woman.

While not all women are as psychically attuned as Joy was, many will be. The undercurrents of duplicity that lying puts into your relationship will inevitably wash away anything good about it. In almost any situation, you will find that the long-term consequences of telling the truth are easier to bear than are the long-term consequences of lying. The bottom line? Don't lie to her.

5. Blaming her for your problems

By this time, the theme of the book should be clear: you are responsible for the quality of your life and the quality of your relationships. Life will always work better for you if you operate from this philosophy.

Sadly, many men like to blame the women in their lives for their problems. This is babyish and immature. In our experience, men who blame their girlfriends or wives for their problems caused 90 percent (or more) of those problems themselves. For instance, Jim blamed his girlfriend, Becky, for not being sexy enough in bed. "It's like I'm stuck with this woman who has no desire," he says. "She must be frigid. I'll tell you one thing, though; she wasn't like this at the beginning. No sir! She couldn't get enough, the little minx. And now what? I'm wearing out my right hand, doing it for myself!" Upon investigation, however, we found that he never did the little things for her anymore, and that he generally treated her like another guy. He had destroyed the romance in the relationship. Not her. After trashing their romance, he blamed her for their lack of a sex life.

We showed Jim how to stop complaining and change his behavior, and he found that Becky warmed up to him sexually once again. He could never have actually solved his problem while he was still blaming her. Before he could change, he had to first realize that he was doing it, and make a decision to stop.

Nine times out of ten, you are more the cause for your problems than you are willing to admit. The tenth time, you are better off acting as though you are the cause anyway. If you blame the woman in your life for your problems, you will just reinforce them and make everything worse.

6. Not being forgiving

In any relationship there will be times when you have to be forgiving. As we've said before, she *will* do things that upset you, just as you will do things that upset her. If you aren't forgiving with her, your behavior will be corrosive to the relationship.

Many people don't know the simple basics of forgiveness. We know how to say "I forgive you," but we don't know how to make the forgiveness really work. We don't know how to let the past be in the past. Most men say they forgive, then bring up their partner's transgression again and again as a way of continual torture.

After Sheila and Gary had been dating for almost a year, they went to a party together where Sheila got more drunk than Gary had ever seen her. She then disappeared with another man. Gary caught them in a back hallway, making out. She drunkenly explained that she didn't know what she was doing, and he took her home.

The next day they talked about what happened, and whether or not their relationship had a future. Gary was understandably angry, and thinking about breaking the relationship off right then and there. He told her "I've passed up other women because I was committed to this relationship! I expect you to do the same, or I want to break up with you." She cried, and apologized, and admitted that she had a problem with alcohol that made her too impulsive when she drank too much. They talked about whether there was a deeper problem in the relationship, and decided there wasn't. She just got really drunk, and did something really stupid. She apologized sincerely, and promised to not drink that much again.

Sheila kept her promise: from then on, she drank little or nothing at the parties they went to. She remained an attentive lover, and a good girlfriend. But this wasn't enough for Gary. He kept bringing up her transgression. Anytime he felt angry, he'd say something like, "I guess I'm not as good as that guy at the party, eh?" or "If you don't like me, I bet that party guy would take you. You seemed pretty into him." For Gary, all conversational roads led back to reminding Sheila of her mistake. Eventually she started defending herself from his attacks, and they fought. Finally they broke up, because of Gary's inability to forgive. "I apologized and apologized," she said later. "But he was never able to let it go."

If you want to truly be forgiving, you must be able to let go of what you have forgiven. This looks like *not talking about it again.* If Gary had really forgiven Sheila, he would never have brought it up again, after their initial conversation. It would be done, over with, finished. If he felt like bringing it up again, a truly forgiving man would have restrained himself. He'd let bygones be bygones, and let the past stay in the past.

This isn't to say that he was wrong in being angry about it. He wasn't. He was absolutely right to make sure she knew that her actions had created a big problem, and it was important that she feel uncomfortable about it, and that she apologize. But after he accepted her apology, he should not have brought it up again, unless she started drinking too much, or flirting too wildly with other men. As long as she kept her promise, he should have let it go.

When you are in a relationship, you will get justifiably angry from time to time. She will do things you have to forgive her for. To keep the relationship alive and happy, you must understand that when you forgive, you give up the right to torment her with what she did. You give up that right *forever.* This may be a sacrifice for you. Left to your own devices, you might bring it up again to "keep her in her place." Don't do it. Allow her transgressions to be over with your forgiveness, and don't drag them into the future. Your relationship will be much happier and have a much greater success rate if you learn to *really* forgive.

DANIEL'S NEWFOUND SUCCESS

Daniel has fulfilled his desire. He meets a woman named Susan, and one year later they are still dating happily. Here's a typical date for them, a year into their relationship:

They've arranged a dinner date for Saturday night, and, on the Wednesday afternoon before the date, Daniel starts to prepare. He calls Susan and tells her "I'd like this Saturday to be a more formal date, if that's okay with you. How about we dress up for it, and make it something special?" "Sure!" she responds. "It'll be a great chance to wear my new outfit!"

Smiling, Daniel hangs up the phone. He calls his friend, Jake, who is about his size, and arranges to borrow his tux for Saturday night. A call to another friend secures a Cadillac for his use on the date as well.

After work he goes by a toy store, and buys her several cheap but fun trinkets, which he will wrap prettily before the date. He also stops by a bookstore and buys her a book she's been interested in. There's no occasion; Daniel simply understands that this is the kind of thing he has to do to keep the relationship exciting and alive. He's happy to do it all, too. After all, it's fun, and it creates moments to remember for both him and Susan.

On the afternoon of the date, he goes by a flower store to get her some flowers. He hasn't bought her anything in a while, so he decides to splurge, and he buys her a dozen red roses.

Well dressed and in a fancy car, he picks Susan up at her house, and she is overwhelmed. The flowers astound her, and she rushes excitedly to put them in water. He holds open doors for her, is the perfect gentleman, and takes her to the restaurant. It's not the best, or most expensive restaurant in town, but it seems more fun to them both because of their fancy dress. People treat them better, too: everyone in the restaurant is amused by their garb, and tries to make their experience even more special. After dinner, over coffee, Daniel gives her one of the little gifts he bought for her. The last one he has reserved for when they get back to her apartment, as a prelude to a night of hot and passionate sex.

You can have what Daniel has, if you desire it. The simple steps described in this chapter will guide you. You, like Daniel, can keep a romance alive, and be more in love each day with the woman of your dreams.

chapter fifteen...
Conclusion

It's now a year later and we see Bob walking down the sidewalk looking like a million bucks. At first glance it is hard to believe that this is the same guy who previously refused to wear nice clothes, had unkempt hair, had a bad attitude, and refused to alter his ways to impress a woman. Now, he is wearing an outfit from GQ magazine, his hair is stylishly done, and he looks and acts confident.

After months of constant failure to meet and date women, Bob decided to finally take our advice and model himself after stylish men in media. He focused on modeling their physiology, thoughts, clothing, attitude, and beliefs about dating. After routine practice he was able to get himself psyched up and "in the zone," and success has become the norm.

A year ago, Bob wouldn't have been caught dead reading and studying men's fashion. Now, even though it is not his favorite topic in life, he has a subscription to several men's fashion magazines. He is always on the look out for ways to improve his looks. At first it felt funny, almost unnatural, to dress fashionably and concentrate on looking good, but after a while Bob noticed that women were treating him differently, and he felt differently about himself. Bob realized, as we hope you have, that the clothes a man wears, and the way he wears them, send a message to women. Before, he was unconsciously saying "stay away from me. I don't care what you think." His strategy was effective, and women kept away. Looking sloppy greatly contributed to his patterns of failure.

Bob also realized that the hot, young, and sexy 21-year-olds he most wanted to date would never consider him a possibility if he dressed messy and didn't project confidence. This realization pushed him to work out frequently, lose weight, and spend a few thousand dollars on clothing. "At first I thought the men's fashion stores were ripping me off, and I left feeling really pissed off. But then, after I thought about it for a while, I figured that it was an investment, like anything else, and it would lead to success down the road. With this attitude I took the advice of the sales clerks and bought several out-fits that looked good on me. Now, I feel powerful when I walk down the street. Women check me out, and I actually feel like a movie star at times. It is fun."

When Bob began to change the way he dressed, he relied on the clothing and hygiene checklist from Chapter Three. This list includes things like glasses both in good repair and fashionable, making sure ear and nose hair are trimmed, making sure lips are soft and kissable, shaving before every date, taking pens out of his shirt pockets before dates, wearing clean underwear, making sure socks match, and keeping all clothing in good repair.

"There were many changes I had to make when I decided to seriously master seduction," Bob reports. "I completely altered my clothing and how I viewed things like exercises and diet. In the past I thought that being a stud was something you were either born with or you could never be. I've changed my tune."

Bob has gained the confidence with women, and in life, that he always wanted. He now knows that action is the key. Bob realized that having close guy friends was also essential for having the life he truly desired. "I always felt distant from other men," he reports. After being coached by us, he says, "I began talking to other men, getting to know them better. There are many topics I can talk about with guys that I can't with women. It has been a great help in seduction to have other men to bounce ideas off of, and egg each other on. I realized how fun it is to kick back, drinking some beers, watch a game and shooting the bull. It energizes me for the other areas of my life. Previously I used to think watching sports was for macho creepheads. Now I know that I too am a creep like everyone else. There's nothing wrong with it—it's great fun!"

Another way Bob gained confidence with women was to admit that he was scared to date women. He was afraid of rejection, afraid that women wouldn't like him, afraid of not knowing how to talk to women, afraid of being viewed as macho and a womanizer. These fears kept him unsuccessful in his pursuit. It was only after he admitted his fears that he was able to move on and change them.

One solution was simply to flirt and talk to women all the time. Bob began doing so every day, and it quickly helped increase his confidence. At first, all he could do was say "hi. " Slowly, he learned to use romantic questions, flirt, smile, memorize lines, and relax. Refusing to let rejections get him down, and having other men egg him on helped him to keep going.

Looking over the year, Bob continued to make hundreds of mistakes, but stayed on track. Most men would have given up, felt bad about themselves, and blamed everyone for their failures. Bob was persistent and things slowly changed for him. He viewed learning seduction like a job, something that took a lot of work on the front end to get results later.

On his first few seduction dates, Bob ignored our warnings that a man must have his car and home set up for romance. He continued to use his car as a roving garbage truck. He stored bottles and cans that would some day arrive at the recycling plant, hamburger wrappers from fast food places, and a collection of tools, all within the confines of his old, loud, rusted, and dented compact car. To make things worse, he had fuzzy dice hanging from his rear view mirror. Any woman who entered his car got out as quickly as she could. He later bought another car and this time modified it to be a certifiable sex mobile. He made sure to keep it clean, got a tape deck installed and purchased romantic music, stored blankets, pillows and wine in the trunk, and, of course, he hid a cache of condoms in the glove box.

Bob's home went through a similar transformation. He realized that a house full of garbage, dirty dishes, ragged furniture, and bad odors, killed the romantic mood every time. Over a few months he replaced all the lamps in the living room and bedroom, making sure they each had a dimmer switch. Bob also purchased some new, soft, and comfortable furniture that invited romance and sensuality. He re-covered other pieces with matching material. His new bed was huge, and was easy to lie on for hours. A nice collection of plants and framed pictures created a romantic mood in both rooms. Bob learned to clean his bedroom and living room before each date, and make sure that clean sheets and pillowcases were on his bed. He felt more comfortable in his home, and several women commented that it was fun and romantic to visit.

He greatly increased both his romance and flirting skills over the year as well. At first it seemed impossible to be effective at either romance or flirting, but after constant reading, practicing, and advice from other men, these skills became easy. In the past, Bob believed that flirting was simply talking without direction that would, hopefully, magically, lead to sex. He thought that since he had never had a one-night stand, and no single conversation had led to sex, he was a failure. Later, Bob realized that the essence of flirting is to play without an attachment to the outcome, and that a man rarely has sex with a woman after one flirting encounter.

When he learned to relax, he was able to flirt, wink, and interact with women with confidence. Bob used flirting to prequalify women to see if they were potentials for dating and sex. He also learned to use flirting to anchor pleasurable feeling in the woman to seeing him. For instance, he began flirting and casually talking to the cashier at the convenience store near his job. Every day, on his lunch break, he decided to go and talk to her about anything romantic. At first he was nervous, only saying a word or two; over time she grew to look forward to his daily visits.

Bob made many botched attempts with flirting before he learned the basics: not using crude humor, not joking as roughly as he would with guys, never joking about her appearance, never indulging in any disgusting behavior in front of her, and never making himself the butt of any joke. In the process of learning, he made all of these mistakes. But he soon learned to make jokes about things at hand, the importance of simply saying "hi," focusing on eye contact, and describing romantic things during conversations.

Learning how to be romantic was equally difficult. In the beginning, he always forgot to make his romantic interest known right away. He often waited a few days before putting on the charm. The women usually felt put off by this behavior, however, having already decided he was a friend. Finally he realized that women usually decide, within the first few minutes of meeting, whether a man is a friend or a lover. Bob even began studying romantic movies, poetry, and novels. He wanted to learn as much as he could. Every week, he gave himself assignments to understand, and learn what women desired in a romantic situation. He decided that it was his job on dates to make the woman feel special, and do the romantic things necessary to achieve the result.

The romantic stories and movies he read confirmed our assertion that romance has the air of the unexpected and unreal. A romantic situation is generous but not needy, goes at her pace, is truly appreciative of her. It demonstrates to a woman that you've put time, energy, and thought into a date.

One of the hardest things for Bob to learn was that women are generally concerned, at first, that a man is dangerous and will hurt them. This fear must be overcome before any further rapport can be built. After many priming and seduction dates, and interviewing female friends, they all proved this to be true.

In the beginning of this book, Bob always complained that there were no places to meet women. He was lonely, but nothing seemed to work for him. After taking our advice, Bob began experimenting with meeting women at alternative places. Some have paid off well, and led to dates, and others were not so productive. In any case, Bob has found that each and every place he goes is a possible place to meet women. He has learned to flirt, and not take it personally if it doesn't lead to anything, or if he is rejected by the woman.

Bob started going to the same coffee shop every day. He became one of the regulars, and this made it easy to talk to women he saw routinely. They already had a connection, the coffee shop. He starting eating at the same restaurants regularly, and going to the gym at the same time to work out. These, too, led to more opportunities to date and flirt. He talked with women at his favorite bookstore, and though it didn't lead to a date, he had some interesting discussions. Bob experimented with attending new-age events; he was even asked to leave one of them for teasing a psychic. He didn't get any sex that day, but he practiced his seduction skills and had fun being obnoxious, so in his mind, it was a success.

He also attended ballroom dance class a few times. He danced with some hot young women. He also met many women at dog training classes. He even signed up for a Japanese cooking class. Bob was the only man in the class. The other students were mostly married, middle-aged women. But Joyce, one of the students, was very friendly. They went out for drinks after one of the classes. Their drinking dates led to a short-term erotic relationship. Though they had little in common, the sex was good, and that was enough for them both.

Bob dated Joyce for a only a month. Though he wanted to date her longer, he knew that if they continued, Joyce would likely want to be his girlfriend. Bob was able to cut off the potential relationship quickly, and Joyce was not surprised when he finally called it quits.

One of Bob's biggest failures was to not notice all the women he came into contact with each day. Previously, he had acted as though there were no women to date. He had failed to notice all the women he talked to, and came into contact with on a daily basis. Now, his days are much more like Bruce in Chapter 4, flirting and dating with women all day and all night long.

As part of his practice, he put out many personals ads in a local paper, and looked for woman on the Internet. The ads led to a few dates; the Internet ad led to no dates, but he did exchange some satisfyingly sexy e-mails.

One of his boldest moves was to attend a poetry reading and get up and read seductive poetry. He wrote several poems about sexuality and romance. He took our advice, and created long poems out of romantic questions, and by describing romantic states. "It shocked me to be up there. I never thought I would be so bold, but it was fun. After, I talked to six or more women. That was the best part. I got a few phone numbers. One woman, Rebecca, was a 20-year-old, tortured-artist type. She was all punky looking with tattoos and piercings on her face. She went home with me that night, and it was my first one-night stand."

Bob also spent time studying magic tricks. He focused on card tricks. It was a perfect way to begin conversations with women. He would pull out a deck of cards while waiting in a line, or sitting on the bus, and use it as a conversation starter. This too, provided opportunities to date and flirt.

He mastered the distinctions between priming and seduction dates. The goal of the first is to prime the woman and generate connection. He saw the importance of keeping that date short. If he went too long, he realized, it was easy to make mistakes, and not develop that connection.

Bob recently took Monica, a woman he met at the gym, on a priming date at a coffee shop. They spent only 45 minutes together, and it worked perfectly. Since she appeared to be having a great time, he decided to end the date even earlier than planned. Bob remembered that it wasn't a time to socialize. The work at hand was asking romantic questions and researching her requirements in a man and a mate. For example, he found out what her first kiss was like, if she believes in love at first sight, what she values in a relationship, and what she looks for in a boyfriend.

Bob, of course, brought his new book to read, in case Monica failed to show up. He knew that many wouldn't show up, and he was prepared, which made it easy for him to relax and be spontaneous. Because he had other women to date, he wasn't too concerned with Monica's reactions to his questions or his behavior. He was able to take it all in stride.

One of Bob's biggest changes is that he is able to be decisive. In the past he always relied on the woman to make the decisions, reasoning that it would make her feel comfortable. Now he realizes that it is crucial that he make decisions during the date.

While the date with Monica went well, he had been on dozens of failed priming dates throughout the year. There were women who were late and didn't show up. He found a way to learn from each mistake he made and each thing he forgot to do. After each date, Bob went through his After-the-Date checklist from the Priming Date chapter. This includes things like looking into the woman's eyes at least four times, asking romantic questions, touching her hand, making sure the date was no longer than 75 minutes, making decisions, making her smile and/or laugh at least once, being early, gathering information about her, and complimenting her at least five times, and many other personal touches. Along with the after the date checklist, he always examined how much he was willing to work to further the relationship. What would it take to move things to the next level? Bob created his own measurements to track the degree to which he was or wasn't interested in a woman.

Bob's next step was to study seduction dates. He wanted to master shifting the focus from building rapport to having sex. With Monica, he knew she was ready to move on. She showed interest in him, flirted frequently, and responded well to his information touch. On the seduction date he made sure to employ the key elements:

making the date into a special event, picking a fun and romantic activity, making it memorable, paying for the date, being flexible with time, giving little gifts, making the woman feel special, planning for success, and making sure the date featured surprises.

Before the date he made sure to do all the pre-work. He assessed the attraction level between the two of them, created sexual goals, made sure the date was at a convenient time, decided how much money to spend, had a back-up plan, was prepared, and used the information from the priming date to guide his choices. During the date, Bob was punctual, polite, affectionate, complimentary, treated her like a woman, talked about upbeat topics, and was fun to be around.

At first Bob failed to get a woman into bed, and when he did it ended up disastrously. Remember the horrid situation with Barb in the Sex chapter? Bob was in bed with her, but didn't know how to touch her sensually. He was too rough, and wanted to quickly move into intercourse. He refused to spend time on foreplay, kissing and petting, and the other necessary elements. While with Monica, however, he kissed her during the seduction date, and they ended up in her bed. Because he had concentrated on learning about sensual touch, women's bodies, and massage, Bob touched Monica just as she desired. He wasn't embarrassed by looking at her, or asking questions. Bob kissed her and Monica moaned loudly. He was full of confidence. His work on attitude in the bedroom paid great dividends.

Bob realizes that his main goal is to be a true playboy. He sees himself in a long-term committed relationship within a few years, but for now, he wants to continue dating and having many short-term erotic relationships. He knows what is needed to make a long-term relationship work, when he is ready: sacrifice, romance, fun experiences, little gifts, and communication skills, especially listening, doing the little things, supporting her fully, maintaining his own sanity. But for now he wants to continue to play the field.

Another important skill Bob has learned, that has come in handy on many dates, is how to handle problem situations and problem women. Before, he would default into the 24 Idiot Mistakes and Stumbling Blocks regarding dating, including not dating more than one woman, not controlling all variables, confronting women when they didn't call him back or initiate enough. He would overwhelm a woman with sexual innuendoes, take the date too seriously, try to get validation and certainty from her, and check out other women when he was with her. He would not set limits and value his time, energy, and/or money. He tried to solve all women's problems, fought incessantly, and defaulted into yelling, screaming, and not managing his anger effectively.

Bob has dated a number of problem women during the year, and has learned to avoid them. He's dated women like the Cry Baby, the Paranoid Police-Caller, the Street Fighter, and the Manipulator/Bitch/Criticizer. He has learned to take his intuition seriously and avoid the women who could be dangerous. He has dated women who had constant emotional problems, who stopped being sexual, who interfered with his work, who degraded his self-respect, who tried to come between him and his buddies , who were overly critical, controlling, and violent. The moment any of these problems arose, he knew to promptly end the relationship.

Bob has also had to face many problems inside himself. The tendency to be a SNAG (Sensitive New-Age Guy), for example, has pestered him for years. He was always trying to get women to have sex with him by being superficially nice, which never worked. He found out that women were looking for a confident man who was not so apologetic, and who was not trying to impress them by being only nice. He also stopped being a control freak and a know-it-all on dates. He no longer lies to himself that he wants a relationship. Bob wants sex, and is not apologetic about it.

Bob credits his success to following our advice carefully, and never ceasing to work. He has faced more problems than most of our students, and he has come out successful with women. By taking the little steps along the way, you too, will be like Bob and change the way you talk, act, and date women. This book is your bible for dating and sexual success. If you use our science and your own intuition, you are destined to succeed.

Index